FROM MOTHER AND DAUGHTER

THE OTHER VOICE IN EARLY MODERN EUROPE

A Series Edited by Margaret L. King and Albert Rabil Jr.

RECENT BOOKS IN THE SERIES

Madeleine and Catherine des Roches

FROM MOTHER AND DAUGHTER
Poems, Dialogues, and Letters of
Les Dames des Roches

Edited and Translated by Anne R. Larsen

THE UNIVERSITY OF CHICAGO PRESS
Chicago & London

Madeleine des Roches, 1520–1587

Catherine des Roches, 1542–1587

Anne R. Larsen is professor of modern and classical languages at Hope College and the editor of the three-volume critical edition of the collected writings of Madeleine and Catherine des Roches.

The University of Chicago Press, Chicago 60637
The University of Chicago Press, Ltd., London
© 2006 by The University of Chicago
All rights reserved. Published 2006
Printed in the United States of America

15 14 13 12 11 10 09 08 07 06   1 2 3 4 5

ISBN: 0-226-72338-0 (paper)
ISBN: 0-226-72337-2 (cloth)

Excerpts from *Les Œuvres* © 1993 by Librairie Droz S.A. All rights reserved.
Excerpts from *Les Secondes Œuvres* © 1998 by Librairie Droz S.A.
All rights reserved.

The University of Chicago Press gratefully acknowledges the generous support of James E. Rabil, in memory of Scottie W. Rabil, toward the publication of this book.

Library of Congress Cataloging-in-Publication Data

Des Roches, Madeleine Neveu, dame, ca. 1520–1587.
[Selections. English. 2006]
From mother and daughter : poems, dialogues, and letters of les dames
Des Roches / Madeleine and Catherine Des Roches ; edited and translated
by Anne R. Larsen.— 1st ed.
p. cm. — (The other voice in early modern Europe)
Includes bibliographical references and index.
ISBN 0-226-72337-2 (cloth : alk. paper) —
ISBN 0-226-72338-0 (pbk. : alk. paper)
I. Des Roches, Catherine Fredonnoit, dame, 1542–1587.
II. Larsen, Anne R. III. Title. IV. Series.
PQ1609.D49A6 2006
841'.3—dc22
2005034483

♾ The paper used in this publication meets the minimum requirements of the American National Standard for Information Sciences—Permanence of Paper for Printed Library Materials, ANSI Z39.48-1992.

To Michael Brinks

CONTENTS

ACKNOWLEDGMENTS

I am deeply grateful for the kind help and encouragement of my colleagues Brigitte Hamon-Porter, Isabelle Chapuis-Alvarez, Vicki De Vries, Sander de Haan, Paulette Chaponnière, Gloria Tseng, Provost James Boelkins, and Dean William Reynolds from Hope College. I thank Sarah Beaubien in the Interlibrary Loan Office at Hope College's Van Wylen Library.

My warmest thanks go as well to Marian Rothstein and Julie Campbell for their careful editing of the introduction, and to Régine Reynolds-Cornell, Diana Robin, Cathy Yandell, and Kirk Read for their insightful comments and suggestions on the introductions to the chapters.

I am grateful to Margaret King and to Albert Rabil Jr. for their enthusiastic support of the project and to the editors, especially Susan Tarcov, who worked with me at the University of Chicago Press. I thank Max Engammare of Librairie Droz for permission to reprint the following copyrighted French texts from my critical editions of Madeleine and Catherine des Roches, *Les Œuvres* (Geneva: Droz, 1993) and *Les Secondes Œuvres* (Geneva: Droz, 1998): from *Les Œuvres*, (by Madeleine) Epistre aux Dames, Epistre à ma Fille, Odes 1, 3, 4, Sonnets 1, 5, 6–9, 11, 15, 16, 20, 22, 35, 36, Epitaphe de feu Maistre François Éboissard, Au Roy, Sonnets V, IV; (by Catherine) Epistre à sa Mere, Sonnets de Sincero à Charite, Sonnets de Charite à Sincero, Pour une Mascarade d'Amazones, Chanson des Amazones, A ma quenoille, A mes escrits, Au Roy, A G. P., A Ma Mere, La Femme forte descritte par Salomon, L'Agnodice; from *Les Secondes Œuvres*, (by Madeleine) A ma Fille, Ode 2, Sonnets 1–4, Poitiers à Messieurs des Grandz Jours, Huitan; (by Catherine) Epistre à sa Mere, Les Responces 1, 3, 4, 6, 9–12, 18, 23, 24, 29–37, 41–44, A Messieurs tenant les Grands Jours à Poitiers, La Puce, Epitaphe 2.

This translation was made possible through the generous support of the National Endowment for the Humanities, a Faculty-Student Collaborative

Research Summer Grant from Hope College which facilitated work on the translations with Michael Brinks, and the Department of Modern and Classical Languages at Hope College as well as Karen Barber-Gibson for additional funding to work with Lauren Hinkle on the transcription of the French poems. I thank as well Julie Ouvrard for help on the index.

This translation is dedicated to Michael Brinks, whose tireless work and artful translations over a summer and a term provided much inspiration to me in bringing the Dames des Roches to an English-speaking audience.

Anne R. Larsen

THE OTHER VOICE IN
EARLY MODERN EUROPE:
INTRODUCTION TO THE SERIES

Margaret L. King and Albert Rabil Jr.

THE OLD VOICE AND THE OTHER VOICE

In western Europe and the United States, women are nearing equality in the professions, in business, and in politics. Most enjoy access to education, reproductive rights, and autonomy in financial affairs. Issues vital to women are on the public agenda: equal pay, child care, domestic abuse, breast cancer research, and curricular revision with an eye to the inclusion of women.

These recent achievements have their origins in things women (and some male supporters) said for the first time about six hundred years ago. Theirs is the "other voice," in contradistinction to the "first voice," the voice of the educated men who created Western culture. Coincident with a general reshaping of European culture in the period 1300–1700 (called the Renaissance or early modern period), questions of female equality and opportunity were raised that still resound and are still unresolved.

The other voice emerged against the backdrop of a three-thousand-year history of the derogation of women rooted in the civilizations related to Western culture: Hebrew, Greek, Roman, and Christian. Negative attitudes toward women inherited from these traditions pervaded the intellectual, medical, legal, religious, and social systems that developed during the European Middle Ages.

The following pages describe the traditional, overwhelmingly male views of women's nature inherited by early modern Europeans and the new tradition that the "other voice" called into being to begin to challenge reigning assumptions. This review should serve as a framework for understanding the texts published in the series the Other Voice in Early Modern Europe. Introductions specific to each text and author follow this essay in all the volumes of the series.

TRADITIONAL VIEWS OF WOMEN, 500 B.C.E.–1500 C.E.

Embedded in the philosophical and medical theories of the ancient Greeks were perceptions of the female as inferior to the male in both mind and body. Similarly, the structure of civil legislation inherited from the ancient Romans was biased against women, and the views on women developed by Christian thinkers out of the Hebrew Bible and the Christian New Testament were negative and disabling. Literary works composed in the vernacular of ordinary people, and widely recited or read, conveyed these negative assumptions. The social networks within which most women lived—those of the family and the institutions of the Roman Catholic Church—were shaped by this negative tradition and sharply limited the areas in which women might act in and upon the world.

GREEK PHILOSOPHY AND FEMALE NATURE. Greek biology assumed that women were inferior to men and defined them as merely childbearers and housekeepers. This view was authoritatively expressed in the works of the philosopher Aristotle.

Aristotle thought in dualities. He considered action superior to inaction, form (the inner design or structure of any object) superior to matter, completion to incompletion, possession to deprivation. In each of these dualities, he associated the male principle with the superior quality and the female with the inferior. "The male principle in nature," he argued, "is associated with active, formative and perfected characteristics, while the female is passive, material and deprived, desiring the male in order to become complete."[1] Men are always identified with virile qualities, such as judgment, courage, and stamina, and women with their opposites—irrationality, cowardice, and weakness.

The masculine principle was considered superior even in the womb. The man's semen, Aristotle believed, created the form of a new human creature, while the female body contributed only matter. (The existence of the ovum, and with it the other facts of human embryology, was not established until the seventeenth century.) Although the later Greek physician Galen believed there was a female component in generation, contributed by "female semen," the followers of both Aristotle and Galen saw the male role in human generation as more active and more important.

In the Aristotelian view, the male principle sought always to reproduce itself. The creation of a female was always a mistake, therefore, resulting from

---

1. Aristotle, *Physics* 1.9.192a20–24, in *The Complete Works of Aristotle*, ed. Jonathan Barnes, rev. Oxford trans., 2 vols. (Princeton, 1984), 1:328.

an imperfect act of generation. Every female born was considered a "defective" or "mutilated" male (as Aristotle's terminology has variously been translated), a "monstrosity" of nature.[2]

For Greek theorists, the biology of males and females was the key to their psychology. The female was softer and more docile, more apt to be despondent, querulous, and deceitful. Being incomplete, moreover, she craved sexual fulfillment in intercourse with a male. The male was intellectual, active, and in control of his passions.

These psychological polarities derived from the theory that the universe consisted of four elements (earth, fire, air, and water), expressed in human bodies as four "humors" (black bile, yellow bile, blood, and phlegm) considered, respectively, dry, hot, damp, and cold and corresponding to mental states ("melancholic," "choleric," "sanguine," "phlegmatic"). In this scheme the male, sharing the principles of earth and fire, was dry and hot; the female, sharing the principles of air and water, was cold and damp.

Female psychology was further affected by her dominant organ, the uterus (womb), *hystera* in Greek. The passions generated by the womb made women lustful, deceitful, talkative, irrational, indeed—when these affects were in excess—"hysterical."

Aristotle's biology also had social and political consequences. If the male principle was superior and the female inferior, then in the household, as in the state, men should rule and women must be subordinate. That hierarchy did not rule out the companionship of husband and wife, whose cooperation was necessary for the welfare of children and the preservation of property. Such mutuality supported male preeminence.

Aristotle's teacher Plato suggested a different possibility: that men and women might possess the same virtues. The setting for this proposal is the imaginary and ideal Republic that Plato sketches in a dialogue of that name. Here, for a privileged elite capable of leading wisely, all distinctions of class and wealth dissolve, as, consequently, do those of gender. Without households or property, as Plato constructs his ideal society, there is no need for the subordination of women. Women may therefore be educated to the same level as men to assume leadership. Plato's Republic remained imaginary, however. In real societies, the subordination of women remained the norm and the prescription.

The views of women inherited from the Greek philosophical tradition became the basis for medieval thought. In the thirteenth century, the supreme Scholastic philosopher Thomas Aquinas, among others, still echoed

---

2. Aristotle, *Generation of Animals* 2.3.737a27–28, in *Complete Works*, 1:1144.

Aristotle's views of human reproduction, of male and female personalities, and of the preeminent male role in the social hierarchy.

ROMAN LAW AND THE FEMALE CONDITION. Roman law, like Greek philosophy, underlay medieval thought and shaped medieval society. The ancient belief that adult property-owning men should administer households and make decisions affecting the community at large is the very fulcrum of Roman law.

About 450 B.C.E., during Rome's republican era, the community's customary law was recorded (legendarily) on twelve tablets erected in the city's central forum. It was later elaborated by professional jurists whose activity increased in the imperial era, when much new legislation was passed, especially on issues affecting family and inheritance. This growing, changing body of laws was eventually codified in the *Corpus of Civil Law* under the direction of the emperor Justinian, generations after the empire ceased to be ruled from Rome. That *Corpus*, read and commented on by medieval scholars from the eleventh century on, inspired the legal systems of most of the cities and kingdoms of Europe.

Laws regarding dowries, divorce, and inheritance pertain primarily to women. Since those laws aimed to maintain and preserve property, the women concerned were those from the property-owning minority. Their subordination to male family members points to the even greater subordination of lower-class and slave women, about whom the laws speak little.

In the early republic, the *paterfamilias*, or "father of the family," possessed *patria potestas*, "paternal power." The term *pater*, "father," in both these cases does not necessarily mean biological father but denotes the head of a household. The father was the person who owned the household's property and, indeed, its human members. The *paterfamilias* had absolute power—including the power, rarely exercised, of life or death—over his wife, his children, and his slaves, as much as his cattle.

Male children could be "emancipated," an act that granted legal autonomy and the right to own property. Those over fourteen could be emancipated by a special grant from the father or automatically by their father's death. But females could never be emancipated; instead, they passed from the authority of their father to that of a husband or, if widowed or orphaned while still unmarried, to a guardian or tutor.

Marriage in its traditional form placed the woman under her husband's authority, or *manus*. He could divorce her on grounds of adultery, drinking wine, or stealing from the household, but she could not divorce him. She could neither possess property in her own right nor bequeath any to her children upon her death. When her husband died, the household property passed not to her but to his male heirs. And when her father died, she had no claim to any family inheritance, which was directed to her brothers or more remote male relatives. The effect of these laws was to exclude women from civil society, itself based on property ownership.

In the later republican and imperial periods, these rules were significantly modified. Women rarely married according to the traditional form. The practice of "free" marriage allowed a woman to remain under her father's authority, to possess property given her by her father (most frequently the "dowry," recoverable from the husband's household on his death), and to inherit from her father. She could also bequeath property to her own children and divorce her husband, just as he could divorce her.

Despite this greater freedom, women still suffered enormous disability under Roman law. Heirs could belong only to the father's side, never the mother's. Moreover, although she could bequeath her property to her children, she could not establish a line of succession in doing so. A woman was "the beginning and end of her own family," said the jurist Ulpian. Moreover, women could play no public role. They could not hold public office, represent anyone in a legal case, or even witness a will. Women had only a private existence and no public personality.

The dowry system, the guardian, women's limited ability to transmit wealth, and total political disability are all features of Roman law adopted by the medieval communities of western Europe, although modified according to local customary laws.

CHRISTIAN DOCTRINE AND WOMEN'S PLACE. The Hebrew Bible and the Christian New Testament authorized later writers to limit women to the realm of the family and to burden them with the guilt of original sin. The passages most fruitful for this purpose were the creation narratives in Genesis and sentences from the Epistles defining women's role within the Christian family and community.

Each of the first two chapters of Genesis contains a creation narrative. In the first "God created man in his own image, in the image of God he created him; male and female he created them" (Gn 1:27). In the second, God created Eve from Adam's rib (2:21–23). Christian theologians relied principally on Genesis 2 for their understanding of the relation between man and woman, interpreting the creation of Eve from Adam as proof of her subordination to him.

The creation story in Genesis 2 leads to that of the temptations in Genesis 3: of Eve by the wily serpent and of Adam by Eve. As read by Christian theologians from Tertullian to Thomas Aquinas, the narrative made Eve responsible for the Fall and its consequences. She instigated the act; she deceived her husband; she suffered the greater punishment. Her disobedience made it necessary for Jesus to be incarnated and to die on the cross. From the pulpit, moralists and preachers for centuries conveyed to women the guilt that they bore for original sin.

The Epistles offered advice to early Christians on building communities of the faithful. Among the matters to be regulated was the place of women. Paul offered views favorable to women in Galatians 3:28: "There is neither Jew nor Greek, there is neither slave nor free, there is neither male nor female; for you are all one in Christ Jesus." Paul also referred to women as his coworkers and placed them on a par with himself and his male coworkers (Phlm 4:2–3; Rom 16:1–3; 1 Cor 16:19). Elsewhere, Paul limited women's possibilities: "But I want you to understand that the head of every man is Christ, the head of a woman is her husband, and the head of Christ is God" (1 Cor 11:3).

Biblical passages by later writers (although attributed to Paul) enjoined women to forgo jewels, expensive clothes, and elaborate coiffures; and they forbade women to "teach or have authority over men," telling them to "learn in silence with all submissiveness" as is proper for one responsible for sin, consoling them, however, with the thought that they will be saved through childbearing (1 Tm 2:9–15). Other texts among the later Epistles defined women as the weaker sex and emphasized their subordination to their husbands (1 Pt 3:7; Col 3:18; Eph 5:22–23).

These passages from the New Testament became the arsenal employed by theologians of the early church to transmit negative attitudes toward women to medieval Christian culture—above all, Tertullian (*On the Apparel of Women*), Jerome (*Against Jovinian*), and Augustine (*The Literal Meaning of Genesis*).

THE IMAGE OF WOMEN IN MEDIEVAL LITERATURE. The philosophical, legal, and religious traditions born in antiquity formed the basis of the medieval intellectual synthesis wrought by trained thinkers, mostly clerics, writing in Latin and based largely in universities. The vernacular literary tradition that developed alongside the learned tradition also spoke about female nature and women's roles. Medieval stories, poems, and epics also portrayed women negatively—as lustful and deceitful—while praising good housekeepers and loyal wives as replicas of the Virgin Mary or the female saints and martyrs.

There is an exception in the movement of "courtly love" that evolved in southern France from the twelfth century. Courtly love was the erotic love between a nobleman and noblewoman, the latter usually superior in social rank. It was always adulterous. From the conventions of courtly love derive modern Western notions of romantic love. The tradition has had an impact disproportionate to its size, for it affected only a tiny elite, and very few women. The exaltation of the female lover probably does not reflect a higher evaluation of women or a step toward their sexual liberation. More likely it gives expression to the social and sexual tensions besetting the knightly class at a specific historical juncture.

The literary fashion of courtly love was on the wane by the thirteenth century, when the widely read *Romance of the Rose* was composed in French by two authors of significantly different dispositions. Guillaume de Lorris composed the initial four thousand verses about 1235, and Jean de Meun added about seventeen thousand verses—more than four times the original—about 1265.

The fragment composed by Guillaume de Lorris stands squarely in the tradition of courtly love. Here the poet, in a dream, is admitted into a walled garden where he finds a magic fountain in which a rosebush is reflected. He longs to pick one rose, but the thorns prevent his doing so, even as he is wounded by arrows from the god of love, whose commands he agrees to obey. The rest of this part of the poem recounts the poet's unsuccessful efforts to pluck the rose.

The longer part of the *Romance* by Jean de Meun also describes a dream. But here allegorical characters give long didactic speeches, providing a social satire on a variety of themes, some pertaining to women. Love is an anxious and tormented state, the poem explains: women are greedy and manipulative, marriage is miserable, beautiful women are lustful, ugly ones cease to please, and a chaste woman is as rare as a black swan.

Shortly after Jean de Meun completed *The Romance of the Rose*, Mathéolus penned his *Lamentations*, a long Latin diatribe against marriage translated into French about a century later. The *Lamentations* sum up medieval attitudes toward women and provoked the important response by Christine de Pizan in her *Book of the City of Ladies*.

In 1355, Giovanni Boccaccio wrote *Il Corbaccio*, another antifeminist manifesto, although ironically by an author whose other works pioneered new directions in Renaissance thought. The former husband of his lover appears to Boccaccio, condemning his unmoderated lust and detailing the defects of women. Boccaccio concedes at the end "how much men naturally surpass women in nobility" and is cured of his desires.[3]

---

3. Giovanni Boccaccio, *The Corbaccio, or The Labyrinth of Love*, trans. and ed. Anthony K. Cassell, rev. ed. (Binghamton, N.Y., 1993), 71.

WOMEN'S ROLES: THE FAMILY. The negative perceptions of women expressed in the intellectual tradition are also implicit in the actual roles that women played in European society. Assigned to subordinate positions in the household and the church, they were barred from significant participation in public life.

Medieval European households, like those in antiquity and in non-Western civilizations, were headed by males. It was the male serf (or peasant), feudal lord, town merchant, or citizen who was polled or taxed or succeeded to an inheritance or had any acknowledged public role, although his wife or widow could stand as a temporary surrogate. From about 1100, the position of property-holding males was further enhanced: inheritance was confined to the male, or agnate, line—with depressing consequences for women.

A wife never fully belonged to her husband's family, nor was she a daughter to her father's family. She left her father's house young to marry whomever her parents chose. Her dowry was managed by her husband, and at her death it normally passed to her children by him.

A married woman's life was occupied nearly constantly with cycles of pregnancy, childbearing, and lactation. Women bore children through all the years of their fertility, and many died in childbirth. They were also responsible for raising young children up to six or seven. In the propertied classes that responsibility was shared, since it was common for a wet nurse to take over breast-feeding and for servants to perform other chores.

Women trained their daughters in the household duties appropriate to their status, nearly always tasks associated with textiles: spinning, weaving, sewing, embroidering. Their sons were sent out of the house as apprentices or students, or their training was assumed by fathers in later childhood and adolescence. On the death of her husband, a woman's children became the responsibility of his family. She generally did not take "his" children with her to a new marriage or back to her father's house, except sometimes in the artisan classes.

Women also worked. Rural peasants performed farm chores, merchant wives often practiced their husbands' trades, the unmarried daughters of the urban poor worked as servants or prostitutes. All wives produced or embellished textiles and did the housekeeping, while wealthy ones managed servants. These labors were unpaid or poorly paid but often contributed substantially to family wealth.

WOMEN'S ROLES: THE CHURCH. Membership in a household, whether a father's or a husband's, meant for women a lifelong subordination to others.

In western Europe, the Roman Catholic Church offered an alternative to the career of wife and mother. A woman could enter a convent, parallel in function to the monasteries for men that evolved in the early Christian centuries.

In the convent, a woman pledged herself to a celibate life, lived according to strict community rules, and worshiped daily. Often the convent offered training in Latin, allowing some women to become considerable scholars and authors as well as scribes, artists, and musicians. For women who chose the conventual life, the benefits could be enormous, but for numerous others placed in convents by paternal choice, the life could be restrictive and burdensome.

The conventual life declined as an alternative for women as the modern age approached. Reformed monastic institutions resisted responsibility for related female orders. The church increasingly restricted female institutional life by insisting on closer male supervision.

Women often sought other options. Some joined the communities of laywomen that sprang up spontaneously in the thirteenth century in the urban zones of western Europe, especially in Flanders and Italy. Some joined the heretical movements that flourished in late medieval Christendom, whose anticlerical and often antifamily positions particularly appealed to women. In these communities, some women were acclaimed as "holy women" or "saints," whereas others often were condemned as frauds or heretics.

In all, although the options offered to women by the church were sometimes less than satisfactory, they were sometimes richly rewarding. After 1520, the convent remained an option only in Roman Catholic territories. Protestantism engendered an ideal of marriage as a heroic endeavor and appeared to place husband and wife on a more equal footing. Sermons and treatises, however, still called for female subordination and obedience.

THE OTHER VOICE, 1300–1700

When the modern era opened, European culture was so firmly structured by a framework of negative attitudes toward women that to dismantle it was a monumental labor. The process began as part of a larger cultural movement that entailed the critical reexamination of ideas inherited from the ancient and medieval past. The humanists launched that critical reexamination.

THE HUMANIST FOUNDATION. Originating in Italy in the fourteenth century, humanism quickly became the dominant intellectual movement in Europe. Spreading in the sixteenth century from Italy to the rest of Europe, it fueled the literary, scientific, and philosophical movements of the era and laid the basis for the eighteenth-century Enlightenment.

Humanists regarded the Scholastic philosophy of medieval universities as out of touch with the realities of urban life. They found in the rhetorical discourse of classical Rome a language adapted to civic life and public speech. They learned to read, speak, and write classical Latin and, eventually, classical Greek. They founded schools to teach others to do so, establishing the pattern for elementary and secondary education for the next three hundred years.

In the service of complex government bureaucracies, humanists employed their skills to write eloquent letters, deliver public orations, and formulate public policy. They developed new scripts for copying manuscripts and used the new printing press to disseminate texts, for which they created methods of critical editing.

Humanism was a movement led by males who accepted the evaluation of women in ancient texts and generally shared the misogynist perceptions of their culture. (Female humanists, as we will see, did not.) Yet humanism also opened the door to a reevaluation of the nature and capacity of women. By calling authors, texts, and ideas into question, it made possible the fundamental rereading of the whole intellectual tradition that was required in order to free women from cultural prejudice and social subordination.

A DIFFERENT CITY. The other voice first appeared when, after so many centuries, the accumulation of misogynist concepts evoked a response from a capable female defender: Christine de Pizan (1365–1431). Introducing her *Book of the City of Ladies* (1405), she described how she was affected by reading Mathéolus's *Lamentations:* "Just the sight of this book . . . made me wonder how it happened that so many different men . . . are so inclined to express both in speaking and in their treatises and writings so many wicked insults about women and their behavior."[4] These statements impelled her to detest herself "and the entire feminine sex, as though we were monstrosities in nature."[5]

The rest of *The Book of the City of Ladies* presents a justification of the female sex and a vision of an ideal community of women. A pioneer, she has received the message of female inferiority and rejected it. From the fourteenth to the seventeenth century, a huge body of literature accumulated that responded to the dominant tradition.

The result was a literary explosion consisting of works by both men and

---

4. Christine de Pizan, *The Book of the City of Ladies*, trans. Earl Jeffrey Richards, foreword by Marina Warner (New York, 1982), 1.1.1, pp. 3–4.

5. Ibid., 1.1.1–2, p. 5.

women, in Latin and in the vernaculars: works enumerating the achievements of notable women; works rebutting the main accusations made against women; works arguing for the equal education of men and women; works defining and redefining women's proper role in the family, at court, in public; works describing women's lives and experiences. Recent monographs and articles have begun to hint at the great range of this movement, involving probably several thousand titles. The protofeminism of these "other voices" constitutes a significant fraction of the literary product of the early modern era.

THE CATALOGS. About 1365, the same Boccaccio whose *Corbaccio* rehearses the usual charges against female nature wrote another work, *Concerning Famous Women*. A humanist treatise drawing on classical texts, it praised 106 notable women: ninety-eight of them from pagan Greek and Roman antiquity, one (Eve) from the Bible, and seven from the medieval religious and cultural tradition; his book helped make all readers aware of a sex normally condemned or forgotten. Boccaccio's outlook nevertheless was unfriendly to women, for it singled out for praise those women who possessed the traditional virtues of chastity, silence, and obedience. Women who were active in the public realm—for example, rulers and warriors—were depicted as usually being lascivious and as suffering terrible punishments for entering the masculine sphere. Women were his subject, but Boccaccio's standard remained male.

Christine de Pizan's *Book of the City of Ladies* contains a second catalog, one responding specifically to Boccaccio's. Whereas Boccaccio portrays female virtue as exceptional, she depicts it as universal. Many women in history were leaders, or remained chaste despite the lascivious approaches of men, or were visionaries and brave martyrs.

The work of Boccaccio inspired a series of catalogs of illustrious women of the biblical, classical, Christian, and local pasts, among them Filippo da Bergamo's *Of Illustrious Women*, Pierre de Brantôme's *Lives of Illustrious Women*, Pierre Le Moyne's *Gallerie of Heroic Women*, and Pietro Paolo de Ribera's *Immortal Triumphs and Heroic Enterprises of 845 Women*. Whatever their embedded prejudices, these works drove home to the public the possibility of female excellence.

THE DEBATE. At the same time, many questions remained: Could a woman be virtuous? Could she perform noteworthy deeds? Was she even, strictly speaking, of the same human species as men? These questions were debated over four centuries, in French, German, Italian, Spanish, and English, by authors male and female, among Catholics, Protestants, and Jews, in ponderous volumes and breezy pamphlets. The whole literary genre has been called the *querelle des femmes*, the "woman question."

The opening volley of this battle occurred in the first years of the fifteenth century, in a literary debate sparked by Christine de Pizan. She exchanged letters critical of Jean de Meun's contribution to *The Romance of the Rose* with two French royal secretaries, Jean de Montreuil and Gontier Col. When the matter became public, Jean Gerson, one of Europe's leading theologians, supported de Pizan's arguments against de Meun, for the moment silencing the opposition.

The debate resurfaced repeatedly over the next two hundred years. *The Triumph of Women* (1438) by Juan Rodríguez de la Camara (or Juan Rodríguez del Padron) struck a new note by presenting arguments for the superiority of women to men. *The Champion of Women* (1440–42) by Martin Le Franc addresses once again the negative views of women presented in *The Romance of the Rose* and offers counterevidence of female virtue and achievement.

A cameo of the debate on women is included in *The Courtier,* one of the most widely read books of the era, published by the Italian Baldassare Castiglione in 1528 and immediately translated into other European vernaculars. *The Courtier* depicts a series of evenings at the court of the duke of Urbino in which many men and some women of the highest social stratum amuse themselves by discussing a range of literary and social issues. The "woman question" is a pervasive theme throughout, and the third of its four books is devoted entirely to that issue.

In a verbal duel, Gasparo Pallavicino and Giuliano de' Medici present the main claims of the two traditions. Gasparo argues the innate inferiority of women and their inclination to vice. Only in bearing children do they profit the world. Giuliano counters that women share the same spiritual and mental capacities as men and may excel in wisdom and action. Men and women are of the same essence: just as no stone can be more perfectly a stone than another, so no human being can be more perfectly human than others, whether male or female. It was an astonishing assertion, boldly made to an audience as large as all Europe.

THE TREATISES. Humanism provided the materials for a positive counterconcept to the misogyny embedded in Scholastic philosophy and law and inherited from the Greek, Roman, and Christian pasts. A series of humanist treatises on marriage and family, on education and deportment, and on the nature of women helped construct these new perspectives.

The works by Francesco Barbaro and Leon Battista Alberti—*On Marriage* (1415) and *On the Family* (1434–37)—far from defending female equality, reasserted women's responsibility for rearing children and managing the house-keeping while being obedient, chaste, and silent. Nevertheless, they served the cause of reexamining the issue of women's nature by placing domestic is-sues at the center of scholarly concern and reopening the pertinent classical texts. In addition, Barbaro emphasized the companionate nature of marriage and the importance of a wife's spiritual and mental qualities for the well-being of the family.

These themes reappear in later humanist works on marriage and the edu-cation of women by Juan Luis Vives and Erasmus. Both were moderately sympathetic to the condition of women without reaching beyond the usual masculine prescriptions for female behavior.

An outlook more favorable to women characterizes the nearly unknown work *In Praise of Women* (ca. 1487) by the Italian humanist Bartolommeo Gog-gio. In addition to providing a catalog of illustrious women, Goggio argued that male and female are the same in essence, but that women (reworking the Adam and Eve narrative from quite a new angle) are actually superior. In the same vein, the Italian humanist Maria Equicola asserted the spiritual equality of men and women in *On Women* (1501). In 1525, Galeazzo Flavio Capra (or Capella) published his work *On the Excellence and Dignity of Women*. This hu-manist tradition of treatises defending the worthiness of women culminates in the work of Henricus Cornelius Agrippa *On the Nobility and Preeminence of the Female Sex*. No work by a male humanist more succinctly or explicitly presents the case for female dignity.

THE WITCH BOOKS. While humanists grappled with the issues pertain-ing to women and family, other learned men turned their attention to what they perceived as a very great problem: witches. Witch-hunting manuals, ex-plorations of the witch phenomenon, and even defenses of witches are not at first glance pertinent to the tradition of the other voice. But they do relate in this way: most accused witches were women. The hostility aroused by sup-posed witch activity is comparable to the hostility aroused by women. The evil deeds the victims of the hunt were charged with were exaggerations of the vices to which, many believed, all women were prone.

The connection between the witch accusation and the hatred of women is explicit in the notorious witch-hunting manual *The Hammer of Witches* (1486) by two Dominican inquisitors, Heinrich Krämer and Jacob Sprenger. Here the inconstancy, deceitfulness, and lustfulness traditionally associated with women are depicted in exaggerated form as the core features of witch be-havior. These traits inclined women to make a bargain with the devil—sealed by sexual intercourse—by which they acquired unholy powers. Such bizarre claims, far from being rejected by rational men, were broadcast by intellectuals. The German Ulrich Molitur, the Frenchman Nicolas Rémy, and the Italian Stefano Guazzo all coolly informed the public of sinister orgies and midnight pacts with the devil. The celebrated French jurist, historian, and political philosopher Jean Bodin argued that because women were especially prone to diabolism, regular legal procedures could properly be suspended in order to try those accused of this "exceptional crime."

A few experts such as the physician Johann Weyer, a student of Agrippa's, raised their voices in protest. In 1563, he explained the witch phenomenon thus, without discarding belief in diabolism: the devil deluded foolish old women afflicted by melancholia, causing them to believe they had magical powers. Weyer's rational skepticism, which had good credibility in the community of the learned, worked to revise the conventional views of women and witchcraft.

WOMEN'S WORKS. To the many categories of works produced on the question of women's worth must be added nearly all works written by women. A woman writing was in herself a statement of women's claim to dignity.

Only a few women wrote anything before the dawn of the modern era, for three reasons. First, they rarely received the education that would enable them to write. Second, they were not admitted to the public roles—as administrator, bureaucrat, lawyer or notary, or university professor—in which they might gain knowledge of the kinds of things the literate public thought worth writing about. Third, the culture imposed silence on women, considering speaking out a form of unchastity. Given these conditions, it is remarkable that any women wrote. Those who did before the fourteenth century were almost always nuns or religious women whose isolation made their pronouncements more acceptable.

From the fourteenth century on, the volume of women's writings rose. Women continued to write devotional literature, although not always as cloistered nuns. They also wrote diaries, often intended as keepsakes for their children; books of advice to their sons and daughters; letters to family members and friends; and family memoirs, in a few cases elaborate enough to be considered histories.

A few women wrote works directly concerning the "woman question," and some of these, such as the humanists Isotta Nogarola, Cassandra Fedele, Laura Cereta, and Olympia Morata, were highly trained. A few were professional writers, living by the income of their pens; the very first among them was Christine de Pizan, noteworthy in this context as in so many others. In addition to *The Book of the City of Ladies* and her critiques of *The Romance of the Rose*, she wrote *The Treasure of the City of Ladies* (a guide to social decorum for women), an advice book for her son, much courtly verse, and a full-scale history of the reign of King Charles V of France.

WOMEN PATRONS. Women who did not themselves write but encouraged others to do so boosted the development of an alternative tradition. Highly placed women patrons supported authors, artists, musicians, poets, and learned men. Such patrons, drawn mostly from the Italian elites and the courts of northern Europe, figure disproportionately as the dedicatees of the important works of early feminism.

For a start, it might be noted that the catalogs of Boccaccio and Alvaro de Luna were dedicated to the Florentine noblewoman Andrea Acciaiuoli and to Doña María, first wife of King Juan II of Castile, while the French translation of Boccaccio's work was commissioned by Anne of Brittany, wife of King Charles VIII of France. The humanist treatises of Goggio, Equicola, Vives, and Agrippa were dedicated, respectively, to Eleanora of Aragon, wife of Ercole I d'Este, Duke of Ferrara; to Margherita Cantelma of Mantua; to Catherine of Aragon, wife of King Henry VIII of England; and to Margaret, Duchess of Austria and regent of the Netherlands. As late as 1696, Mary Astell's *Serious Proposal to the Ladies, for the Advancement of Their True and Greatest Interest* was dedicated to Princess Anne of Denmark.

These authors presumed that their efforts would be welcome to female patrons, or they may have written at the bidding of those patrons. Silent themselves, perhaps even unresponsive, these loftily placed women helped shape the tradition of the other voice.

THE ISSUES. The literary forms and patterns in which the tradition of the other voice presented itself have now been sketched. It remains to highlight the major issues around which this tradition crystallizes. In brief, there are four problems to which our authors return again and again, in plays and catalogs, in verse and letters, in treatises and dialogues, in every language: the problem of chastity, the problem of power, the problem of speech, and the problem of knowledge. Of these the greatest, preconditioning the others, is the problem of chastity.

THE PROBLEM OF CHASTITY. In traditional European culture, as in those of antiquity and others around the globe, chastity was perceived as woman's quintessential virtue—in contrast to courage, or generosity, or leadership, or rationality, seen as virtues characteristic of men. Opponents of women charged them with insatiable lust. Women themselves and their defenders—

without disputing the validity of the standard—responded that women were capable of chastity.

The requirement of chastity kept women at home, silenced them, isolated them, left them in ignorance. It was the source of all other impediments. Why was it so important to the society of men, of whom chastity was not required, and who more often than not considered it their right to violate the chastity of any woman they encountered?

Female chastity ensured the continuity of the male-headed household. If a man's wife was not chaste, he could not be sure of the legitimacy of his offspring. If they were not his and they acquired his property, it was not his household, but some other man's, that had endured. If his daughter was not chaste, she could not be transferred to another man's household as his wife, and he was dishonored.

The whole system of the integrity of the household and the transmission of property was bound up in female chastity. Such a requirement pertained only to property-owning classes, of course. Poor women could not expect to maintain their chastity, least of all if they were in contact with high-status men to whom all women but those of their own household were prey.

In Catholic Europe, the requirement of chastity was further buttressed by moral and religious imperatives. Original sin was inextricably linked with the sexual act. Virginity was seen as heroic virtue, far more impressive than, say, the avoidance of idleness or greed. Monasticism, the cultural institution that dominated medieval Europe for centuries, was grounded in the renunciation of the flesh. The Catholic reform of the eleventh century imposed a similar standard on all the clergy and a heightened awareness of sexual requirements on all the laity. Although men were asked to be chaste, female unchastity was much worse: it led to the devil, as Eve had led mankind to sin.

To such requirements, women and their defenders protested their innocence. Furthermore, following the example of holy women who had escaped the requirements of family and sought the religious life, some women began to conceive of female communities as alternatives both to family and to the cloister. Christine de Pizan's city of ladies was such a community. Moderata Fonte and Mary Astell envisioned others. The luxurious salons of the French *précieuses* of the seventeenth century, or the comfortable English drawing rooms of the next, may have been born of the same impulse. Here women not only might escape, if briefly, the subordinate position that life in the family entailed but might also make claims to power, exercise their capacity for speech, and display their knowledge.

THE PROBLEM OF POWER. Women were excluded from power: the whole cultural tradition insisted on it. Only men were citizens, only men bore arms, only men could be chiefs or lords or kings. There were exceptions that did not disprove the rule, when wives or widows or mothers took the place of men, awaiting their return or the maturation of a male heir. A woman who attempted to rule in her own right was perceived as an anomaly, a monster, at once a deformed woman and an insufficient male, sexually confused and consequently unsafe.

The association of such images with women who held or sought power explains some otherwise odd features of early modern culture. Queen Elizabeth I of England, one of the few women to hold full regal authority in European history, played with such male/female images—positive ones, of course—in representing herself to her subjects. She was a prince, and manly, even though she was female. She was also (she claimed) virginal, a condition absolutely essential if she was to avoid the attacks of her opponents. Catherine de' Medici, who ruled France as widow and regent for her sons, also adopted such imagery in defining her position. She chose as one symbol the figure of Artemisia, an androgynous ancient warrior-heroine who combined a female persona with masculine powers.

Power in a woman, without such sexual imagery, seems to have been indigestible by the culture. A rare note was struck by the Englishman Sir Thomas Elyot in his *Defence of Good Women* (1540), justifying both women's participation in civic life and their prowess in arms. The old tune was sung by the Scots reformer John Knox in his *First Blast of the Trumpet against the Monstrous Regiment of Women* (1558); for him rule by women, defects in nature, was a hideous contradiction in terms.

The confused sexuality of the imagery of female potency was not reserved for rulers. Any woman who excelled was likely to be called an Amazon, recalling the self-mutilated warrior women of antiquity who repudiated all men, gave up their sons, and raised only their daughters. She was often said to have "exceeded her sex" or to have possessed "masculine virtue"—as the very fact of conspicuous excellence conferred masculinity even on the female subject. The catalogs of notable women often showed those female heroes dressed in armor, armed to the teeth, like men. Amazonian heroines romp through the epics of the age—Ariosto's *Orlando Furioso* (1532) and Spenser's *Faerie Queene* (1590–1609). Excellence in a woman was perceived as a claim for power, and power was reserved for the masculine realm. A woman who possessed either one was masculinized and lost title to her own female identity.

THE PROBLEM OF SPEECH. Just as power had a sexual dimension when it was claimed by women, so did speech. A good woman spoke little. Excessive speech was an indication of unchastity. By speech, women seduced men. Eve had lured Adam into sin by her speech. Accused witches were commonly accused of having spoken abusively, or irrationally, or simply too much. As enlightened a figure as Francesco Barbaro insisted on silence in a woman, which he linked to her perfect unanimity with her husband's will and her unblemished virtue (her chastity). Another Italian humanist, Leonardo Bruni, in advising a noblewoman on her studies, barred her not from speech but from public speaking. That was reserved for men.

Related to the problem of speech was that of costume—another, if silent, form of self-expression. Assigned the task of pleasing men as their primary occupation, elite women often tended toward elaborate costume, hairdressing, and the use of cosmetics. Clergy and secular moralists alike condemned these practices. The appropriate function of costume and adornment was to announce the status of a woman's husband or father. Any further indulgence in adornment was akin to unchastity.

THE PROBLEM OF KNOWLEDGE. When the Italian noblewoman Isotta Nogarola had begun to attain a reputation as a humanist, she was accused of incest—a telling instance of the association of learning in women with unchastity. That chilling association inclined any woman who was educated to deny that she was or to make exaggerated claims of heroic chastity.

If educated women were pursued with suspicions of sexual misconduct, women seeking an education faced an even more daunting obstacle: the assumption that women were by nature incapable of learning, that reasoning was a particularly masculine ability. Just as they proclaimed their chastity, women and their defenders insisted on their capacity for learning. The major work by a male writer on female education—that by Juan Luis Vives, *On the Education of a Christian Woman* (1523)—granted female capacity for intellection but still argued that a woman's whole education was to be shaped around the requirement of chastity and a future within the household. Female writers of the following generations—Marie de Gournay in France, Anna Maria van Schurman in Holland, and Mary Astell in England—began to envision other possibilities.

The pioneers of female education were the Italian women humanists who managed to attain a literacy in Latin and a knowledge of classical and Christian literature equivalent to that of prominent men. Their works implicitly and explicitly raise questions about women's social roles, defining problems that beset women attempting to break out of the cultural limits that had bound them. Like Christine de Pizan, who achieved an advanced education through her father's tutoring and her own devices, their bold questioning makes clear the importance of training. Only when women were educated to the same standard as male leaders would they be able to raise that other voice and insist on their dignity as human beings morally, intellectually, and legally equal to men.

THE OTHER VOICE. The other voice, a voice of protest, was mostly female, but it was also male. It spoke in the vernaculars and in Latin, in treatises and dialogues, in plays and poetry, in letters and diaries, and in pamphlets. It battered at the wall of prejudice that encircled women and raised a banner announcing its claims. The female was equal (or even superior) to the male in essential nature—moral, spiritual, and intellectual. Women were capable of higher education, of holding positions of power and influence in the public realm, and of speaking and writing persuasively. The last bastion of masculine supremacy, centered on the notions of a woman's primary domestic responsibility and the requirement of female chastity, was not as yet assaulted—although visions of productive female communities as alternatives to the family indicated an awareness of the problem.

During the period 1300–1700, the other voice remained only a voice, and one only dimly heard. It did not result—yet—in an alteration of social patterns. Indeed, to this day they have not entirely been altered. Yet the call for justice issued as long as six centuries ago by those writing in the tradition of the other voice must be recognized as the source and origin of the mature feminist tradition and of the realignment of social institutions accomplished in the modern age.

We thank the volume editors in this series, who responded with many suggestions to an earlier draft of this introduction, making it a collaborative enterprise. Many of their suggestions and criticisms have resulted in revisions of this introduction, although we remain responsible for the final product.

PROJECTED TITLES IN THE SERIES

Isabella Andreini, *Mirtilla*, edited and translated by Laura Stortoni

Tullia d'Aragona, *Complete Poems and Letters*, edited and translated by Julia Hairston

Tullia d'Aragona, *The Wretch, Otherwise Known as Guerrino*, edited and translated by Julia Hairston and John McLucas

Francesco Barbaro et al., *On Marriage and the Family*, edited and translated by Margaret L. King

LES DAMES DES ROCHES.

An eighteenth-century lithograph of Madeleine and Catherine des Roches (Collection Laruelle, vol. 106). Reproduced by permission of the Bibliothèque Nationale de France, Paris.

VOLUME EDITOR'S
INTRODUCTION

THE OTHER VOICE

The Dames des Roches, *mère et fille* (mother and daughter), as they were commonly called, rank among the best known and most prolific French women writers of the sixteenth century. Celebrated for their learning and their uncommon collaborative mother-daughter bond, they distinguished themselves for their bold assertion of women's right to *auctoritas* (poetic authority) in the realm of belles lettres. At a time when few intellectual women had their writings printed, they took pride in counting themselves among the few:[1] "whereas there are plenty of men who write," asserts Catherine in her dedicatory letter to her mother, "there are few women who get involved in such an exercise, and I've always desired to be counted among the few."[2] Although aware of their exceptionality, they retained a heightened sense of a common feminine condition, and their writings are suffused with an engaging feminist consciousness. They spent their entire lives in the southwestern city of Poitiers where they belonged to an elite circle of members of the upper gentry and the nobility of the robe (lawyers and royal officials). There, together, they wrote and published three volumes of writings in a wide variety of genres including poems, translations of Latin and Italian works, letters, prose dialogues, a pastoral drama, and a tragicomedy based on the biblical apocryphal story of Tobias. These volumes were published in the late 1570s and 1580s when they had already attained celebrity status for their learning and their coterie. Among the first in France, their literary circle paved the way for the

---

1. Women's writings make up less than one percent of the total number of printed editions in sixteenth-century France, see Susan Broomhall, *Women and the Book Trade in Sixteenth-Century France* (Aldershot: Ashgate, 2002), 1.

2. "Il y a bien assez d'hommes qui escrivent, mais peu de filles se meslent d'un tel exercice, et j'ay toujours desiré d'estre du nombre de peu," *Epistle to Her Mother* (see chap. 2).

flowering of the salon in the next century. In continuous dialogue with each other, with local and visiting members of their coterie, and with their times, they became astute political commentators: they addressed the issues of their day, the ravages of the religious civil wars,[3] the necessity for greater justice and equity before the law,[4] the weak monarchy, women's education, marriage and the family, violence against women, and the status of female intellectuals. Through their collaborative engagement in shared public discourse, the Dames des Roches modeled moral, political, and literary agency.

LIFE, WORKS, AND CONTEXT

Little is known about Madeleine des Roches's birth, childhood, and early life.[5] Born Madeleine Neveu into a bourgeois family of notaries ca. 1520, she was somehow fortunate enough to receive a good education. She was married twice. First, in 1539, she married André Fradonnet, a *procureur* (public prose-cutor) and the father of her three children, Nicolles, baptized on 17 March 1540; Catherine, baptized on 15 December 1542; and Lucrèce, baptized on

---

3. The Dames des Roches lived through seven civil wars from the first in 1562–63 to the last during their lifetime in 1579–84. Iconoclastic vandalism and desecration of churches, summary executions, drownings and hangings, the pillage and desolation of the countryside, and the sieges of cities (including Poitiers) were daily occurrences during the wars. Mother and daughter became through necessity caustic observers of the chaos around them. See Nicole Vray, *La guerre des religions dans la France de l'Ouest. Poitou, Aunis, Saintonge 1534–1610* (La Crèche: Geste Éditions, 1997); R. J. Knecht, *The French Civil Wars, 1562–1598* (London: Longman, 2000).

4. As active businesswomen buying land and houses, lending money, and collecting revenues, the Dames des Roches were frequently engaged in lawsuits against debtors. Their letters and poems include numerous references to jurists, the law, and the restitution of personal property.

5. On the Dames des Roches' lives and milieu, see George Diller, *Les Dames des Roches. Étude sur la vie littéraire à Poitiers dans la deuxième moitié du XVIe siècle* (Paris: Droz, 1936); Anne R. Larsen, "The French Humanist Scholars: Les Dames des Roches," in *Women Writers of the Renaissance and Reformation*, ed. Katharina Wilson (Athens: University of Georgia Press, 1987), 232–59; Tilde Sankovitch, *French Women Writers and the Book: Myths of Access and Desire* (Syracuse: Syracuse University Press, 1988); Eve-lyne Berriot-Salvadore, *Les femmes dans la société française de la Renaissance* (Geneva: Droz, 1990); Ann Rosalind Jones, *The Currency of Eros: Women's Love Lyric in Europe, 1540–1620* (Bloomington: Indiana University Press, 1990); Kirk Read, "French Renaissance Women Writers in Search of Community: Literary Constructions of Female Companionship in City, Family and Convent. Louise Labé Li-onnoize, Madeleine and Catherine des Roches, mère et fille, Anne de Marquets, Sœur de Poissy" (Ph.D. diss., Princeton University, 1991); Colette H. Winn, "Mère/fille/femme/muse: maternité et créativité dans les œuvres des Dames des Roches," *Travaux de Littérature* 4 (1991): 53–68; Kendall Tarte, "'Mes Rochers hautains': A Study of Madeleine and Catherine des Roches and the Culture of Renaissance Poitiers" (Ph.D. diss., University of Virginia, 1997); Madeleine Lazard, "Deux féministes poitevines au XVIe siècle: Les Dames des Roches," in *Joyeusement vivre et honnêtement penser. Mélanges offerts à Madeleine Lazard. Choix d'articles*, ed. Marie-Madeleine Fragonard and Gilbert Schrenck (Paris: Champion, 2000), 267–79; Cathy Yandell, *Carpe Corpus: Time and Gender in Early Modern France* (Newark: University of Delaware Press, 2000).

22 October 1547. Only Catherine survived infancy. After Fradonnet died in 1547, Madeleine married three years later François Éboissard, seigneur de la Villée. An *advocat* at the *présidial* (appeals court), originally from Brittany, Éboissard was elected in the 1560s as one of the seventy-five bourgeois who made up the municipal council at the city hall of Poitiers. He was taxed at 50 sols which represented a sufficient but not a great income.[6] Upon his death from a pulmonary disease during the summer of 1578, Madeleine wrote a mournful sonnet and an epitaph lauding his nobility, learning, and friendship for her.[7] In this striking epitaph, Madeleine's deceased husband speaks mostly about her rather than himself in his representation of her as an irreproachable widow.[8] It was upon the death of Éboissard that mother and daughter first allowed their works to appear in print. They adopted the quasi-noble name of Des Roches taken from a family property, located some seven kilometers east of Châtellerault, that Madeleine had inherited. Going public with such a surname highlighted their self-representation as members of a noble elite of letters whose modus vivendi they had adopted with the creation of their coterie.[9]

EDUCATION. Madeleine des Roches's education is a matter of speculation. She was a studious young woman, for in her first ode, collected and published with her other poems in *Les Œuvres* (1578–79), she admits her great disappointment at having to curtail her studies when she married. She likely

6. François Éboissard's income level can be compared with that of André Fradonnet, who was taxed at 7 sols. In marrying *maistre* Éboissard, Madeleine achieved a comfortable living for herself and her daughter. On the Des Roches' finances, see Diller, *Dames des Roches*, 168–69; George Huppert, *Les Bourgeois Gentilshommes: An Essay on the Definition of Elites in Renaissance France* (Chicago: University of Chicago Press, 1977), 123.

7. Sonnet 1, *Les Œuvres* (1579), ed. Anne R. Larsen (Geneva: Droz, 1993), 174; *Epitaph for Master François Éboissard, Lord of La Villée, her Husband* (see chap. 1). On the publication of the Des Roches' *Œuvres* in 1578 and 1579, see below.

8. See Colette H Winn on this epitaph, "Écriture, veuvage et deuil. Témoignages féminins du XVIᵉ siècle," in *Veufs, veuves et veuvage dans la France d'Ancien Régime. Actes du colloque de Poitiers (11–12 juin 1998)*, ed. Colette Winn and Nicole Pellegrin (Paris: Champion, 2003), 293. Madeleine's persona as an inviolate widow reflects her knowledge of customary law that dictated that a widow could retain her *douaire* and administer alone her wealth on the condition that she led an exemplary life. On widows and the law, see Jean-Marie Augustin, "La protection juridique de la veuve sous l'Ancien Régime," in *Veufs, veuves et veuvage dans la France d'Ancien Régime*, 25–45.

9. Families that rose into the nobility of the robe often dropped the family name, substituting that of a fief; see Nancy Roelker, *One King, One Faith. The Parlement of Paris and the Religious Reformations of the Sixteenth Century* (Berkeley: University of California Press, 1996), 26. While Madeleine continued to use her paternal surname Neveu in her (unpublished) correspondence, Catherine frequently signed only with the maternal surname Des Roches. A transcription of a sample unpublished letter by the mother and the daughter can be found in their *Missives* (1586), ed. Anne R. Larsen (Geneva: Droz, 1999), 70–71.

benefited from the intellectual renewal and enthusiasm for poetry that turned Poitiers into a cultural center from 1546 to 1554. The *poètes du Clain* (from the Clain river passing through Poitiers) included long-term poets from Poitou like Jean Salmon Macrin (1490–1557), Scévole de Sainte-Marthe (1536–1623) and Jean Boiceau de La Borderie (1513–91), as well as publishers and writers Jacques Bouchet (1476–ca. 1558) and Guillaume Bouchet (1514–92) and poets passing through Poitiers like Marc-Antoine Muret (1526–85), who studied law and taught poetry at the university; Joachim du Bellay (1522–60); the philosopher-scientist Jacques Peletier du Mans (1517–82), who resided in the city from 1549 to 1552; Jacques Tahureau (1527–55), who arrived in 1552; Jean-Antoine de Baïf (1532–89); and Jean Bastier de La Péruse (1529–54).[10] Madeleine probably continued learning in her spare time by making use of the private libraries of local lawyers and physicians, and certainly that of her husband François Éboissard. Such collections belonging to professionals, most notably jurists,[11] would have contained many legal works, the Church Fathers, works by humanist poets and writers such as Erasmus, Boccaccio, Petrarch, and Ariosto, Plato's works translated into Latin and interpreted by Marsilio Ficino and Pico della Mirandola, the Greek and Latin poets Hesiod, Horace, Ovid, and Virgil, and especially historians such as Plutarch, Herodotus, Sallust, Josephus, and Justin. Both Catherine des Roches and especially Madeleine des Roches establish their literary authority by citing abundantly from these sources. The humanist philologist Joseph-Juste Scaliger (ca. 1540–1609), who lived in Poitou for close to two decades (1574–93), recalls Madeleine in these terms:

> Madame des Roches the mother, who knows more than Madame her daughter, is more learned and has read and remembered more history, in my estimation, than any Frenchman; and she converses as elegantly, effortlessly, and eloquently as is possible. In short, she is the most learned person in Europe, among those who know only one language.[12]

---

10. On the *école du Clain* (school of the Clain), as it was called, see Alice Hulubei, *L'églogue en France au XVI* siècle, 1515–1589 (Paris: Droz, 1938), chap. 10; Trevor Peach, "Autour des *Amours de Francine*: quelques notes d'histoire littéraire," *Bibliothèque d'Humanisme et Renaissance* 44 (1982): 81–95; Jean Brunel, *Un poitevin poète, humaniste et soldat à l'époque des guerres de religion. Nicolas Rapin (1539–1608)*, 2 vols. (Paris: Champion, 2002), vol. 1, chap. 4.

11. The most important libraries in Paris belonged to members of the legal profession and to wealthy merchants. See Henry-Jean Martin, "What Parisians Read in the Sixteenth Century," in *French Humanism, 1470–1600*, ed. Werner L. Gundersheimer (New York: Harper, 1969), 134.

12. "Madame des Roches la mere, qui en sçait plus que Madame sa fille, est plus docte et a plus leu et retenu d'histoires, à mon jugement, qu'aucun François et parle autant proprement, facilement, et éloquemment qu'il est possible. Bref c'est la plus docte personne, pour ne sçavoir qu'une langue, qui soit en l'Europe." *Prima Scaligerana* (1595), 341, cited by Diller, *Dames des Roches*, 13.

Madeleine took charge of Catherine's education. Humanist pedagogy legitimized the authority of the mother in the care of infants and the young. Madeleine nursed her own daughter, thereby fulfilling the directives of humanist pediatric literature.[13] She took her responsibilities very seriously and in matters of instruction was far more daring than the majority of mothers of her social class. While she adhered to humanist views on the centrality of the mother's role, she deliberately disregarded their strictly utilitarian goals. She did not groom her daughter for marriage, the exclusive focus of the majority of parents of the time for whom the merger of two families was an economic and political investment. Instead, she inspired in Catherine a thirst for learning coupled with an ambition for poetic fame. She urges Catherine in her dedicatory *Epistle to My Daughter (Œuvres)* "to do your duty / Toward the Muse and divine learning"[14] so that someday Catherine would become "immortal" through her "virtue." Daughters of the upper gentry and urban nobility were sometimes sent to convent schools or more rarely tutored at home by a governess or male instructors. While likely home-tutored, Catherine was guided and inspired primarily by her learned mother, to the awe of contemporary commentators. Scévole de Sainte-Marthe, a cousin of the Des Roches, admiringly describes "the mother instructing her daughter and speaking to her of all the sciences with equal authority and ease."[15] Catherine may have had private tutors in Latin and Italian. It seems highly improbable, however, that she would have known Greek. She mastered Latin, even translating into French alexandrine verse for the first time two complete Latin classical texts, Pythagoras's *Symbola* (Symbols)[16] and Claudian's *De raptu Proserpinae* (On the

---

The one language is presumably Latin (possibly, but less likely, Italian), since Madeleine's native French would have been taken for granted.

13. In a sonnet of *Les Œuvres* of 1579 (see chap. 1), Madeleine conjures her ill daughter to get well soon "by [my] maternal love, by the sweet milk drawn from [my] breast, and [my] womb which bore you for nine months." On the nursing of children urged upon mothers by humanist pedagogues, see for instance Erasmus, "The New Mother" (1526), in *Erasmus on Women*, ed. Erika Rummel (Toronto: University of Toronto Press, 1996), 156–73; Juan Luis Vives, *The Education of a Christian Woman*, ed. and trans. Charles Fantazzi, Other Voice in Early Modern Europe (Chicago: University of Chicago Press, 2000), 2.10.131; Berriot-Salvadore, *Les Femmes dans la société française de la Renaissance*, 82–90. For an analysis of this sonnet, see chap. 1.

14. "Faire ton devoir / Envers la Muse et le divin sçavoir," *Epistle to My Daughter* (see chap. 1).

15. "La Mere instruire la fille, et luy parler de toutes les sciences avec autant de suffisance que de facilité." Scévole de Sainte-Marthe, *Éloges des hommes illustres, qui depuis un siecle ont fleury en France dans la profession des Lettres. Composez en Latin ... et mis en François, par G. Colletet* (Paris: Sommaville, 1644) (original Latin edition in 1596), in "Les Éloges des Dames des Roches sous l'ancien régime," in Des Roches, *Missives*, 361.

16. *Les Secondes Œuvres*, ed. Anne R. Larsen (Geneva: Droz, 1998), 127–42. Catherine also produced a French adaptation of Pythagoras's *Carmina aurea* (Golden Verse), which had been translated by Jean-Antoine de Baïf in 1574 and Barthélémy Fournier in 1577; see *Secondes Œuvres*, 122–26.

Rape of Proserpina).[17] In both adaptations, Catherine adds her own distinctive point of view, injecting a subjective tone into Pythagorean wisdom and Greco-Roman mythology.

LEGAL AND FINANCIAL DIFFICULTIES From 1560 into the 1570s, the Dames des Roches encountered legal and financial challenges. Madeleine refers four times in *Les Œuvres* to a thirteen-year lawsuit and in her letters mentions other court cases related to uncollected *rentes* (government bonds) and loans, as well as sales of properties. As members of the elite, they invested in parcels of land, loans to individuals, and *rentes* that allowed them to loan money at interest while helping to alleviate the royal debt. Their income from moneylending in the single year 1580–81 amounted to 551 livres 13 sous 4 deniers (or 8 percent) for an invested capital of 6,618 livres. The revenues from their landholdings on the other hand amounted to little more than 66 livres a year.[18]

To these legal and financial concerns were added the iconoclastic ransacking of Poitiers's churches and monasteries by Protestant armies in May 1562 and the siege of the city in 1569 by Admiral Gaspard de Coligny (1519–72) that led to the destruction of two of Madeleine's houses on the outskirts of the city. In 1578, the year of her second widowhood, Madeleine included in her first volume of collected poems an outspoken request to King Henri III for an indemnity for these properties that "may well have been worth two thousand pounds, / More than the worth of my pen and my books combined."[19] She was finally awarded a royal grant in February 1587, the year of her death. In odes 6 and 8 and a number of sonnets written during the 1560s,[20] Madeleine reflects on the ravages of the civil wars, particularly in connection with the attacks on Poitiers. She criticizes the Protestants as traitors to family, country, and crown, invoking in ode 2 the patricide of Oedipus and the matricide of Orestes. Her dramatic account of the 1569 siege of Poitiers (ode 8), the only female-authored response to this event, highlights incidents and heroic feats by various warriors, particularly the young Henri de Guise (1550–88). These events are also described by contemporary historians, both Catholic and Protestant, such as Marin Liberge, François de La Noue, Lancelot de La Popelinière, and Agrippa d'Aubigné. Her 187-

---

17. *Missives*, 212–87.

18. Diller, *Dames des Roches*, 174–75; Huppert, *Bourgeois Gentilshommes*, 123.

19. "Bien valoir deux mille livres, / Plus que ne m'ont valu ma plume ny mes livres" *Au Roy* (To the King) (see chap. 1).

20. Odes 6 and 8, *Œuvres* (1578–79); sonnets 15 to 20 (see chap. 1).

alexandrine narrative epitaph on the death of Timoléon de Cossé, comte de Brissac, a favorite at the court of Charles IX, who was killed at the age of twenty-six at the siege of Mussidan in Périgord on 28 April 1569, competes rhetorically with the outpouring of verse on this event by court and Pléiade poets.[21] Replete with mythological, historical, and political citations, as well as military references to celebrated battles fought by a host of sixteenth-century French nobles from François I, Henri II, and Henri III to the ducs de Guise (*père* and *fils*) and Antoine de Bourbon, king of Navarre, this epitaph circulated widely and must have attained a certain celebrity for it was included in a court manuscript collection.[22] In these and other instances such as her sonnets addressed to monarchs Charles IX and Henri III[23] and her unpublished poem to the Queen Mother Catherine de Médicis,[24] Madeleine des Roches entered public discourse as an astute political commentator and historiographer of her times. Her skill at applying serious historical research to the genre of epideictic verse enabled her to assert her agency on matters of social and public concern.

COTERIE AND PUBLICATIONS. The Dames des Roches' first publications appeared in the late 1570s after their literary coterie was established. Their house in Saint Michael's parish, close to the cathedral Notre Dame la Grande, was well situated to welcome daily the visitors who came to their home. Years later, Scévole de Sainte-Marthe recalled:

> The home of these two illustrious Ladies in Poitiers was an Academy of honor where daily there congregated a great many men of excellence

---

21. Examples include the collection *Epitaphes et regrets sur le trespas de Monsieur Thimoleon de Cossé, Comte de Brissac* (Paris: Gabriel Buon, 1569) that includes verse by Jean Dorat, Jean-Antoine de Baïf, Scévole de Sainte-Marthe, Amadis Jamyn, and others; Philippe Desportes, *Epitaphe de Timoléon de Cossé, Comte de Brissac* in *Cartels et masquerades. Epitaphes*, ed. Victor Graham (Geneva: Droz, 1958), 54; François de Belleforest, *Deploration de la France, sur la mort de tres-hault et puissant Seigneur Timoleon de Cossé, comte de Brissac* (Paris: Jean Hulpeau, 1569), and many others.

22. *Épitaphe de feu Monsieur le Comte de Brissac, Œuvres* (1578–79), 158–70. This poem appears in a court album (BNF, Fonds français 22.563, fols. 95–100).

23. Sonnets 10 to 14 (see chap. 1).

24. This unpublished sonnet to Catherine de Médicis appears in an elegant court manuscript of 47 folios (BNF, ancien fonds français 862, fols. 31–34) containing other poems by the Dames des Roches that were published in *Les Œuvres*. The album, composed between 1578 and 1584, contains poems to François d'Alençon (1554–84), King Henri III's younger brother, and to other members of the royal family; many are written anonymously but several bear the names of court poets such as Philippe Desportes (1546–1606) and Jacques Davy du Perron (1556–1618). Several anonymous sonnets are addressed to Charite, Catherine des Roches's coterie pseudonym. On the transcription of the manuscript poems related to the Dames des Roches, see Diller, *Dames des Roches*, appendix 3.

and where all those who professed *belles lettres* were welcomed with friendly entertainment and joy. And one can truthfully say that everyone who was introduced there, as learned and polished as he may have been upon arrival, left having gained even more learning and finer manners.[25]

Étienne Pasquier states admiringly that the Des Roches led disciplined lives allowing them to manage their household, study, write, *and* entertain on a daily basis: "In the mornings, you will find the mother and her daughter, after having ordered their household, bring out their books and write here a proper verse, there a well-appointed letter. After dinner and in the evenings, their door is open to any courteous man. There one discusses various matters, sometimes Philosophy, or history, or the weather, or some lively tales."[26] Although neither Sainte-Marthe nor Pasquier mention other women in attendance besides the Des Roches, there were a number of them, close family connections or learned friends. These would have included Catherine's aunt Perrine Chasteigner and her two daughters Madeleine (a poet in her own right) and Françoise Chémeraut, the two sisters Françoise and Marie Grené[27] (the former was the "Francine" of Jacques-Antoine de Baïf's love sonnets and the latter "L'Admirée" of Jacques Tahureau), the poet Suzanne Cailler, sister of Raoul Cailler and niece of the poet lawyer Nicolas Rapin (1539–1608), possibly Jeanne de Boulet, baronne de Germoles, who may have accompanied her husband, Jacques de Germigny, on his trips to Poitiers,[28] and a number of wives, daughters, and sisters of legists who visited the salon during the Grands Jours of 1579.[29]

In 1571, Caye-Jules de Guersens (ca. 1543–83), a distinguished member of their salon and a suitor of Catherine (who was then twenty-nine years old), published a play, *Panthée*, to which Madeleine appended a liminary quatrain. Guersens dedicated his play to Catherine, declaring that he had merely "put

---

25. "La maison de ces deux illustres Dames estoit à Poitiers, une academie d'honneur, où se trouvoient tous les jours plusieurs excellents hommes, et où tous ceux qui faisoient profession des belles lettres estoient reçeus avec caresse, et avecque joye. Et l'on peut dire en verité, que pas un n'y estoit introduict, pour docte et pour poly qu'il fust, qu'il n'en sortist avec plus de doctrine et plus de politesse." Scévole de Sainte-Marthe, *Éloges des hommes illustres*, in Des Roches, *Missives*, 362.

26. "Le matin, vous trouverez la mere et la fille, aprés avoir donné ordre à leur mesnage, se mettre sur les livres, puis tantost, faire un sage vers, tantost une epistre bien dictée. Les aprés-disnées et souppées, la porte est ouverte à tout honneste homme. Là l'on traite divers discours, ores de Philosophie, ores d'histoire, ou du temps, ou bien quelque propos gaillards." *Lettre à Pierre Pithou*, in *Les Lettres* (Paris: Abel L'Angelier, 1586), vol. 6, letter 11, in Des Roches, *Missives*, 348.

27. And not Françoise and Marie de Gennes. Trevor Peach rectifies the error, "Autour des *Amours de Francine*," 93.

28. On the couple, see letter 25 (see chap. 5).

29. On the Grands Jours, see below.

it in order" while she actually wrote it. He may have said this to flatter her into marrying him. Claude Pellejay (1542–1613), a mathematician, musician, and the son of a lawyer from Poitiers, also a suitor of Catherine and the same age, dedicated a manuscript collection of love sonnets and an *Hymne de la Beauté* (Hymn to Beauty) to her, now lost. Catherine's sonnet sequence *Sonnets from Sincero to Charite* and *From Charite to Sincero*, and her *Dialogue between Sincero and Charite*, refer to herself—her coterie pseudonym was Charite, a Greek term for Grace, as in the three Graces—and possibly Claude Pellejay,[30] although the character of Sincero could be an amalgam of traits constituting the typical Petrarchan lover. In this highly unusual love sequence, Sincero ends up praising Charite's learned writings so that she will bring him fame; he claims to derive his very existence from her tales which give her the power to withhold or confer immortality.[31] Catherine refused Pellejay's suit, as she would all others, preferring to remian a lifelong companion to her mother, unencumbered by the strictures of marriage.

Catherine experimented with political verse when in 1574 she addressed the ode *To the King* (*Œuvres*) to Henri III (1551–89), who, upon his return to Paris on 30 May from a brief sojourn in Poland, was crowned king following the death of his brother Charles IX (1550–74). As in the genre of the "mirror for princes," Catherine adopts the persona of a *conseiller* instructing the king on his duties and praising him especially—a trait not generally found in the genre—for his filial devotion to the Queen Mother Catherine de Médicis. As Susan Broomhall reminds us, rare was the woman writer who dared to advise a king; among those who did, only authoritative members of the royal family such as Marguerite de Navarre and Catherine de Médicis could offer in writing legitimate counsel.[32] Catherine's daring self-representation as critical advisor to the king is founded on her connection to legal circles where, as Donald Kelley has stated, the *advocats du roi*, particularly those of the Paris Parlement, "together with their more anonymous notarial colleagues, constituted the ideological shock-troops of the monarchy."[33] They

---

30. George Diller argues for this identification in "Un amant de Catherine des Roches: Claude Pellejay," in *Mélanges de littérature, d'histoire et de philologie offerts à Paul Laumonier* (Paris: Droz, 1935), 287–303.

31. For an analysis of this sequence, see chap. 2.

32. Susan Broomhall, "'In my opinion': Charlotte de Minut and Female Political Discussion in Print in Sixteenth-Century France," *Sixteenth-Century Journal* 31, no. 1 (2000): 33. Christine de Pizan was a notable exception when during the Hundred Years War she addressed numerous epistles and works to members of the royal family pleading with them to bring about a lasting peace.

33. Donald R. Kelley, *The Beginning of Ideology: Consciousness and Society in the French Reformation* (Cambridge: Cambridge University Press, 1981), 182.

were integral to the fashioning of French kingship, justifying the expansion of royal power and centralization. Although a woman, Catherine exploited her connection with this service elite to speak publicly, and in her social position as learned writer and hostess of a famous coterie she exercised her authority.

In 1575, polymaths Scévole de Sainte-Marthe and Joseph-Juste Scaliger translated Catherine's ode to the king, the former into Latin and the latter into Greek. By harnessing the prestige of these humanists and participating in the flurry of publications lauding the newly crowned king, Catherine signaled her desire to engage in political discourse and become better known among court and literary circles in the capital. Her aspiration was fulfilled when, in 1577, the city of Poitiers hosted the royal family and the court for three months from 2 July to 5 October. During this time Henri III negotiated and ratified the Peace of Bergerac. The treaty, known as the Edict of Poitiers, was signed on 14 September, bringing to an end the sixth war of religion (1576–77).[34] During the court's sojourn, sessions of the Palace Academy were regularly held at Henri III's dinner table. The principal lecturer, Pontus de Tyard (1521–1605), discussed the origins of the world and the four elements which make up the universe.[35] Tyard's *discours* on one of these elements—water—may have inspired Catherine's *Hymne de l'Eau à la Roine* (Water Hymn to the Queen) in honor of Queen Louise of Lorraine (1553–1601), consort of Henri III. She addressed to the queen mother an *Imitation de la mere de Salomon à la Roine Mere* (Imitation of the Mother of Solomon to the Queen Mother) whose immediate source, Proverbs 31:1–9, features a queen mother offering advice to her royal son. Des Roches adopts the persona of Catherine de Médicis counseling her son to uphold justice, remain faithful to his wife if he wishes to have an heir, and refrain from war: "What's the use," she writes, "of seeing our land / Strewn with so many corpses?"[36] Catherine could have also composed her feminist *For a Masquerade of Amazons* and *Song of the Amazons* to commemorate court entertainments performed at Poitiers. Her poems cele-

34. The Edict of Poitiers and the later Treaty of Nérac (February 1579) represent, more than any other pacification decrees during the civil wars, a matrix from which the drafters modeled the Edict of Nantes in 1598, bringing a final end to the wars of religion. Henri de Navarre, as governor of Guyenne and later king of France, was present at all three negotiations. See Gregory Champeaud, "The Edict of Poitiers and the Treaty of Nérac, or Two Steps towards the Edict of Nantes," *Sixteenth-Century Journal* 32, no. 2 (2001): 319–34.

35. On the Academy's sessions held in Poitiers, see Robert Sealy, *The Palace Academy of Henry III* (Geneva: Droz, 1981), 81–134.

36. "Et que sert-il de voir nostre terre semée / De tant de corps humains?" *Œuvres*, 326.

brate the defiance of the mythical Amazons who refuse to submit to the god of love and eschew male control of their lives.[37]

The Dames des Roches published these and other poems in 1578 in *Les Œuvres de Mes-dames des Roches de Poetiers, Mere et Fille* (The Works of Mesdames des Roches of Poitiers, Mother and Daughter). It may seem surprising that they elected to publish in Paris rather than their native Poitiers. At mid-century, Poitiers was a thriving commercial city of sixteen thousand inhabitants and twenty-eight parishes, with a major university, a celebrated law school, and numerous printers and booksellers.[38] However, the civil wars had wreaked havoc in the region, and according to Joseph-Juste Scaliger on a visit to Poitiers in 1576, "I see there only a great solitude in regard to letters, and a great instability and promptness for sedition."[39] Abel L'Angelier, a rising star in the Parisian book market, contacted them first. A *privilege du roi* was accorded to him on 12 July 1578 for the publication of the volume.[40] L'Angelier sought to make a name for himself with a volume containing works already known in manuscript form among the king's entourage and in Parisian literary society. Furthermore, an early version of Catherine's *Hymne de l'Eau à la Roine* had appeared in Paris in 1578 in a volume containing a translation of Longus's *Daphne and Chloe* and Louise Labé's *Debate of Folly and Love*.[41] The volume of the Des Roches' *Œuvres* has two sections, one containing the mother's works prefaced by a dedicatory letter to her daughter, the other her daughter's works prefaced by a dedicatory epistle to her mother. This pat-

---

37. For an analysis of these poems, see chap. 2.

38. In 1552, Poitiers had four printers and twenty-seven booksellers; see Jean-Pierre Andrault, *Poitiers à l'âge baroque 1594–1652*, 2 vols. (Poitiers: Société des antiquaires de l'ouest, 2003), 1:266. The university, with its complement of fifty doctors and master regents who taught in thirteen colleges, had a large, fairly well-off student body. Poitiers's bishopric was the richest in the Gallican Church, and the income of such institutions as the collegiate church of St. Hilaire and the monastery of Sainte Croix was on a huge scale.

39. "Je n'y voy qu'une grande solitude de lettres, et une grande legereté et promptitude à faire sédition." Letter to Claude du Puy (25 September 1576), cited by Richmond Lauren Hawkins, "The Friendship of Joseph Scaliger and François Vertunien," *Romanic Review* 8, no. 2 (1917): 135.

40. On Abel L'Angelier's status in the Parisian book market and his relationship with the Dames des Roches, see Jean Balsamo, "Abel L'Angelier et ses dames. Les Dames des Roches, Madeleine de L'Aubespine, Marie Le Gendre, Marie de Gournay," in *Des femmes et des livres: France et Espagne, XIVᵉ–XVIIᵉ*, ed. Dominique de Courcelles and Carmen Val Julián (Paris: École des Chartes, 1999), 117–36.

41. Louise Labé, *Debate of Folly and Love* (Paris: Jean Parent, 1578). The *Hymne de l'eau à la Roine* evidently circulated in manuscript form among Parisian circles. Titled *Louange des eaux* in Jean Parent's edition, it contains a number of minor differences from the version printed in *Les Œuvres*. This volume was presumed lost by George Diller. However, there are two extant copies, one at the Bibliothèque Mazarine in Paris and one at the Bibliothèque de Lyon, fond Coste.

tern, repeated in each subsequent volume, underscores the familial community which they used to legitimize their writings. The cautionary editorial
strategy of dedicating their books to each other invokes the convention of
the female sponsor or "chaperon" frequently found in Renaissance women's
writings. It also indicates the collaborative nature of the Des Roches' venture.
None of their works, however, is co-authored, as the symmetrical layout of
their books makes clear. *Les Œuvres* includes on Madeleine's part nine odes,
thirty-six sonnets, and epitaphs for her deceased husband François Ebois-
sard, the comte de Brissac, and the baron d'Anguervaques. For her portion
Catherine chose six dialogues, a sequence of twenty-six sonnets from Sincero to Charite and vice versa that includes as well three *chansons* and a *bla-
son*, two poems on the Amazons, the sonnets *To My Distaff* and *To My Writings*,
the *Chanson de la Musique* (Song of Music), the poems written for the king's
entourage described above, *The Strong Woman as Described by Solomon* (a para-
phrase of the Song of the Valiant Woman in Proverbs 31), which Catherine
dedicates to her mother, the narrative poem *Agnodice*, and epitaphs for Medea,
Clytemnestra, Lucretia, and Niobe translated from the Italian.[42]

This first volume was quickly followed in 1579 by a second edition, also
published by Abel L'Angelier, that includes new sonnets, Madeleine's request
for an indemnity from the king for her two destroyed townhouses, and
Catherine's *Un acte de la tragicomedie de Tobie* (One Act of the Tragicomedy of
Tobias). In this drama, Catherine revises the biblical apocryphal story by
turning Sarah, Tobias's bride, and her mother into major characters who at-
tempt to supplant the love relation between Tobias and Sarah with their own

---

42. *Œuvres* (1578–79), 342–46. Catherine des Roches was familiar with Italian contemporary
poets. She found the four epitaphs in Bernardo Accolti's *Verginia. Comedia* (Vinegia: Zoppino,
1530), fols. 47v–48v. Catherine also translated a sonnet blazon on the hand, *O bella man*, by Giovanni Mozzarello found in Girolamo Ruscelli, *I fiori delle rime de' poeti illustri* (Venice: Giovambat-
tista and Melchior Sessa, 1558) (further edition in 1579, fol. 281). This translation is included
in *Les Secondes Œuvres*, 347–48. Letter 63 in *Missives* (204) refers to a saying by Francesco Maria
Molza (1489–1544), a poet from Modena, whose verse Catherine may have read in Ruscelli's anthology. Mother and daughter refer to the characters of Logistilla, symbol of reason, the good
sorceress Melissa, and Alcina, symbol of sensuality in Lodovico Ariosto's *Orlando Furioso*, which
gained enormous popularity during the 1570s in the Parisian literacy circles of Catherine de
Clermont and Madeleine de L'Aubespine. Finally, in her feminist *Dialogue between Placide and Severe*
(*Secondes Œuvres*), she invokes as exemplary models of female professionalism four Italian learned
women, Cassandra Fedele, Laura Terracina, Ippolita Taurella, and Olympia Morata. On their
significance for Des Roches's oeuvre, see chap. 4. On the popularity of *Orlando Furioso* and its
French translators who included Nicolas Rapin, one of the guests of the Des Roches' coterie, see
Rosanna Gorris, "'Je veux chanter d'amour la tempeste et l'orage': Desportes et les *Imitations de
l'Arioste*," in *Philippe Desportes (1546–1606). Un poète presque parfait entre Renaissance et Classicisme*, ed.
Jean Balsamo (Paris: Klincksieck, 2000), 173–211.

economy of creative exchange. In the end, however, Sarah's father asserts the cultural norm of marriage. Des Roches's implicit critique is that marriage and separation from the mother lead to unhappiness, the destruction of the mother-daughter bond, and the silencing of women's voices.

Unlike the 1578 edition of *Les Œuvres* of which there are only seven extant copies in library collections, the 1579 edition has twenty-two extant copies and shows differences from the first edition in ornamentation, typography, punctuation, and orthography. This new amplified edition, appearing so soon after the first, highlights the growing national reputation of the mother-daughter team from Poitiers.[43]

THE FLEA OF THE GRANDS JOURS AND FINAL PUBLICATIONS. The Dames des Roches' coterie acquired even greater prestige when from 10 September to 18 December 1579, the Grands Jours or Great Assizes courts brought influential jurists to Poitiers from the Paris Parlement. Henri III commissioned these Parisian lawyers to relieve the congestion of the local courts due to the property damage caused by the civil wars. Since Poitiers did not have a *parlement* of its own, the Grands Jours were intended to assert the authority of the king over the city and the region and serve as an institution with jurisdiction in criminal matters. Two of the legists, Étienne Pasquier (1529–1615) and Antoine Loisel (1536–1617), headed for the Des Roches home upon arriving in Poitiers. Their lively conversation with the two ladies produced one of the best-known episodes in social literary history. Pasquier, seeing a flea on Catherine's breast, proposed that each immortalize the insect in a poetic exchange. No sooner had both complied and read their work in a salon gathering than a number of the Parisian legists and several of the local habitués of the salon began to produce odes, sonnets, epigrams, and blazons punning in Latin, Greek, and French on the erotic peregrinations of the *puce* (flea) over the body of the fair *pucelle* (maiden). These poems were later collected by Jacques de Sourdrai and published by Abel L'Angelier in a ninety-three-folio collection *La Puce de Madame des-Roches* (The Flea of Madame des Roches). L'Angelier obtained a royal privilege on 7 November 1582 and had a small number of copies issued before the end of the year with the bulk of the edition printed at the beginning of 1583. Catherine's poem *The Flea* opens the volume, offering a highly original tale of resistance and empowerment.

Nine poems or "responses" of Catherine des Roches, included in the col-

---

43. As scion of a publishing house founded by his father and uncle in collaboration with their wives, Abel L'Angelier did business with a network of printers and booksellers in many other cities, most notably Lyons.

laborative volume of *La Puce,* appear along with another seven responses on the flea in the *Secondes Œuvres de Mes-dames des Roches de Poictiers, Mere et Fille* (Second Works of Mesdames des Roches of Poitiers, Mother and Daughter). This volume, published in 1583, was sold by Nicolas Courtois, the newly appointed publisher for the University of Poitiers. Although Madeleine des Roches had asked L'Angelier to publish this second volume, the latter demurred. It is possible that he thought the volume of lesser quality, but a more plausible explanation for his refusal is that the printers working for him at the time may have been too busy with other book projects, or that the collection as a whole focused too much on Poitiers. Indeed Poitiers is at the center, its siege in 1569, its Grands Jours and the flea contest as well as other local events pertaining to the Des Roches' coterie. In her portion of the volume, Madeleine includes two odes, five sonnets, and several quatrains and octets; she exalts the illustrious guests who frequented her salon and praises Poitiers for its institutions as well as for its famous resistance to the army of Admiral Coligny during the 1569 siege (she thus contributes to the relatively new poetic emphasis at the time on cities and urban sites). In *La Mesme ville au Roy* (The Same City to the King),[44] Madeleine's female speaker represents Poitiers pleading with the king to reinstate a *parlement* or sovereign court, which had been so central to the city's administrative life in 1418–36, when Poitiers was the French capital under King Charles VII. Such an institution, Madeleine writes, would grant Poitiers even more authority to crush the "rebel Huguenots" and maintain law and order.[45]

Catherine des Roches includes in her portion two feminist pedagogical dialogues on the education of girls, translations of Pythagoras's *Vers dorez* (Golden Verses) and *Enigmes* (Symbols), two prayers for before and after dinner, two canticles to the Virgin, several epitaphs and sonnets, two songs (one from Sincero and one from Charite), forty-six "Responses," and a pastoral drama entitled *Bergerie.* In the pastoral, Des Roches delights in presenting a virtuous and learned beloved (Amaranthe) formed in her own image who is the undisputed mistress of a male admirer (Violier). Amaranthe is free to arbitrate her own destiny while her lover is left to strike a balance between his restless passion and his duty to serve her. Mirroring salon conversation and activities, shepherds and shepherdesses mingle, sing, and discuss different

---

44. *Secondes Œuvres,* 101–4.

45. On a parlement in Poitiers, see Hilary J. Bernstein, *Between Crown and Community. Politics and Civic Culture in Sixteenth-Century Poitiers* (Ithaca: Cornell University Press, 2004), 168–71. I was unable to benefit from this important study that appeared after this book's completion.

views on love: Marguerite and Fleurion embody sensuality, Pensée remains skeptical, disengaged from love, and single (she defends the celibate and independent female self), and Roseline believes that one can maintain rational control over one's desires. Des Roches's pastoral offers an idealized version of an egalitarian mixed community where friendship between men and women as well as *amour honnête* is in full display.

In 1586, the Dames des Roches had their last work, *Les Missives de Mesdames des Roches de Poictiers, Mere et Fille* (The Letters of the Dames des Roches of Poitiers, Mother and Daughter), published in Paris by Abel L'Angelier. They were the first women in France to publish their private letters, rewritten for publication to be sure. They adapted two epistolary traditions, the humanist letter intended to influence public opinion and make a name for oneself, and the *lettre mondaine* (courtly letter) modeled by such court secretaries as Étienne du Tronchet (ca. 1500–1584) whose *Lettres missives et familieres* (Familiar Letters and Missives) (1569) dominated the epistolary market into the next century.[46] The Des Roches' last volume contains ninety-six letters, Catherine's ambitious translation *Le Ravissement de Proserpine*, and several responses, epitaphs, and imitations by both mother and daughter. The translation into 1,480 alexandrines of the late Latin poet Claudian's unfinished epic *De raptu Proserpinae* (On the Rape of Proserpina) provides Des Roches with grounds to retell the powerful story of the rape and separation of Proserpina from her mother, Ceres. By elaborating on the violence of the abduction and the horror of Ceres at being torn from her daughter, Des Roches evokes the deep bonds between mothers and daughters and especially the fact that, in Tilde Sankovitch's words, Madeleine and Catherine's "poetic creativity is made possible by their inseparability, which nothing or nobody is to interrupt or disrupt."[47]

In the summer of 1587, the plague reached Poitiers. When they became ill, the Dames des Roches dictated their last testament on 8 October and both died before the end of November. They were buried in an unmarked common grave. Posthumous *elogia* state that they died together on the same day. As life had united the mother and her daughter, so they were inseparable in death: "Death itself, deaf and inexorable," writes Scévole de Sainte-Marthe,

---

46. For an analysis of the Des Roches' letters, see chap. 5.

47. Tilde Sankovitch, "Catherine des Roches's *Le Ravissement de Proserpine*. A Humanist/Feminist Translation," in *Renaissance Women Writers. French Texts / American Contexts*, ed. Anne R. Larsen and Colette H. Winn (Detroit: Wayne State University Press, 1994), 57.

"could not refuse the ardent and noble desire of these two generous Ladies who sought so passionately to live and die together."[48]

THE OEUVRE OF THE DAMES DES ROCHES: MAJOR THEMES

Three major themes, crystallizing around the terms *vertu* (virtue), *loi* (law), and *plume* (pen), are to be found in the writings of the Dames des Roches. Each acquires its specificity from the Des Roches' sociopolitical connection to an urban elite for whom education and ennoblement played a central defining role.[49] Their entourage consisted mostly of educated family members and professionals— physicians, university professors, and especially the upwardly mobile office-holding members of the emerging nobility of the robe, including lawyers, judges, mayors of Poitiers, *échevins* and officers of the king, *conseillers présidiaux*, members of the *sénéchaussée* court, and royal administrators. This "open" service nobility, which emerged in the course of the century as a new governing elite, posed a threat to the older hereditary nobility of the sword, which had come under attack for its disreputable conduct during the wars of religion.[50] Political commentators of the period, many of them members of the new elite, called for a more modern view of the nobility based on an alliance of education, merit,[51] civility, and the cultivation of virtue. In Donna Bohanan's words, "culture itself became a new *marque de noblesse.*"[52] The catchall phrase "to live nobly" epitomized the aspirations of this urban elite, whose class boundaries at the time were fluid. This new style of living was neither that of the bourgeois merchant intent on monetary gain nor that of the *gentilhomme de race.* It connoted a separate ideal of nobility founded on civility and letters.[53] Educated women were considered instru-

---

48. "La mort mesme toute sourde et toute inexorable qu'elle est, n'a peu resister aux ardans et nobles desirs de ces deux genereuses Dames, qui ne souhaittoient rien plus passionnément que de vivre et de mourir ensemble." *Éloges des hommes illustres,* in Des Roches, *Missives,* 363.

49. As Robert Favreau indicates, Poitiers was dominated by the legal profession: "Les valeurs dominantes y sont celles de l'office et de l'anoblissement" (The dominant values are those of legal office and ennoblement). *Histoire de Poitiers* (Paris: Privat, 1985), 189.

50. For the criticism of the old nobility, see Ellery Schalk, *From Valor to Pedigree. Ideas of Nobility in France in the Sixteenth and Seventeenth Century* (Princeton: Princeton University Press, 1986), chaps. 4–5.

51. "Merit" signified both virtue, or a person's superior qualities, and generosity, assessed in his or her relation to someone else. See Jay Smith, *The Culture of Merit: Nobility, Royal Service, and the Making of Absolute Monarchy in France, 1600–1789* (Ann Arbor: University of Michigan Press, 1996), 20–21.

52. Donna Bohanan, *Crown and Nobility in Early Modern France* (New York: Palgrave, 2001), 14.

53. Huppert, *Bourgeois Gentilshommes,* chap. 8; Elizabeth Goldsmith, *Exclusive Conversations: The Art of Interaction in Seventeenth-Century France* (Philadelphia: University of Pennsylvania Press, 1988), 8–9.

mental in promoting this new ideal and "the integration of new individuals into the elite."[54] The Dames des Roches participated in these discussions in their role as "promoters of civility," a role they viewed as a social and moral responsibility. By means of their coterie and their writings, they came to embody *civilité mondaine* (worldly civility).[55] Agrippa d'Aubigné, who visited their coterie during the Grands Jours, admired their "elegance,"[56] and for seventeenth-century panegyrist Hilarion de Coste their home was "l'escole du sçavoir, l'Academie d'honneur, et la demeure des Muses" (the school for learning, the Academy of honor, and the dwelling of the Muses [in Poitiers]), even resembling a sort of "Academie des Sciences,"[57] while for Madeleine de Scudéry it was quite simply "le Temple des Muses" where reigned "la vertu, l'esprit et la beauté" (virtue, wit, and beauty).[58]

The Des Roches underscore the Platonic notion of learning as a means to virtue, defined by Randle Cotgrave as "worth, merit, valor, talent," with the added notion of sexual purity and chastity when applied to a woman. In their letters, they frequently associate eloquence with virtue, as in letter 2 where Madeleine lauds her male interlocutor for his "excellences en vertu, doctrine, et courtoisie" (excellence in virtue, learning, and courtesy), or in letter 17 to a lawyer whose "singulieres vertus" (singular virtues) are attributed to the "divines graces qui reluisent en vos escrits" (divine grace so evident in your writings). This same acquisition of virtue through letters applies to women who in the Des Roches' oeuvre study not merely to avoid idleness, as prescribed in humanist conduct books, but to "exercise an important public role"[59] and

54. Carolyn C. Lougee, *Le Paradis des Femmes. Women, Salons, and Social Stratification in Seventeenth-Century France* (Princeton: Princeton University Press, 1976), 41. While Lougee writes predominantly of seventeenth-century salon women, her view holds as well for sixteenth-century provincial coterie women like the Des Roches. Even though Madeleine's origins were in the gentry, she was perceived on account of her learning and her coterie as belonging to the urban nobility. Madeleine de Scudéry, in a telling remark, describes Madeleine as having "toûjours l'air fort noble" (always a very noble air about her). *Conversations nouvelles sur divers sujets, dediée au roy* (Paris: Claude Barbin, 1684), in *'De l'air galant' et autres conversations. Pour une étude de l'archive galante,* ed. Delphine Denis (Paris: Champion, 1998), 263.

55. For an overview of women's roles in the early modern French salon, see Steven Kale, "Women, the Public Sphere, and the Persistence of Salons," *French Historical Studies* 25, no. 1 (2002): 115–48.

56. Agrippa d'Aubigné, "À mes filles touchant les femmes doctes de nostre siecle," in *Lettres touchant quelques poincts de diverses sciences* (1616), in *Œuvres complètes,* ed. H. Weber, J. Bailbé, and M. Soulié (Paris: Gallimard, Bibliothèque de la Pléiade, 1969), 851–54; see Des Roches, *Missives,* 358.

57. Hilarion de Coste, *Les eloges et les vies des Reynes, des Princesses, et des Dames illustres . . .,* 2 vols. (Paris: Sebastien Cramoisy, 1647), 2:232–37; see Des Roches, *Missives,* 369, 372.

58. Madeleine de Scudéry, *Conversations nouvelles sur divers sujets,* 263; see Des Roches, *Missives,* 378.

59. Yandell, *Carpe Corpus,* 211.

acquire "immortalité." In addition to depicting accomplished female heroines noted for their learning (the "femme forte" of *The Strong Woman described by Solomon*, Agnodice, Pasithée, Sarra in the *Tragicomedie de Tobie*, Amaranthe and Pensée in the *Bergerie*), Catherine is especially fond of addressing letters and *responce* poems to contemporary learned women: she praises a female correspondent for attaining "le plus hault degré de ceste admirable eloquence" (the highest level of that admirable eloquence) which belonged to the Gallic Hercules, a symbol of linguistic nationalism;[60] another she calls a "miracle entre les autres filles" (miracle among young girls) for combining beauty, poetic writing, painting, and music in such a way that "you can with the pen and the brush grant immortality to mere mortals, thus making yourself immortal as well."[61] In a response to her cousin, the poet Madeleine Chémeraut, she rejoices that in celebrating in print her cousin's "gracieuse Muse," "purité de tes meurs" (purity of morals), and "Ame sage et sçavante" (wise and learned soul), she profits doubly: she brings honor to her cousin and sings her own praise as well.[62] Catherine's adaptation of the topos of *exegi monumentum* (I have erected a monument) to female learning is thus a radical revision of the Pléiade gender-bound principle that the *male* poet alone can bestow immortality.

Second, the Des Roches' knowledge of ancient and contemporary humanist letters afforded them an education in rhetoric. Considered an instrument of politics, rhetoric prepared them to enter into political discourse. Rhetoric was viewed in the Renaissance as an art of persuasion aimed at producing action in the world and engaged with basic social and political concerns.[63] Susan Broomhall notes that publications by women on political issues were prevalent between 1560–69 and 1585–89 when political turmoil wreaked havoc in war-torn France. Most of these publications took the form of pamphlets and letters written usually by noblewomen whose personal experiences of destruction of property and family entitled them to a public voice on the matter.[64] Few women, however, ventured beyond the expression of personal loss to address outright the political issues of their time. The Dames des Roches were exceptions in advising officeholders. Cognizant of the literature that linked rhetoric and eloquence with rulers whose chief duty

---

60. Catherine des Roches, letter 14 (see chap. 5).

61. "Vous pouvez avec la plume et le pinceau donner immortalité aux mortels, vous rendant immortelle aussi." Catherine des Roches, letter 49 (see chap. 5).

62. Catherine des Roches, response 10 (see chap. 3).

63. On rhetoric as implicated in the social and political order it produces, see Wayne Rebhorn, *The Emperor of Men's Minds: Literature and the Renaissance Discourse of Rhetoric* (Ithaca: Cornell University Press, 1995), 9–12.

64. Broomhall, *Women and the Book Trade*, 96–99.

was the preservation of the *laws* at the foundation of the state,[65] they remind government officials, judges, lawyers, and the king himself to apply the rule of law. Madeleine addresses the king as "God's lieutenant" whose divinely appointed mission is to join "la rigueur à la douce clemence" (the rule of law and gentle clemency), indicating thereby her knowledge of contemporary political thought on monarchical power.[66] The Des Roches' admiration for the jurists of the Grands Jours is founded on the latter's embodiment of justice: Madeleine praises them for knowing more laws than Lycurgus and Solon, while Catherine likens them to "Dieux de paix et de guerre" (gods of peace and war) punishing "Hommes dépravez" (depraved men) and protecting the good.[67] The law is the glue that holds a society together and the king, as the law's overseer, writes Catherine in her ode to Henri III, has in him the "discours de raison, et le pouvoir supreme / Que vous donnez aux loix" (lessons of reason, and the supreme power / That you give to the laws). On account of his power, the king has a duty to apply the law equally to all citizens.[68] Disobeying the law leads to chaos, a term frequently found in Madeleine's verse. The Dames des Roches therefore criticize all those who practice injustice and exploit rhetoric for selfish gain, be they courtiers using flattery to gain royal favors,[69] law officials dispensing justice only when bribed,[70] lovers exploiting Petrarchan parlance to win over their lady,[71] husbands mistreating and humiliating their wives,[72] or Protestant preachers "seducing" worshipers into believing their lies.[73] Madeleine even goes so far as to comment on the theological foundation of the law when she states that "one faith" and "one law" led the blind man of the Gospel to obey Christ's command so as to regain his lost sight.[74]

---

65. Wayne Rebhorn, ed. and trans., *Renaissance Debates on Rhetoric* (Ithaca: Cornell University Press, 2000), introduction; William Farr Church, *Constitutional Thought in Sixteenth-Century France: A Study of the Evolution of Ideas* (New York: Octagon Books, 1969), 195–226.

66. Madeleine des Roches, sonnet 14 (see chap. 1).

67. Madeleine des Roches, sonnet 3 (see chap. 3); Catherine des Roches, *To the Gentlemen Judges at the Grands Jours* (see chap. 3).

68. Catherine des Roches, *To the King*, ll. 56–57, 49 (see chap. 2).

69. Ibid., ll. 9–18.

70. Catherine des Roches, *Dialogue between Poverty and Hunger* (see chap. 4).

71. Catherine des Roches, *Dialogue between Sincero and Charite* (see chap. 4).

72. Madeleine des Roches critiques the "laws of marriage" that rob women of freedom and happiness. In a personalized aside, she states: "My God, my God, how much suffering / I don't care to remember here! / It is enough if I can make men see / How much their laws do violence to us." Ode 1, ll. 53–56 (see chap. 1).

73. Madeleine des Roches, sonnet 16 (see chap. 1).

74. Madeleine des Roches, sonnet 18, *Œuvres*, 137–38.

The Dames des Roches adhered closely to the motto of the Politiques party, *une foi, une loi, un roi* (one faith, one law, one king), whose principles according to Nancy Roelker were "constitutional, absolutist, Stoic, and Gallican."[75] The defining elements of the Politiques' loosely connected network were loyalty to the monarchy, opposition to the ultramontane position that threatened Gallican liberties, pacifism, and a certain degree of tolerance of those who entertained differing religious beliefs.[76] Even in the face of the ruthless destruction of their city in 1562 and again in 1569 by Protestant armies, the Dames des Roches remained pacifists, critical of the necessity for war. In her *Imitation de la Mere de Salomon*, addressed to Catherine de Médicis, Catherine has the queen mother counseling the king to avoid placing his trust in armies: "Qui fait guerre à autruy, / Il sent premierement la guerre dedans luy" (He who wars against others, / Is first at war within himself).[77]

The third dominant theme in the works of mother and daughter is the intellectual woman's relation to her *pen*, to writing and literary production. Writing for the Dames des Roches was neither an occasional activity nor a matter of enlightened amateurism. Writing, especially during their coterie years in the 1570s and 1580s, constituted the center of their lives, and they can rightly be considered, with Christine de Pizan, among the first professional women writers of the early modern period. They differed from Pizan in that they did not openly make a living from their pen. However, they welcomed commissions and did receive payments for their writings on behalf of others. They wrote continuously over a period of almost two decades, negotiating space and time for writing and forming support networks. Three strategic interconnected alliances enabled them to write and publish: their familial mother-daughter collaborative bond, their coterie, and their geocultural situation in Poitiers. Long before 1578 when they became a financially independent, fatherless, and husbandless team, they developed, in Kirk Read's words, "a feminine family community"[78] where, depending first and foremost on each other, they lived out their determined resolve. Contemporaries admired their resolute attention to writing and to adapting their learning to the twin principles of *docere* and *delectare* (teaching and pleasing). Éti-

---

75. Roelker, *One King, One Faith*, 326. The Politiques formed in the 1570s a group of moderate Catholics and Protestants who advocated negotiated settlement to bring about an end to the wars of religion. See Christopher Bettinson, "The *Politiques* and the *Politique* Party: A Reappraisal," in *From Valois to Bourbon Dynasty: State and Society in Early Modern France*, ed. Keith Cameron (Exeter: Exeter University Press, 1989), 35–49.

76. Roelker, *One King, One Faith*, 328.

77. Catherine des Roches, *Imitation de la Mere de Salomon*, *Œuvres*, 326.

78. Read, "French Renaissance Women Writers in Search of Community," 123.

enne Pasquier states that they wrote daily and that their learning, although classically grounded, "savant," and extensive, on a par with that of their male guests, seemed so unaffected and "naïf" (natural) that Catherine in particular, he declared, "is a [walking] book; she possesses a mind that is so natural and fertile in beautiful [literary] flowers that she has no need to go beg for the Ancients' authority and wise sayings to supply any lack in her conversation."[79] As coterie hostesses, they were adept at modulating their learning to the social imperatives of *conversation mondaine* and therefore persuaded their male guests of the acceptability of their ambition to become known as independent writers. Not content with their own celebrity, they sought to effect agency in other women. They challenged their female readers to "choisir l'ancre et la plume / Pour l'employer doctement" (choose ink and pen / And to employ these learnedly) so as to "vous venger de la mort blesme / Sans mendier l'escrivain" (take revenge on pale Fate / Without having to beg another writer [to do it for you]).[80]

The Des Roches' coterie gave them the civic support and public endorsement of an influential community which found useful the social distinction that such a circle gave. Its nature is exemplified particularly during the Grands Jours when a host of Parisian jurists mingled with habitués of the Poitiers region vying for recognition. Madeleine's letter 20, possibly addressed to a young lawyer visiting the salon at that time, compliments him on seeking out "les plus gentils personnages de la France afin que, les admirant, vous fussiez admiré par eux" (the noblest people in France so that, in admiring them, you might be admired by them).[81] One of the means to social distinction was the use of literature as a cultural marker of good taste and superior intellect. Promotion for an ambitious young lawyer depended on the ability to demonstrate his eloquence; for more established professionals, a show of learning lent symbolic status.[82] Like the learned gatherings of humanists and Pléiade poets at the court of Marguerite de France, the sister of Henri II, at Henri III's Palace Academy, or at the Parisian house of Jean de Morel and his

---

79. "Mais la fille est les livres mesmes; elle a un esprit si naïf et abondant de belles fleurs, qu'il ne fault point qu'elle aille mandier, des Autheurs anciens, leurs authoritez et sentences, pour suppléer le defaut de ses propos." *Lettre à Pierre Pithou*, in *Lettres*, vol. 6, letter 8; see Des Roches, *Missives*, 344. This comment reveals the extent to which the Des Roches team defied current notions of what women could or could not do.

80. Madeleine des Roches, ode 3, ll. 47–48, 53–54 (see chap. 1).

81. See chap. 5.

82. Barbara Diefendorf, *Paris City Councillors in the Sixteenth Century: The Politics of Patrimony* (Princeton: Princeton University Press, 1983), 112–19; George Hoffmann, *Montaigne's Career* (Oxford: Clarendon Press, 1998), chap. 6.

wife Antoinette de Loynes,[83] the Des Roches' circle offered an academy-like setting for serious philosophical and political discussion. A number of their guests such as Étienne Pasquier, Scévole de Sainte-Marthe, Nicolas Rapin, and possibly Agrippa d'Aubigné attended likewise the Parisian "salon vert" (green-tendered salon) of Claude-Catherine de Clermont, maréchale de Retz,[84] and the court coterie of Madeleine de L'Aubespine.[85] Like these circles, the Poitiers coterie included *divertissements*, musical offerings, poetry readings, the composition of witty "response" poems "faite[s] promptement" (improvised on the spot),[86] anagrams, plays, and dialogue performances. Catherine on a number of occasions sang her poetry while playing the lute and likely performed in her dialogues, pastoral drama, and *Tragicomedie de Tobie*. The contemporary annotator who wrote in the margins of his copy of the Des Roches' *Œuvres* and *Secondes œuvres* notes that he personally heard Catherine sing and saw her dance at gatherings at her house during the Grands Jours.[87] The Des Roches' performative practices mirrored those of court circles: like the "Nine Muses" (female participants) of the maréchale de Retz's coterie, they used pseudonyms (Charite for Catherine, Sincero for possibly Claude Pellejay), offered musical soirées, read, wrote, and discussed poetry. Court poets included them in their collections: Jacques Peletier du Mans dedicated to them a sonnet and a poem in his *Œuvres poëtiques intitulez Loanges* (1581),[88] Guy Le Fèvre de la Boderie dedicated a translation in his *Diverses Meslanges poëtiques* (1582), containing many poems to court members,[89] and Pierre L'Anglois, in his *Discours*

83. See Clark Keating, *Studies on the Literary Salon in France, 1550–1615* (Cambridge: Harvard University Press, 1941).

84. On Catherine de Clermont's salon album and on her guests, see her *Album de poésies (Manuscrit français 25455 de la BNF)*, ed. Colette H. Winn and François Rouget (Paris: Champion, 2004).

85. Ronsard probably came across Catherine's *Sonnets of Sincero and Charite* in manuscript form at one of the gatherings held at Madeleine de L'Aubespine's summer residence in Conflans. Catherine reports that he wrote a sonnet (now lost) in honor of Sincero, letter 42 (see chap. 5).

86. A number of such poems are qualified as such in the volume of *La Puce*.

87. "Ladicte dame avoyt bonne voix, entendoyt la musique, et jouoyt du lut mediocrement. Je luy ay veu faire tous ces exercices, avec beaucoup de grace, et en oultre sçavoit bien danser" (This lady had a good voice, understood music, and played well on the lute. I saw her perform all these activities with a good deal of grace, and she even danced well). *Chanson de Sincero, Secondes Œuvres*, 263 n. 4. On the two annotators of the Des Roches' oeuvre, see "Note on the Translation."

88. *Aus Dames des Roches, Mere et Fille* and *Louange des trois Graces*, in Jacques Peletier du Mans, *Œuvres poëtiques intitulez Loanges* (Paris: Robert Coulombel, 1581), 17v. Peletier was an equally strong supporter of Louise Labé. See his prefatory sonnet to the collection of 24 poems written by admirers of Labé in her collected *Œuvres complètes*, ed. François Rigolot (Paris: Garnier-Flammarion, 1986), 141.

89. *Les Roses. À Madame des Roches de Poictiers la Jeune*, in Guy Le Fèvre de la Boderie, *Diverses meslanges poëtiques* (Paris: Robert le Mangnier, 1582), fols. 60v–62r, ed. Rosanna Gorris (Geneva: Droz, 1993), 256–59.

des Hieroglyphes aegyptiens, emblemes, devises, et armoiries (1583), compares the phoenix to "Ces deux Dames de vertu rare, / Jointes d'un lien si heureux / Que ce n'est qu'une d'elles deux" (These two Ladies of rare virtue, / Joined with such a happy bond / That of the two there is but one).[90] The Des Roches's coterie enabled its hostesses and other female participants to showcase their *érudition* at a unique moment in social literary history when the lines demarcating the later all-male academies from the salons run by women were still fluid.[91]

The Des Roches' geocultural situation in Poitiers was also integral to their self-representation. Like their predecessor "Louise Labé Lyonnaise," mother and daughter were continuously identified as the "Dames des Roches de Poitiers" on the title page of their publications and in contemporary and posthumous *elogia*. At a time when urban centers and nation-states were consolidating their identities, the appeal to civic and national pride constituted a strong incentive for women to write. The bibliographer La Croix Du Maine describes the Des Roches in his *Bibliothèque Française* (1584) as "both so erudite and learned, that France can pride herself, in engendering them, for having produced the two pearls of all of Poitou, a region abundant in all [good] things, especially in individuals with wit among whom these ladies have obtained the first rank for their learning."[92] And for Pasquier, the "Dames des Roches, mother and daughter," are "truly the honor of the city of Poitiers and of our century."[93]

Madeleine and Catherine des Roches were extraordinarily skilled in creating a writer's life for themselves and in asserting their creative agency. They

90. Pierre L'Anglois, *Discours des Hieroglyphes* . . . (Paris: Abel L'Angelier, 1683), fols. 58v–59.

91. Italian precedents for women's participation in academies and salon-like gatherings were highly influential in France during the Renaissance. The career poet Laura Terracina, for instance, whom Catherine des Roches considers an exemplary writer in her *Dialogue between Placide and Severe* (*Secondes Œuvres*) belonged to the Accademia degli Incogniti in Naples. Many other Italian women writers frequented academies and hosted coteries in their native cities (see Irma B. Jaffe, *Shining Eyes, Cruel Fortune: The Lives and Loves of Italian Renaissance Women Poets* [New York: Fordham University Press, 2000]). On the distinctions between academies and salons in seventeenth-century France, see Erica Harth, *Cartesian Women: Versions and Subversions of Rational Discourse in the Old Regime* (Ithaca: Cornell University Press, 1992). On the depreciation of a classical, humanist culture for women in the seventeenth century, see Linda Timmermans, *L'accès des femmes à la culture (1509–1715). Un débat d'idées de Saint François de Sales à la Marquise de Lambert* (Paris: Champion, 1993).

92. "Toutes deux si doctes et si sçavantes, que la France peut se vanter les ayant engendrées, d'avoir produit en elles les deux perles de tout le Poictou, qui est une région abondante en toutes choses, et sur-tout en personnes d'esprit, entre lesquelles celles-ci doivent obtenir le premier rang pour leur sçavoir." *Bibliothèque Françoise* (Paris: Abel L'Angelier, 1584), in *Les Bibliothèques Françoises de La Croix du Maine et de Du Verdier sieur de Vauprivas*, ed. Rigoley de Juvigny, 6 vols. (Paris: Saillant, 1772), 2:71; see Des Roches, *Missives*, 341.

93. "Honneurs vrayement, et de la ville de Poitiers, et de nostre siecle." *Lettre à Pierre Pithou*, in *Lettres*, vol. 6, no. 8; see Des Roches, *Missives*, 344.

did so by bridging apparently antithetical roles and sociocultural sites of learning: they used the rhetoric of *in utramque partem* (both sides) to model the woman as writer and as household manager and were noted throughout their lives for their uncommon ability at combining the life of the mind with their household tasks; their coterie became a point of connection between provincial intellectuals and Parisian literary networks. They were considered exemplary in aligning themselves with the interests of their class, their king, and their faith. Alongside the newly emerging class of the *noblesse de robe*, they were engaged in political commentary as they sought in their writings to strengthen national consciousness and the glory of the monarchy. They were devoted Roman Catholics, critics of the Protestant reform, and pacifists. They belonged to the party of the Moderns, which defended the superiority of French culture. They were linked, like Italian learned women before them, to the civic pride of their native city. Exceptionally learned, they rank high in catalogues of illustrious women until the nineteenth century. Their writings provide a glimpse into the development of early modern feminism and abundant evidence of the vitality of humanist learning among members of the provincial upper gentry and urban nobility.

THE FORTUNES OF THE DAMES DES ROCHES

The Dames des Roches were renowned in their own day. Immediately following their death in 1587, they were eulogized by Louis Le Grand, a nobleman from Touraine, who compares them favorably to Ronsard and declares that throughout their lives and writings they overcame "time, fate, fortune, and envy."[94] In calling attention to their creative bond, Le Grand describes a salon ritual that Madeleine would perform to showcase her daughter's learning: by making believe that she had forgotten a passage from a poem or a book that she was discussing, she would let Catherine take her place in informing the audience of the forgotten lines. Another near contemporary of the Des Roches, Marie Le Gendre, Dame de Rivéry (dates unknown), wrote a Neoplatonic *Dialogue des chastes Amours d'Eros et de Kalisti* (Dialogue on the Chaste Love of Eros and Kalisti) inspired by Catherine's *Dialogue between Love, Beauty, and Physis*. Unlike Catherine's character Beauty who rejects Love and eschews marriage, Le Gendre's heroine Kalisti is led by her mother Sophie to accept Eros's suit in marriage.[95]

---

94. "Le temps, le sort, la fortune, et l'envie," in Louis Le Grand, *Elegie sur le Trespas de Mesdames des Roches de Poictiers mere et fille* (Paris: Estienne Prevosteau, 1587); see Des Roches, *Missives*, 350, l. 18.

95. Marie Le Gendre, *Dialogue des chastes Amours d'Eros, et de Kalisti*, in *L'Exercice de l'âme vertueuse* (1596), ed. Colette H. Winn (Paris: Champion, 2001).

The Des Roches were frequently cited and anthologized throughout the next two centuries. Contemporaries who knew them such as Agrippa d'Aubigné (1616), Antoine Mornac (1619), Étienne Pasquier (1621), and Scévole de Sainte-Marthe (1644) included them in historical accounts on the well-known writers and thinkers of their age. They were praised in unpublished biographies and bibliographies such as Guillaume Colletet's *Vies des poetes françois* (first half of the seventeenth century), or Père Louis Jacob's *Bibliothèque des femmes illustres par leurs ecrits* (1646). Compendia like those of Hilarion de Coste (1647), Jean de La Forge (1663), Titon du Tillet (1732), P.-F. Beauchamps (1735), Claude-Pierre Gouget (1752), Dreux du Radier (1754), and Joseph de La Porte (1769) contain entries on the Des Roches.[96]

Of great interest is the Des Roches' influence on later seventeenth- and eighteenth-century female intellectuals. In her catalogue of learned women, Jacquette Guillaume (dates unknown) includes among contemporary famous women the Dames des Roches; Charlotte des Ursins, vicomtesse d'Auchy; Marie de Gournay; and Madeleine de Scudéry.[97] She then draws on the popular genre of the portrait to describe the varied intellectual interests of *mondaines* (society women) and anonymous female friends by discussing their preference for the sciences and anthologizing their writings. According to Linda Timmermans, Jacquette Guillaume's compilation is the first anthology of scientific texts written by women and one of a growing number of works on the intellectual aspirations of elite women.[98]

Madeleine de Scudéry (1607–1701) writes at length about the Des Roches. Jane Donawerth and Julie Strongson have indicated that Scudéry's salon gatherings were influenced especially by the "salon vert" of Claude-Catherine de Clermont, maréchale de Retz, since many of the same performative activities took place in both circles.[99] It is important to note, however, that Scudéry was equally, if not more, influenced by the Des Roches' coterie and their views on female learning. In *Conversations nouvelles sur divers sujets* (1684), Scudéry has one of her salon participants, the comte de Lemos, praise the Des Roches pair as "the honor of their sex in France." After describing their home as the temple of the Muses, he describes their defining attributes as

---

96. See Des Roches, *Missives*, appendix 2.

97. Jacquette Guillaume, *Les Dames Illustres où par bonnes et fortes raisons, il se prouve, que le sexe féminin surpasse en toute sorte de genre le sexe masculin* (Paris: Thomas Jolly, 1665), 291. See Des Roches, *Missives*, 377.

98. Timmermans, *L'accès des femmes à la culture*, 279.

99. Madeleine de Scudéry, *Selected Letters, Orations, and Rhetorical Dialogues*, ed. and trans. Jane Donawerth and Julie Strongson, Other Voice in Early Modern Europe (Chicago: University of Chicago Press, 2004), 14.

a knowledge without pride, virtue without prudishness, wit without overzealousness, and a friendship for each other in which their age difference presents no obstacle and that perfectly unites them. . . . They write extremely well in prose and in verse; but they preserve so perfectly the modesty of their sex that this doubles the admiration that one has for them; they have thus gained the esteem of the poets, the Ronsards and the Du Bellays and in general of all *honnestes gens.*[100]

The Des Roches' exemplarity is held up as a mirror in Scudéry's world for all women to imitate. One of the female participants endorses the comte of Lemos's epideictic portrait with a final pronouncement: "What a great and beautiful idea [put forth] by two persons of my sex! I would not fear being [known as] a great wit of that sort."[101] A comparison of the Des Roches' works with Scudéry's *Twentieth Harangue. Sapho to Erinne,* in *Illustrious Women, or the Heroic Harangues* (1642), indicates Scudéry's possible firsthand knowledge of their works. Sapho contrasts for instance the rewards of writing poetry with the paltry recognition and fading glory of a "beautiful face."[102] And to Erinne's query whether "it is not glory enough for a beautiful woman to be praised in verse by all the great poets of her time without getting involved herself in creating her own portrait," she replies:

it is better to give immortality to others than to receive it from someone else, better to find glory within yourself than to wait for it from elsewhere. The portraits made of you of that kind might some day be considered by posterity as tableaux made for amusement. The poet's imagination would be admired more than your beauty, and the copies would eventually pass for the originals. But if you leave traces of yourself from your own hand, you will live forever honored in the memory of all men.[103]

100. "Du sçavoir sans orgueil, de la vertu sans severité, de l'esprit sans empressement, et une amitié l'une pour l'autre, à qui la difference d'age ne fait nul obstacle, et qui les unit parfaitement. . . . Elles ecrivent toutes deux fort bien, et en prose, et en vers; mais elles conservent si parfaitement toute la modestie de leur sexe, que cela redouble l'admiration qu'on a pour elles; aussi ont-elles acquis l'estime particulière des Ronsard, des Du Bellay, et en general de tous les honnestes gens." *Conversations nouvelles sur divers sujets,* 263–64.

101. "Voilà une grande et belle idée de deux personnes de mon sexe, et je ne craindrois pas d'estre bel esprit de cette sorte-là." Ibid., 265; see Des Roches, *Missives,* 380.

102. Madeleine de Scudéry, *The Twentieth Harangue from Les Femmes illustres, ou, les harangues héroïques,* in *The Story of Sapho,* trans. Karen Newman, Other Voice in Early Modern Europe (Chicago: University of Chicago Press, 2003), 138.

103. Ibid., 142.

Catherine des Roches's principal legacy, which Madeleine de Scudéry has understood so well, is that women should "take the trouble to write" without "making their serfs [lovers] compose in their stead," and that "honor, goodness, and glory" reside in "words, deeds, and writings."[104] Madeleine as well challenged her female contemporaries to "choose ink and pen" so that "on your own you can / Take revenge on pale Fate / Without having to beg another writer."[105]

Finally, the novelist, historian, and translator Louise de Kéralio (1758–1821) included the Des Roches' life story in her remarkable fourteen-volume *Collection des Meilleurs Ouvrages François, composés par des Femmes* (Collection of the Best French Works Composed by Women), a series on the lives and works of French women writers that she dedicated to her mother and published during the three years leading to the French Revolution.[106] "Leur histoire est peu connue" (their story is little known), she states about the mother and daughter.[107] After describing their salon in a Poitiers that "dans ce temps-là n'étoit pas aussi désert qu'à présent" (at that time was not as deserted as it now is) and their relationship to each other, she transcribes a great number of poems, dialogues, and letters—the Des Roches' works occupy one hundred pages of the four-hundred-page fourth volume. One senses delight in Louise de Kéralio's discovery of "ces deux intéressantes femmes" (these two interesting women), as she calls them. Louise de Kéralio was an only child whose learned mother was a writer and a translator. Like Catherine, she chose the single life and, according to Carla Hesse, became "a virtuoso at bending the rules of both gender and genre as far as they could bend without breaking them."[108]

Nineteenth-century eulogists of the Des Roches on the other hand are more interested in their mother-daughter relations and in their adherence to the notion of "la femme au foyer" (the housewifely woman) than in their works. While Édouard Renaudin thinks that Catherine's refusal to marry (hence to begin a family of her own) turns her into a "précieuse" (a precious

---

104. Catherine des Roches, *Epistle to Her Mother* (see chap. 2); response 34 (see chap. 3).

105. Madeleine des Roches, ode 3 (see chap. 1).

106. Louise de Kéralio, *Collection des Meilleurs Ouvrages François, composés par des Femmes, Dédiée aux Femmes Françoises,* 14 vols. (Paris: La Grange, 1786–89), 4:74–183. Kéralio initially planned thirty-six volumes. Of the fourteen volumes, one is devoted to Madeleine de Scudéry and the last six to Mme. de Sévigné; she left volumes 7 and 8 blank in the hope of returning to them.

107. Ibid., 4:74.

108. Carla Hesse, "Revolutionary Histories: The Literary Politics of Louise de Kéralio (1758–1822)," in *Culture and Identity in Early Modern Europe (1500–1800): Essays in Honor of Natalie Zemon Davis,* ed. Barbara B. Diefendorf and Carla Hesse (Ann Arbor: University of Michigan Press, 1993), 238–39.

woman, harking back to Molière's precious damsels), critics Jules de La Marsonnière, Léon Feugère, and Camoin de Vence insist on the legitimacy of her filial sentiments and her devotion to domestic values.[109] According to Feugère, "under the influence of her tender feelings [for her mother], Catherine avoided pedantry, a common pitfall for women authors."[110] In the early twentieth century, George Diller produced the first monograph on the life and works of the Des Roches, which remains essential reading. However, he judges negatively Catherine's "coldly intellectual temperament" and her "abnormal" attachment to her mother.[111]

Since the mid-nineteen eighties, on the other hand, the Dames des Roches' reception has grown tremendously. They have been studied from different perspectives such as their adaptation and revision of generic conventions; their negotiative strategies aimed at developing a writer's identity and widening the educational prospects for intellectual women; their engagement with the political, religious, and literary discourses of their time; and their mother-daughter bond, coterie, and urban community of learning.

---

109. Édouard Renaudin, "Des Roches," in *Nouvelle biographie générale*, ed. F. Didot (Paris: Didot, 1854–77), 4:904–5; Jules de La Marsonnière, "Le salon de Mesdames des Roches aux Grands Jours," *Bulletin de la société des antiquaires de l'ouest* 7, 1st series (1841): 37–58; Léon Feugère, *Les femmes poètes au XVIe siècle* (Paris: Didier, 1860), 39–61; Camoin de Vence, "Deux femmes de lettres au XVIe siècle," *L'Investigateur* 52 (1882): 213–23.

110. "Sous l'influence de ces tendres sentiments, elle échappa au pédantisme, cet écueil ordinaire des femmes auteurs." *Les femmes poètes*, 52.

111. Diller, *Dames des Roches*, 150, 52.

VOLUME EDITOR'S
BIBLIOGRAPHY

PRIMARY SOURCES

Agrippa, Cornelius. *Declamation on the Nobility and Preeminence of the Female Sex.* Ed. and trans. Albert Rabil Jr. Other Voice in Early Modern Europe. Chicago: University of Chicago Press, 1996.

Alciati, Andrea. *A Book of Emblems: The Emblematum Liber in Latin and English.* Ed. and trans. John F. Moffitt. Jefferson, N.C.: McFarland, 2004.

Ariosto, Lodovico. *Orlando Furioso (The Frenzy of Orlando).* 2 vols. Translated with an introduction by Barbara Reynolds. Harmondsworth: Penguin Books, 1975.

Aubigné, Agrippa d'. *Œuvres complètes.* Ed. H. Weber, J. Bailbé, and M. Soulié. Paris: Gallimard, Bibliothèque de la Pléiade, 1969.

Baïf, Jean-Antoine de. *Les amours de Francine.* Ed. Ernesta Caldarini. Geneva: Droz, 1966.

Billon, François de. *Le fort inexpugnable de l'honneur du sexe feminin.* Introduction by M. A. Screech. New York: Johnson Reprint, 1970.

Boccaccio, Giovanni. *Famous Women.* Ed. and trans. Virginia Brown. I Tatti Renaissance Library. Cambridge: Harvard University Press, 2001.

Campiglia, Maddalena. *Flori, A Pastoral Drama.* Ed. Virginia Cox and Lisa Sampson, trans. Virginia Cox. Other Voice in Early Modern Europe. Chicago: University of Chicago Press, 2004.

Castiglione, Baldassare. *The Book of the Courtier.* Trans. Charles Singleton. New York: Anchor Books, 1959.

Clermont, Claude-Catherine de (Maréchale de Retz). *Album de poésies. Manuscrit français 25455 de la BNF.* Ed. Colette H. Winn and François Rouget. Paris: Champion, 2004.

Coignard, Gabrielle de. *Spiritual Sonnets: A Bilingual Edition.* Ed. and trans. Melanie E. Gregg. Other Voice in Early Modern Europe. Chicago: University of Chicago Press, 2004.

Coste, Hilarion de. *Les eloges et les vies des Reynes, des Princesses, et des Dames illustres. . . .* 2 vols. Paris: Sebastien Cramoisy, 1647.

Crenne, Helisenne de. *A Renaissance Woman: Helisenne's Personal and Invective Letters.* Ed. and trans. Marianna M. Mustacchi and Paul J. Archambault. Syracuse: Syracuse University Press, 1986.

Des Roches, Dames (Madeleine Neveu and Catherine Fradonnet). *Les Missives.* Ed. Anne R. Larsen. Textes Littéraires Français. Geneva: Droz, 1999.

———. *Les Œuvres* (1579). Ed. Anne R. Larsen. Textes Littéraires Français. Geneva: Droz, 1993.

———. *Les Secondes œuvres.* Ed. Anne R. Larsen. Textes Littéraires Français. Geneva: Droz, 1998.

Du Bellay, Joachim. *Deffence et Illustration de la langue françoyse.* Ed. Henri Chamard. Paris: Didier, 1970.

Du Four, Antoine. *Les Vies des femmes célèbres.* Ed. G. Jeanneau. Geneva: Droz, 1970.

Du Tronchet, Étienne. *Lettres missives et familieres.* Paris: Lucas Breyer, 1569.

Erasmus, Desiderius. *Adages.* In *The Collected Works of Erasmus,* trans. Margaret Mann Phillips and R.A. B. Mynors. Toronto: University of Toronto Press, 1989.

Fedele, Cassandra. *Letters and Orations.* Ed. and trans. Diana Robin. Other Voice in Early Modern Europe. Chicago: University of Chicago Press, 2000.

Ficino, Marsilio. *Commentary on Plato's Symposium on Love.* Trans. Sears Jayne. Dallas: Spring Publications, 1985.

Fonte, Moderata. *The Worth of Women.* Ed. and trans. Virginia Cox. Other Voice in Early Modern Europe. Chicago: University of Chicago Press, 1997.

Gournay, Marie de. *Apology for the Woman Writing and Other Works.* Ed. and trans. Richard Hellman and Colette Quesnel. Other Voice in Early Modern Europe. Chicago: University of Chicago Press, 2002.

Guillaume, Jacquette. *Les Dames Illustres où par bonnes et fortes raisons, il se prouve, que le sexe féminin surpasse en toute sorte de genre le sexe masculin.* Paris: Thomas Jolly, 1665.

Hyginus. *Fabulae: The Myths of Hyginus.* Trans. Mary Grant. Lawrence: University of Kansas Publications, 1960.

Kéralio, Louise de. *Collection des Meilleurs Ouvrages François, composés par des Femmes, Dédiée aux Femmes Françoises.* 14 vols. Paris: La Grange, 1786–89.

Labé, Louise. *Complete Works.* Trans. and ed. Edith R. Farrell. Troy, N.Y.: Whitston, 1986.

———. *Debate of Folly and Love.* Trans. Anne-Marie Bourbon. New York: Peter Lang, 2000.

———. *Œuvres complètes.* Ed. François Rigolot. Paris: Garnier-Flammarion, 1986.

La Croix du Maine et Du Verdier. *Les Bibliothèques Françoises de La Croix du Maine et de Du Verdier sieur de Vauprivas.* 6 vols. Ed. Rigoley de Juvigny. Paris: Saillant, 1772.

Le Gendre, Marie. *L'Exercice de l'âme vertueuse.* Ed. Colette H. Winn. Paris: Champion, 2001.

Le Grand, Louis. *Elegie sur le Trespas de Mesdames des Roches de Poictiers mere et fille.* Paris: Estienne Prevosteau, 1587.

Marinella, Lucrezia. *The Nobility and Excellence of Women and the Defects and Vices of Men.* Ed. and trans. Anne Dunhill. Introduction by Letizia Panizza. Other Voice in Early Modern Europe. Chicago: University of Chicago Press, 1999.

Morata, Olympia. *The Complete Writings of an Italian Heretic.* Ed. and trans. Holt N. Parker. Other Voice in Early Modern Europe. Chicago: University of Chicago Press, 2003.

Pasquier, Étienne. *Les lettres.* Paris: Abel L'Angelier, 1586.

———. *Lettres familières.* Ed. Dorothy Thickett. Geneva: Droz, 1974.

Peletier, Jacques. *Œuvres poëtiques intitulez Loanges.* Paris: Robert Coulombel, 1581.

Petrarca, Francesco. *Petrarch's Lyric Poems: The Rime Sparse and Other Lyrics.* Ed. and trans. Robert Durling. Cambridge: Harvard University Press, 1976.

Pizan, Christine de. *The Book of the City of Ladies.* Trans. Earl Jeffrey Richards. New York: Persea, 1982.

Romieu, Marie de. *Premieres œuvres poëtiques.* Ed. André Winandy. Geneva: Droz, 1972.

Ronsard, Pierre de. *Œuvres complètes.* Ed. Jean Céard, Daniel Ménager, and Michel Simonin. 2 vols. Paris: Gallimard, Bibliothèque de la Pléiade, 1993.

————. *Œuvres complètes.* Ed. P. Laumonier, R. Lebègue, and I. Silver. 20 vols. Paris: Hachette-Didier, 1914–74.

Sainte-Marthe, Scévole de. *Éloges des hommes illustres, qui depuis un siecle ont fleury en France dans la profession des Lettres. Composez en Latin . . . et mis en François, par G. Colletet.* Paris: Sommaville, 1644.

Scève, Maurice. *Délie.* Ed. I. D. McFarlane. Cambridge: Cambridge University Press, 1966.

Scudéry, Madeleine de. *Conversations nouvelles sur divers sujets, dediée au roy.* Paris: Claude Barbin, 1684. In *"De l'air galant" et autres conversations. Pour une étude de l'archive galante,* ed. Delphine Denis. Paris: Champion, 1998.

————. *Selected Letters, Orations, and Rhetorical Dialogues.* Ed. and trans. Jane Donawerth and Julie Strongson. Other Voice in Early Modern Europe. Chicago: University of Chicago Press, 2004.

————. *The Twentieth Harangue from Les Femmes illustres, ou, les harangues héroïques.* In *The Story of Sapho,* trans. Karen Newman. Other Voice in Early Modern Europe. Chicago: University of Chicago Press, 2003.

Sigea, Luisa. *Dialogue de deux jeunes filles sur la vie de court et la vie de retraite.* Ed. and trans. Odette Sauvage. Paris: Presses Universitaires de France, 1970.

————. *Duarum virginium colloquium de vita aulica et privata.* Ed. Manuel Serrano y Sanz. Madrid: Biblioteca de Autores Españoles, 1903.

Terracina, Laura. *Discorso sopra tutti i primi canti di "Orlando Furioso."* Venice: Giolito, 1549.

Tyard, Pontus de. *Les erreurs amoureuses.* Ed. John McClelland. Geneva: Droz, 1967.

————. *Solitaire premier.* Ed. S. F. Baridon. Geneva: Droz, 1950.

Valois, Marguerite de. *Correspondance 1569–1614.* Ed. Éliane Viennot. Paris: Champion, 1998.

Vives, Juan Luis. *The Education of a Christian Woman.* Ed. and trans. Charles Fantazzi. Other Voice in Early Modern Europe. Chicago: University of Chicago Press, 2000.

SECONDARY SOURCES

Altman, Janet Gurkin. "The Letter Book as a Literary Institution, 1539–1789: Toward a Cultural History of Published Correspondences in France." *Yale French Studies* 71 (1986): 17–62.

————. "Women's Letters in the Public Sphere." In *Going Public: Women and Publishing in Early Modern France,* ed. Elizabeth Goldsmith and Dena Goodman, 99–115. Ithaca: Cornell University Press, 1995.

Balsamo, Jean. "Abel L'Angelier et ses dames. Les Dames des Roches, Madeleine de l'Aubespine, Marie le Gendre, Marie de Gournay." In *Des femmes et des livres: France et Espagne, XIVᵉ–XVIIᵉ.* Ed. Dominique de Courcelles and Carmen Val Julián, 117–36. Paris: École des Chartes, 1999.

Benson, Pamela Joseph, and Victoria Kirkham, eds. *Strong Voices, Weak History: Early Modern Women Writers and Canons in England, France, and Italy.* Ann Arbor: University of Michigan Press, 2005.

Bernstein, Hilary J. *Between Crown and Community. Politics and Civic Culture in Sixteenth-Century Poitiers.* Ithaca: Cornell University Press, 2004.

Berriot-Salvadore, Evelyne. "Les femmes dans les cercles intellectuels de la Renaissance: De la fille prodige à la précieuse." In *Mélanges Petti-Ferrandi. Études corses, études littéraires,* 210–37. Paris: Le Cerf, 1989.

———. "Les femmes et les pratiques de l'écriture de Christine de Pisan à Marie de Gournay. 'Femmes sçavantes et savoir féminin.'" *Réforme, Humanisme, Renaissance* 16 (1983): 52–69.

———. "Les héritières de Louise Labé." In *Louise Labé. Les voix du lyrisme,* ed. Guy Demerson, 93–106. Saint-Étienne: Publications de l'Université de Saint-Étienne, 1990.

———. "La problématique histoire des textes féminins." *Atlantis* 19 (1993): 11–15.

Bettinson, Christopher. "The *Politiques* and the *Politique* Party: A Reappraisal." In *From Valois to Bourbon Dynasty: State and Society in Early Modern France,* ed. Keith Cameron, 35–49. Exeter: Exeter University Press, 1989.

Bohanan, Donna. *Crown and Nobility in Early Modern France.* New York: Palgrave, 2001.

Boucher, Jacqueline. *La cour de Henri III.* Rennes: Éditions Ouest-France, 1986.

———. *Société et mentalité autour de Henri III.* 4 vols. Paris: Champion, 1981.

Broomhall, Susan. "'In my opinion': Charlotte de Minut and Female Political Discussion in Print in the Sixteenth-Century France." *Sixteenth-Century Journal* 31, no. 1 (2000): 25–45.

———. *Women and the Book Trade in Sixteenth-Century France.* Aldershot: Ashgate, 2002.

Brunel, Jean. *Un poitevin poète, humaniste et soldat à l'époque des guerres de religion. Nicolas Rapin 1539–1608.* 2 vols. Paris: Champion, 2002.

Castor, Grahame. *Pléiade Poetics: A Study of Sixteenth-Century Thought and Terminology.* Cambridge, Mass.: Cambridge University Press, 1964.

Chang, Leah. "Catherine des Roches' Two Proserpines: Textual Production and the Ravissement de Proserpine in the Missives de Mes-Dames des Roches (1586)." *Symposium* 58, no. 4 (2005): 203–22.

Church, William Farr. *Constitutional Thought in Sixteenth-Century France: A Study of the Evolution of Ideas.* New York: Octagon Books, 1969.

Clarke, Danielle. *The Politics of Early Modern Women's Writing.* London: Longman, 2001.

Couchman, Jane. "What Is 'Personal' about Sixteenth-Century French Women's Personal Writings?" *Atlantis* 19, no. 1 (1993): 16–22.

Crampe-Casnabet, Michèle. "A Sampling of Eighteenth-Century Philosophy." In *A History of Women in the West: Renaissance and Enlightenment Paradoxes,* ed. Natalie Zemon Davis and Arlette Farge, 315–47. Cambridge: Harvard University Press, 1993.

Cox, Virginia. "The Single Self: Feminist Thought and the Marriage Market in Early Modern Venice." *Renaissance Quarterly* 48, no. 3 (1995): 513–81.

Davis, Natalie Zemon. *The Gift in Sixteenth-Century France.* Madison: University of Wisconsin Press, 2000.

Dewald, Jonathan. *Aristocratic Experience and the Origins of Modern Culture: France, 1570–1715.* Berkeley: University of California Press, 1993.

Diefendorf, Barbara. *Paris City Councillors in the Sixteenth Century: The Politics of Patrimony.* Princeton: Princeton University Press, 1983.

Diller, George E. "Agrippa d'Aubigné à Poitiers en 1579." *Bibliothèque d'Humanisme et Renaissance* 2 (1935): 172–74.

———. "Un amant de Catherine des Roches: Claude Pellejay." In *Mélanges de littérature, d'histoire et de philologie offerts à Paul Laumonier*, 287–303. Paris: Droz, 1935.

———. *Les Dames des Roches. Étude sur la vie littéraire à Poitiers dans la deuxième moitié du XVIe siècle.* Paris: Droz, 1936.

Duchêne, Roger. "The Letter: Men's Genre, Women's Practice." In *Women Writers in Pre-Revolutionary France: Strategies of Emancipation*, ed. Colette H. Winn and Donna Kuizenga, 315–34. New York: Garland, 1997.

Ezell, Margaret J. M. *Writing Women's Literary History.* Baltimore: Johns Hopkins University Press, 1993.

Feugère, Léon. *Les femmes poètes au XVIe siècle.* Paris: Didier, 1860.

Fontaine, Marie-Madeleine. "Les Antiquitez chez les dames des Roches: *Les Sonets sur les ruines de Luzignan* d'Odet de Turnèbe (1579)." *Œuvres et Critiques* 20, no. 1 (1995): 197–208.

Frémy, Edouard. *L'Académie des derniers Valois.* Geneva: Slatkine Reprints, 1969.

Fumaroli, Marc. *Le genre des genres littératures française: la conversation.* Oxford: Clarendon Press, 1992.

———. *Trois institutions littéraires.* Paris: Gallimard, 1994.

Glenn, Cheryl. *Rhetoric Retold. Regendering the Tradition from Antiquity through the Renaissance.* Carbondale: Southern Illinois University Press, 1977.

Goldberg, Jonathan. *Writing Matter: From the Hands of the English Renaissance.* Stanford: Stanford University Press, 1990.

Goldsmith, Elizabeth. *Exclusive Conversations: The Art of Interaction in Seventeenth-Century France.* Philadelphia: University of Pennsylvania Press, 1988.

———, and Dena Goodman, eds. *Going Public: Women and Publishing in Early Modern France.* Ithaca: Cornell University Press, 1995.

Gorris, Rosanna. "'Je veux chanter d'amour la tempeste et l'orage': Desportes et les *Imitations* de l'Arioste." In *Philippe Desportes (1546–1606). Un poète presque parfait entre Renaissance et Classicisme*, ed. Jean Balsamo, 173–211. Paris: Klincksieck, 2000.

Grafton, Anthony. *Joseph Scaliger: A Study in the History of Classical Scholarship.* Oxford: Clarendon Press, 1983.

Gray, Floyd. *Gender, Rhetoric, and Print Culture in French Renaissance Writing.* New York: Cambridge University Press, 2000.

Harth, Erica. *Cartesian Women: Versions and Subversions of Rational Discourse in the Old Regime.* Ithaca: Cornell University Press, 1992.

Hoffmann, George. *Montaigne's Career.* Oxford: Clarendon Press, 1998.

Hulubei, Alice. *L'églogue en France au XVIe siècle, 1515–1589.* Paris: Droz, 1938.

Huppert, Georges. *Les Bourgeois Gentilshommes. An Essay on the Definition of Elites in Renaissance France.* Chicago: University of Chicago Press, 1977.

Jaffe, Irma B. *Shining Eyes, Cruel Fortune: The Lives and Loves of Italian Renaissance Women Poets.* New York: Fordham University Press, 2000.

Jones, Ann Rosalind. "Assimilation with a Difference: Renaissance Women Poets and Literary Influence." *Yale French Studies* 62 (1981): 135–53.

———. "Contentious Readings: Urban Humanism and Gender Difference in *La Puce de Madame Des-Roches* (1582)." *Renaissance Quarterly* 48, no. 1 (1995): 109–28.

———. *The Currency of Eros: Women's Love Lyric in Europe, 1540–1620.* Bloomington: Indiana University Press, 1990.

———. "Enabling Sites and Gender Difference: Reading City Women with Men." *Women's Studies: An Interdisciplinary Journal* 19, no. 2 (1991): 239–49.

———. "The Muse of Indirection. Feminist Ventriloquism in the Dialogues of Catherine Des Roches." In *The Dialogue in Early Modern France, 1547–1630: Art and Argument,* ed. Colette H. Winn, 190–222. Washington, D.C.: Catholic University of America Press, 1995.

———. "Nets and Bridles: Early Modern Conduct Books and Sixteenth-Century Women's Lyrics." In *The Ideology of Conduct: Essays on Literature and the History of Sexuality,* ed. Nancy Armstrong and Leonard Tennenhouse, 39–72. New York: Methuen, 1987.

———. "Surprising Frame: Renaissance Gender Ideologies and Women's Lyric." In *The Poetics of Gender,* ed. Nancy K. Miller, 74–95. New York: Columbia University Press, 1986.

———, and Peter Stallybrass, eds. *Renaissance Clothing and the Materials of Memory.* Cambridge: Cambridge University Press, 2000.

Jouanna, Arlette. *Le devoir de révolte. La noblesse française et la gestation de l'État moderne.* Paris: Fayard, 1989.

Kale, Steven. "Women, the Public Sphere, and the Persistence of Salons." *French Historical Studies* 25, no. 1 (2002): 115–48.

Keating, Clark. *Studies on the Literary Salon in France, 1550–1615.* Cambridge: Harvard University Press, 1941.

Kelley, Donald R. *The Beginning of Ideology: Consciousness and Society in the French Reformation.* Cambridge: Cambridge University Press, 1981.

Kettering, Sharon. "Gift-Giving and Patronage in Early Modern France." *French History* 2, no. 2 (1988): 131–51.

King, Margaret L. "Book-Lined Cells: Women and Humanism in the Early Italian Renaissance." In *Beyond Their Sex: Learned Women of the European Pasted.* Patricia H. Labalme, 66–90. New York: New York University Press, 1980.

Kupisz, Kazimierz. "Dans le sillage de Louise Labé et Catherine des Roches." In *Il Rinascimento a Lione,* ed. Antonio Possenti et Guilia Mastrangelo, 2:529–47. 2 vols. Rome: dell' Ateneo, 1988.

Kushner, Eva. "The Dialogue of Dialogues." In *The Dialogue in Early Modern France, 1547–1630: Art and Argument,* ed. Colette H. Winn, 259–83. Washington, D.C.: Catholic University of America Press, 1995.

———. "The Dialogue of the French Renaissance: Work of Art or Instrument of Inquiry?" *Zagadniena Rodzajou Literackich* 20 (1977): 23–35.

———. "Trois locutrices du XVIe siècle; deux 'miroirs.'" *Dalhousie French Studies* 52 (2000): 14–21.

Landry, Diane. "Le dialogue chez Louise Labé et Catherine des Roches, 1555–1583." Master's thesis, University of Montreal, 2000.

Larsen, Anne R. "Catherine des Roches (1542–1587): Humanism and the Learned Woman." *Journal of the Rocky Mountain Medieval and Renaissance Association* 8 (1987): 97–117.

————. "Catherine des Roches, the Pastoral, and Salon Poetics." In *Women Writers in Pre-Revolutionary France: Strategies of Emancipation*, ed. Colette H. Winn and Donna Kuizenga, 227–41. New York: Garland, 1997.

————. "Les Dames des Roches: The French Humanist Scholars." In *Women Writers of the Renaissance and Reformation*, ed. Katharina M. Wilson, 232–59. Athens: University of Georgia Press, 1987.

————. "Legitimizing the Daughter's Writing: Catherine Des Roches's Proverbial Good Wife." *Sixteenth-Century Journal* 21, no. 4 (1990): 559–74.

————. "On Reading *La Puce de Madame Des-Roches*: Catherine des Roches's *Responces* (1583)." *Renaissance and Reformation / Renaissance et Réforme* 22, no. 2 (1998): 63–75.

————. "Reading/Writing and Gender in the Renaissance: The Case of Catherine des Roches (1542–1587)." *Symposium* 41, no. 4 (1987–88): 292–307.

————. "La Réfléxivité dans les dialogues de Catherine des Roches (1583)." In *Dans les miroirs de l'écriture: la réfléxivité chez les femmes écrivains d'Ancien Régime*, ed. Jean-Philippe Beaulieu and Diane Desrosiers-Bonin, 61–71. Quebec: Université de Montréal, 1998.

Lazard, Madeleine. *Les avenues de Fémynie: les femmes et la Renaissance*. Paris: Fayard, 2001.

————. "Les Dames des Roches: une dévotion réciproque et passionnée." In *Autour de Mme de Sévigné: Deux colloques pour un tricentenaire: Rapports mère-fille au XVIIᵉ siècle et de nos jours*, ed. Roger Duchêne and Pierre Ronzeaud. Papers on French Seventeenth-Century Literature 105 (1997): 9–18.

————. "Deux féministes poitevines au XVIᵉ siècle: Les Dames des Roches." In *Joyeusement vivre et honnêtement penser. Mélanges offerts à Madeleine Lazard. Choix d'articles*, ed. Marie-Madeleine Fragonard and Gilbert Schrenck, 267–79. Paris: Champion, 2000.

Lougee, Carolyn C. *Le Paradis des Femmes. Women, Salons, and Social Stratification in Seventeenth-Century France*. Princeton: Princeton University Press, 1976.

Macdonald, Katherine M. "Broderie sur la traduction feminine: *Le ravissement de Proserpine de Catherine des Roches* (1586)." *Nouvelle revue du XVIᵉ siècle* 22, no. 2 (2004): 83–93.

Maclean, Ian. *The Renaissance Notion of Woman: A Study in the Fortunes of Scholasticism and Medical Science in European Intellectual Life*. Cambridge: Cambridge University Press, 1980.

Marsh, David. *Classical Tradition and Humanist Innovation*. Cambridge: Harvard University Press, 1980.

Martin-Ulrich, Claudie. *La "persona" de la princesse au XVIᵉ siècle*: personnage littéraire et personnage politique. Paris: Champion, 2004.

Matthieu-Castellani, Gisèle. *La quenouille et la lyre*. Paris: José Corti, 1998.

Nephew, Julia Anne. "The Portrayal of Women's Education: Christine de Pizan to the Dames des Roches (1400–1587)." Ph.D. diss., University of Wisconsin–Madison, 1999.

Neuschel, Kristen B. *Word of Honor: Interpreting Noble Culture in Sixteenth-Century France*. Ithaca: Cornell University Press, 1986.

Olson, Todd P. "La Femme à la Puce et la puce à l'oreille: Catherine Des Roches and the Poetics of Sexual Resistance in Sixteenth-Century French Poetry." *Journal of Medieval and Early Modern Studies* 32, no. 2 (2002): 327–42.

Panizza, Letizia, ed. *Women in Italian Renaissance Culture and Society*. Oxford: European Humanities Research Center, 2000.

————, and Sharon Wood, eds. *A History of Women's Writing in Italy*. Cambridge: Cambridge University Press, 2000.

Peach, Trevor. "Autour des *Amours de Francine*: quelques notes d'histoire littéraire." *Bibliothèque d'Humanisme et Renaissance* 44 (1982): 81–95.

Piéjus, Marie-Françoise. "La création du féminin dans le discours de quelques poétesses du XVIe siècle." In *Dire la création. La culture italienne entre poétique et poïétique*, ed. D. Budor, 79–90. Lille: Presses Universitaires de Lille, 1994.

Pieper, Julia. "'Madeleine et Catherine des Roches, mère et fille.' Aspekte der Legitimierung weiblicher Autorschaft in der Renaissance." In *Geschlechterdifferenzen*, ed. Katharina Hanau et al., 33–41. Bonn: Romanistischer Verlag, 1999.

————. *Zwischen Bildungslust und Konvention: Gelehrsamkeit, Tugend, und weibliche Autorschaft im Werk der Dames des Roches*. Pfaffenweiler: Centaurus, 1998.

Pree, Julia K. "Préciosité et dédoublement: vers une nouvelle lecture des Dames des Roches." *Romance Notes* 32, no. 3 (1992): 255–62.

Read, Kirk. "French Renaissance Women Writers in Search of Community: Literary Constructions of Female Companionship in City, Family and Convent. Louise Labé, Lionnoize, Madeleine and Catherine des Roches, mère et fille, Anne de Marquets, Soeur de Poissy." Ph.D. diss., Princeton University, 1991.

————. "Mother's Milk from Father's Breast: Maternity without Women in Male French Renaissance Lyric." In *High Anxiety: Masculinity in Crisis in Early Modern France*, ed. Kathleen P. Long, 71–92. Sixteenth Century Essays and Studies. Kirksville, Mo.: Truman University Press, 2002.

Rebhorn, Wayne. *The Emperor of Men's Minds: Literature and the Renaissance Discourse of Rhetoric*. Ithaca: Cornell University Press, 1995.

————, ed. and trans. *Renaissance Debates on Rhetoric*. Ithaca: Cornell University Press, 2000.

Roelker, Nancy. *One King, One Faith: The Parlement of Paris and the Religious Reformations of the Sixteenth Century*. Berkeley: University of California Press, 1996.

Sankovitch, Tilde. "Catherine Des Roches's Le Ravissement de Proserpine: A Humanist/Feminist Translation." In *Renaissance Women Writers: French Texts / American Contexts*, ed. Anne R. Larsen and Colette H. Winn, 55–66. Detroit: Wayne State University Press, 1994.

————. *French Women Writers and the Book: Myths of Access and Desire*. Syracuse: Syracuse University Press, 1988.

————. "Inventing Authority of Origin: The Difficult Enterprise." In *Women in the Middle Ages and the Renaissance: Literary and Historical Perspectives*, ed. Mary Beth Rose, 227–43. Syracuse: Syracuse University Press, 1986.

Schalk, Ellery. *From Valor to Pedigree: Ideas of Nobility in France in the Sixteenth and Seventeenth Century*. Princeton: Princeton University Press, 1986.

Schutz, Alexander Herman. "The Group of the Dames des Roches in Sixteenth-Century Poitiers." *Publications of the Modern Language Association* 48, no. 3 (1933): 648–54.

Scognamiglio, Concetta Menna. "La fortuna nell'opera di Madeleine e Catherine des Roches." In *Il Tema della Fortuna nella letteratura francese e italiana del Rinascimento. Studi in memoria di Enzo Giudici*, 123–33. Florence: Leo Olschki, 1990.

Sealy, Robert. *The Palace Academy of Henry III*. Geneva: Droz, 1981.

Smarr, Janet Levarie. *Joining the Conversation: Dialogues by Renaissance Women.* Ann Arbor: University of Michigan Press, 2005.

Smith, Jay. *The Culture of Merit: Nobility, Royal Service, and the Making of Absolute Monarchy in France, 1600–1789.* Ann Arbor: University of Michigan Press, 1996.

Solterer, Helen. *The Master and Minerva: Disputing Women in French Medieval Culture.* Berkeley: University of California Press, 1995.

Sommers, Paula. "Female Subjectivity and the Distaff: Louise Labé, Catherine des Roches, and Gabrielle de Coignard." *Explorations in Renaissance Culture* 25 (1999): 139–50.

Sonnet, Martine. "A Daughter to Educate." In *A History of Women in the West: Renaissance and Enlightenment Paradoxes,* ed. Natalie Zemon Davis and Arlette Farge, 101–31. Cambridge: Harvard University Press, 1993.

Tarte, Kendall Bracy. "Early Modern Literary Communities: Madeleine des Roches's City of Women." *Sixteenth-Century Journal* 35, no. 3 (2004): 751–69.

———. "*Mes rochers hautains:* A Study of Madeleine and Catherine Des Roches and the Culture of Renaissance Poitiers." Ph.D. diss., University of Virginia, 1997.

Timmermans, Linda. *L'accès des femmes à la culture (1598–1715). Un débat d'idées de Saint François de Sales à la Marquise de Lambert.* Paris: Champion, 1993.

Tomarken, Annette. *The Smile of Truth: The French Satirical Eulogy and Its Antecedents.* Princeton: Princeton University Press, 1990.

Vaillancourt, Luc. *La lettre familière au XVIe siècle. Rhétorique humaniste de l'épistolaire.* Paris: Champion, 2003.

Winn, Colette H. "Aux origines du discours féminin sur l'amitié. Marguerite de Navarre, *La Coche* (1541)." *Women in French Studies* 7 (1999): 9–24.

———, ed. *The Dialogue in Early Modern France, 1547–1630: Art and Argument.* Washington, D.C.: Catholic University of America Press, 1993.

———. "Mère/fille/femme/muse: maternité et créativité dans les œuvres des Dames des Roches." *Travaux de Littérature* 4 (1991): 53–68.

———, and Nicole Pellegrin, eds. *Veufs, veuves et veuvage dans la France d'Ancien Régime. Actes du colloque de Poitiers (11–12 juin 1998).* Paris: Champion, 2003.

Yandell, Cathy. "'L'Amour au féminin?' Ronsard and Pontus de Tyard Speaking as Women." In *Ronsard. Figure de la variété. En mémoire d'Isidore Silver,* ed. Colette H. Winn, 65–83. Geneva: Droz, 2002.

———. *Carpe Corpus: Time and Gender in Early Modern France.* Newark: University of Delaware Press, 2000.

———. "'Des ames sans cors, et des cors sans ames': la pédagogie dialectique de Catherine des Roches." In *Lectrices d'Ancien Régime,* ed. Isabelle Brouard-Arends, 557–66. Rennes: Presses Universitaires de Rennes, 2002.

———. "Of Lice and Women: Rhetoric and Gender in *La Puce de Madame Des Roches.*" *Journal of Medieval and Renaissance Studies* 20, no. 1 (1990): 123–35.

Yates, Francis. *The French Academies of the Sixteenth Century.* London: Wartburg Institute, 1947.

Zarri, Gabriella. "The Third Status." In *Time, Space, and Women's Lives in Early Modern Europe,* ed. Anne Jacobson Schutte et al., 181–99. Sixteenth-Century Essays and Studies, no. 57. Kirksville, Mo.: Truman State University Press, 2001.

NOTE ON TRANSLATION

The translation of Catherine des Roches's eight dialogues and of the Des Roches' selected poems from *Les Œuvres* (1579) and *Les Secondes Œuvres* (1583) follow the copy of both texts bound together and owned by the Bibliothèque de l'Arsenal in Paris (4° BL 2912). This is the copy that was also used in my critical edition of these texts. This copy was annotated by two different readers. The first reader inscribed on the title page of *Les Œuvres* "Ex Biblioteca Petri Cadotii Equit. 1597" (From the library of Pierre Cadot Esquire 1597) and on the back page of *Les Secondes Œuvres* "Emptus an. 1586 mense Maio" (Bought in the month of May 1586). Internal evidence gleaned from the marginal notations indicates that Pierre Cadot was the son of a magistrate of the Grands Jours and that he attended the Des Roches' salon along with his mother and sister. His many marginal comments include his memories of the mother and daughter and the jurists who were their guests. A philologist, he corrects errors of spelling, notes a rare word or suggests another more appropriate to the content, and explains obscure metaphors and images. He cites many sources, indicating thereby his vast knowledge of ancient and contemporary texts. The second annotator wrote his marginal comments in the early seventeenth century and unlike the first annotator did not personally know the Des Roches. He writes in shorthand and includes the dates of death of famous jurists such as Achille de Harlay in 1616 and Antoine Loisel in 1617, and refers to the heroine of Saint François de Sales's *Introduction de la vie dévote* (Introduction to the Devout Life, 1609). I include comments from the first annotator in a few reference notes.[1]

1. For the comments of both annotators, see the reference notes in my critical edition of the *Œuvres*, Textes Littéraires Français (Geneva: Droz, 1993), and *Les Secondes Œuvres*, Textes Littéraires Français (Geneva: Droz, 1998).

The translation of the selected letters follows the 1586 copy of *Les Missives* owned by the Bibliothèque Nationale de France in Paris (Rés. Ye. 527). This was the text used in my critical edition of *Les Missives*. In the translations, I have retained the capital letters for nouns that are capitalized in the original and the French *Monsieur* and *Madame* as forms of address, but I have modified the punctuation to allow for greater readability in English. I have imported some of the notes of my critical editions but have included many new ones to reflect the most recent scholarship on Renaissance women writers.

I

SELECTED POEMS OF MADELEINE
DES ROCHES FROM *LES ŒUVRES* (1579)

I prefer writing to spinning.

—Madeleine des Roches, sonnet 8

INTRODUCTION

Madeleine des Roches's dedicatory epistle to *Les Œuvres* is addressed *Aux Dames* (To the Ladies). Who were they? It is tempting to think that they constituted primarily Parisian upper gentry and court "doctes dames" (learned ladies).[1] Two reasons would have impelled the Dames des Roches to address them. *Les Œuvres* appeared a year after the royal court's three-month sojourn in Poitiers, and publishing in the capital would have been a reminder of that fortunate occurrence.[2] They would also have found a larger and more sympathetic audience in an environment where the phenomenon of the learned woman and women's participation in literary coteries were not exceptional. Madeleine's letter, however, appeals for the patronage of possibly two conjoined groups of imagined female readers. She addresses ladies whom she depicts as contemptuous of her "humbles vers" (humble verse) and to whom she is indebted in friendship: "I have wanted, in this little work wherein I have depicted myself, to take the time to assure you of the true friendship which I have always felt for you, my ladies, that is, if some of you deign to read my humble verse."[3] It is possible to identify these ladies as superior in status and erudition and as part of the Parisian audience whose criticism Des Roches forestalls. A second group consists of those who admonish their peers not to meddle in writing and publishing since "silence, the ornament of woman, can cover errors of the tongue and of understanding."[4] These readers differ from the Parisian reader whose patronage Des Roches hopes to interest. A clue to their identity is offered in ode 3, also addressed "aux dames," where Madeleine criticizes women who disparage female intellectuals: "Some Satyr's tongue, / That loves to mock, / Will emphatically state: / Enough! All a woman needs to know is how / To spin and do her housework; / Such a woman is much more profitable" (ll. 25–30).[5] Other women who derive importance from incessant quarreling or from clothes are summoned to more worthwhile occupations: "But there is something far more worthy / For the lady of Poitiers / Than the gallant garment: / Already she has made it her habit / To choose ink and pen / And to employ these learnedly" (ll. 43–48).[6] Des Roches's inclusion of provincial female readers is a tactical ploy to herald those among them who, like her, are part of a new "docte echole" (learned school).

From the outset, Madeleine des Roches positions herself in her published works in the *querelle des femmes* controversy, a plurivocal debate on the nature of the female sex. To the disapproval, hesitation, and even fear of intimidation of her imagined female readers, Madeleine responds in her prefatorial letter: "[le silence] peut bien empescher la honte, mais non pas accroistre l'honneur, aussi que le parler nous separe des animaux sans raison" (silence may well prevent shame but cannot increase honor, and . . . speech distinguishes us from the reasonless beasts). She identifies with the third voice in this discursive tradition: women differ from men not because they are by nature inferior (the misogynist track), or because they are superior (the feminist angle), but because of long-ingrained cultural prejudices and practices.[7] Since women possess reason, they are capable of moral and intellectual improvement; it follows that like men they should receive moral training and education in rhetoric, the sciences, and the arts to acquire virtue, honor, and a good reputation.

Madeleine des Roches's views on women's education are founded upon humanistic principles. Following Erasmus, she considered nature, education, and exercise as the three fundamentals in the training of men and women. In her dedicatory Epistle to My Daughter, she writes a poetic "mirror" or "institution" in which she briefly outlines the broad principles in the education of a daughter, her own. Taking Catherine as her exemplary model, she evokes first the humanist notion of the innate qualities inherited at birth. Catherine's heart, she states, is "né à la vertu" (naturally inclined to virtue); she resembles her mother in body and in the "gracious compatibility" of their minds. This leads Madeleine to emphasize yet another Erasmian principle that physical and moral resemblance must be cultivated through religious instruction as well as an education in *bonae litterae* (letters). Like Erasmus and Vives, Madeleine des Roches is concerned with the education of the Christian woman whose dominant trait is *sagesse* (propriety or decorum), an epithet that admirers consistently applied to Catherine.[8] Instruction in belles lettres focuses above all on the acquisition of virtue: "It is not enough, however, to be wellborn,/ Acquired knowledge makes us well-mannered.../Letters can change the vice-ridden,/ Letters can increase the courage of the virtuous."[9] Catherine has demonstrated this amply by showing herself an exemplary daughter, offering "since childhood/Love, counsel, support, and obedience."[10] As a reward for her services, her mother bestows upon her the rare "gift" of allowing her to devote herself to "la Muse et le divin sçavoir" (the Muse and divine learning), rare because such erudition was more appropriate for male professionals and for women of the aristocracy and /or of independent means.[11] Ciceronian *otium literatum* (literary leisure), opposed to *negotium* (business), was the privilege of the male professional, before evolving in the Renaissance and seventeenth century into worldly leisure reserved for the aristocratic habitués of literary circles and salons. This prized *otium* probably is the reason that Catherine's output amounts to over two-thirds of the combined works of the two women. Then, in a syncretist linking of Erasmian virtue to Greco-Roman mythopoetics, Madeleine des Roches ends her epistle by invoking the literary immortality conferred upon such learning and virtuous conduct: "And may the Daemon,[12] who began this work in you,/ So well guide your thoughts and actions,/ That posterity may know/How much honor you will have merited./ May you some day become immortal through your virtue./ It is thus that I have always wanted you to be."[13] Des Roches's speaker connects humanist ideology with Pléiade poetics: she draws on the Greco-Roman concept of *exegi monumentum* (I have raised a monument), which Ronsard evokes for instance in his praise of Marguerite de France, the learned sister of Henry II: "Your mind is always taking pleasure / In the saintly studies of the Muse, / Who, despite the tomb, / Will render your name even more renowned."[14] Madeleine's wish for her daughter is couched in terms strikingly similar to those of Ronsard for the king's sister. Madeleine furthermore taps into terminology particular to noble discourse. For the urban nobility, dedication, services rendered to another, educational achievement, and virtue constituted merit deserving recompense.[15] Madeleine's pride in Catherine's achievements leads her to apply the rhetoric of class merit to the praise of her daughter.

Nowhere throughout her writings does the mother enjoin her daughter to marry. To the contrary, she bluntly critiques the unjust "laws of marriage," which robbed her of her own youthful literary aspirations (ode 1). Unlike Catherine, she published late in life (she was fifty-eight when *Les Œuvres* appeared) and wrote only poetry. Her worldview, that of her generation in fact, is pessimistic. The wars of religion, which ravaged the southwest of France and the region of Poitou in particular, fueled feelings of insecurity and distress. Madeleine comments frequently on the disorders of the civil wars (sonnets 15, 16, 20), her bouts of ill health when she was plagued with migraines (ode 4, sonnets 7, 8), numerous lawsuits[16] (*Epistle to My Daughter*, sonnet 5), and the death of loved ones and friends (*Epitaph for Her Husband*, sonnet 36). She critiques the lack of equity, or fairness, toward women that led to their juridical incapacity and dependency: "As for my country, I am powerless;/ Men have all the authority,/ Against reason and against fairness."[17] On the other hand, in her catalogue of women worthies (ode 3), she emphasizes the contributions to civilization of ancient female rulers, goddesses, and especially inventors of laws, such as Carmenta and Ceres. As Kendall Tarte has shown, she juxtaposes in ode 3 two communities of women, the actual historical community of ladies of Poitiers whom she challenges to a life of the mind, and a fictional literary community not unlike Christine de Pizan's ideal city.[18] The latter models the building blocks of a civilized society founded upon the rule of law maintained by women, women's learning, and women's fame.

In the selected sonnets, Madeleine defends the Gallican principle "one faith, one law, one king" (sonnet 14), arguing for the strengthening of the monarchy, and showing her preference for Politiques thought.[19] Her fierce opposition to the Huguenot warring armies is based on what she perceives as their attacks on the core values of the monarchy. In sonnet 15, she states: "It is not Byzantium, Spain, or Rome,/ It is not Scotland, England, or Germany/ Who have sacked us and caused us so much suffering./ It is the French mutineers who have done the damage,/ Not worrying about injuring a young and just King,/ After having polluted everything that is holy."[20] She critiques Huguenot teachings, preachers, and iconoclastic military operations. Like Étienne Pasquier, however, who was uniformly polite in his letters to Protestant scholars, Madeleine was on friendly terms with Protestant humanists who were welcome at her salon. These included the philologist Joseph-Juste Scaliger, the physician François de Saint-Vertunien, the lawyer Jean Boiceau de La Borderie, and the then young poet Agrippa d'Aubigné.

The sense of social disintegration that fueled the pessimism of so many at the time also gave rise to a new nationalism and patriotic awareness both politically and in the realm of literature. The latter is linked to the Pléiade school that in the 1550s engendered the drive toward the enrichment of the French language. Madeleine des Roches's strong nationalist commitments are evident in her bold critique of the anticipated marriage of François d'Alençon (1554–84), Henri III's younger brother, to Queen Elizabeth I in the late 1570s (sonnet 11). Such a marriage with "barbarous England," she argues, is unsustainable for a defender of "the Holy Roman See" and traitorous to Gallican principles. Nationalist pride leads her to assert the notion of *translatio studii et imperii* (transferal of letters and dominion) as a way of proclaiming her belief in the superiority of French culture: "So shall France become the most learned of them all," she declares. "Just as our prince has overcome by arms / The Spanish, the English, and Roman men of arms, / So shall the French Toga take the first prize."[21] Hence, like the humanist Guillaume Budé and Pléiade poets Joachim du Bellay and Pierre de Ronsard, Madeleine evokes, in ode 2 of *Les Secondes œuvres*, the "Gallic Hercules" as a figure authorizing linguistic nationalism.

Finally, Madeleine ends her portion of the 1579 volume of *Les Œuvres* with two sonnets to her daughter. In the first, she laments the unjust burden on Catherine of helping her mother withstand the pressure of her lawsuit. In the second, she pleads with her to recover from an illness and thus spare her mother further anguish. She beseeches her "by [my] maternal love, / By the sweet milk drawn from [my] breast, / And [my] womb which bore you for nine months."[22] The image of her nursing child now grown author daughter becomes a metaphor for her continual nurturance of Catherine's literary talent. In ending her contribution to their common volume with this image, Madeleine underscores the role of maternal sustenance in literary creation. She rescripts here what Kirk Read has called the "self-sufficient paradigm of literary sustenance and reproduction," coopted by French Renaissance male poets to empower their writing.[23] Poets of the period used such feminine imagery to assert their control over textual reproduction while at the same time effacing women altogether from that process. Thus Ronsard for instance addresses his mentor Jean Dorat, expressing his gratitude at having been able "To suckle the savory milk / Of your fertile breast!"[24] Madeleine reclaims the topos of the "nursing mother" to assert the primacy of female nurturance of women poets. Maternalized mentorship is affirmed continuously throughout the oeuvre of the Des Roches as they evoke mothers nurturing their daughters to assume control of their lives and writings.

᠄᠊

EPISTRE AUX DAMES

Si le marbre bien taillé, ou les couleurs du pinceau employé d'une docte main, nous ont fait congnoistre, non la seule beauté du corps, mais encores les moeurs et complexions de ceux qu'ils ont representez, j'ay pensé que la parolle, vraye image de l'ame, et la voix fuyante arrestée par la plume sur le papier, donnoit un certain indice, non seullement de la richesse de l'esprit et de ses sens acquis ou naturels, mais de l'integrité naïfve de ceux qui parlent ou escrivent Pour ceste cause, j'ay voulu en ce petit tableau où je me suis depeinte, arrester ma parolle, pour vous asseurer de l'amitié entiere que j'ay tousjours portée à vous (Mesdames) si aucunes de vous daignez lire mes humbles vers. Et si, m'estant plus charitables, vous m'advisez que le silence, ornement de la femme, peut couvrir les fautes de la langue et de l'entendement, je respondray qu'il peut bien empescher la honte, mais non pas accroistre l'honneur, aussi que le parler nous separe des animaux sans raison. Au fort j'espere de voz courtoisies que si vous ne me jugez digne d'estime, vous ne penserez pas que je merite grande reprehension, pource que si c'est peu de mes escrits pour la valeur, aussi n'est-ce point beaucoup pour la longueur. Ainsi vous me trouverez aucunement excusable; mais il vaut mieux que je trouve la fin de mon epistre assez pres du commencement, de crainte que vous ennuiant pour sa longueur, elle contredise à moy-mesme et à vostre désir, de sorte qu'il me fallust chercher excuse à mon excuse. Adieu mes Dames.

EPISTRE À MA FILLE

Les anciens amateurs de sçavoir
Disoient qu'à Dieu faut rendre le devoir,
Puis au pays, et le tiers au lignage,
Les induisant à force de courage,
Soit quelques fois pour souffrir passion,   5
Soit pour dompter la forte affection.
Au Seigneur Dieu je porte reverence,
Pour mon pays, je n'ay point de puissance,
Les hommes ont toute l'autorité,
Contre raison et contre l'equité.   10
Mais envers toy, fille qui m'es si proche,
Ce me seroit un grand blasme et reproche
De te conduire au sentier plus battu,
Veu que ton cueur est né à la vertu.
Il ne suffit pourtant d'estre bien nées,   15
Le sens acquis nous rend morigenées,
Et le flambeau dans nostre ame allumé,

[DEDICATORY EPISTLE BY MADELEINE DES ROCHES]
EPISTLE TO THE LADIES

If the well-chiseled marble, or the colors of a paintbrush employed by a skilled hand, acquaint us with not only the physical beauty but the manners and traits of those they depict, it is my opinion that the word, true image of the soul, and the fleeting voice recorded by the pen onto paper, give a certain indication not only of the richness of the mind and of its acquired or natural capacities but of the natural[25] integrity of those who speak or write. For this reason, I have wanted, in this little work wherein I have depicted myself, to take the time to assure you of the true friendship which I have always felt for you, my ladies, that is, if some of you deign to read my humble verse. And if, out of greater charity for me, you advise me that silence, the ornament of woman,[26] can cover errors of the tongue and of understanding, I will answer you that silence may well prevent shame but cannot increase honor, and that speech distinguishes us from the reasonless beasts.[27] At least I count on your courtesy, that if you do not judge me worthy of esteem, you will not think that I should be greatly reprehended, for if the value of my writings is not great, neither is their length. Therefore, you will find me somewhat worthy of excuse; but I had better end my letter near its beginning for fear that by boring you on account of its length, I contradict myself and your wishes, and I must then apologize for my excuse. Adieu, Mesdames.

EPISTLE TO MY DAUGHTER

Ancient lovers of wisdom
Said that to God one must do one's duty,
Then to one's country, and finally to one's lineage;
Leading [their listeners] by dint of courage,
Sometimes to endure suffering,   5
And other times to overcome their strong longings.
I revere Almighty God;
As for my country, I am powerless;
Men have all the authority,
Against reason and against fairness.[29]   10
But in what concerns you, my daughter who are so dear to me,
I would be subject to great blame and reproach
Were I to lead you down the beaten path,
For your heart is naturally inclined to virtue.
It is not enough, however, to be wellborn;   15
Acquired knowledge makes us well-mannered,
And the fire burning in our soul,

Sans le sçavoir est bientost consommé.
La lettre sert d'une saincte racine,
Pour le regime, et pour la Medecine: 20
La lettre peut changer le vitieux,
La lettre accroist le cueur du vertueux,
La lettre est l'art qui prenant la matiere
Luy peut donner sa forme plus entiere.
Ce brief discours sur un tel argument   25
Soit bien reçeu de ton entendement,
Ma fille unique, et de moy cher tenue,
Non pour autant que tu en es venue
Et que dans toy je me voy un pourtraict
Du poil, du teint, de la taille, et du traict,   30
Façon, maintien, parolle, contenance,
Et l'aage seul en faict la difference;
Ny pour nous voir tant semblables de corps,
Ny des esprits les gracieux accords,
Ny ceste douce aymable sympathie,   35
Qui faict aymer la semblable partie,
N'ont point du tout causé l'entier effect
De mon amour envers toy si parfaict,
Ny les efforts mis en moy par nature,
Ny pour autant qu' és de ma nourriture.   40
Mais le penser, qu'entre tant de mal-heurs,
De maux, d'ennuis, de peines, de douleurs,
Sujection, tourment, travail, tristesse,
Qui puis[28] treze ans ne m'ont point donné cesse,
Tu as, enfant, apporté un cueur fort,   45
Pour resister au violent effort
Qui m'accabloit, et m'offris dès enfance
Amour, conseil, support, obeissance.
Le tout puissant à qui j'eu mon recours,
A faict de toy naistre mon seul secours.   50
Or je ne puis de plus grands benefices
Recompenser tes loüables offices,
Que te prier de faire ton devoir
Envers la Muse et le divin sçavoir.
"Mais le vray centre et globe de l'estude,   55
"C'est de donner à vertu habitude,
"Et se vouloir en elle insinuer;

When deprived of learning is soon consumed.
Letters can be a sacred resource
For one's health, and for medicinal use;   20
Letters can change the vice-ridden,
Letters can increase the courage of the virtuous,
And letters are the art that give
To matter its most perfect form.
May this brief discourse on such a topic   25
Find in you a warm welcome,
My only daughter, so precious to me,
Not because you come from me,
And because in you I see my reflection
In hair, complexion, build, and trait,   30
Manner, bearing, word, countenance,
And only age distinguishes us;
Nor the sight of so great a physical resemblance,
Nor the gracious compatibility of our minds,
Nor this sweet amiable sympathy   35
That makes us love the one who is like us,
Can fully account for the extent
Of my perfect love for you,
Or the strength that nature has given me,
Or the fact that such strength is my sustenance.   40
But the thought that amidst so many calamities,
Ills, troubles, sorrows, pains,
Subjection, torment, work, sadness,
Which for thirteen years have given me no respite,[30]
You, child, have shown a strong heart,   45
Resisting the violent travail
That overwhelmed me, and you have offered me since childhood
Love, counsel, support, and obedience.
The Almighty in whom I took my refuge
Has made you the sole source of my succor.   50
To reward you for your worthy services
I cannot grant you a greater gift
Than to urge you to do your duty
Toward the Muse and divine learning.
"But the true aim and goal of study   55
Is to make out of virtue a habit
And to want to become part of it;

L'abit se faict difficile à muer.
Tu es au temps pour apprendre bien née,
Et sembles estre aux Muses inclinée.   60
Le Ciel te face avoir tant de desir
Des sainctes moeurs, le seul juste plaisir,
Et le Dœmon, qui l'oeuvre a commencée,
Guide si bien l'effect de ta pensée,
Que tesmoignant à la posterité   65
Combien d'honneur tu auras merité,
Tu sois un jour par vertu immortelle,
Je t'ay tousjours souhaitée estre telle.

ODE 1
Si mes escris n'ont gravé sur la face
Le sacré nom de l'immortalité,
Je ne l'ay quis³³ non plus que merité,
Si je ne l'ay de faveur ou de grace.

Je ne descry Neptune en sa tourmente,   5
Je ne peins pas Jupiter irrité,
Le vase ouvert, la fuite d'equité,
Dont nostre terre à bon droict se lamente.

L'enfant venu de Porus et Poenie,
Qu'on dit brusler le plus froid des glaçons,   10
Se plaist d'ouyr les superbes chansons.
Et je me play d'une basse armonie.

Mais qui pourroit, chargé de tant de peine,
L'esprit geenné de cent mille malheurs,
Voir Apollon reverer les neuf Seurs,   15
Et dignement puiser en leur fontaine?

Le Ciel a bien infuz dedans nostre Ame
Les petits feux, principes de vertu:
Mais le chaud est par le froid combatu,
Si un beau bois n'alimente la flame.   20

Nature veut la lettre et l'exercice
Pour faire voir un chef-d'oeuvre parfaict;

For such a habit is then difficult to break."[31]
You are born at an auspicious time for learning,
And you seem inclined to the Muses.   60
May Heaven give you such a longing
For saintly living, the only source of just pleasure,
And may the Daemon,[32] who began this work in you,
So well guide your thoughts and actions,
That posterity may know   65
How much honor you will have merited.
May you some day become immortal through your virtue.
It is thus that I have always wanted you to be.

ODE 1[34]

If my writings do not have engraved on their cover
The sacred name of immortality,
Neither have I acquired nor earned that name,
Unless it were by favor or by grace.

I do not depict Neptune in his torments,   5
Nor do I paint angry Jupiter,
The open vase,[35] the flight of equity,[36]
Which our land rightly laments.

The child of Porus and Penia[37]
Who is said to burn up the coldest of ice,   10
Delights to hear lofty songs;
Yet I am content with a humbler harmony.

But who, weighed down by so much sorrow,
With mind racked by a hundred thousand misfortunes,
Could ever behold Apollo revere the nine Sisters,[38]   15
And draw from their fountain in a worthy manner?

Heaven has indeed infused within our Soul
Small sparks, principles of virtue;[39]
But heat is often overcome by cold
If a good supply of wood doesn't feed the flame.   20

Nature requires that both learning and exercise
Combine to perfect a chef-d'oeuvre;

Elle, bien sage en toutes choses, faict
Ses premiers traits limer à l'artifice.

Noz parens ont de loüables coustumes,   25
Pour nous tollir l'usage de raison,
De nous tenir closes dans la maison
Et nous donner le fuzeau pour la plume.

Trassant noz pas selon la destinée,
On nous promet liberté et plaisir: 30
Et nous payons l'obstiné desplaisir,
Portant le dot sous les loix d'Hymenée.

Bientost apres survient une misere
Qui naist en nous d'un desir mutuel,
Accompagné d'un soing continuel,   35
Qui suit tousjours l'entraille de la mere.

Il faut soudain que nous changions l'office
Qui nous pouvoit quelque peu façonner,
Où les marys ne nous feront sonner
Que l'obeir, le soing, et l'avarice.   40

Quelcun d'entr' eux, ayant fermé la porte
A la vertu, nourice du sçavoir,
En nous voyant craint de la recevoir
Pource qu'ell' porte habit de nostre sorte.

L'autre reçoit l'esprit de jalousie,   45
Qui, possesseur d'une chaste beauté,
Au nid d'Amour loge la cruauté,
En bourellant sa propre fantasie.

Pyrrha choisist une claire semence
Pour repeupler le terrestre manoir,   50
Et Deücal sema le caillou noir,
Dont le Ciel mesme a faict experience.

Mon Dieu, mon Dieu, combien de tolerance
Que je ne veux icy ramentevoir!

She, wise in every way, demands that
Craftsmanship join talent to shape a work of art.[40]

Our parents have laudable customs[41]   25
To deprive us of the use of our reason:
They lock us up at home
And hand us the spindle instead of the pen.

Conforming our steps to our [female] destiny,
They promise us liberty and pleasure: 30
But we reap continuous displeasure,
When we lose our dowry to the laws of Marriage.[42]

Then soon after comes a new misery,
Born within us of mutual desire,
Accompanied by those continuous cares   35
That always burden the mother's womb.

Suddenly we must reorder all those tasks
That fashioned our lives in some way,
For our husbands will harangue us to the tune of
Obedience, hard labor, and stinginess.   40

One such husband, because he closed his door
To virtue, mother of learning,
On seeing us fears to welcome her back
Because she wears the garb of our sex.

Another, filled with jealousy,   45
Now in possession of a beautiful chaste lady,
Resorts to cruelty in the nest of Love,
Tormenting his own misguided fantasies.

Pyrrha chose a light seed
To repopulate the earth,   50
But Deucalion sowed black stones
As Heaven itself knows well. [43]

My God, my God, how much suffering
I don't care to remember here!

Il me suffit aux hommes faire voir   55
Combien leurs loix nous font de violence.

Les plus beaux jours de noz vertes années
Semblent les fleurs d'un printems gracieux,
Pressé d'orage, et de vent pluvieux,
Qui vont borner les courses terminées.   60

Au temps heureux de ma saison passée,
J'avoy bien l'aile unie à mon costé:
Mais en perdant ma jeune liberté,
Avant le vol ma plume fut cassée.

Je voudroy bien m'arester sur le livre,   65
Et au papier mes peines souspirer.
Mais quelque soing m'en vient tousjours tirer,
Disant qu'il faut ma profession suivre.

L'Agrigentin du sang de Stesichore
A dignement honoré le sçavoir.   70
Qui envers nous feit semblable devoir,
Pareil miracle on reverroit encore.

Dames, faisons ainsi que l'Amarante
Qui par l'hyver ne pert sa belle fleur:
L'esprit imbu de divine liqueur   75
Rend par labeur sa force plus luisante.

Pour supporter les maux de nostre vie,
Dieu nous feit part de l'intellect puissant
Pour le reduire à l'intellect agent
Maugré la mort, la fortune, et l'envie.   80

ODE 3
Heureux fardeau qui aporte
Tant d'honneur; fussé-je forte
Pour chanter d'un ton divin
L'astre clair, dont la lumiere
Est d'esclairer coustumiere   5
Le rivage Poëtevin.

It is enough if I can make men see   55
How much their laws do violence to us.

The most beautiful years of our verdant youth
Seem but the flowers of a gracious springtime,
Pressed in by storms and rainy winds,
That halt in the end the course of life.   60

In the happy moments of my yesteryear,
I bore my wings close by my side:
But, in losing my youthful freedom,
My feathered pen was clipped before I flew.[44]

I so long to spend time with my books   65
And, sighing, cast my sorrows onto paper.
But some distracting trouble always diverts me,
Claiming that I must pursue a wife's vocation.

The Agrigentan worthily honored
The learning of the daughters of Stesichorus.   70
He who would do the same to us
Would bring about a similar miracle.[45]

Ladies, let us live as the amaranth[46]
That does not lose its beautiful flower in winter:
The mind imbued with a divine sap,   75
Through labor makes its strength shine brightly.

To help us bear the misfortunes of life,
God imparts to us a mighty intellect
That we are to turn into an active force
In spite of death, fortune, and envy.[47]   80

ODE 3
Happy the burden that brings
Such great honor! Would that I were strong enough
To praise with a heavenly voice
The brilliant sun whose light
Illuminates every day   5
The riverbanks of Poitiers.

Mais je n'ay pas la puissance
Egalle à la connoissance,
Ainsi que faut le pouvoir;
Si ce que je puis je donne,   10
Je vous pry qu'on me pardonne
Si je ne fay mon devoir.

Quand par plus claires bucines,
Dames graves et insignes,
Vostre loz sera chanté,   15
Ne desdaignez pas l'ouvrage
Qui vous porte tesmoignage
De ma bonne volonté.

Au moins, mes Dames, ne faictes
Comme Judée aux prophetes   20
A eux peculiers donnez;
Les vers que bas je souspire
Sur les fredons de ma lyre,
Ne soyent ainsi guerdonnez.

Quelque langue de Satyre,   25
Qui tient banque de mesdire,
Dira tousjours, il suffit:
Une femme [est]⁴⁸ assez sage
Qui file et faict son mesnage;
L'on y fait mieux son profit.   30

L'autre tient que c'est office
De plus loüable exercice
Se lever un peu matin,
Dire mal de sa Cousine,
Quereler à sa voisine,   35
Ou festier Sainct Martin.

L'autre un peu mieux avisée
Se sent beaucoup plus prisée
D'un habit bien etofé,
D'une belle decoupure,   40

But my strength is not
Equal to my knowledge,
Lacking power as I do;
If I give what I can,   10
I beg you to forgive me
If I do not do my duty.

When, to the sound of a more worthy trumpet,
Solemn and illustrious Ladies,
Your honors shall be sung,   15
Do not disdain this work
That bears witness to you
Of my goodwill.

At least, my Ladies, do not act
As Judah did to the prophets   20
Who were sent to her;[49]
The lowly verses that, sighing, I strum
On the strings of my lyre,
Should not be thus rewarded.

Some Satyr's tongue   25
That loves to mock[50]
Will emphatically state:
Enough! All a woman needs to know is how
To spin and do her housework;
Such a woman is much more profitable.   30

Another insists that it is her duty
And a more laudable activity
To get up early each morning,
To speak ill of her Cousin,
Quarrel with her neighbor,   35
Or celebrate the feast of Saint Martin.[51]

Yet another, a bit better advised,
Feels much more prized
If she wears a beautiful dress,
Well cut and stitched,   40

D'un Carquan, d'une dorure,
D'un chaperon bien coifé.

Mais quelque chose plus digne
A la dame Poïtevine
Que le brave acoutrement: 45
Jà desjà ell' faict coustume
De choisir l'ancre et la plume
Pour l'employer doctement.

Aussi le Ciel qui a cure
De vous, mes Dames, vous jure,   50
Et ne jure point en vain,
Que vous pourrez de vous-mesme
Vous venger de la mort blesme
Sans mendier l'escrivain.

Le Clain et sa rive mole,   55
Admirant la docte échole
D'une si douce leçon:
Furiant contre l'envie
Donnera pour jamais vie
Aux vers de vostre façon.   60

Je vay par un riche Temple
Pour raporter quelque exemple
Des Dames d'exellent pris;
Mais pour le trop d'abondance
Ou pour mon insuffisance   65
Je n'en ay beaucoup apris.

J'y ay pourtant sçeu aprendre
Comme la mere d'Evandre
Les Arcades gouverna,
Par le moyen des loix sainctes   70
De religion etraintes
Que sagement leur donna.

On voit par le rond du monde
Le nom de Ceres la blonde

With a necklace besides or some other finery,
And fancy headgear.

But there is something far more worthy
For the lady of Poitiers
Than the gallant garment: 45
Already she has made it her habit
To choose ink and pen
And to employ these learnedly.

The Heavens, therefore, that take good care
Of you, my Ladies, swear to you,   50
And do not swear in vain,
That on your own you can
Take revenge on pale Fate
Without having to beg another writer.[52]

The river Clain's peaceful banks,   55
Home to the learned school[53]
That teaches such sweet lessons,
Rages against envy
By granting long life
To the verses you will write.   60

I'll visit a rich Temple
To bring back some examples
Of Ladies of excellent talent.
But because of its exceeding abundance,
Or on account of my insufficiency,   65
I have not learned enough about them.

I have, however, learned
How Evander's mother[54]
Governed the Arcadians
By means of sacred laws   70
Founded on religion
That she wisely gave them.

We see that throughout the world
The name of blond Ceres

De temps en temps refleurir,   75
Qui garda, tant ell' sçeut faire,
Porte-blez et Legifere,
Corps et ames de perir.

De la grand' Deesse armée,
Le loz et la renommée   80
Se borne par l'univers;
Moins ne se chante la gloire
Des neuf Filles de Memoire,
Ornement des plus beaux vers.

Celle que la Grece vante   85
Belle, docte, bien disante,
Qui tant de bon-heur acquit
Le prix qui, grave, la pare,
Porte le nom de Pindare
Qu'en Olympe elle vainquit.   90

Qui se taira de Camille,
De Tomiris, et de Mille,
Du siecle digne ornement;
Du Nil et de Babylone,
Et de celle dont Ausone   95
Escrit veritablement.

Voyez les Dames de France
Qui ce monstre d'ignorance
Ont froissé en tant de pars,
Que leur quittant la carriere   100
Il saute sur la barriere,
Esloigné de leurs rampars.

Voy, ma fille, ma chere ame,
Fortune, Vertu, et Fame,
Se parer de ce beau nom;   105
Foy, Esperance, Concorde,
Pieté, Misericorde,
Toutes d'immortel renom.

Flowers time and time again.   75
Bearer of wheat and Maker of laws,[55]
She kept bodies and souls from perishing
As she knew how to do so well.

The praise and renown
Of the great armed Goddess[56]   80
Are limited by the universe only;
In equal manner is sung the glory
Of the nine Daughters of Memory,[57]
Who embellish the most beautiful poems.

She of whom Greece boasts,   85
Beautiful, learned, and well spoken,
Who so happily won
The prize that, solemnly, adorns her,
Bears the name of Pindar
Whom on Olympus she vanquished.[58]   90

Who can fail to speak of Camilla,[59]
Of Tomyris[60] and of all those
Who were illustrious in their time,
Those from the Nile region and from Babylon,
And her whom   95
Ausonius praised in his writings.[61]

See the Ladies of France
Who have torn into so many pieces
That monster Ignorance;
Abandoning the playing field to them,   100
He jumps over the barrier,
And flees from their ramparts.[62]

See, my daughter, my dearest soul,
Fortune, Virtue, and Fame
Are adorned with that beautiful name;[63]   105
Faith, Hope, Concord,
Piety, and Mercy,
Are all of immortal renown.

ODE 4

Quel sorcier rempli d'envie
Sur ma languissante vie
A versé tant de poison,
Que l'ame aux sens asservie
Brusle comme le tison.   5

Le Mercure, ainsi que l'onde
Fusile en sa forme ronde,
Se voit sans fin agité,
Et ma tristesse profonde
N'a point de cours arresté.   10

Je voy tousjours l'Hydre preste
A me marteler la teste
Par contraire mouvement:
Car quand l'un guerir s'appreste,
L'autre prend accroissement.   15

L'esprit lent, mort et labile,
Le corps sec, froid, et debile,
Souffrent plus que je ne dis:
Si je me tire de Scylle,
Je retombe en Carybdis.   20

Du chef jusques à la plante
Une humeur froide se plante
Par le millieu de mes os
Dont la douleur trop pressante
M'oste repas et repos.   25

Le penser qui ne repose,
Le triste effect de la cause
Raporte continuel
Que ma paupiere fut close
Au sommeil perpetuel.   30

Ma nef en ce dur orage
Perd le voile et le cordage
Dedans ce fleuve inconnu:

ODE 4

What sorcerer filled with envy,
On my listless life
Has poured out so much poison,
That my soul, enslaved to my senses,
Burns like a branding iron?   5

Mercury, like the waves of the sea,
Shoots around in circular motion,
And sees itself endlessly tossed to and fro;
And my profound sadness
Has no end in sight.   10

Before me I always see the Lernaean Hydra
Ready to pound my head
By constant adverse movement;
While one of its heads is on the mend,
Another keeps growing stronger.[64]   15

My mind sluggish, dead, and unstable,
My body so dry, cold, and feeble,
Suffer more than I can bear;
If I escape from Scylla,
I fall back again into Charybdis.[65]   20

From my head to the soles of my feet,
A frigid humor implants itself [66]
In the middle of my bones,
Whose pain is so overwhelming
That I can neither sleep nor eat.   25

My mind finds no rest,
The sad outcome of my suffering
Keeps telling me
That my eyelids were shut out
Of never-ending sleep.   30

My ship in this bitter storm[67]
Loses its sail and rigging,
In these unknown waters;

He Dieu! je fay le naufrage
Quand le serain est venu.   35

Je seray saine et entiere
Quand la forme et la matiere
Par leur alteration
Feront la terre heritiere
D'autre generation.   40

SONNET 1

Le Moteur eternel, de ce grand univers
Commencement et fin, la divine pensée
Qui tient dessous ses pieds la terre balancée,
Et qui au fond du cœur voit les secrets ouvers,
Reserva en ce temps, amer, dur et divers,
Où semble que l'Astrée est de chacun chassée,
À montrer la vertu du haut Ciel abaissée
Pour ceindre ton beau chef de rameaux toujours vers.
Bien qu'icy nous voyons, Neron et Domitie,
Et qu'un nouveau Breüs ait la terre obscurcie,
Ton honneur grave et sainct luist de si clair flambeau,
Que le Siecle est heureux, où tu es descendue
Pour miracle nouveau, car Dieu t'a deffendue
Du vice, de l'oubly, du temps, et du tombeau.

SONNET 5

Ayant souffert treze ans d'une injuste puissance,
L'ennuy et le travail, la peine et la douleur
Ont pris si forte place au centre de mon coeur,
Que je n'y trouve lieu pour la seule esperance.
On me dit que le temps guerit la violence,
Et qu'un mal coustumier n'a plus tant de vigueur.
Cela est vain en moy; je sens mesme rigueur,
Bien qu'ores je ne voy que douceur et clemence.
Pource que si longtemps mon mal-heur a eu place,
En le voulant chasser, il laisse telle trasse
Qu'on ne peut relever l'edifice destruit.
La triste passion, dont j'ay l'ame offensée,
M'a tant blessé le corps, l'esprit, et la pensée,
Que ce bien tard venu n'aporte point de fruict.

O God! I am shipwrecked
Just as calm waters are in sight.   35

I shall be safe and sound
When form and matter
By their alteration
Will lead the earth on to
Another generation.   40

SONNET 1 [TO CATHERINE DES ROCHES][68]

The eternal Motor, of this immense universe
The beginning and the end, the divine mind
Who holds beneath his feet the earth in its balance
And sees in the recesses of the heart open secrets,
Began, in these bitter, hard, and troubled times
Where Astrea seems to be chased away by all,[69]
To bring down virtue from high heaven
So as to crown your lovely brow with ever-verdant boughs.
Although at present we see the likes of Nero and Domitian,
And a new Briareus obscure the earth,[70]
Your solemn and saintly honor shines with a flame so bright
That the Century in which you came down is pleased,
For as a miraculous new being, God kept you
From vice, neglect, time, and the tomb.

SONNET 5[71]

Thirteen years have I suffered an unjust burden.
Vexation and toil, sorrow and pain
Have rooted themselves so strongly in my heart
That I find no room for a single ray of hope.
They tell me that time heals all wounds,
And that a customary evil loses its vigor.
But this doesn't hold true for me; my suffering remains unabated,
Even though now only gentleness and clemency surround me.
Because my misfortune has lasted so long,
Attempting to root it out has left such a gaping hole
That it's impossible to reconstruct the destroyed building.
The sad affliction that has injured my soul
Has so wounded my body, spirit, and mind
That this late-coming happiness bears no real fruit.[72]

SONNET 6

Sera jamais la fortune assouvie
Du mal sans fin en mon coeur renaissant,
Las! que j'endure? (O Seigneur tout puissant!)
Guide mon ame en l'eternelle vie.
Voy à mes sens ma raison asservie,
Ma foible force, et mon travail pressant.
Si mon prier (o Dieu) m'estoit decent,
J'ay, Seigneur, j'ay de mourir bonne envie.
O bien-heureux, dont la mortalité
Par foy se guide à la Divinité,
Purifiant ceste tache imparfaicte.
Heureux qui plein de prudence et raison,
Par vive foy dit en son oraison:
Du Seigneur Dieu la volonté soit faicte!

SONNET 7

Pleurant amerement mon douloureux servage
Qui tient mon corps mal sain, mon esprit en souci,
Le coeur comblé d'amer, le visage transi,
Cachant l'ombre de vie en une morte image,
Je cherche vainement qui l'esprit me soulage;
Le Medecin du corps j'esprouve vain aussi;
D'un front saturnien, d'un renfrongné sourci,
Je trouve tout amy en amitié volage.
Voyant donc mes mal-heurs croistre en infinité,
N'eprouvant rien qu'ennuy, peine et adversité,
Un celeste desir esleve ma pensée,
Disant, il ne faut plus en la poudre gesir;
Il faut chercher au Ciel le bien-heureux plaisir,
"N'espere pas salut en une nef cassée.

SONNET 8

Quelqu'un mieux fortuné dira de ma complainte,
Mes douloureux soupirs, et mon gemissement:
Cette-cy n'eut jamais que mal-contentement;
On ne voit que rigueur dessus sa charte peinte.
Est-ce une histoire vraie, ou une fable feinte,
Se veut-elle exercer sur un triste argument?
La perte du repos me faict plus de tourment

SONNET 6

Will Fortune ever be satiated
By the unrelenting suffering that I continually feel in my heart?
Alas! How can I bear it? O Lord Almighty,
Guide my soul into eternal life!
See my reason enslaved to my senses,
My feeble strength, and my pressing labor.
If my prayer, O God, were acceptable,
I wish, O Lord, I wish so much to die.
O blessed are those whose mortal life,
Guided by faith to Heaven above,
Is purified of its imperfection.
Happy is the one who full of reason and prudence,
Through an ardent faith says in his prayer:
May the Lord God's will be done!

SONNET 7

As I bitterly cry over the painful servitude
That keeps my body in pain, my spirit worried,
My heart filled with bitterness, and my face paralyzed,
Its dead composure masking life itself,
I search in vain for someone to relieve my spirit;
The Doctor of the body I search for in vain;
With their saturnine foreheads and their frowning eyebrows,
I find all my friends fickle in their friendship.
Thus, as my misfortunes grow infinite,
And I find nothing but annoyance, sorrow, and adversity,
A celestial desire elevates my thoughts,[73]
It says: you must no longer lie here in the dust;
Look to Heaven for happy pleasures,
"Do not hope for health in a broken vessel."

SONNET 8

Someone with better luck will say of my complaining,
My painful sighs, and my groaning:
This woman never had anything but disquiet;
One finds only unpleasantness written on her chart.
Is she telling the truth, or is this a made-up lie?
Are her sad words mere rhetorical exercise?
The loss of rest causes me torment

Cent et cent mille fois que je ne fay de plainte.
Par le repos perdu j'ay la raison blessée,
J'ay le discours rompu, la memoire offencée,
L'aprehension faict mon cerveau distiller.
Le feu de mon esprit perd sa douce lumiere,
Et ne me reste plus de ma forme premiere
Sinon que j'ayme mieux escrire que filer.

SONNET 9

Les Prestres de Memphis pillerent de l'Indie
De leur docte sçavoir le premier rudiment,
La Grece de l'Egypte eut son commencement,
Passant ses geniteurs d'une audace hardie.
Puis le peuple de Mars connut la maladie
Qui vient de l'ignorance, et embla doucement
Des trois et de l'Hebrieu le plus digne ornement,
Le François la faveur de ces quatre mendie.
Mais tout ainsi que l'or qui par le feu s'affine
Est plus clair et luisant qu'au sortir de sa mine,
Le François se verra mieux que nul autre apris.
D'autant que nostre prince a surmonté en armes
L'Espaignol, les Anglois, et les Romains gens-d'armes,
La Togue de la France aura le premier prix.

SONNET 11

O Prince, aymé de Dieu, quittez-vous nostre terre?
Laissez-vous ce grand Roy, vostre frere germain,
Ores que Dieu et luy, et vostre heureuse main
Avez tiré la paix du ventre de la guerre?
Avez-vous tant à coeur la barbare Angleterre,
Vous qui estes clement, courtois, doux, et humain,
Vous qui estes l'apuy du sainct siege Romain,
De l'Eglise de Dieu, de la foy de sainct Pierre?
Monsieur, l'Anglois s'est veu le meurdrier de ses Rois,
Contempteur du vray Dieu, ennemy de ses loix,
Et fleau capital du repos de la France.
Au moins, souvenez-vous que leur dernier seigneur
Par un semblable nœud, n'esprouvant que mal-heur,
Detestoit le païs, le peuple, et l'alliance.

A hundred and a hundred thousand times more than I complain of.
My reason is troubled by lack of sleep,
My words are faltering, my memory is injured,
Fear turns my brain into mush.
My keen mind grows dim,
And of my former self I am left with nothing except
That I prefer writing to spinning.

SONNET 9[74]
The Priests of Memphis pillaged from India
The basis of their erudite learning.
Greece took her beginnings from Egypt,
Surpassing her progenitors with an audacious boldness.
Then the people of Mars[75] endured the ill health
That comes from ignorance, and carefully stole
From the former three and from the Hebrews their most worthy ornament.
France is the begging inheritor of these four nations.
But just as gold that is refined by fire
Is clearer and more luminous than upon extraction from the mine,
So shall France become the most learned of them all.
Just as our prince has overcome by arms
The Spanish, the English, and Roman men of arms,
So shall the French Toga take the first prize.[76]

SONNET 11
O Prince, beloved of God, are you departing from our land?[77]
Are you leaving behind our great King, your kindred brother,
Now that God, and he, and your skillful hand
Have wrested peace from the very clutches of war?
Are you so fond of barbarous England,
You, so clement, courteous, gentle, and humane,
You, the sustainer of the Holy Roman See,
Of the Church of God, of the faith of Saint Peter?
Monsieur, England has murdered her kings,
She holds in contempt the one true God, is the enemy of His laws,
And the chief enemy of France's tranquility.
At least, remember that the last to become England's master[78]
In such a union found only unhappiness, and
Detested the country, the people, and its alliance.

SONNET 14

Les legitimes Rois sont envoyez des Cieux
Pour Lieutenans de Dieu, en supreme puissance:
Ils joignent la rigueur à la douce clemence,
Car la saincte Justice est mignonne des Dieux.
Sire, le tige sainct des antiques ayeux,
Qui vous ont mise au chef la couronne de France,
Ont tenu l'un et l'autre en egale balance,
Et jeune vous passez l'honneur des siecles vieux.
Vostre effigie entr' eux n'a point trouvé de place
Au Palais de Paris; la vertu et la grace
Vous ont plus qu'à eux tous d'heur et honneur promis.
C'est qu'apres voz ans vieux, Dieu prenant l'ame insigne,
Vostre corps dans le Ciel sera faict nouveau signe,
Et sur les saincts autels voz portraicts seront mis.

SONNET 15

Le debord des ruisseaux dont le mont Pyrenée
Feit jadis denommer la gentille Aquitaine,
Predit l'evenement des mutins de Guienne,
Et que Saturne et Mars regiroient sur l'année.
Sacrileges, larrons, nous ont la loy donnée
Sous le pretexte faux d'une opinion vaine;
Orleans, Tours, et Blois, sont causes de la peine
Dont ma pauvre Cité se pleint mal-fortunée.
Ce n'est le Bisantin, l'Espaignol, ou Romain,
Ce n'est pas l'Escossois, l'Anglois, ou le Germain
Qui nous ont mis au sac, cause de tant de plaintes.
C'est le mutin François qui a faict le deroy,
Ne craignant d'offencer un jeune et juste Roy,
Apres avoir polu toutes les choses sainctes

SONNET 16

Cambises, et Brenus, devinrent maniacles.
L'un blessant à Memphis le Dieu Egyptien,
L'autre pillant aux Grecs le temple Delphien
Où Apollon rendoit le vain de ses oracles.
Des vaisseaux profanez les sacre-saincts miracles
Osterent vie et regne au Babylonien.
Artrayctes, volant le sepulcre ancien,

SONNET 14[79]

Legitimate Kings are sent by the Heavens
To be God's Lieutenants, with supreme power:
They join together the rule of law and gentle clemency,
For holy Justice is dearest to the gods.
Sire, you are the holy heir of your ancient forebears,
Who crowned you as king of France,
And have granted equal weight to law and clemency;
Though young, your honor surpasses that of your ancestors.
Your effigy among theirs has found no place
In Paris's Palace of Justice; virtue and grace
Have promised you more than to them happiness and honor.
In the twilight years, God welcomes meritorious souls:
So you will become a new sign in Heaven,
And on holy altars your portraits will be placed.

SONNET 15[80]

The overflowing of the streams to which the Pyrenees
In times past gave the name of noble Aquitaine
Predicted the advent of the mutineers of Guyenne,[81]
And that Saturn and Mars would rule the year.[82]
Sacrilegious thieves have given us our laws
Under the false pretext of their vain opinions;
Orleans, Tours, and Blois share in the sorrow
Of which my poor City laments.
It is not Byzantium, Spain, or Rome,
It is not Scotland, England, or Germany
Who have sacked us and caused us so much suffering.
It is the French mutineers who have done the damage,
Not worrying about injuring a young and just King,
After having polluted everything that is holy.

SONNET 16

Cambyses[83] and Brennus[84] became maniacal.
The former wounded at Memphis the Egyptian God,
The latter pillaged the Delphian temple of the Greeks
Where Apollo issued his oracles in vain.
Because he profaned the sacrosanct, miraculous vessels,
The Babylonian's life and reign were taken away.[85]
Artraÿctes,[86] who plundered the ancient sepulcher,

En lieu profane ou sainct n'eut de seurs receptacles.
Si ce grand Dieu permit l'effect de sa vengeance
Pour ce qui n'a de soy vertu, force, ou puissance,
Saincte ceremonie, esperance, ny foy,
Ne vous punira-t-il, violeurs des saincts temples,
Qui avez des Payens pris les cruels exemples,
Offençant l'Eternel, le pays, et la Loy?

SONNET 20
Multiplier parolles sans science
N'est agreable à la Divinité,
Invectiver sur la tranquilité,
Subtiliser pour une indiference.
Une syncere et bonne conscience,
Un coeur benin rempli de charité,
Gardent la seure et sage verité
Par qui de Christ le beau regne s'advance.
Mais depriser toutes traditions,
Ne reigler point ses imperfections,
Trainer à soy la sotte multitude,
Sont les projets de ces prescheurs rusez,
Qui ont du nom de Vertu deguisez
L'ambition, l'erreur, l'ingratitude.

SONNET 22
Comme parfois la mere du grand Typhoée,
Ayant reçeu la celeste clarté,
Tient un broüillaz dans la nue arresté
Pour estre trop du soleil eschaufée,
Ainsi voit-on la raison estoufée
Par le sensible et par la Volupté,
Cachant le ray de la Divinité
Dont l'ame fut richement etoffée.
Plongez, perdus dans le gouffre d'Alcine,
Logistile est la vraye medecine
Pour nous tirer de l'obscure prison.
Comme Phoebus consomme la fumiere,
L'esprit remis en sa clarté premiere,
Le cheval blanc gouverne la raison.

No longer found a sure refuge in either holy or profane places.
If this great God exacted his vengeance
On that which in itself has neither virtue, strength, nor power,
Holy ceremony, hope, nor faith,
Will he not punish you, violators of holy temples,
Who have taken from Pagans their cruel examples,
Offending God, the country, and the Law?

SONNET 20

To babble on without knowledge
Is displeasing to God.
So is reviling peace, and plotting
How to make everyone indifferent to it.
A good and sincere conscience,
A benign heart filled with charity,
Ensure that certain and wise truth
Will let Christ's beautiful reign advance.
But to disdain all traditions,
In no way to moderate one's imperfections,
To drag after oneself the besotted multitude,
Are the plans of these wily preachers,
Who have, in the name of Virtue, disguised
Ambition, error, and ingratitude.

SONNET 22[87]

Just as the mother of the great Typhon,
Upon whom shines the celestial light,
Sometimes stops the mist, holding it in one place,
So as not to be burned by the sun,
In the same way do we see Reason suffocated
By the sensible and the sensual,
That veil the heavenly rays
With which the soul was once richly filled.[88]
Plunged, lost as we are in Alcina's chasm,
Logistilla is the true medicine
To free us from the dark prison.[89]
Just as Phoebus[90] makes vapor disappear,
So the spirit is restored to its former self,
The white horse rules over reason.[91]

SONNET 35

O Seigneur Dieu! esleve ma pensée,
Fay que j'embrasse en grand' devotion
Ta douloureuse et saincte passion,
Payement seur de la loy transgressée.
A toy, mon Dieu, ma priere est dressée:
Ayde, Seigneur, mon imperfection,
Delivre-moy de tant d'affliction,
Qui m'a du Ciel vers la terre abaissée.
Grave en mon coeur ta juste verité,
Guide mes pas au sentier d'equité,
Benin Seigneur en qui seul je me fie.
Je veux offrir à ton sacré autel,
O Dieu vivant, mon esprit immortel,
Qui mort en moy en toy se vivifie.

SONNET 36

Las! où est maintenant ta jeune bonne grace,
Et ton gentil esprit plus beau que la beauté?
Où est ton doux maintien, ta douce privauté?
Tu les avois du Ciel, ils y ont repris place.
O miserable, helas, toute l'humaine race
Qui n'a rien de certain que l'infelicité!
O triste que je suis, o grande aversité,
Je n'ay qu'un seul appuy en cette terre basse!
O ma chere compaigne et douceur de ma vie,
Puisque les Cieux ont eu sur mon bon-heur envie,
Et que tel a esté des Parques le decret:
Si apres nostre mort le vray amour demeure,
Abaisse un peu tes yeux de leur claire demeure
Pour voir quel est mon pleur, ma plainte et mon regret.

EPITAPHE DE FEU MAISTRE FRANÇOIS ÉBOISSARD, SEIGNEUR DE LA VILLÉE, SON MARY

Veux-tu sçavoir, passant, quel a esté mon estre?
Sçaches que la nature, et fortune, et les Cieux,
Noble, riche, et sçavant autrefois m'ont fait maistre,
Me rendant possesseur de leurs dons precieux.
Apres avoir vescu d'une loüable vie,   5
Je fus pris d'un catere, et maintenant le sort

SONNET 35[92]

O Lord God! Elevate my thoughts,
Make it so that I may embrace in great devotion
Your painful and holy passion,
Sure payment for the law that was transgressed.
To you, my God, my prayer is addressed:
Lord, help my imperfection,
Deliver me from this affliction,
Which has from Heaven lowered me to earth.
Engrave upon my heart your just truth,
Guide my steps on the path of equity,
Kind Lord in whom alone I trust.
I wish to offer on your holy altar,
O living God, my immortal spirit,
Which, dead in me, in you is given life.

SONNET 36[93]

Alas! Where is your graceful young self now,
And your noble spirit more beautiful than beauty itself?
Where your gentle demeanor, your sweet acquaintance?[94]
You were given them by Heaven, and they have returned there.
O how miserable, alas, is the entire human race
For it is sure of nothing but infelicity!
How sad I am! O great adversity!
I have but one refuge on this lowly earth!
O my dearest friend, the sweetness of my life,
Since the Heavens were envious of my happiness,
And such has been the decree of Fate,
If after our death true love remains,
Lower your eyes a bit from their luminous dwelling
To see how I cry for, moan, and miss you.

EPITAPH FOR MASTER FRANÇOIS ÉBOISSARD, LORD OF LA
VILLÉE, HER HUSBAND

Do you wish to know, passerby, what my life has been?[95]
Know that nature, and fortune, and the Heavens,
Noble, rich, and erudite, occasioned me to be master[96] in another era,
Making me the possessor of their precious gifts.
After living a praiseworthy life,   5
I was taken by a rheumatism, and now the fate

Des Parques me guerit de ceste maladie:
Je mourois en ma vie, et je vis en ma mort.
Je fus trente ans Breton; vingt et huict mon espouse
Me retint dans Poëtiers lié de chaste amour.   10
Mon ame devant Dieu maintenant se repose,
Et mon corps en ce lieu attend le dernier jour.
Mon corps n'est pas tout seul souz ceste froide tombe;
Le coeur de ma compaigne y gist avec le mien.
Jamais de son esprit nostre amitié ne tombe,   15
La mort ne trenche point un si ferme lien.
O Dieu, dont la vertu dedans le Ciel enclose
Enclost mesme le Ciel; vueillez que ma moitié
Toutes ses actions heureusement dispose,
Honorant pour jamais nostre saincte amitié.   20

AU ROY

Sire, durant l'effort de la guerre civille,
Je plaignois le malheur de nostre pauvre ville:
J'eslevois jusque au ciel ma parole et mes yeux,
Ayant le cueur espoint d'un ennuy soucieux.
Mais, helas! cependant que ma triste pensée,   5
De tant de maux publics griefvement offencée,
Alloit sur les autels, j'apperçeu deux maisons
Que j'avois au faubourg, n'estre plus que tisons.
Et si ce n'eust esté que la perte commune
M'estoit cent mille fois plus aspre et importune: 10
A peine eussé-je pu m'apaiser promptement,
Voyant mon peu de bien se perdre en un moment.
Ces maisons pouvoient bien valoir deux mille livres,
Plus que ne m'ont valu ma plume ny mes livres
Qui seront inutils s'ils n'ont ceste faveur,   15
Que vostre majesté estime leur labeur.
Depuis, j'ay entendu que vostre main Royalle,
A ceux qui ont perdu, se monstre liberalle,
Et que vostre bonté les veut recompenser.
Voilà l'occasion qui m'a fait avancer,   20
Sire, pour vous offrir ma treshumble requeste,
Priant le Seigneur Dieu vous couronner la teste
De l'heur de Salomon, comme de ces vertus;
De voir vos ennemis à vos pieds abbatus;

Of the Parcae[97] has cured me of this illness;
I died while in life and now live in death.
For thirty years I was a Breton; for twenty-eight my wife
Kept me in Poitiers bonded in chaste love.   10
My soul before God now rests,
And my body in this place awaits the last day.[98]
My body is not alone beneath this frigid grave:
The heart of my companion there rests with mine.
Our friendship will never forsake her spirit;   15
Death cannot break such a strong bond.
O God, whose virtue, cloistered in Heaven,
Cloisters Heaven itself, may it be your will that my better half
Do well in all her actions,
Forever honoring our holy friendship.   20

TO THE KING[99]
Sire, during the troubles of the civil war,
I lamented the misfortune of our poor city;
I raised to Heaven both my words and my eyes,
As my heart was moved by such distressing anxiety.
But, alas! While I, with sad thoughts,   5
Grievously offended by so many public evils,
Was going to church [to pray], I saw two houses
I owned on the outskirts of town reduced to rubble.
And if I had not felt the common loss
To be a thousand times more grave and pressing,   10
I scarcely would have been able to contain myself,
Seeing that what little I possessed was lost in a moment.
These houses may well have been worth two thousand pounds,
More than the worth of my pen and my books combined,
Which shall remain useless if not granted this favor   15
That Your Majesty will esteem the value of their labor.
Since then, I have heard that your Royal hand
Proves itself generous[100] to those who have suffered loss,
And that your kindness wishes to compensate them.
This is the occasion for my coming forward,   20
Sire, to offer you my ever-so-humble request,
Praying the Lord God to crown your head
With the good fortune and virtues of Solomon;[101]
May your enemies be vanquished at your feet;

D'acomplir un tres beau et tres long cours de vie   25
Sans avoir de mourir ny crainte, ny envie;
D'establir pour jamais ce regne ferme et seur,
Et d'y laisser de vous un digne successeur.

SONNET

Triste penser, qui me rends taciturne,
Que dans mon sein tu glissas promptement,
Quand un procez consu à clous d'aimant
Me feit changer Apolon pour Saturne.
Depuis ce jour, le ciel et la fortune,
L'air et la terre et tout autre Element
Ont conjuré l'incroyable tourment,
Dont toy, mon cueur, sens la peine commune.
Mon dieu! faut-il que ta belle jeunesse,
Et ta douceur, du malheur qui me presse,
Indignement sente le dur effect?
Ainsi Cadmus feit au serpent l'outrage,
Et une voix menace le lignage
Pour le peché que l'Ayeul avoit faict.

SONNET

Si quelquefois ta gentille jeunesse,
Par ses discours naifvement bien faits,
A soulagé le miserable faix
Qui abortif avança ma vieillesse;
Le rhume froid, qui maintenant te blesse
M'en fait payer l'usure à si grand fraicts,
Que je ne sçay (pauvre moy) que je fais,
Tant je ressens ta peine et ma tristesse!
Dea, mon doux soin, reprends un peu ta force,
Ayes pitié de ceste frelle escorce;
Je te suply par ta chaste beauté,
Par ta douceur, par l'amour maternelle,
Par le doux suc tiré de la mamelle,
Et par les flancs qui neuf mois t'ont porté.

May you live a very long and very pleasing life,   25
Neither wishing for death nor fearing it;
May you permanently establish your reign firm and sure,
And leave behind you a worthy successor.[102]

SONNET [TO CATHERINE DES ROCHES, ON A LAWSUIT][103]
Sad thought that makes me taciturn,
You slipped promptly into my breast
When a lawsuit sewn up tight with magnet nails
Made me switch from Apollo to Saturn.[104]
Since that day, heaven and fortune,
The air, earth, and every other Element
Have conjured up such incredible torment
That you, my dearest one, feel its communal pain.
My God! Must your fair youth,
And sweet disposition, of the misery that afflicts me
Unworthily suffer the same effects?
In like manner did Cadmus inflict outrage on the serpent,
And judgment threaten his lineage
On account of the sin their Ancestor committed.[105]

SONNET [TO CATHERINE DES ROCHES, ON THE
LATTER'S ILLNESS]
If at times your sweet youthful self,
By offering me naturally well-said counsel,
Has lightened the miserable burden
That, abortive, made my old age advance,
The wretched cold that assails you now
Is forcing me to pay up at such great cost [for your advice]
That (poor me) I don't know what I'm doing,
I feel so much your distress and my sadness!
Good God, my sweet care, recover your strength a little,
Take pity on my frail appearance;[106]
I beseech you by your chaste beauty,
By your gentleness, by [my] maternal love,
By the sweet milk drawn from [my] breast,
And [my] womb which bore you for nine months.

I I

SELECTED POEMS OF CATHERINE DES
ROCHES FROM *LES ŒUVRES* (1 5 7 9)

I write of your worth, distaff, my care,
As I hold in my hand my spindle and my pen.

—Catherine des Roches, *To My Distaff*

She answered me that she would never be alone since she always had her books and her
papers with her, which were her perpetual companions.

—Étienne Pasquier, *Letter to Pierre Pithou*

INTRODUCTION

Catherine des Roches's poetry is marked by a sustained meditation on and
defense of her status as a single learned woman who dared to publish.
Her bold dedicatory letter to her mother in *Les Œuvres* sets the tone for her
work. Against critics who she states would say to her that she "shouldn't have
written about anything at all, especially in these days when we see so many
writers in France,"[1] she declares her pride of membership among the few
women who did write. Furthermore, against those who would condemn her
for writing love poetry with the moralistic admonition that if she is truly in
love, she should not reveal the fact, and if she is not, she should not pretend
she is, she counters that it is not real-life experience that matters in poetic
creation but inspiration and imagination. Her concept of the imagination,
founded on Pléiade theory, holds that it is the "making" power of the intellect and the ability to create images.[2] In the twenty-six sonnets she writes for
Sincero and Charite, imagination surely takes over, for in the power relations
between the lovers rhetorical control is assigned to Charite, a stark reversal
of gender relations in real life. Des Roches distances herself from both moralistic and Petrarchan orthodoxy through the dominance she accords to
Charite, in whom converge the roles of beloved, pedagogue, scholar, and

80

writer. Rather than pining away for an inaccessible and passive object of desire, Sincero proclaims his gratitude to his lady whose writings "weave an excellent web" that will bring *him* fame.[3] As Ann Rosalind Jones aptly puts it, in Catherine's Neoplatonic system, "a quiet revolution is being carried out."[4] The woman poet fashions a textual lover whose sole purpose is to mirror her desires and legitimize her poetic endeavors.

In Des Roches's *For a Masquerade of Amazons* and *Song of the Amazons*, likely composed during Henri III's visit to Poitiers in 1577, warrior women aggressively invoke the same values of glory, fame, dominion, and power as do male rulers. The figure of the legendary Amazon, popular in court entertainments where Henri III and his male entourage often disguised themselves as female warriors, served the political purpose of honoring the "femme forte" (strong woman), especially the Queen Mother Catherine de Médicis, for her capacity to govern, by reconciling the traditional opposites of feminine virtue and male valor.[5] In *For a Masquerade of Amazons*, Catherine des Roches emphasizes the Amazons' pairing of female chastity and male prowess that "never surrenders to sensuality" (1. 25). She conflates these women warriors with women writers in that both are crowned with laurel leaves, symbols of poetic and military glory (ll. 5–6).[6] Des Roches further singles out Orithya from among the nine Amazon queens for her perpetual virginity and identification with her mother, Martesia, implicit references to her own situation as an unmarried daughter devoted to a life of perpetual company with her learned mother. Contemporaries' ambivalence about Catherine's extraordinary devotion to her mother, which led her to reject all suitors, is reflected in Étienne Pasquier's critical remarks concerning her foiling of the normal circulation of body and property: "she has been asked for her hand in marriage by a great number of highly placed men, yet has refused all proposals; she is resolved to live and to die with her mother," he states ruefully.[7] With Camille de Morel (1547–after 1611) and later Marie de Gournay (1565–1645), Catherine des Roches is the first major woman writer in France to refuse marriage.[8] Des Roches thus valorizes the mother-daughter bond as a political site of power and literary agency.

Spinning or weaving, the principal activity of *mulier economica*, and the spindle or distaff, a cultural icon of the domesticated woman, occasion point counterpoint and a final synthesis in Catherine des Roches's frequently anthologized *A ma Quenoille* (To My Distaff). The distaff signaled women's exclusion from public discourse and rule in early modern France[9] and was perceived as antithetical and inferior to the pen, a symbol of the learned man.[10] It is interesting that Catherine does not refer in her sonnet to needlework which, contrary to the distaff, appealed to high-ranking women as a form of virtuous femininity.[11] At the end of *Epistle to Her Mother*, Catherine declares that she ought to display the gifts that her mother has imparted to her which include writing and fine stitchery: "I have not abandoned my clews of string for the pen, nor have I stopped working with wool, silk, and gold thread when they have been needed, or when you have asked me to."[12] Fine needlework occasioned among the high gentry and noblewomen the public display of artistic virtuosity: Louise Labé's speaker describes her ability to "avec l'esguille peindre" (paint with the needle),[13] and Catherine de Médicis was often seen working on exquisite embroidery as she listened to the conversations around her.[14] Needlework for noblewomen was considered a corollary to learning: Ronsard urges Marguerite de France to "connect in equal measure / The needle to the book, / And to follow in double manner / Pallas's two professions;"[15] As with mythical Pallas Athena, goddess of learning and textile work, Des Roches argues in her distaff sonnet both sides, using the rhetorical device of the *argumentum utramque partem*, a discursive practice founded on a skeptical epistemology deeply "tentative, exploratory, and dialogic."[16] The final line of this sonnet, "Ayant dedans la main, le fuzeau, et la plume" (As I hold in my hand my spindle and my pen), evokes a tentative and highly awkward act of balancing *negotium* with *otium*, the tasks of the household with writing. Does Des Roches reconcile the spindle and the pen, according equal value to both poles of a woman writer's life? Or does she subtly undermine the former, arguing, as Cathy Yandell does, that "the distaff poem constitutes a subversion under the guise of reconciliation"?[17]

In either case, the distaff sonnet must be read in conjunction with its sequel, *À mes Escrits* (To My Writings), in which Des Roches questions the enduring value of her oeuvre: will it survive the "efforts de l'oubly, ny du temps" (effects of forgetfulness, or of time)? Should it not remain by her side rather than wander the world in printed form?[18] This is a rhetorical reflection connected with the humility topos as well as a philosophical question.[19] By calling her writings "mes petits enfans" (my little children), she regenders the Platonic trope of the book as child used by Pléiade poets to signify their proud sense of the ongoing sustenance of their production. The issue that subtends this sonnet is the matter of the "exchange value" of Catherine's poetic enterprise. As Danielle Clarke points out, women's published writings in the early modern period confronted a double risk: either they were relegated to the marginalized category of "women's poetry" or the name of the author was threatened with erasure.[20] While participating in the shared cultural discourse of her time, Catherine des Roches sensed that she and her mother were writing a new text founded on a poetics of a different order whose precariousness threatened to marginalize them.

To counter the perceived obstacles that would sever her from her writerly ambition, Catherine des Roches composes propitiatory texts where conventional ideals of womanly behavior are invoked and praised. This is the case with the narrative poem *The Strong Woman as Described by Solomon*, an adaptation of the Song of the Valiant Woman in Proverbs 31:10–31, which Catherine dedicates to her mother. She selects a canonical biblical text depicting the ideal wife to situate her mother, and by extension herself, within a reassuringly conservative bourgeois environment in which both are seen to perform their expected roles of mother/wife and dutiful daughter. Her message is that her lifestyle conforms to cultural expectations. However, this piece gives her the occasion to offer an interpretative feminist subtext that deviates from contemporaries' exegesis, particularly in her evaluation of the Valiant Woman's standing in the public domain. She highlights the latter's public visibility and renown, her eloquence and "divine mind," while standard sixteenth-century theological interpretation muted and negated such traits.

In *Agnodice*, Catherine des Roches defends women's learning against critics who, embodying allegorical Envy, are depicted as tyrannical husbands forbidding their wives to read.[21] The women begin to suffer a number of physical ailments, chief among these the pain of childbirth, and, forced into isolation, are left only with the solitary occupation of spinning: "Les femmes (o pitié!) n'osoient plus se mesler / De s'aider l'une l'autre, on les faisoit filler" (The women (what a pity!) did not dare / To help one another; they were made to spin) (ll. 78–79). Agnodice takes pity on them and goes off to the medical school, disguised as a man. Her efforts to help the women upon her return are thwarted by Envy, who incites the men to kill Agnodice. She reveals to them her true identity and, on account of her modesty and her wish to serve the common good, succeeds in obtaining their promise to grant their wives access to books and learning. Patriarchal norms are respected since learned wives will become even more conscientious in their marital duties. But the underlying political subtext is that all women should be allowed to study and form a community of learning such as the one that the women create with Agnodice upon her return to them.

☙

EPISTRE A SA MERE

MA MERE, je sçay que vous ensuivant, je pourroy suivre un exemple de vertu suivy de bien peu de personnes; mais pource que je ne puis vous imiter, ny me tirer si promptement de la multitude, à tout le moins en cecy je fuiray la commune façon de la plus grand part de ceux qui escrivent, lesquels ont accoustumé de prier les lecteurs d'avoir leurs oeuvres pour agreables, comme s'ils vouloient par leurs courtoisies mendier les faveurs. Or quant à moy je leur donnerois volontiers licence de penser et dire de mes escrits tout ce que bon leur semblera, mais je croy qu'ils n'ont point besoing de ma permission. S'il y en a qui les reprennent avecques juste occasion, j'essairay de me corriger, tirant profit de leur censure; si quelques-uns en jugent sans advis et discretion, je penserois estre sans discretion et advis de m'arrester à leur jugement. Ils diront peut-estre que je ne devois pas escrire d'amour, que si je suis amoureuse il ne faut pas le dire, que si je ne suis telle il ne faut pas le feindre; je leur respondray à cela, que je ne le suis, ny ne feins de l'estre; car j'escry ce que j'ay pensé, et non pas ce que jay veu en Syncero, lequel je ne connoy que par imagination. Mais comme il est advenu à quelques grands personnages de representer un Roy parfaict, un parfaict orateur, un parfaict courtisan, ainsi ai-je voulu former un parfaict amoureux; et si l'on dit que pour avoir pris exemple de tant d'excellens hommes, je les ay mal ensuyvis, je diray aussi que les Roys, estant personnes publiques, doivent par leurs vertus estre l'ornement de leurs peuples, que les orateurs et courtisans ayant à paroistre devant les grands ont besoing de se pourvoir de toutes perfections qui les facent remerquer des sages et du vulgaire; mais Syncero ne veut plaire qu'à sa dame seulement, que j'ay formée à son patron le plus qu'il m'a esté possible, imitant nostre grand Dieu, lequel apres qu'il eut creé le pere Adam, luy donna une femme semblable à luy.

Beaucoup diront volontiers que je ne devoy point escrire de quelque suject que ce soit, mesme en ce temps que nous voyons tant de Poëtes en la France. Je ne veux faire autre responce à ce propos là, sinon qu'il y a bien assez d'hommes qui escrivent, mais peu de filles se meslent d'un tel exercice, et j'ay tousjours desiré d'estre du nombre de peu; non pas que j'aye tant d'estime de moy que de me vouloir parangonner aux plus excellentes non plus qu'aux moindres: car je ne veux juger de moy ny par audace, ny par vilité de cueur. Au moins je ne me sentiray point coupable d'avoir perdu beaucoup de temps à composer un si petit ouvrage que cettuy-cy, pource que je n'y ay jamais employé d'heures, fors celles que les autres filles mettent à visiter les compaignies pour estre veües de leurs plus gentils serviteurs, desirant qu'ils puissent devenir dignes chantres de leurs beautez, encores qu'elles ayent bien la puissance de se chanter elles-mesmes. Toutesfois elles dedaignent de s'y prendre,

EPISTLE TO HER MOTHER

MOTHER, I know that in emulating you, I shall be able to follow an example of virtue matched by very few. But because I can neither imitate you nor elevate myself so easily above the common crowd, at the very least I'll not follow the normal way of the majority of those who write. That is, I'll not ask my readers to find my works agreeable, as if I could by such courtesies beg for their favors. Now, as far as I'm concerned, I'll freely give them permission to think and say whatever they like of my writings, but I don't believe they need my permission. If there are some who justly feel that there is room for improvement, I'll try to correct what I've written and take advantage of their critique. If others judge my work to be without sense or discretion, I'd be without discretion or sense in paying attention to them. Perhaps my readers will say that I should not have written about love, that if I am in love I must not say so, and if I am not, I should not pretend to be. To this I'll answer that I neither am in love nor pretend to be. For in Sincero I write what I have thought, not what I have actually seen, since I know him only through my imagination.[22] But just as it has happened that certain great writers have represented a perfect king, a perfect orator, or a perfect courtier,[23] so I have tried to fashion a perfect lover. And if some say that I have fallen short of the examples set by so many excellent men, I shall respond that kings, being public persons, must through their virtues be the ornament of their people, that orators and courtiers, having to appear before the great, need to outfit themselves with every kind of perfection, thus enabling them to be distinguished by both the wise and the common man. But Sincero wishes only to please his lady, whom I have fashioned to conform to him as much as was possible. In this way I have imitated our great God who, after He created father Adam, gave him a wife resembling him.[24]

Many will likely say that I shouldn't have written about anything at all, especially in these days when we see so many writers in France. All I wish to say to this is that whereas there are plenty of men who write, there are few women who get involved in such an exercise, and I've always desired to be counted among the few. It's not that I judge myself so highly that I'd want to compare myself to the most excellent of women, or to the least; I don't wish to judge myself with either presumption or baseness of heart. However, I will at least not feel guilty for having wasted a lot of time composing a work as little as this one, since the time I spent working on it is the time other girls spend with their most obliging suitors, desiring these men to become worthy acclaimers of their beauty, even though they're quite capable of lauding their own beauty themselves. Nevertheless they disdain all attempts to do so, thus exemplifying (it seems to me) the attitude of Zosimus,[25] who judged Roman

approuvant (ce croi-je) l'opinion de Zinzime qui ne pouvoit estimer les Gentils-hommes Romains pour estre bien instruits en la musique à saulter et voltiger, pource que les seigneurs de Turquie faisoient faire tels exercises à leurs esclaves. Ainsi quelques-unes des Damoiselles de ce temps, sans vouloir prendre la peine d'escrire, se contentent de faire composer leurs serfs, attisant mille flammes amoureuses dans leurs cueurs, par la vertu desquelles ils deviennent Poëtes mieux que s'ils avoient beu toute l'onde sacrée de la fontaine des Muses.

Mais quant à moy, qui n'ay jamais faict aveu d'aucun serviteur, et qui ne pense point meriter que les hommes se doivent asservir pour mon service, j'ay bien voulu suivre l'advis de la fille de Cleomenes qui reprenoit les Ambassadeurs Persans, dont ils se faisoient accoustrer par des Gentils-hommes, comme s'ils n'eussent point eu de mains. Aussi je m'estimerois indigne de ce peu de graces que Dieu m'a donné par vostre moyen (ma mere) si de moy-mesme je n'essaïois de les faire paroistre; ce n'est pas que j'espere me tracer avec la plume une vie plus durable que celle que je tien de Lachesis; aussi n'ay-je point quitté pour elle mes pelotons, ny laissé de mettre en oeuvre la laine, la soye, et l'or quand il en a esté besoing, ou que vous me l'avez commandé. J'ay seulement pensé de vous monstrer comme j'employe le temps de ma plus grande oisiveté, et vous supplie humblement (ma mere) de recevoir ces petits escrits qui vous en rendront tesmoignage; si vous en trouvez quelques-uns qui soient assez bien nez, avoüez-les s'il vous plaist pour voz nepveux, et ceux qui ne vous seront agreables, punissez-les à l'exemple de Jacob qui condemna la famille d'Isachar pour obeir à ses autres enfans.

SONETS DE SINCERO À CHARITE

1

Madame, voz beautez si parfaictement belles
Sont nées dans le Ciel. Mais pource que les Dieux
Vous alloient regardant d'un oeil trop curieux,
Brulant dans la clarté de vos flames jumelles,
Jupiter, prevoyant les diverses querelles
Qui pourroient advenir aux Citoyens des Cieux,
Vous feit venir icy, doux paradis des yeux
Qui peuvent contempler voz graces immortelles.
Et maintenant les Dieux, irritez contre nous,
Espris du feu d'amour, et d'un ardant courroux,
Mesme de Jupiter deffient le tonnerre,
Et nous vont menaçant de mill' et mille morts.
Mais il faut bravement soustenir leurs efforts
Pour garder le tresor du Ciel et de la terre.

gentlemen less than praiseworthy for their skills in music and dance because the lords of Turkey made their slaves do such things. In the same way some of the ladies of our time, without wishing to take the trouble to write, are content to make their serfs[26] compose in their stead. They kindle a thousand amorous flames in the hearts of their suitors, by virtue of which these men become even better poets than if they had drunk all the sacred water of the fountain of the Muses.

But as far as I'm concerned, since I have never admitted to having a suitor, nor think that I merit that men be made slaves in my service, I have willingly followed the advice of Cleomenes' daughter, who rebuked the Persian ambassadors for letting themselves be dressed by the gentlemen of their retinue as if they had no hands of their own.[27] Therefore I would judge myself unworthy of the few talents God has given me on account of you (my Mother) if I did not put them to good use. It is not that I hope to trace with the pen a more lengthy life than the one I hold from Lachesis;[28] thus I have not abandoned my clews of string for the pen, nor have I stopped working with wool, silk, and gold thread when they have been needed, or when you have asked me to.[29] I have only thought of showing you how I employ my idle time,[30] and humbly beseech you (my Mother) to receive this little collection of writings that bears witness to you; if you find some of them well enough conceived, please acknowledge them as your very own progeny,[31] and those that you do not find agreeable, punish them in the same way Jacob condemned the family of Issachar to serve his other children.[32]

SONNETS BY SINCERO TO CHARITE

1

My lady, your beauty, so perfectly lovely,
Was born in Heaven.[33] But because the gods
Were watching you with too curious a gaze,
As they burned in the light of your twin flames,
Jupiter, foreseeing the many quarrels
That might break out among Heaven's Citizens,
Had you sent here, a sweet paradise for eyes
That now can contemplate your immortal graces.[34]
But now the gods, irritated at us,
Seized by the fire of love and by a scorching wrath,
Defy even Jupiter's thunder,
And threaten us with a thousand deaths.
Yet we must bravely withstand their threats
To protect Heaven and earth's new treasure.

2

Las! Je suis mort en moy, mais c'est pour vivre en vous,
Charite, mon honheur, ma vie et ma lumiere,
Vostre rare beauté des beautez la premiere
Tient mon esprit ravy d'un ravissement doux.
De voz cheveux dorez les agreables nœuds,
Et de voz yeux divins la rigueur humble-fiere,
Serrent tant doucement mon ame prisonniere
Que moy-mesme je suis de moy-mesme jaloux.
Mon corps est envieux de l'honneur de mon ame
Qui brule dedans vous d'une tant saincte flame,
Que d'un homme mortel je deviens un grand Dieu.
O bien-heureuse mort, cause de double vie!
Heureux amour qui fais que mon ame ravie
Heureusement se meurt pour vivre en si beau lieu.

3

Honneur de mes pensers, honneur de mes propos,
Honneur des mes escrits, Charite, ma chere ame,
Charite mon soleil, ma singuliere Dame,
Royne de mon plaisir, douceur de mon repos.
Charite qui tenez mon cueur comme un depos,
Mon coeur environné d'une si douce flame,
Et qu'un amoureux traict si doucement entame,
Que plus il est blessé plus je me sens dispos.
Charite que je sers, que j'honore, et que j'ayme,
Charite que je tiens plus chere que moy-mesme,
Helas! je sens pour vous tant de pensers divers,
Helas! j'ay si grand pœur, chaste et belle Charite,
Que vous me connoissant de trop peu de merite
Desdaignez mes pensers, mes propos et mes vers.

4

Bouche dont la douceur m'enchante doucement
Par la douce faveur d'un honneste[37] soubs-rire;
Bouche qui souspirant un amoureux martyre,
Apaisez la douleur de mon cruel tourment.
Bouche de tous mes maux le seul allegement,
Bouche qui respirez un gratieux Zephire,
Qui les plus eloquens surpassez à bien dire
À l'heure qu'il vous plaist de parler doctement.

2

Alas! if I have died to myself, it is to live in you,[35]
Charite, my honor, my life, and my light,
Your rare beauty, among beauties the foremost,
Holds my spirit gently ravished.
The lovely knots in your golden hair,
And the humble-proud rigor of your divine eyes,
So softly bind my imprisoned soul
That I myself am jealous of myself.
My body is envious of the honor given my soul
Which burns within you with such a holy flame
That from a mortal man I have become a great god.
O blessed death, source of double life!
Happy love, that makes my ravished soul
Die content to live again in such a wondrous place.

3

Honor of my thoughts, honor of my words,
Honor of my writings, Charite, my dearest soul,
Charite my sun, my singular Lady,
Queen of my pleasure, sweetness of my repose.
Charite who hold my heart in trust,
My heart surrounded by such a gentle flame;
An amorous arrow so gently pierces me
That the more I am wounded, the better I feel.
Charite whom I serve, Charite whom I honor and love,
Charite whom I hold dearer than myself,
Alas! for you I feel such different sensations,
Alas! I am so fearful, chaste and lovely Charite,
That finding me so unworthy of you,
You'll scorn my thoughts, my words, and my verse.[36]

4

Mouth whose sweetness enchants me sweetly
Through the sweet favor of a virtuous smile;
Mouth that by the sighs of an amorous affliction
Appease the pain of my cruel torment.
Mouth, the only one to lessen my pain,
Mouth that breathe in a graceful Zephyr
And that surpass in word the most eloquent,
Whenever it pleases you to speak learnedly.

Bouche plaine de lys, de perles, et de roses,
Bouche qui retenez toutes graces encloses,
Bouche qui recelez tant de petits Amours,
Par voz perfections, ô bouche sans pareille,
Je me perds de douceur, de crainte et de merveille
Dans voz ris, voz souspirs, et voz sages discours.

5

Penser qui m'es plus doux que les fleurs à l'Abeille,
Et le soleil aux fleurs, penser en qui je voy
L'angelicque beauté qui me desrobe à moy,
Ravi par les soupirs d'une bouche vermeille.
Penser de mes esprits l'agreable merveille,
Penser des mes pensers le seigneur et le Roy,
Penser heureux, penser qui commande ma foy,
Serve de la douceur d'une voix nompareille.
Penser mon cher mignon, ma faveur, mon plaisir,
Penser que ma Charite a bien daigné choisir
Pour renger un portraict de sa beauté exquise.
En luy representant son exquise beauté,
Fay-luy paroistre aussi ma ferme loyauté,
Afin que me prenant elle demeure prise.

6

O que j'ayme voz yeux, doux tirans de ma vie,
Et que j'ayme voz mains qui m'ont pris et lié.
Que j'ayme vostre poil blond crespe et delié
Qui tient dedans ses laqs ma liberté ravie.
Vous tenez tellement ma raison asservie
Par un regard meslé de honte et de pitié,
Voz mains serrent si fort le nœud de l'amitié
Et vostre poil doré si doucement me lie,
Que plustost que sortir de ma captivité,
Que plustost que manquer à ma fidelité,
Que plustost que faillir à si digne maistresse,
Je veux mourir cent fois en ma douce prison,
Laissant ma liberté, ma vie et ma raison
Dans voz yeux, dans vos mains et vostre blonde tresse.

7

Printemps aporte fleurs, dont la riche peinture
Imite la couleur de la robe d'Iris,

Mouth, home to lilies, pearls, and roses,
Mouth that hold within you all the graces,
Mouth that conceal so many budding Loves,
Through your perfections, O peerless mouth,
I am lost in delight, fear, and marvel,
Amid your laughter, your sighs, and your wise discourses.

5

Thought, sweeter to me than flowers to the Bee
And sun to the flowers, thought, in whom I see
The angelic beauty that robs me from me,
Ravished by the sighs of a vermilion mouth.
Thought, that lovely marvel within my spirit,
Thought, the lord and King of my thoughts,
Happy thought, thought that commands my trust,
That serves a sweet voice beyond compare.
Thought, my dearest, my favor, my pleasure,
Thought that my Charite has deemed worthy of choosing
To draw a portrait of her exquisite beauty;
In portraying her marvelous beauty,
Let her know of my steadfast loyalty,
So that in taking me, taken she will be.

6

O how I love your eyes, gentle drawstrings of my life,
And how I love your hands, which have captured and bound me.
How I love your curly and fine blond hair,
That holds my ravished freedom in its locks.
You hold my reason so enslaved
To your gaze of shame and pity mixed,
Your hands squeeze so tightly the knot of friendship
And your golden hair binds me so gently,
That rather than escape from my captivity,
That rather than be found faithless to my trust,
That rather than fail such a worthy mistress,
I want to die a hundred times in my sweet prison,
And leave behind my freedom, my life, and my reason
In your eyes, in your hands, and in your blond tresses.

7

Spring brings flowers whose rich portrait
Imitates the color of Iris's dress,[38]

Printemps suivy du jeu, de la dance, et du ris
Qui follatre tousjours dans ta gaye verdure;
Printemps, fils du soleil, cher mignon de nature,
Delice des humains, qui doucement nourris
Tant et tant d'animaux qui fussent tous peris
Sans tes herbes et fleurs qu'ils ont pour nourriture;
Printemps, honneur des prez, des champs, et des jardins,
Quand tu baises les doigts delicats et rosins
De ma belle Charite en pillant les fleurettes,
Oeilladant la splendeur de ses divins regards,
Tu deviens un esté pauvre, tu brule et ards,
Admirant le parfaict de ses beautez parfaictes.

8

Vrayement, je reprendrois vostre oeil de trahison.
Mais ce n'est pas bien faict que d'accuser son maistre,
C'est faict encore pis de receler un traistre
Et le tenir enclos en si douce prison.
Charite, voz beaux yeux, seigneurs de ma raison,
Cachent Amour dans eux; le tyran y veut estre
Afin d'estre plus seur, plus fort, et plus adextre,
Recevant la faveur de si belle maison.
Apres qu'il m'a tiré maintes et maintes sagettes,
Apres qu'il m'a lancé maintes flames secrettes,
Je meurs et repren vie au brasier allumé:
Ainsi l'unique oiseau qui brule dans sa flame
Reprend corps de son corps, et ame de son ame,
Renaissant par le feu qui l'avoit consommé.

9

Ma nef au gré des vens dedans l'onde poussée
Erroit de toutes parts quand vostre heureuse main,
Piteuse de mon mal, me retira soudain,
En me sauvant des flotz de la mer courroucée.
Follement aveuglé d'une erreur insensée,
Monstrant que la raison m'estoit donnée en vain,
Je me laissois guider d'un erreur incertain
Lorsque vostre bel œil arresta ma pensée.
Maintenant je mourrois en mon cruel tourment.
Mais de voz doux propos le doux enchantement
De cet aspre douleur promptement me delie.

Spring, harbinger of games, dances, and laughter
That always frolics in your merry foliage;
Spring, son of the sun, nature's dear minion,
Delight of humans, which gently nourish
So many animals that would all have perished
Without the grass and flowers you give them as food;
Spring, honor of meadows, of fields, and of gardens,
When you kiss the delicate and rosy fingers
Of my beautiful Charite as she picks blossoms,
When you glance at the splendor of her divine gaze,
You become a poor summer, you set on fire and burn
As you admire the excellence of her perfect beauty.

8

Truly, I could indict your gaze for treason.
But if it's unbecoming to accuse one's master,
It's even worse to hide a traitor
And hold him in so sweet a prison.
Charite, your beautiful eyes, masters of my reason,
Hide Love in them; that tyrant wants to settle there
To gain more security, strength, and skill,
As he receives the favor of such a lovely dwelling.
After aiming numberless arrows at me,
After burning me with his secret flames,
I die and am reborn in the burning embers:
Thus the fabulous bird that burns in its flames
Regains body from its body, and soul from its soul,
As it is reborn through the fire that had consumed it.[39]

9

My ship, tossed at random among the waves,
Veered in every wrong direction until your blessed hand,
Taking pity on my suffering, suddenly rescued me,
And saved me from the waves of the angry sea.[40]
Insanely blind, in meaningless error,
Proving that reason had been given me in vain,
I was letting myself go into unknown wandering
Till your lovely eye centered my thought.[41]
Now I was dying in my cruel torment.
But the sweet enchantment of your words
Promptly free me from this grievous pain.

Ainsi le sainct honneur de voz perfections,
Conduisant sagement toutes mes actions,
Commande sur mes sens, mes pensers, et ma vie.

10

Belle, plustost les eaux enflameront la terre
Et le feu glacera les fruicts, herbes et fleurs,
Les aveugles plustost jugeront des couleurs,
Et plustost sans verdeur on verra le l'hyerre
La paix sera plustost bonne que la guerre,
Venus ira sans grace, et l'Amour sans douceurs,
Les Princes seront serfs, et les serfs Empereurs
Qui frapperont les Dieux avec le tonnerre.
Plustost seront les Cieux à la terre pareils,
Plustost aparoistront mill' et mille soleils
Dans le centre profond de cette lourde masse,
Plustost seront tousjours les hommes sans couroux,
Tous les pensers plustost se liront en la face,
Que je puisse jamais aymer autre que vous.

11

Ce qui me rend pour vous le cueur tant allumé,
Charite, mon doux feu, c'est qu'une mesme flame
Embrase vostre cueur, vostre esprit, et vostre ame,
Et que je suis de vous uniquement aymé.
Je me sens tres-heureux de me voir estimé
Par voz doctes escris, et connoy bien, Madame,
Que vous pouvez ordir une excellente trame
Qui rendra par voz vers mon renom animé.
Alceste racheta de son mary la vie,
Voulant mourir pour luy, mais vous avez envie
De racheter la miene avec plus heureux sort.
Pource que sans mourir, chaste, sçavante, et belle,
Vous filez pour nous deux une vie immortelle,
Qui vaincra les efforts du temps et de la mort.

12

Je confesse vrayement que l'Amour sçait bien peindre,
Et non pas Sincero, car je vous sens trop mieux
Gravée dans mon cueur qu'en mill' et mille lieux,
Où j'ay tant essayé de pouvoir vous depeindre.

And so the holy honor of your perfections,
Wisely controlling all of my actions,
Rules over my senses, my thoughts, and my life.

10

My beauty, sooner will the seas burn up the earth[42]
And fire freeze fruits, grass, and flowers,
The blind judge different colors,
And the ivy lose its foliage;
Peace will sooner be considered less desirable than war,
Venus lose her courtliness, and Love his sweetness,
Princes become servants, and servants Emperors
Who will strike the Gods with thunder;
The Heavens will sooner be no different from the earth,
Thousands upon thousands of suns will shine
From the bottomless center of this heavy mass;
Men lose their anger,
And all thoughts become transparently clear,
Than I will ever love a lady other than you.

11

What makes my heart so ardent for you,
Charite, my sweet fire, is that one and the same flame
Burns in your heart, your mind, and your soul,
And that I am your one and only love.
I feel my good fortune when I see myself esteemed
In your learned writings, and I am well aware, Madame,
That you can weave an excellent web
Which, through your verse, will give life to my renown.[43]
Alcestis won back her husband's life
By offering to die in his place, but you desire
To redeem my life through a better fate.[44]
For without dying, chaste, learned, and beautiful,
You spin out for us both life immortal,
Which will vanquish the ravages of time and death.

12.

I confess that Love alone can paint a true portrait
And not Sincero, for you are more deeply
Engraved upon my heart than in a thousand other places
Where I have tried in vain to depict you.

Helas! je ne sçay rien que me douloir et plaindre,
Charite, mon soucy, les flambeaux de voz yeux
Ont versé dans les miens tant d'esclairs radieux
Que je brule tousjours sans me pouvoir esteindre.
Il y a fort long que ces flambeaux ardans
M'eussent tout consommé tant dehors que dedans:
Mais une froide pœur qui veut que je languisse
Me rend glacé, craignant que voz perfections,
Desdaigneuses de voir tant de seditions,
S'envolent dans les Cieux avecques la justice.

FIN DES VERS DE SINCERO À CHARITE. S'ENSUIVENT CEUX DE
CHARITE À SINCERO

1

Je veux que Sincero soit gentil et accord,
Né d'honnestes parens, je veux que la noblesse
Qui vient de la vertu orne sa gentillesse,
Et qu'il soit temperant, juste, prudent, et fort.
Je veux que Sincero m'ayme jusqu'à la mort,
Me retenant du tout pour unique maistresse.
Je veux que la beauté avecques la richesse
Pour le favoriser se trouvent d'un accord.
Je veux en Sincero une douce eloquence,
Un regard doux et fin, une grave prudence,
Un esprit admirable, et un divin sçavoir,
Un pas qui soit gaillard, mais toutesfois modeste,
Un parler gracieux, un agreable geste,
Voilà, qu'en le voyant, je desire de voir.

2

Sincero, mon desir, et mon coeur, et ma vie,
Excusez-moy de grace, et ne vous offencez
Si poursuivant le cours de mes vers commencez,
J'accompaigne l'amour avec la jalousie.
Sincero, mon desir, je n'eu jamais envie
D'aymer autre que vous: mais aussi ne pensez
D'aymer autre que moy, et ne vous avancez
De chercher autre nœud que celuy qui nous lie.
Ne vous arrestez point aux propos envieux
Qui veulent reformer la grace de voz yeux,

Alas! I know only how to suffer and complain,
Charite, my care, the torches of your eyes
Shone so many bright beams into mine
That still burning, I cannot extinguish the fire.
These fiery flames a long time ago
Would have consumed me both within and without:
But a cold fear that wants me to languish
Turns me to ice. I worry that your perfections,
Contemptuous of so much strife,
May fly off to Heaven, taking justice along with them.[45]

END OF THE VERSES FROM SINCERO TO CHARITE. THOSE OF CHARITE TO SINCERO FOLLOW

1

I want Sincero to be courteous and affable,
Born of honorable parents, I want the nobility
That comes from virtue to adorn his gentility,
And I want him temperate, just, prudent, and strong.
I want Sincero to love me until death,
Keeping me always as his one and only mistress.
I want beauty, and also wealth,
To favor him in equal measure.[46]
I want in Sincero an agreeable eloquence,
A gentle and witty gaze, a dignified prudence,
An admirable mind, and divine learning,
A step that is lively, but nonetheless even,
A gracious speech, pleasant gestures,
That is what, seeing him, I want to see.

2

Sincero, my love, my heart, and my life,
Forgive me, I pray, do not be angry
If as I write these verses that I have begun,
I add jealousy to my love for you.
Sincero, my desire, I never wanted
To love anyone other than you: but don't you dare think of
Loving anyone but me, and don't go
Seeking another bond than the one that unites us.
Pay no attention to those envious folk
Who want to alter the graciousness of your eyes,

Leur finesse et douceur ne sont dignes de blasme.
Leur finesse demonstre une sincerité,
Leur douceur represente une sincerité,
Car les yeux, Sincero, sont fenestres de l'ame.

3

Dittes-moy, Sincero, que c'est qu'il vous en semble,
Dittes si c'est mon oeil qui vous a retenu,
Ou mon cueur, ou ma bouche, ou s'il m'est advenu
Pource que j'ay uni leurs trois forces ensemble.
Mon œil dit que mon cueur estoit tout en un tremble,
Ma bouche sans discours, et qu'il a soustenu,
Luy seul, tous les effors de ce Dieu inconnu
Qui d'une saincte amour sainctement nous assemble.
Mon cueur jure qu'il s'est pour le vostre changé,
Et que luy seul vous tient à nostre amour rangé,
Ma bouche maintenant veut affermer pour elle
Que si ce n'eust esté son gracieux acceuil,
Ny la force du cueur, ny la force de l'oeil,
N'eussent peu arrester cette flame nouvelle.

4

Puisque le ferme nœud d'une amitié tant saincte
Vous doit unir à moy, faictes vostre devoir
D'egaller voz vertus à vostre grand sçavoir,
Et que ce ne soit point une aparence feinte.
Si vous estes meschant, las! je seray contrainte
De vous abandonner: car je craindroy d'avoir
Un amy vitieux, et je ne veux point voir
Mon honneste amitié compaigne de la crainte.
La vertu seulement rend l'homme bien-heureux,
Soyez donc s'il vous plaist de vertu desireux,
Suivant de l'ypsilon la moins commune adresse.
Faictes que la raison commande à vos desirs,
En esperant de moy les honnestes plaisirs
Que l'on doit esperer d'une chaste maistresse.

5

Amy, je ne sçaurois rompre ce doux lien,
Ce doux lien d'amour dont vous me tenez prise.
Aussi ne veux-je point faire telle entreprise,

Their fineness and gentleness are not worthy of reproach.
Their fineness is proof of your sincerity,
Their gentleness evokes that same sincerity,
For eyes, Sincero, are the windows of the soul.[47]

3

Tell me, Sincero, just what you think,
Tell me if my eyes attracted you,
Or my heart, or my mouth, or if it happened that
You were drawn to all three at once.
My eyes tell me that my heart was all atremble,
My mouth speechless, and that it was my heart that,
Alone, bore the attacks of that unknown god
Who with a sacred love united us in a sacred bond.[48]
My heart swears it changed for yours,
And that, alone, it keeps you in love with me,
My mouth now wants to confirm
That if it hadn't been for its gracious welcome,
Neither the strength of my heart, nor the power of my eyes,
Could have put a stop to this new flame.

4

Since the firm knot of our sacred friendship[49]
Must bind you to me, do your duty then
By ensuring that your virtues equal your vast learning,
And that you do not pretend it so.
If you are unworthy, alas, I'll be compelled
To abandon you: I'm afraid that I'd have
A villain as friend, and I don't want to see
Fear a companion to my honorable friendship.
Virtue alone makes a man blessed,
Please then, seek virtue,
And follow the least trodden path of the epsilon.[50]
Make reason command all your desires,
And expect from me only those honorable pleasures
That one ought to expect from a chaste mistress.

5

Friend, I could never break this sweet bond,
This sweet bond of love in which you hold me fast.
And I do not even want to undertake such an enterprise,

Puisque tous mes efforts n'y serviroient de rien.
Je vous ayme, et honore, et voy assez combien
La troupe des neuf soeurs sur tout vous favorise,
Mais si dessus voz mœurs on faict quelque reprise,
Le blasme n'en sera non plus vostre que mien.
Pour vous retirer donc de l'ecole du vice,
Je voudroy ressembler une sage Melice,
Et vous pouvoir conduire en plus heureux sentier.
Pour les fautes d'un serf on s'en prend à son maistre,
Et si vous estes mien, ou desirez de l'estre,
Soyez donc, Sincero, en moeurs pur et entier.

6

Si je veux m'acquiter, on ne me doit reprendre
De ce dont est repris le prodigue donneur,
Qui depend follement et richesse et honneur
Sans esperer le bien qu'il en pourroit attendre.
Recevant un amour, un amour je veux rendre
A vous, mon Sincero, et confesse mon heur
D'avoir sçeu rencontrer un si rare sonneur
Pour nostre affection dignement faire entendre.
Or je doy vous aymer pour trois occasions,
Pource que vous m'aymez, pour voz perfections,
Pource que je vous suis liée de promesse:
Et vous payant ainsi, je ne vous donne rien,
Que pourrois-je donner? Vous estes tout mon bien,
Vous estes mon honneur, mon plaisir, ma richesse.

7

Mais d'où vient, Sincero, qu'estant si loing d'ici,
Vous ne m'escrivez point? La douce souvenance
De nostre chaste amour, est-elle en oubliance?
N'avez-vous plus de moy pensement ny souci?
Vrayement, si j'apperçoy que vous soyez ainsi,
Volage et indiscret, vous n'aurez la puissance
De me vaincre en oubly, car par vostre inconstance
Je veux estre inconstante, et le seray aussi.
Doncques si vous m'aymez, pensez que je vous ayme
Autant comme mon coeur, autant comme moy-mesme:
Mais si vous ne m'aymez, je ne vous ayme point,
Si vous me haïssez, je hay plus que la rage,

For all my efforts would be utterly useless.
I love and honor you, and I recognize too how much
The troupe of the nine sisters[51] favors you above all others;
But if someone were to raise some objection to your morals,
The blame will not fall on you more than me.
So to retrieve you from the school of vice,
I'd like to resemble wise Melissa,[52]
And be able to guide you to a happier path.
For the faults of a servant, one blames his master,
If then you are really mine, or desire to be so,
Sincero, be pure and wholeheartedly good.

6

In acquitting myself of a debt, I shouldn't be reproached
For what the prodigal spender is blamed for,
When foolishly he wastes his wealth and his honor
Without thinking of the good he might reap instead.
In receiving a love, a love I want to return
To you, my Sincero, and I confess my happiness
In meeting such a rare songster[53]
Who can so worthily make our affection known.
Now I must love you for three reasons,
Because you love me, for your perfections,
And because I'm bound to you by a promise:
By thus repaying you, I really give you nothing,
For what could I give? You are all that is precious to me,
You are my honor, my pleasure, and my wealth.

7

But how is it, Sincero, that being so far away,
You don't write to me? Is the sweet remembrance
Of our chaste love now forgotten?
Do you no longer think or care for me?
In truth, if I discover that you've become
Fickle and indiscreet, you won't be able
To outdo me in forgetting, for if you're faithless
I want to be faithless, and faithless will I be.
So if you love me, know that I love you
As much as my own heart, as much as myself:
But if you don't love me, I don't love you at all,
If you hate me, I hate you more than fury,

Je hay plus que l'enfer vostre mauvais courage,
Ainsi l'amour me bleçe, et la hayne me point.

8

Vous voyant exposer aux dangers de la guerre,
Helas! j'ay si grand pœur que vostre amoureux nœud
Soit trenché par le fer, que vostre amoureux feu
Soit esteint par le feu de ce double tonnerre!
J'importune les Dieux du Ciel et de la terre,
De l'air et des enfers, je fay maint piteux vœu,
Esperant vous ayder et delier un peu
Les liens de la pœur qui tient mon cœur en serre.
Et s'il m'advient bientost par la faveur des Dieux
De vous revoir icy, doux plaisir de mes yeux,
À l'heure vous pourrez me donner delivrance,
À l'heure vous pourrez m'affranchir de la pœur
Qui va tyrannisant vostre cœur, et mon cœur,
Puisque le vostre en moy fait tousjours demeurance.

9

Si je connois en vous quelque imperfection,
Si je connois en vous quelque penser volage,
Si je connois en vous un superbe courage
Qui mesprise le cours de vostre passion;
Si je connois en vous une presomption,
Grande peste des cueurs que l'on met en servage,
Si je vous voy changer de mœurs et de langage,
Vous me voirrez bientost manquer d'affection.
Si vous m'estes constant, je vous seray constante,
Si vous voulez changer, hé bien j'en suis contente,
Cherchez une autre amie et moy un autre amy.
Cherchez une maistresse honneste, aymable, et belle,
Et moy un serviteur sage, accort, et fidelle:
Car je ne veux jamais que l'on m'ayme à demy.

10

Sincero, mon doux feu, si j'ay peu attirer
De voz perfections une amitié non feinte,
Et si j'ay doucement escouté vostre pleinte,
Craignant que vostre mal peut croistre ou empirer,
Dittes-moy, s'il vous plaist, qui vous peut retirer

I hate more than hell your feeble cowardice,
In such a way love wounds me and hate pierces my heart.

8

In seeing you exposed to the dangers of war,
Alas! I'm so afraid that our amorous bond
Will be cut by the sword, that your amorous flame
Will be put out by the fire of the cannon!
I plead with the Gods of both Heaven and earth,
Of the air and of hell itself, I make all kinds of pitiful vows,
Hoping to help you and undo a little
The bonds of fear that tear at my heart.
And if it soon happens that by the favor of the Gods
I see you again, sweet pleasure of my eyes,
Then promptly will you deliver me,
Promptly will you free me from the fear
That tyrannizes your heart and mine,
Since your heart in mine always dwells.[54]

9

If I find in you some imperfection,
If I find in you some fickle thought,
If I find in you cowardly arrogance
That scorns the course of your passion;
If I find in you any conceit,
That plague of hearts subservient to love,
If I see you've changed your behavior and your speech,
You'll soon see me losing all affection for you.
If you're faithful to me, I'll be faithful to you,
If you want a change, well then I'm quite content,
Find another love, I'll find another, too.
Seek out a chaste, amiable, and lovely mistress,
And I'll look for a wise, witty, and faithful suitor:
For I refuse to be loved halfway.

10

Sincero, my sweet love, if I've won
From your perfections an unfeigned friendship,
And if I gently listened to your lament,
For fear that your pain might increase or worsen,
Tell me, please, who can withdraw you

De mon affection inviolable et saincte?
Avez-vous point senti quelque nouvelle atteinte
Qui pour un autre amour vous face souspirer?
Et que peut-ce estre donc qui de moy vous esloigne?
Mais ne seroit-ce point que le Roy de Pouloigne
Vous eut faict oublier vostre amoureuse foy?
Ha! mon Dieu, que je crain que cet excellent Prince,
Pour honorer de vous sa nouvelle province,
Vous derobe à la France, à l'amour, et à moy.

11

S'il est vray, Sincero, que la perseverance
Demeure dedans vous, si vous avez tousjours
Dans la bouche mon nom, dans l'esprit mes amours,
Dans les yeux mon pourtraict, au cueur mon aliance,
Faictes-le-moy connoistre avec plus d'asseurance,
Sans me laisser conter les heures et les jours,
Et composer en moy mille fascheux discours,
Pensant et repensant à vostre longue absence.
Le terme es jà passé que vous avez promis
De retourner icy visiter voz amis.
Qui vous peut empescher de faire ce voyage
Sinon faute d'amour? Doncques s'il est ainsi,
Je quitte vostre bouche, et vostre esprit aussi,
Voz yeux, et vostre cueur inconstant et volage.

12

Jamais, mon Sincero, je ne prendray plaisir
De vous assujectir à des loix rigoureuses.
Ha! vrayement je hay trop ces ames langoureuses
Qui sans cause d'espoir renforcent leur desir.
Je vous sçauray bon gré, s'il vous plaist, de choisir
Le temps le plus commode aux œuvres serieuses.
Mais ne me racontez voz plaintes amoureuses
Sinon quand vous serez aux heures de loisir.
La plus grand part du temps demeurez à l'estude,
Puis quand vous serez las de vostre solitude,
De raisonner en vous, et de penser en moy,
Allez voir le Palais, et la paume, et l'escrime,
Et les Dames d'honneur, de vertu, et d'estime,
Gardant tousjours l'amour, l'esperance, et la foy.

From my inviolable and sacred affection?
Have you not felt some new attraction
That would make you sigh for some other love?
And what is it then that is separating you from me?
But is it not the King of Poland[55]
Who has made you forget your amorous promise?
Ah! my God, how I worry that this excellent prince,
To honor his new province with you,
Steals you from France, from love, and from me.

11

If it's true, Sincero, that perseverance
Remains your hallmark, that you always carry
My name on your lips, my love in your mind,
My portrait before your eyes, my alliance in your heart,
Let me be more certain of it,
Without making me count the hours and days
As I compose a thousand angry lines,
Thinking and brooding over your long absence.
The time has already passed that you promised
To return here to visit your friends.
What then could prevent you from making this voyage
Besides lack of love? If that's the case,
I refuse your lips, and your mind as well,
Your eyes, and your inconstant and fickle heart.

12

Never, Sincero, would I take pleasure
In subjecting you to rigorous laws.
Ah! truly, I simply hate those languishing souls
That without any cause for hope reinforce their desires.[56]
I'd be obliged to you, please, for choosing
The most appropriate time for serious study.
But don't tell me your amorous complaints
Except in moments of leisure.
Devote the greater part of your time to your studies,
Then, when you're tired of being alone,
Of reasoning to yourself, and thinking of me,
Go visit the Palace, and watch the handball and swordplay,[57]
And the Ladies, esteemed for their honor and virtue,
And above all remain true to love, hope, and faith.[58]

13

Ouvrez-moy, Sincero, de voz pensers la porte.
Je desire de voir si l'Amour de son traict
Vous engrave aussi bien dans le cueur mon pourtraict,
Comme vostre beau vers à mes yeux le raporte.
Je ne veux pas pourtant que hors de vous il sorte,
Ny que par la faveur d'un gracieux attrait
Vostre cueur soit jamais d'avec le mien distrait
Pour bruler d'une flamme, ou plus douce, ou plus forte.
Ouvrez donc s'il vous plaist: ha! mon Dieu! je me voy!
Ha! mon Dieu! que de bien, que d'honneur je reçoy!
Apres que vous m'avez par mille vers chantée,
Je me voy dans voz yeux, et dedans voz escrits,
Et dedans vostre cueur, et dedans voz esprits,
Par la Muse, et l'amour, si bien representée.

RESPONCE AU DERNIER SONNET DE CHARITE

Regardez-vous en moy, Charite, ma Deesse,
Regardez vostre front, heureux siege d'amour,
Regardez voz beaux yeux, ma lumiere, et mon jour,
Qui commandent mon cueur d'une œillade maistresse.
Regardez l'or frisé de vostre blonde tresse,
Regardez voz sourcils courbez d'un demi-tour,
Regardez mille traicts recelez à l'entour
Pour servir le tyrant de ma jeune allegresse.
Mais surtout regardez vostre gracieux ris,
Qui par sa grand' douceur ouvre le Paradis
Où veullent demeurer les bien-heureuses ames.
Ha! n'y regardez plus, Madame, car j'aye pœur
Que vous reconnoissant si parfaicte en mon cueur,
Vous-mesme ne brulez dans voz propres flammes!

POUR UNE MASCARADE D'AMAZONES

Apres avoir acquis tant d'honneur, et de gloire,
Apres avoir gaigné une double victoire,
Apres avoir lié ces superbes guerriers,
Apres avoir monstré tant de braves vaillances,
Par les traits de noz yeux, et l'effort de noz lances,   5
Nous rapportons en main les Myrthes et Lauriers.

13

Open to me, Sincero, the door of your thoughts.
I want to see if Love's arrow
Has etched my portrait on your heart
The same way that your lovely verse reveals it to my eyes.
And I don't want my likeness ever to leave you,
Nor, attracted by the gracious favors of another,
Your heart ever to be distracted from me,
To burn with either a gentler or a stronger flame.
So open up, please: ah! my God! I see myself!
Ah! my God! what delight and what honor are given me!
After you've sung me in a thousand verses,
I see myself now in your eyes, and in your writings,
And in your heart, and in your soul,
By the Muse, and by love, so well portrayed.[59]

RESPONSE TO CHARITE'S LAST SONNET

Look at yourself in me, Charite, my goddess,
Look at your forehead, love's blessed seat,
Look at your lovely eyes, my light and my sun,
Which rule my heart with their commanding gaze.
Look at the braided gold of your blond tresses,
Look at your brows, arched in half circles,
Look at the thousand arrows hidden all around
To serve [Love] the tyrant of my youthful elation.
But above all, look at your graceful laugh,
Which, in its melting sweetness, opens up Paradise
Where blessed souls long to dwell.
Ah! look no longer, Madame, for I fear
That seeing yourself so perfectly engraved upon my heart,
You yourself may burn up in your own flames![60]

FOR A MASQUERADE OF AMAZONS

After acquiring so much honor and glory,[61]
After winning a double victory,
After binding these arrogant warriors,
After showing so much brave valiance,
By the arrows of our eyes and the strength of our lances,   5
We bring back in our hands Myrtle and Laurel.[62]

L'Amour audacieux, desirant que ses flames
Alentissent du tout la vertu de noz ames,
Elançoit dens noz cœurs mille flambeaux ardans:
Mais nostre chasteté qui gardoit cette place   10
Changeoit incontinent les ardans feux en glace,
Empeschant que l'amour ne logeast au dedans.

Voyant la chasteté qui forte le repousse,
Amour tout desdaigneux se depite et courrouce,
Et dechassé du cueur il s'adresse à noz yeux: 15
Mais le pauvret (helas) y a laissé en gage
Et son arc, et ses traicts, comme pour tesmoignage
Que noz yeux ont esté sur luy victorieux.

Demeurant despoüillé de ses plus fortes armes,
Il s'en va chercher Mars au millieu des alarmes,   20
Le priant humblement de luy donner secours:
Mars, esmeu de pitié, amena de sa terre
Grand nombre de soldats pour nous faire la guerre,
Et n'y gaigna non plus que le Dieu des amours.

Un cueur qui n'ouvre point aux voluptez la porte,   25
Un penser genereux, une puissance forte,
Nous preserve tousjours de l'Amour et de Mars:
Aussi en toutes parts la femme ne resonne
Que du pouvoir hautain de la Roine Amazone
Qui faict marcher les Dieux dessous ses estendars.   30

Son nom est Otrera, fille de Martesie,
Qui tient pour la servir cette trouppe choisie,
Voulant par sa proüesse eterniser son nom:
Elle retient du tout le souverain Empire
De la grande cité nommée Themyscire,   35
Enceinte par les bras du fameux Thermodon.

CHANSON DES AMAZONES
Nous faisons la guerre
Aux Rois de la terre,
Bravant les plus glorieux,
Par nostre prudence

Audacious Love, wishing that his flames
Utterly mollify the virtue of our souls,
Launched at our hearts a thousand blazing torches:
But our chastity, always standing guard,   10
Suddenly transformed these ardent flames into ice,
Thus preventing Love from forcing his way in.

Seeing Chastity push him decisively back,
Love, disdainful, frets and fumes,
And driven from our hearts, he looks us in the eye: 15
But the wretch (alas) has thrown down his glove
And his bow, and his arrows, for he is forced to admit
That our gaze has gained victory over him.

Deprived of his strongest weapons,
He goes searching for Mars in the midst of the fray,   20
Humbly begging for his help:
Mars, moved with pity, brought forth from his lands
A great number of soldiers to make war on us,
But he had no more luck than did the God of love.

A heart that never surrenders to sensuality,   25
A generous mind and powerful strength,
Forever protect us from Love and from Mars:
And so everywhere, all women speak only
Of the proud rule of the Queen of the Amazons,
Who makes the very Gods march beneath her banners.   30

Her name is Orithya, daughter of Martesia,[63]
Who commands this chosen army to serve her,
For she wishes by her prowess to immortalize her name:
She retains the sovereign Empire
Of that great city of Themyscira,   35
Encircled by the arms of the famous river Thermodon.

SONG OF THE AMAZONS

We wage war
Against the Kings of the earth,
And we defy the most glorious among them,
By our prudence

Et nostre vaillance.   5
Nous commandons en maints lieux,
Domptant les efforts
Des plus hardis et forts
D'un bras victorieux.

Nous chassons les vices,   10
Par les exercices
Que la vertu nous aprend,
Fuyant comme peste
Le brandon moleste
Qui autour du cueur se prend: 15
Car la pureté
De nostre chasteté
Pour jamais le defend.

Nous tenons les hommes,
Des lieux où nous sommes,   20
Tous empeschez à filer:
Leur lasche courage
D'un plus bel ouvrage
N'est digne de se mesler.
Si quelcun de vous   25
S'en fache contre nous,
Qu'il vienne quereller.

A MA QUENOILLE

Quenoille mon souci, je vous promets et jure
De vous aimer tousjours, et jamais ne changer
Vostre honneur domestic pour un bien estranger,
Qui erre inconstamment et fort peu de temps dure.
Vous ayant au costé je suis beaucoup plus seure
Que si encre et papier se venoient aranger
Tout à l'entour de moy, car pour me revanger
Vous pouvez bien plustost repousser une injure.
Mais quenoille m'amie, il ne faut pas pourtant
Que pour vous estimer, et pour vous aimer tant
Je delaisse du tout cest' honneste coustume
D'escrire quelquefois; en escrivant ainsi,
J'escri de voz valeurs, quenoille mon souci,
Ayant dedans la main, le fuzeau, et la plume.

And our valor.   5
We rule in many places,
Taming the efforts
Of the most daring and the strongest,
By our victorious arm.

We chase away the vices,   10
By means of practices
That virtue teaches us,
We flee as from the plague
Love's grievous flame
That ravages the heart: 15
For the purity
Of our chastity
Forbids Love ever to enter.

We keep the men
In the places we rule,   20
All busily spinning:[64]
Their cowardly wits
Do not deserve
To take up more beautiful work;
If any among you   25
Wish to argue with us,
Let him come forward.

TO MY DISTAFF[65]

Distaff, my care,[66] I promise you and swear
That I'll love you forever, and never exchange
Your domestic honor for a good which is strange,
And which, inconstant, wanders aimlessly and does not endure.
With you at my side, I am far more secure
Than with ink and paper arrayed all around me,
For, if I needed defending, you would be there,
You are much better at repelling an assault.
But distaff, my love, it is not really necessary,
That in order to value you and love you so,
I abandon entirely that honorable custom
Of writing sometimes; for by writing as I do,
I write of your worth, distaff, my care,
As I hold in my hand my spindle and my pen.

A MES ESCRITS

Je ne pensay jamais que vous eussiez de force
Pour forcer les efforts de l'oubly, ny du temps.
Aussi je vous escry comme par passe-temps,
Fuyant d'oisiveté la vitieuse amorce.
Et pource mes escrits, nul de vous ne s'efforce
De vouloir me laisser, car je le vous deffens.
Où voudriez-vous aller? He mes petits enfans,
Vous estes abillez d'une si foible escorce.
Je croy que vous pensez me faire quelque honneur
Pour m'emporter aussi, envieux du bon-heur
Que deux freres ont eu portant leur mere au temple:
Lors qu'ell' en demanda digne loyer aux Dieux,
Un sommeil eternel leur vint siler les yeux,
Et cela (mes enfans) vous doit servir d'exemple.

AU ROY   ·

Apres avoir reçeu (o lumiere des Princes)
Les honneurs meritez aux estranges Provinces,
Jeune vous retournez dans le pays aymé:
Vous changez maintenant d'un agreable eschange,
Pour le sceptre Gaulois une couronne estrange,   5
Et un peuple sans ame à un peuple animé.

À vostre heureux retour tout le monde s'apreste,
Epoint d'une allegresse à vous faire grand feste:
Mais quelques-uns aussi vous offrent de leur bien,
Esperant d'en avoir plus grande recompense,   10
Cent et cent mille fois que ne vaut leur depense,
Et vous donnant de mesme, ils ne vous donnent rien.

Ceux qui vous font present par une tromperie,
D'argent, de perles, d'or, de riches pierreries,
Au lieu de les donner, vous les vendent bien cher: 15
Et si vous ne payez leur belle marchandise
D'un autre plus grand don, l'avare convoitise
Ne leur permettra plus de vous venir chercher.

Sire, si mon present vous peut estre agreable,
À moy qui le vous donne il sera honorable,   20

TO MY WRITINGS

I never thought that you had strength enough
To undo the effects of forgetfulness, or of time.
Hence I write as a pastime,
To flee the vicious bait of idleness.[67]
Therefore, my writings, may none of you try
To leave me, because I forbid it.
Where would you go? Ah, my little children,[68]
You are protected by such a thin cover.
It seems you think that you can honor me
By carrying me, envious of the happiness those two brothers had
Who carried their mother to the temple:
When she asked the Gods for a worthy reward,
An eternal sleep came and covered their eyes,
And this (my children) must serve as a lesson.[69]

TO THE KING[70]

After receiving (O light of Princes)
The honors bestowed by foreign Provinces,
You return, young, to your beloved country:
In an advantageous swap, you now exchange
A foreign crown for the French scepter,   5
And a soulless people for a lively one.

The world readies itself for your joyful return,
Our happiness moves us to throw you a great party:
But some also offer you their possessions
In hopes of receiving a much greater reward,   10
A hundred thousand times more than what they've given,
But in giving thus, they really give you nothing.

Those who in deceit offer you gifts,
Of silver, pearls, gold, or precious stones,
Instead of offering them, are really selling them to you at a high price: 15
And if you don't pay for their beautiful merchandise
With another, greater gift, insatiable greed
Will prevent them from further seeking your favor.[71]

Sir, if my gift pleases you,
To me who give it, it shall bring honor,   20

À vostre peuple mesme il pourra profiter:
Car vostre Royauté est le souverain temple
Où voz subjects prendront un singulier exemple
De vouloir pour jamais voz vertus imiter.

Pour chastier l'Anglois et le subject rebelle,   25
Un de noz Roys prit bien l'advis d'une Pucelle.
Donques je vous supply de vouloir escouter
Ce que vostre vertu divinement inspire
Dans mes foibles esprits, afin de le vous dire,
Et vous pourrez ainsi voz haineux surmonter.   30

Monstrant que vous avez une ame tres-Chrestienne,
Honorez tousjours Dieu à la mode ancienne,
Tousjours obeissez à ses divines loix:
Presentez-vous à luy franc et pur de tout vice,
Offrez-luy voz pensers pour humble sacrifice,   35
Car Dieu dedans sa main tient le pouvoir des Rois.

Donnez à voz parens les charges les plus belles,
Et celles d'importance aux serviteurs fidelles
De vostre majesté, à vostre entendement
Le soing de vostre vie, à vostre vigilance   40
L'espoir de voz sujects, et l'honneur de la France,
Donnez-le à vostre sage et prudent jugement.

L'ornement d'un grand Roy, son honneur, sa noblesse,
Vient d'aymer la vertu, trop plus que la richesse,
Aymer un bon conseil, trop plus qu' un grand present,   45
Plus qu' un plaisir volage, aymer la Temperance,
Avoir devant les yeux, les yeux de la Prudence
Qui voit le temps passé, le futur, et present.

La rigueur de la loy, et la douceur du livre,
Induisent quelquefois les privez à bien vivre,   50
Avec le chastiment de leurs proches parens,
Le soing de leurs amys qui les veulent aprendre,
L'injure des hayneux qui les vienent reprendre,
Montrant de toutes pars leurs defaux apparans.

And even profit to your people:
For your Royal Highness is the sovereign temple
Where your subjects shall find a singular example
And wish forever to imitate your virtues.

To punish the English and all rebellious subjects,   25
One of our Kings wisely took the advice of a chaste Maiden.[72]
I beseech you then to hear
What your virtue divinely inspires
In my feeble mind, so that I can write it to you,
And you can thus triumph over those who bear you ill.   30

To show to all that you have a true Christian soul,
Always honor God in the old-fashioned way,
By always obeying His divine commands:
Come before Him openly and free from every vice,
Offer Him your thoughts as a humble sacrifice,   35
For God holds the power of Kings in his hand.

Assign to your family the most prominent charges,
And those of importance to the ever-loyal servants
Of Your Majesty, to your understanding
Entrust your life, to your vigilance   40
The hope of your subjects, and the honor of France
To your wise and prudent judgment.

The greatness of a King, his honor and his nobility,
Come from loving virtue much more than wealth,
Loving good counsel much more than a great gift,   45
More than fickle pleasure, loving Temperance,
Having before one's eyes the eyes of Prudence
Which sees times past, future, and present.

The severity of the law and the benefits of the book
Sometimes help private citizens to live well,   50
As also the admonition of their close relatives,
The care of their friends who wish to teach them,
Even the insults and rebukes of those who hate them
Warning them of their obvious faults.

Mais vous (Prince excellent) vous avez en vous-mesme   55
Des discours de raison, et le pouvoir supreme
Que vous donnez aux loix: puis vous avez aussi
Le vertueux amour de vostre sage mere,
L'humble fidelité que vous doit vostre frere,
Et de voz bons sujets le gracieux souci.   60

Vostre grandeur sçait bien que le plus vray office
D'un Roy sage et parfaict, c'est d'aimer la justice,
Delivrer ses sujets de leur calamité,
Favoriser les bons, faire aux meschans la guerre,
Maintenir son pouvoir, et accroistre sa terre: 65
Voilà qui tient un Roy en son autorité.

Si vous ne desdaignez les escris d'une fille,
J'espere bien qu' un jour de mode plus gentille,
D'une plus forte voix j'entonneray les sons
De voz rares valeurs, de voz graces divines.   70
Si bien qu'à l'avenir les Nimphes Poëtevines
En diront sur le Clain mill' et mille chansons.

À G. P.
Vous dictes que je vends ces vers à leurs hautesses,
Non, je ne les vend point: le present est entier.
Car je proteste Dieu que Princes ny Princesses
Ne m'ont jamais donné la valeur d'un denier.

À MA MERE
Je vous fays un present de la vertu supreme,
Depeinte proprement par un Roy tres-parfaict,
(Ma mere) et vous offrant cest excellent pourtraict,
C'est vous offrir aussi le pourtraict de vous-mesme.

LA FEMME FORTE DESCRITTE PAR SALOMON
Heureux qui trouvera la femme vertueuse,
Surpassant de valeur la perle precieuse,
Le cueur de son mary d'elle s'esjouïra,
Plein d'honneurs, plein de biens, content il joüira
Du fruict de son labeur, tous les jours de sa vie,   5
Il l'aura pour compaigne et servante et amie.

But you (excellent Prince) have in you 55
The lessons of reason, and the supreme power
That you give to the laws: you also have
The exemplary love of your wise mother,[73]
The humble loyalty owed you by your brother,[74]
And the kind thoughts of your good subjects. 60

Your grandeur well knows that the truest duty
Of a wise and perfect King is to love justice,
To deliver his subjects from calamity,
To favor the good, and to make war on the bad,
To maintain his power, and to acquire more land; 65
That is how a King holds onto his authority.[75]

If you do not scorn the writings of a mere young girl,
I truly hope that someday in a more gracious way,
With a stronger voice I'll sing a song
About your exceptional worth and your divine graces. 70
So much so that in future times the Nymphs of Poitiers
Will sing a thousand songs about them on the river Clain.[76]

TO G. P.
You say that I sell these verses to their royal highnesses,[77]
No, in no way do I sell them: they are simply a gift.
For I protest before God that neither Princes nor Princesses
Have ever paid me as much as a sou.

TO MY MOTHER
Here is a gift of supreme virtue,
Perfectly depicted by an ever so perfect King,
(My mother) and in offering you this excellent portrait,
I am also offering you a portrait of yourself.

THE STRONG WOMAN AS DESCRIBED BY SOLOMON[78]
Happy the man who finds himself a virtuous wife,
She is far more precious than the pearl,
The heart of her husband will rejoice in her,
Full of honor and goods, he will enjoy
The fruit of her labor all the days of his life, 5
He will have her for companion, servant, and friend.

Fuyant le doux languir du paresseux sommeil,
Ell' se leve au matin, premier que le soleil
Monstre ses beaux rayons, et puis faict un ouvrage,
Ou de laine, ou de lin, pour servir son mesnage,   10
Tirant de son labeur un utile plaisir.
Ses servantes aussi qu'elle a bien sçeu choisir,
Chassant l'oisiveté, sont toutes amusées
A cherpir, à peigner, à tourner leurs fusées,
Faire virer le trueil, comme un petit moulin,   15
Le chastelet aussi pour devider le lin.
Comme l'on voit sur mer la vagante navire
Raporter au marchand le profit qu'il desire,
Le bled, le vin, le bois, afin qu'à son besoing
Il le trouve chez luy sans le chercher plus loing,   20
Ainsi la Dame sage ordonne sa famille,
Afin que son mary, et ses fils, et sa fille,
Ses servans, ses sujects, puissent avoir tousjours
Le pain, le drap, l'argent, pour leur donner secours
Contre la faim, le froid, et maintes autres peines,   25
Qui tourmentent souvent les pensées humaines.
Ayant bien disposé l'estat de sa maison,
Dependant par mesure, espargnant par raison,
Elle va voir aux champs la brebis porte-laine,
Et le boeuf nourricier qui traine par la plaine   30
Le soc avant-coureur de l'espy jaunissant.
Elle regarde apres si le fruict meurissant
Dedans le boys tortu, promet que cette année
On puisse rencontrer une bonne vinée.
Et ne desdaignant point de travailler aussi,   35
Elle prend d'y planter la peine, et le souci.
Vous la verriez parfois r'accourcir sa vesture,
Troussée proprement d'une forte ceinture,
Et revirer apres ses manches sur les bras
Qui paroissent charnus, poupins, doüillets, et gras: 40
Car il ne faut penser que la delicatesse
Se trouve seulement avecques la paresse.
La femme mesnagere est plus belle cent fois
Que ne sont ces Echo qui n'ont rien que la voix.
Or cette diligente ayant tel avantage,   45
Elle est plus belle aussi, d'autant qu'elle est plus sage:

Escaping from the sweet idleness of lazy sleep,
She rises promptly at dawn, before the sun
Shines forth its lovely rays, and then sets to work
On wool or on flax, to serve her household,   10
For she finds pleasure in this useful task.[79]
Her maidservants, too, whom she has chosen with care,
Spurn idleness and are all happily occupied in
Tousing, combing, and turning their spools,
And like miniature windmills they twirl their spindles,   15
And use the bobbin to wind up their fibers.
Like a merchant's ship roaming the seas,
That brings from afar the riches he seeks
So that whenever he may need wheat, wine, or wood,
He'll find them close at hand in his very home,   20
In like manner the wise Lady provides for her family.
Her husband, her sons and her daughter,
Her servants and all her subjects will always have
Bread, cloth, and money, to protect them
From hunger, cold, and many other ills   25
That often afflict the human spirit.
Having ascertained that all's well at home,
For she has spent moderately and saved wisely,
She goes down to her fields, sees the wool-bearing flock,
And the sustaining oxen that guide through the plain   30
The plow, that harbinger of golden wheat.
She then inspects the ripening fruit
On the twisted branch, to see if this year
It will produce a good vintage.
She doesn't think manual work beneath her,   35
She takes the trouble and the care to plant.
You'd see her now and then drawing up her gown
And tucking it in neatly with her sturdy belt,
And then rolling up her sleeves that reveal arms
Looking plump and rosy, soft and full: 40
For you mustn't think that delicacy
Is found only among the idle.
The housewifely woman is a hundred times lovelier
Than those mere Echoes who have only a voice.[80]
Now this diligent woman, so richly blessed,   45
Is all the more beautiful for her prudence:

Prenant provision des beaux fruicts de ses champs,
Elle en mesure aussi pour les vendre aux marchands.
Sa lampe n'esteint point, ains tousjours la lumiere
Est dedans son logis d'esclairer coustumiere,   50
Pource qu'il faut veiller et travailler souvent
Pour faire des linceuls, et des draps qu'elle vend.
Sa liberale main se monstre favorable
Aux pauvres affligez, dont l'estat miserable
Est digne de pitié. En ne refusant pas   55
De prendre la quenoille, ell' n'espargne ses pas
Pour aller et venir autour de ses servantes,
Et loüant leurs labeurs les rendre diligentes.
Elle donne à chascune un bon accoustrement,
En les encourageant d'advancer promptement,   60
De faire des tapys, couvertes, et courtines.
À elle seulement pour accoustremens dignes
De ses rares valeurs, le pourpre est suffisant:
Mais elle a un habit qui luy est mieux duisant
De sage Temperance, et de saincte Justice,   65
De Fortitude aussi, qui faict la guerre au vice,
De Prudence guidant toutes ses actions,
Chascun la reconnoist pour ses perfections.
Son mary est prisé en tous lieux de la ville,
Pour estre possesseur de femme si gentille.   70
Ell' a dessus sa langue un coulant fleuve d'or,
Et tient en son esprit un precieux tresor,
De graces et vertus, sa parfaicte eloquence
Monstre par ses propos la vraye sapience.
Ell' est douce, benigne, et conduit sagement   75
Le train de sa maison, non pas oysivement,
Car elle faict avoir, et le pain, et la peine,
Voulans que le travail un doux repos ameine.
Ses enfans sont autour qui reverent sans fin
Le discret jugement de son esprit divin.   80
Son mary, la voyant sur toutes admirable,
Confesse qu'en la terre elle n'a de semblable:
Plusieurs Dames pourtant, on faict digne recueil
De graces et beautez qui plaisent fort à l'œil.
Mais tu les passes tant (o Dame d'excellence)!   85
D'autant qu'un bon propos surpasse le silence,

She stores the lovely fruit from her fields,
And puts some aside to sell to the merchants.
Her lamp is never put out; it always casts
Its daily glow in every corner of her house, 50
For she stays up and works long hours
To make and sell both sheets and cloth.
She opens her generous hands
To the poor and afflicted whose misery
Is worthy of pity. She is not averse 55
To working with the distaff, she comes and goes
Amidst her maidservants, praising them
And encouraging their labors to make them more diligent.
She gives to each fine clothing,
As a reward to incite them not to tarry in the making 60
Of wall hangings, coverlets, and curtains.
The purple alone is sufficient
As a worthy garment for her rare qualities:
But better fitting yet is her apparel
Of wise Temperance, and of saintly Righteousness, 65
Of Fortitude also which battles vice,
And Prudence, the guide to all her actions.[81]
Everyone acknowledges her accomplishments.
Her husband is honored throughout the city,
For possessing such an affable wife. 70
From her lips flows a river of gold,
Her mind is a precious treasure,
Of graces and virtues, her perfect eloquence
And her speech reveal true wisdom.
She is gentle and good; she manages her household 75
Wisely, never giving way to idleness,
For she knows there's no bread without toil,
And she desires that gentle rest follow upon hard work.
Her children all around her revere endlessly
The discreet good judgment of her divine mind. 80
Her husband, seeing how she surpasses all others,
Confesses that on earth she has no equal:
"Many Ladies have indeed received
All manner of grace and beauty so pleasing to the eye.
But you outdo them all by far (most excellent Lady)! 85
For as a good word is superior to silence,

D'autant qu'un jour luisant passe l'obscure nuict,
Ta rarité d'autant sur les autres reluit.
La beauté se flestrist, la grace est decevable,
Et de tous leurs attraits ce n'est rien qu'une fable: 90
Mais la femme qui ayme, et qui craint le Seigneur,
Merite recevoir un immortel honneur:
Sus doncques! rendez-luy la gloire meritée!
Sa loüange ne soit de bornes limitée.
Faictes-luy voisiner la grand' voute des Cieux,   95
Puisqu'elle est en ce monde un miracle à voz yeux,
Que sa perfection un tel loyer demande,
Rendez-le prontement, car Dieu vous le commande.

L'AGNODICE

Il n'y a passion qui tourmente la vie
Avec plus de fureur que l'impiteuse Envie.
De tous les autres maux on tire quelque bien:
L'avare enchesné d'or se plaist en son bien;
Le superbe se fond d'une douce allegresse,   5
S'il voit un grand seigneur qui l'honore et caresse;
Le voleur, epiant sa proye par les champs,
Soubsrit à son espoir, attendant les marchands;
Le gourmand prend plaisir au manger qu'il devore,
Et semble par les yeux le devorer encore;   10
Le jeune homme surpris de lascives amours,
Compose en son esprit mille plaisans discours;
Le menteur se plaist fort s'il se peut faire croire;
Le jureur en bravant se pompe dans sa gloire.
Mais, o cruelle Envie, on ne reçoit par toy   15
Sinon le desplaisir, la douleur, et l'esmoy.
A celuy qui te loge, ingrat' et fiere hotesse,
Tu laisse pour payement le dueil et la tristesse;
A celuy qui te donne à repaistre chez luy,
Tu payes pour escot le chagrin et l'ennuy;   20
De noz premiers parens tu espris le courage,
Espandant le venin de ta feilleuse rage
Sur les divins autels, quand le bras fraternel
Tua le pauvre Abel invoquant l'eternel.
Depuis, en te coulant aux autres parts du monde,   25
Tu semas en la terre une race feconde

And the light of day better than the dark night,
So your uniqueness shines high above the others."
Beauty fades, charm is deceitful,
Their allure amounts to no more than a lie: 90
But the woman who loves and who fears the Lord
Deserves immortal honor.
Come then! Give her the glory she merits!
Let her praise be boundless!
Place her in the great dome of the Heavens,   95
And because you see in her a miracle on earth,
And her perfection should receive such praise,
Bestow it on her promptly, for God commands you to do so.

AGNODICE[82]
There is no other passion that torments life
With more fury than pitiless Envy.
From all other evils one can derive some good:
The greedy chained to his gold finds pleasure in his wealth;
The proud man is overcome with sweet delight   5
When he sees a great lord honor and flatter him;
The thief, spying his prey in the fields,
Smiles at his good luck as he waits for the [unsuspecting] merchants;
The glutton takes pleasure in eating what he devours,
And seems by the look in his eyes to devour it still;   10
The young man trapped by his lecherous love,
Composes in his mind a thousand pleasing phrases;
The liar is greatly pleased when he can make himself believed;
The one who swears in his bravado is puffed up with glory.
But, O cruel Envy, one receives from you   15
Only displeasure, pain, and sorrow.
To whoever takes you in, ungrateful and proud guest,
You leave as payment only mourning and sadness;
To whoever gives you food at his home,
You give in return only grief and chagrin;   20
You invaded the heart of our first ancestors,
By spreading the venom of your furious rage
Upon the holy altars, when a brother's arm
Killed poor Abel while he prayed to the Almighty.[83]
Since then, in reaching to other parts of the world,   25
You sowed on the earth a plentiful mix

D'ires, de cruautez, de geines, et de morts
Qui font aux vertueux cent et cent mille torts.
Mais sur tous autres lieux, c'est la Contrée Attique
Qui tesmoigne le plus de ta puissance inique,   30
Nenny point pour Thesé de ses parens trahy,
Pour le juste Aristide injustement hay,
Ny pour que Themistocle ait fuy dans la terre
D'un Roy que tant de fois il poursuivit en guerre;
Ny pour voir Miltiade à tort emprisonné,   35
Pour Socrate non plus qui meurt empoisonné;
Mais pour toy (Phocion) qui n'eus pas sepulture
Au pays tant aymé où tu pris nourriture.
Une Dame estrangere, ayant la larme à l'œil,
Reçeut ta chere cendre, et la meit au cercueil,   40
Honorant tes vertus de loüanges supremes,
Elle cacha tes oz dedans son fouyer mesmes,
Disant d'un triste cueur, humble et devotieux:
Je vous appelle tous, o domestiques Dieux,
Puisque de Phocion l'ame s'est desliée   45
Pour aller prendre au ciel sa place dediée,
Et que ses citoyens, causes de son trespas,
L'ayant empoisonné ores ne veulent pas
Qu'il soit ensevely dedans sa terre aymée,
Se montrant envieux dessus sa renommée.   50
Aymons ce qui nous reste, honorons sa prison,
Le feu s'en est volé, gardons bien le tison.
L'Envie, regardant cette dame piteuse,
Dans soy-mesme sentit une ire serpenteuse;
Roüant ses deux grans yeux pleins d'horreur et d'effroy,   55
Ah! je me vengeray, ce dit-elle, de toy,
He! tu veux donc ayder (sotte), tu veux deffendre
Phocion, dont je hay encor la morte cendre;
Saches qu'en peu de temps je te feray sentir
De ton hastif secours un tardif repentir.   60
Car en despit de toy j'animeray les ames
Des maris, qui seront les tyrans de leurs femmes,
Et qui leur deffendant le livre et le sçavoir,
Leur osteront aussi de vivre le pouvoir.
Aussitost qu'elle eut dit, elle glisse aux moüelles   65
Des hommes qui, voyans leurs femmes doctes-belles,

Of anger, cruelty, torture, and death,
Which upon the virtuous inflicts a thousand wrongs.
But more than all other places, it is the Country of Attica[84]
That bears witness to your unequaled power,   30
Not only over Theseus, who was betrayed by his relatives,[85]
Or just Aristides who was unjustly hated,[86]
Themistocles who had to flee to the land
Of a King he had pursued so many times in war;[87]
Miltiades who was wrongfully imprisoned,[88]   35
Or even Socrates, who died of poison;[89]
But especially over you (Phocion) who received no sepulcher[90]
In the beloved country where you were born and raised.
It was a foreign Lady who, with tears in her eyes,
Took your precious ashes and placed them in a tomb,   40
Honoring your virtues with highest praises,
She hid your bones within her very home,
Saying with a sad, humble, and devoted heart:
"I call on you all, domestic Gods,
For Phocion's soul has departed   45
To go take its prepared place in the heavens;
The citizens of this country, who have caused his death
By poisoning him, now refuse
To have him buried in his beloved land,
Because they envy his renown.   50
Let us treasure his remains, let us honor his new prison,
The fire has left it, let us guard his ashes."
Envy, gazing upon this pitiful lady,
Felt a poisonous anger well up inside;
Rolling her two great eyes full of horror and terror,   55
"Ah! I'll avenge myself on you," she said;
"So, you foolish woman, you seek to help and protect
Phocion, whose dead ashes I still hate;
Know that soon I'll force you to feel
For your promptness in helping him a tardy regret.   60
For to spite you I'll incite
Husbands to become the tyrants of their wives;
By keeping learning and books from them,
They'll take away their very desire to live."
As soon as she had spoken, Envy slips into the hearts   65
Of men who, seeing their wives smart and beautiful,

Desirent effacer de leur entendement
Les lettres, des beautez le plus digne ornement;
Et ne voulant laisser chose qui leur agrée,
Leur ostent le plaisir où l'ame se recrée.   70
Que ce fust à l'Envie une grand' cruauté
De martirer ainsi cette douce beauté!
Les dames aussitost se trouverent suivies
De fiebvres, de langueurs, et d'autres maladies,
Leur faisoit supporter incroyables tourmens.   75
Aymant trop mieux mourir que d'estre peu honteuses
Contant aux Medecins leurs peines langoureuses,
Les femmes (o pitié!) n'osoient plus se mesler
De s'aider l'une l'autre, on les faisoit filler.
Leurs marys, les voyans en ce cruel martyre,   80
Ne laissoient pas pourtant de gaucer et de rire;
Peut-estre desirant deux nopces esprouver,
Ils n'avoient plus de soing de les vouloir sauver.
En ce temps il y eut une Dame gentille,
Que le ciel avoit faict belle, sage, et subtile,   85
Qui, piteuse de voir ces visages si beaux,
Prontement engloutis des avares tombeaux,
Les voulant secourir couvrit sa double pomme
Afin d'estudier en accoustrement d'homme,
Pource qu'il estoit lors aux femmes interdit   90
De pratiquer les arts, ou les voir par escrit.
Ceste Dame, cachant l'or de sa blonde tresse,
Aprist la medecine, et s'en feit grand maistresse.
Puis se resouvenant de son affection,
Voulut effectuer sa bonne intention,   95
Et guerir les douleurs de ses pauvres voisines
Par la vertu des fleurs, des fueilles et racines,
D'une herbe mesmement qui fut cueillie au lieu
Où Glauque la mengeant d'homme devint un Dieu.
Ayant tout preparé, la gentille Agnodice   100
Se presente humblement pour leur faire service.
Mais les Dames pensant que ce fut un garson,
Refusoient son secours d'une estrange façon.
L'on cognoissoit assez à leurs faces craintives
Qu'elles craignoient ses mains comme des mains lassives.   105
Agnodice, voyant leur grande chasteté,

Seek to erase from their minds
All learning, that most worthy ornament of beauty;
And by not leaving them this pleasant occupation,
They rob from them the very pleasure in which the soul recreates itself.   70
How cruel it was for Envy
To martyrize sweet beauty in this way!
The women soon found themselves beset
By fevers, faintness, and other illnesses,
Envy forced them to bear incredible torments.[91]   75
They preferred death to the shame of
Telling the [male] Doctors about their debilitating troubles.
The women (what a pity!) did not dare
To help one another, they were made to spin.
Their husbands, observing them in this cruel martyrdom,   80
Did not refrain from mocking and jeering at them;
And perhaps hoping to marry again,
They did not care at all to save them.
Now in that time, there lived a noble young Lady,[92]
Whom Heaven had made beautiful, wise, and subtle,   85
Who, full of pity at the sight of so many beautiful faces
Soon to be engulfed by the greedy tomb,
Wanted to rescue them. She hid the twin apples [of her bosom],
So that she could study, disguised as a man,
Because it was then forbidden for women   90
To practice the arts, or even to read about them.
This young woman, hiding the gold of her blond locks,
Learned medicine, and became quite expert at it.
Then, remembering her original intent,
She wanted to carry out her plan   95
To heal the sufferings of her poor sisters
By the special virtues of flowers, leaves, and roots,
Especially with an herb picked on the very spot
Where Glaucus from a man became a God after eating it.[93]
Having prepared everything, the noble Agnodice   100
Humbly offers her services to the Ladies.
But they, thinking she was a man,
Harshly refused her help.
It was readily apparent from their timorous faces
That they feared her hands as lustful hands.   105
Agnodice, seeing their great chastity,

Les estima beaucoup pour ceste honnesteté;
Lors descouvrant du sein les blanches pommes rondes,
Et de son chef doré les belles tresses blondes,
Monstre qu'elle estoit fille, et que son gentil cueur   110
Les vouloit delivrer de leur triste langueur.
Les Dames, admirant ceste honte naïfve,
Et de son teint doüillet la blanche couleur vive,
Et de son sein poupin le petit mont jumeau,
Et de son chef sacré l'or crepelu tant beau,   115
Et de ses yeux divins les flammes ravissantes,
Et de ses doux propos les graces attirantes,
Baiserent mille fois et sa bouche et son sein,
Recevant le secours de son heureuse main.
On voit en peu de temps les femmes et pucelles   120
Reprendre leurs teins frais, et devenir plus belles.
Mais l'Envie, presente à cest humain secours,
Proteste de bientost en empescher le cours:
Elle mangeoit son cueur, miserable viande,
Digne repas de ceux où son pouvoir commande,   125
Et tenoit en la main un furieux serpent
Dont le cruel venin en tous lieux se respand.
Son autre main portoit une branche espineuse,
Son corps estoit plombé, sa face despiteuse,
Sa teste sans cheveux où faisoient plusieurs tours   130
Des viperes hideux qui la mordoient tousjours.
Trainant autour de soy ses furieuses rages,
Elle s'en va troubler les chastes mariages,
Car le repos d'autruy luy est propre malheur.
Aux hommes elle mist en soupçon la valeur   135
De la belle Agnodice et ses graces gentilles,
Disant que sa beauté de leurs femmes et filles
Avoit plus de faveur que ne doivent penser
Celles qui ne voudroient leurs honneurs offencer.
Eux, eprix de fureur, saisirent Agnodice   140
Pour en faire à l'Envie un piteux sacrifice.
Helas! sans la trouver coulpable d'aucun tort,
Ils l'ont injustement condemnée à la mort.
La pauvrete, voyant le malheur qui s'appreste,
Descouvrit promptement l'or de sa blonde teste,   145
Et monstrant son sein beau, aggreable sejour

Esteemed them all the more for their virtue,
And uncovering then the white round apples [of her bosom],
And the beautiful blond tresses of her golden head,
Showed that she was a maiden, and that her kind heart   110
Wished to deliver them from their sad predicament.
The Ladies, admiring her innocent modesty,
And the lively whiteness of her soft complexion,
And the little twin mounts of her adorable breasts,
And the beautiful golden shine of her blessed head,   115
And the ravishing flames of her divine eyes,
And the engaging gracefulness of her sweet words,
Kissed a thousand times both her mouth and her breast,
As they received help from her blessed hands.
Soon, one could see wives and maidens   120
Regain their glowing complexion, and become even more beautiful.
But Envy, who was present at this scene of human assistance,
Vowed soon to prevent it from continuing:
She ate out her heart, a wretched food,
A meal worthy only of those she commands,   125
And she held in her hand a raging serpent
Whose cruel venom she spread everywhere.
Her other hand held a thorny branch,
Her body was leaden, her face full of spleen,
And her bald head was surrounded by several crowns of   130
Hideous vipers who kept biting her.
Dragging along her raging furies,
She set out to bring turmoil to chaste marriages,
For the peace of another is to her a misfortune.
She made the men suspicious of the worth   135
And the gentle grace of beautiful Agnodice,
Telling them that Agnodice's beauty held more sway
Over their wives and daughters than was becoming
To women mindful of their honor.
The men, filled with fury, seized Agnodice   140
To make of her a pitiful sacrifice to Envy.
Alas! Without finding her guilty of any wrong,
They unjustly condemned her to death.
The poor creature, seeing the misfortune awaiting her,
Promptly uncovered the gold of her blond tresses,   145
And, showing them her beautiful breasts, graceful abode

Des Muses, des vertus, des graces, de l'amour,
Elle baissa les yeux pleins d'honneur et de honte;
Une vierge rougeur en la face luy monte;
Disant que le desir qui la faict desguiser   150
N'est point pour les tromper, mais pour authoriser
Les lettres qu'elle apprist voulant servir leurs Dames;
Que de la soupçonner de crimes tant infames,
C'est offencer nature et ses divines loix.
Depuis qu'elle eut parlé, oncq une seulle voix   155
Ne s'esleva contre elle; ains toute l'assistance
Monstroit d'esmerveiller ceste rare excellence;
Ils estoient tous ravis, sans parler ny mouvoir,
Ententifs seulement à l'ouyr et la voir.
Comme l'on voit parfois apres un long orage,   160
R'asserener les vents, et calmer le rivage,
Quand les freres jumeaux qui regardoient sur mer
Une piteuse nef en danger d'abismer,
La sauvant de peril des flots l'ont retirée
Pour luy faire aborder la rive desirée,   165
Les hommes, tout ainsi vaincus par la pitié,
Rapaisent la fureur de leur inimitié;
Faisant à la pucelle une humble reverence,
Ils luy vont demander pardon de leur offence.
Elle, qui ressentit un plaisir singulier,   170
Les supplia bien fort de faire estudier
Les Dames du pays, sans envier la gloire
Que l'on a pour servir les filles de Memoire.
L'Envie, congnoissant ses efforts abbatus
Par les faicts d'Agnodice et ses rares vertus,   175
A poursuivy depuis d'une haine immortelle
Les Dames qui estoient vertueuses comme elle.

Of the Muses, of virtue, of grace, and of love,
She lowered her eyes, filled with an honorable shame;
A virginal blush came over her face;
She declared that her intent in taking on a disguise   150
Is not to deceive them, but only to allow her
To study and to learn, wishing to serve their wives;
And to suspect her of such infamous crimes
Was an offense against nature and her divine laws.
After she had spoken, not a single voice   155
Was raised against her; on the contrary, the entire audience
Marveled at her rare excellence;
Everyone was filled with wonder, and no one moved or made a sound,
Attentive only to hearing and seeing her.
In like manner one sometimes sees, after a long storm,   160
The winds die down, and the waves become calm,
As when the twin brothers who looked out over the sea[94]
Noticed a pitiful ship in danger of sinking,
Saved it from shipwreck, pulled it back from the waves
And made it land on the longed-for shore,   165
So the men, all overcome with pity,
Appease the fury of their enmity,
And humbly kneeling down before the maiden,
They ask her forgiveness for the harm they have done.
Agnodice, who felt a singular pleasure,   170
Beseeched them urgently to allow
The Ladies of the land to study, without envying the glory
Given to those who serve the daughters of Memory.[95]
Envy, recognizing that she had lost the battle
To Agnodice and to her rare virtues,   175
Has ever since persecuted with an everlasting hatred
All Ladies as virtuous as she.[96]

III

SELECTED POEMS OF MADELEINE DES ROCHES AND CATHERINE DES ROCHES FROM *LES SECONDES ŒUVRES* (1583)

I think that happiness depends solely upon us,
Madame, and that we can all forge our own destiny.

—Madeleine des Roches, sonnet 4

The divine Muses
Might avenge themselves,
If we thought ourselves worthy
Of the honor you bestow upon us.

—Catherine des Roches, response 37

INTRODUCTION

Critics have pointed out that while a humanistic and rhetorical education produced and reinforced power for men, it had the opposite effect for women.[1] Advocates of female education emphasize a "domesticated" version, barring women from the study of logic and rhetoric that would facilitate the application of their skills in the public sphere. Dominant in advice manuals is the injunction that women use deferential forms of speech and learning to show respect for male authority.[2] For their part, women writers seeking to effect poetic agency needed to do so conditionally: like their education, their circulated texts tended to reinforce the status quo rather than challenge it. Faced with such sociopolitical imperatives, the Dames des Roches adapted official definitions of womanly conduct through their practice of indirection, a "mixed life"[3] or a propitiatory "bricolage"[4] that facilitated their bid for social promotion and fame. The poems selected from *Les Secondes Œuvres* exemplify the artifices they used to maintain a pose of deference yet assert at the same time their agency.

Madeleine des Roches's poetic contribution in *Les Secondes Œuvres*, very much smaller than her daughter's, consists of fifteen short poems (sonnets, octets, sixtains, odes, an epitaph), several of them written a decade earlier, in which she focuses largely on topics close to home: her poor health, her husband's and daughter's illnesses, the religious wars and the loss of her properties, Poitiers and the 1579 Grands Jours. To overcome her personal troubles, she has recourse to a Christianized Neostoicism largely in vogue at the time. She draws on the works of Seneca and especially Epictetus and Marcus Aurelius who could be read in translation.[5] Treatises on Stoic thought in Plutarch's *Moralia*, translated by Jacques Amyot whom Madeleine cites by name in sonnet 10 of her *Œuvres*, and Guy du Faur de Pibrac's celebrated *Quatrains moraux* (1574) inspired her search for inner tranquility. Her syncretist œuvre reflects her reading of Platonic cosmology, Empedocles and Heraclitus on the mutability of the universe which she likely found in book 9 of Diogenes Laertius's *Lives of Eminent Philosophers*, Plato's *Timaeus*, Ronsard, and the Bible. Madeleine frequently invokes the Gospels and even briefly offers an exegesis of the second-century apologist Saint Justin Martyr's defense of Christianity against pagan persecution.[6] Her implicit message is that the Protestant cause is an affront to "nostre sainte Theologie" (our holy theology). She thereby bypasses prescriptive literature's interdiction against women's concerning themselves with theology. Poitiers and the Grands Jours hold a major place in her writings: in five poems (sonnets 1 through 3, and two untranslated quatrains), Madeleine des Roches addresses the lawyers of the famous circuit court, exhibiting a consummate flair (as does her daughter) in sidestepping compliment while bestowing praise on her admirers; in *Poitiers to the Gentlemen of the Grands Jours* she assumes the voice of her beloved city to showcase its ramparts, churches, and legal and educational institutions, and to praise the legists whom she compares to Orpheus, fabled singer, musician, and poet, "Qui tirant de l'oubly mes gloires estoufées, / Me font luyre partout comme un astre divin" (Who by bringing back into the limelight my [Poitiers's] forgotten glories, / Make me shine everywhere like a heavenly star).

Two odes by Madeleine des Roches on the Grands Jours (*Aux Poëtes chante-Puce* [To the poet songsters of the Flea] and a final untitled poem addressed to Étienne Pasquier)[7] appeared in the collaborative volume of *La Puce de Madame Des-Roches* in 1582/83 under Catherine's name.[8] The former poem, which evidently circulated in manuscript form, contains numerous typographical errors in its printed version in *La Puce*. By including these poems in *Les Secondes Œuvres*, it is clear that Madeleine wished to rectify errors of transcription and to reclaim her own work. Catherine evidently shared this same desire, for she included and corrected in her *Responces* (Responses) in *Les Secondes Œuvres* all nine of her pieces that had appeared in the group-authored collection, adding seven new poems that she had also composed for the gatherings of the coterie during the Grands Jours. By publishing her responses in a volume of her own, she sought to resist the effacement of her name that had already taken place when individual poets published their "Flea" verses and that would occur again some thirty years later when Pasquier claimed the *Flea* volume as his own, eliminating Des Roches's name altogether from its title.[9]

Included here are twenty-four of Catherine's forty-six *Responses*.[10] Six of these are addressed to the lawyers of the Grands Jours. Also included are her ode *Poitiers to the Gentlemen of the Grands Jours* and her poem *The Flea* which opened the group composition, authorizing the outpouring of verses in Greek, Latin, French, Italian, and Spanish in which the judges attempted to outdo each other in mock heroic punning and erotic lyrics in honor of Catherine's flea. The paradoxical encomium, a genre founded on Greek and Latin lyric, enjoyed an uncommon vogue at court and among Pléiade writers: it enabled poets to display their wit, poetic skill, and mastery of classical antecedents by using as pretext a lowly, mundane object.[11] Dramatized in this salon verbal ritual was the art of compliment and clever repartee which, while ostensibly directed to Catherine, was really focused on a celebratory exchange among professional men seeking social promotion.[12] Catherine for her part walked a tightrope. Against her guests' repeated usage of the Ovidian script of female rape, she invents "an authority of origin,"[13] a tale of emancipation that resists their depiction of her body as a locus of male conquest, all the while balancing, as Ann Jones puts it, "witty affability with modesty by means of an imperturbable Neoplatonism and a didactic rather than participatory attitude toward love."[14]

Catherine des Roches's strategic use of the response genre links her to the medieval topos of the woman respondent replying to a male partner.[15] The etymology of the "responce," from the Latin verb *respondere*, "to reciprocate," is apparent in several Provençal genres during the eleventh and twelfth centuries that included dialogues and debate poems such as the *tenso*, a favorite among the *trobaritz* (women troubadours). The *pièce responsive*, popular among poets of the *groupe marotique*[16] attached to the courts of François I and Henri II, was also a common device in Petrarchist poetry. In the Italian *ridotto* (salon), male and female participants improvised verse responses "per le rime" or dabbled in *centone* compositions piecing together lines from other lyrics.[17] The chief characteristic of the response is that it is a "corrigé" or a correction of a preceding piece.[18] Thus, in her responses, Catherine des Roches affirms her agency by "correcting" and even contradicting her male addressees. For example, in sonnets 10 and 11 of a sequence that the young lawyer Odet de Turnèbe wrote on the ruins of the legendary castle of Lusignan,[19] Turnèbe shifts from the poetry of ruins to a *carpe diem* love lament in which he bemoans his incapacity to move "une beauté cruelle, ingrate et fiere" (a cruel beauty, ungrateful and proud).[20] In her response 30, Des Roches contradicts Turnèbe's rhetoric of earthly love with an emphasis on the celestial Venus or spiritual, Neoplatonic love: Turnèbe, she states, through his learned writing on the ruined castle, has invited into it "la sage Logistile, / Les Muses, les Vertus, les Graces, et l'Amour / Je dy l'Amour venu de la Venus celeste" (wise Logistilla,[21] / The Muses, the Graces, and Love, / I mean the Love that comes from the celestial Venus) (ll. 14–15). Her final rejoinder is that Turnèbe should find satisfaction in his "excellent work" whose worth is guaranteed by his "virtue." She shifts the discursive terrain from his focus on short-lived physical/bodily love to the acquisition of immortality through writing and virtue.

Catherine des Roches affirms her writerly authority by positioning her replies with other responses written on other occasions and addressed to other readers besides the lawyers. In doing so, she disengages her production from the fetishist, univocal conversation on "her" flea. Several responses are addressed either to welcome admirers (1, 12, 36, 41) or to unwelcome suitors (4, 32, 37). Others concern more mundane matters: she sends René Brochart, her legal representative, a bouquet with a long ode attached to it (6); or she writes sympathetic advice to a female friend distraught over her husband's infidelities (42). The rest of the selected responses are to learned women (18, 34, 44), including her cousin Madeleine Chémeraut, a poet in her own right (10, 11), and to Jeanne de Bourbon, the noble abbess of the convent of Sainte Croix in Poitiers (29).

A response to a female admirer (3) seems to allude to love between women, an extremely rare topic in the Renaissance:[22] "I need no other Poet," Catherine writes, "and I wish no greater happiness / Than to call myself yours. / . . . One finds many Men / In love with a sweet flame, / But a woman loving a girl, / No other can pride herself on that."[23] While male poets such as Ronsard and Pontus de Tyard ventriloquize the female voice in their depiction of female-female desire, and the historian Brantôme refers to the lesbian practices of court women,[24] women poets generally desexualized the representation of the erotic. This is the case in Catherine's *Agnodice* (*Œuvres*) where the wives who have been freed by their female healer-turned-doctor embrace her, kissing "mille fois et sa bouche et son sein" (a thousand times both her mouth and her breast) (l. 115). The breast here evokes the image of the "nursing breast," symbolic source of knowledge in humanist child-care books. Catherine uses the same image of the nourishing breast in her poem *La Puce* (The Flea): whereas the breast is a fetishized, erotic site in the flea poems of the judges of the Grands Jours, her flea sucks "le sang incarnat / Qui colore un sein delicat" (the deep red blood / That colors such a delicate breast), finding there a "place honorable" (honorable place) for "nourriture et enseignement" (nourishment and learning).[25] How then should one read response 3? It is important to note that same-sex friendships in the early modern period, both men's and women's, found expression in a lexicon marked by an intense, almost physical attraction. In Orest Ranum's words: "For an individual of the early modern period, there could be no true friendship without such affection of one body for another."[26] Noble correspondences between same-sex friends included avowals of love and devotion proffered in a spirit similar to Catherine des Roches's to her admiring female friend.[27]

Lastly, Catherine des Roches's responses are marked by a refusal to be politically coopted. In an interesting discussion of the group publication of *La Puce*, Todd Olsen argues that the flea contest functions allegorically as a competition between the king's men, Parisian Parlementaires seeking the consolidation of royal power represented by the colonizing (male) flea, and the provincial "pucelle" (maiden) resisting royal political intervention.[28] Through her use of humanist citation and the rhetoric of exemplarity, Catherine disrupts her guests' "parasitic narrative." Her (female) flea in her poem *La Puce* abdicates all "cruel" bites (l. 37) and, metamorphosed into the Ovidian "chaste young maiden" Syrinx (l. 69), seeks refuge from rape and mental entrapment in Diana's virginal safe haven, none other than Des Roches's speaker. This female-to-female encounter functions doubly as political foil—the flea is a stand-in for feminine Poitiers[29]—and as the expression of feminine solidarity, a mirror image of the autonomy of the mother and daughter with respect to men.

SELECTED POEMS OF MADELEINE DES ROCHES

A MA FILLE

MAMIE, je sçay que la reverence, l'amour, et l'honnéte pudeur, ne vous permetent étre sans moy au papier des Imprimeurs, et qu'il vous plaît mieux que je suive mon devoir, mon desir, et ma coutume. Marchons doncques en cete union qui nous a toujours maintenues, et prions la Divine puissance, qu'elle vueille guider l'oeuvre, la pensée, et la parole de nous deux, nous preservant (s'il luy plaît) de toutes calomnies, et du venin de l'ingrate dent de l'Envie.

ODE 2

Esprit gentil, docte, expié
Ferme sur Arete apuié,
Amy aimé des Muses,
Pour mes passions enchanter,
Veuillez-moy de Grace préter   5
Vos excellentes ruses.

Ce grand Grec étoit enchanteur,
Ce grave et sage correcteur
Des mignons d'Uranie,
Qui par le Vice combatu,   10
Rapella du Ciel la Vertu,
Par sa douce Harmonie.

Si fut Orphé', et Amphion:
Et le pensé d'Amphytrion,
Par sa douce Eloquence,   15
A mieux le Gaulois surmonté,
Que le Romain ne l'a domté,
Par l'éfort de sa lance.

Courte d'argent et de raison,
Je veus bâtir une Maison,   20
Et trouver une bourse,
En creusant un vieux Fondement
D'un miserable bâtiment,
Qui n'a point de resource.

SELECTED POEMS OF MADELEINE DES ROCHES

TO MY DAUGHTER

LOVE, I know that out of reverence, love, and honorable modesty, you will not send anything to the printers' shop without me,[30] and that you would rather I follow my duty, my desire, and my customary ways. Let us continue then in that union which has always kept us together, and let us pray that the Divine Power may always guide us in our work, our thoughts, and our words, protecting us, if it pleases Him, from all calumny, and from the venom of ungrateful Envy.

ODE 2[31]

Noble, learned, and pure spirit,[32]
Firmly supported by Arete,[33]
Friend beloved of the Muses,
To enchant my passions,
Lend me, I beg you,   5
Your excellent wiles.

That famed Greek was an enchanter,
A grave and wise reformer
Of the minions of Urania,[34]
Who to combat Vice,   10
Brought down Virtue from Heaven,
With his sweet Harmony.

Thus were Orpheus[35] and Amphion;[36]
And Amphitryon who with his intellect, [37]
And his gentle Eloquence,   15
Vanquished the Gaul better
Than could the Roman who tried to do so
With the force of his lance.

Short on money and on reason,
I'd like to build a House,   20
And find myself a purse,
To dig out the old Foundation
Of a decrepit building,
That has lost its worth.[38]

La fievre tient mon cher souci,   25
Je languis de la fievre aussi,
Mon Mari d'un caterre;
La maladie a pris acces,
Ah! Medecins, Juges, proces,
Trois pestes de la Terre.   30

Au lieu de manger et dormir,
Le plaint, le pleur, et le gemir
Me servent de viande;
Je n'oy qu'un propos ennuyeux,
Je n'ay qu'un penser odieux   35
Qui, maitre, me commande.

Mes maux se suivent de si pres,
Que du seul funeste cypres,
Maintenant j'ay envie,
Si le conseil et le repos,   40
Qui vient de vos sages propos,
Ne rassure ma vie.

Vous donc, Esprit saint et divin,
Honneur du sejour Poitevin,
Amy aimé des Muses,   45
Pour mes passions enchanter,
Veuillez-moy de Grace préter
Vos excellentes ruses.

SONNETZ
1
La sacre-sainte Deité,
Aux veux des Humains tant propice,
Exerce vers nous son ofice,
Par une douce Charité.
Mais pourtant la Divinité
Du beau Soleil de sa justice,
Ne veut pas afubler le Vice
Du manteau de la Verité,
Ainsi que vous, qui par louange
Faites souvent d'un Diable un Ange,

A fever takes hold of my dearest love,[39]   25
I too languish in fever,
My Husband suffers from a rheumatism;
Sickness has made its way in,
Ah! Doctors, Judges, lawsuits,
The three plagues of the Earth!   30

Instead of eating and sleeping,
Moaning, crying, and groaning
Serve as my daily sustenance;
I hear only wearisome words,
I think only hateful thoughts   35
Which are my master and control me.

My misfortunes follow one another so closely
That now I want nothing
But the cypress of death,
If counsel and rest,   40
Which come from your wise words,
Do not save my life.

You, therefore, saintly and divine Spirit,
Honor of our native Poitou,
Friend beloved of the Muses,   45
To enchant my passions,
Lend me, I beg you,
Your excellent wiles.

SONNETS

1[40]

The sacrosanct Deity,
So auspicious to the wishes of Humans,
Exercises on our behalf His mercy
By means of a sweet Charity.
But beware, for the Divinity,
With the beautiful light of His justice,
Does not wish to dress up Vice
Under the cloak of Truth,
As you do, who with your praise,
Often make an Angel out of a Devil,

Par un argument plus subtil.
Je suy en tout la Doriéne,
Car pour la fraze Helleniéne,
Je n'ay l'Esprit assez gentil.

2

Celuy qui, d'un clin d'oeil, forma la terre et l'onde,
Qui fait luyre sur nous les celestes flambeaux,
Qui, du vent de sa voix, fit les ornemens beaux,
Dont l'accord discordant tient les membres du monde,
Voit ores, par quel art, vostre plume feconde
Donne vie et honneur à deus Rochers nouveaux;
Je crains qu'il vous punisse avec ses justes fleaux,
Comme larron du feu de la grand' torche blonde.
Prenéz donc, s'il vous plaît, un plus digne sujet,
Vray, acomply, sacré, saint et louable objet,
Qui fera bien en vous renaistre un autre foye:
Non comme Promethé pour la terre amollir,
Ny pour vouloir un roc parer et embellir,
Que d'un aigle nouveau vous ne soiez la proye.

3

Tout ainsi qu'Eumetis, et la docte Aspasie,
Ont pris des sçavants Grecz le plus digne ornement,
Vous me voulez donner forme et entendement,
Par les excellents traitz de vostre poesie.
La grande Diotime a eu l'ame saisie
De ce Dœmon qui va les ames transformant,
Et sage vous allez le vice reformant
Par la sainte raison, vostre guide choisie.
Vous sçavez plus de loix que Lycurgue, et Solon;
Vous estes eslevé sur le char d'Apollon;
Vous estes favory de la plus chaste Muse.
Si je veus faire voir vostre renom tant beau,
C'est monstrer le Soleil avecques un flambeau.
Ainsi le non pouvoir me servira d'excuse.

4

Je croy que le bonheur ne dépend que de nous,
Madame, et que chascun peut forger sa fortune:
Le fol trop indiscret se la rend importune,

Through your very wily arguments.
In everything I follow the Dorian,[41]
Because for the Hellenic phrase,
I don't own a sweet enough Mind.

2

He who, in the twinkling of an eye, created earth and sea,
Who makes bright stars to shine upon us
And, by the wind of His voice, breathes beauty all around,
Whose discordant accord[42] holds the parts of the world together,
He, then, sees by what art your fertile pen
Gives life and honor to two new rocks;[43]
I fear He may punish you with His righteous judgments,
In the same way as the thief who stole fire from the great heavenly torch.[44]
Choose then, I pray, a worthier subject,
A true, accomplished, sacred, holy, and laudable object,
That will cause another liver to be reborn within you:
Not like Prometheus to soften the earth,
Or to adorn or beautify a rock,
So you may not be the prey of a new eagle.

3

Just as Eumetis[45] and the learned Aspasia[46]
Took from Greek scholars their most worthy knowledge,
You wish to give me form and understanding
Through the excellence of your poetry.
Great Diotima had her soul filled[47]
By this Daemon who goes about transforming souls,[48]
And wise, you go about reforming vice
Through sacred reason, your chosen guide.
You know more laws than Lycurgus and Solon;[49]
You have found a place on Apollo's chariot;
You are favored by the most chaste Muse.
Should I wish to reveal your glorious renown,
It would be like illuminating the sun with a torch.
And so my inability will serve as excuse.

4

I think that happiness depends solely upon us,[50]
Madame, and that we can all forge our own destiny:
The fool, too indiscreet, renders his troublesome,

Le sage la conduit d'un mouvement plus dous.
La preuve s'en fait claire aux actions de tous.
Au theatre mondain de la fable commune,
Tous les humains, enclos soubz le Ciel de la Lune,
Trament leur bien et mal, leur plaisir, et courrous.
Celle qui a de l'heur sans estre mariée,
Elle est heureuse aussi en se trouvant liée
Aux sainctes loix d'Hymen, et si amour l'esprit
Avec l'heureux flambeau d'un chaste mariage,
Elle est heureuse encor en son simple veufvage,
Pource que son bonheur depend de son Esprit.

POITIERS À MESSIEURS DES GRANDZ JOURS

Ny mes Rochers hautains qui voisinent les Cieux,
Ny de mes chams fleuris l'abondance fertille,
Ny du Passe-lourdin[51] la demarche subtille,
Ny de mes dous Zephirs le soupir gracieux,
Ny mes espris locauls, mes tutelaires Dieux,
Ny de ma chere Echo la voix douce-gentille,
Ny de mes Citoyens la police civile,
Ny de mes temples saintz le choeur devotieux,
Ny de ma grand' Themys la prudence honorée,
Ny de mes sages loix la force reverée,
Ny du Ciel favorable un oeil tousjours benin,
Ne sçauroient m'animer autant que ces Orphées,
Qui tirant de l'oubly mes gloires estoufées,
Me font luyre partout comme un astre divin.

HUITAIN

Vous avez violé le droit et l'equité,
Renonçeant à la foy promise à nostre France,
Vous voiant sans la foy, l'espoir vous a quité,
Pouviez-vous esperer pardon de telle offense?
Et puis vous demandez des villes d'asseurance
Au Roy que vous avez tant de fois irrité,
Mais puisque vous n'avez la foy, ny l'esperance,
Vous ne meritez pas d'avoir la charité.

The wise guides it with a steadier hand.
The proof is made clear by the actions of all.
In the worldly theater of familiar fables,
All humans, enclosed beneath the Moon's Heaven,
Weave together good and evil, pleasure and pain.
A woman happy enough without being married,
Is also happy in finding herself bound
To Hymen's holy laws, and if love overtakes her
With the happy flame of a chaste marriage,
She's still happy even in her widowhood,
Because her contentment depends on her spirit.

POITIERS TO THE GENTLEMEN OF THE GRANDS JOURS

Neither my high boulders that approach the Heavens,
Nor the fertile abundance of my flowery fields,
Nor the subtle progression of my rocky pass,
Nor the graceful sighs of my gentle Zephyrs,
Nor the surrounding spirits, my protective Gods,
Nor the sweet, gentle voice of my dear Echo,[52]
Nor the civil policies of my citizens,
Nor the devoted choirs of my holy temples,
Nor the honorable prudence of my great Themis,[53]
Nor the revered strength of my wise laws,
Nor the always-kind eye looking down from Heaven,
Could enliven me as much as these Orpheuses,[54]
Who by bringing back into the limelight my forgotten glories,
Make me shine everywhere like a heavenly star.[55]

OCTET[56]

You have violated the law and justice,
By renouncing the faith promised to our France,
Seeing you without faith, hope has left you,
Could you expect forgiveness for such an offense?
And then you ask for places of refuge
From the King you have irked so many times,
But since you have neither faith nor hope,
You do not deserve charity.[57]

SELECTED POEMS OF CATHERINE DES ROCHES

EPISTRE A SA MERE

MA MERE, vous m'avez animée comme Promethé, l'image de terre que luy-mémes forma, et n'est point d'un feu desrobé : car il vous fut donné des Cieux. Or connoissant que je tiens de vous, non seulement ceste mortelle vie, mais encore la vie de ma vie, je vous suy partout comme l'ombre le cors: Et tout ainsi que le cors en ses proportions, ny l'ombre en son estandue ne sont point veus sans la faveur de la lumiere, ainsi la vive clarté de vostre entendement nous fait voir par un sentier non gueres frequenté, où je prie Dieu, MA MERE, que nous puis- [11v°] sions trouver plus d'Oliviers que de Houx. La branche paisible de l'arbre de Pallas nous est autant necessaire que l'estoit à Enée, le rameau d'or enseigné par Deiphobe. Je sçay que l'Or, filz de la Terre, fait trouver beaucoup de credit chez sa mere, mais nous avons aussi les vers dorez du sage Samien qui demonstre, en ses escris, et recommande ce que vos admirables vertus font voir à tous ceux qui vous connoissent. Pource qu'il desire de parler, je me tairay, MA MERE, apres avoir humblement supplié la bonté divine, qu'il luy plaise rendre vos jours longs en prospere fortune afin que vous soiez longtemps sur terre, exemple des graces du Ciel.

LES RESPONCES

1

Comme Dieu rend toute divine
L'Ame qu'il luy plait d'atirer,
L'Amant subtilise et afine
Celle qu'il monstre desirer.
Dieu, par sa puissance eternelle,   5
Enflame, agite les Espris,
L'Amant, d'une Grace immortelle,
Embellit le Beau qui l'a pris.
Ce ne sont les vertus des Ames
Qui les elevent dans les cieux,   10
Ce ne sont les beautez des Dames
Qui font Amour victorieux.
Celle qui n'a rien d'estimable
Sinon qu'elle plait seulemant,
Par une puissance admirable   15
Se voit Divine en son Amant.
Doncques, ô beautez Printanieres,
Durant la fleur des jeunes ans,

SELECTED POEMS OF CATHERINE DES ROCHES

EPISTLE TO HER MOTHER

MOTHER, you gave me life as Prometheus did to the earthen image which he himself formed, and neither was the fire lacking, for that was given to you by Heaven.[58] Now, knowing that I have received from you not only this mortal life but the life of my life, I follow you everywhere as the shadow follows the body. And just as neither the body in all its proportions nor the shadow in its projection can be seen without the grace of light, so the brilliant clarity of your mind illumines for us the narrow path where, MY MOTHER, I hope we will gather more olive branches than holly.[59] The peace-bearing branch of the tree of Pallas is as necessary to us as was to Aeneas the golden bough divulged to him by Deiphobus.[60] I know that Gold, the son of Earth, brings great credit to his mother, but we have the golden verse of the wise Samian[61] who demonstrates and recommends in his writings what your admirable virtues make clear to all those who know you. Since he wishes to speak, I'll be silent, MY MOTHER, after humbly beseeching God that it please Him to lengthen and prosper your days so that you may live a long life, an example of the graces of Heaven.

RESPONSES

   1 [To an admirer][62]

Just as God makes divine
The soul it pleases Him to attract,
So a lover perfects and adorns
Her whom he desires.
While God, with His eternal power,   5
Inspires and stirs our Minds,
A lover, with an immortal Grace,
Embellishes the Beauty who has captured him.
Hence, it is not the Soul's virtues
That lift it up to the heavens,   10
It is not Women's beauty
That renders Love all victorious.
She who has no inherent worth
Other than that she's pleasing,
Finds that she becomes Divine   15
Through her Lover's admirable eloquence.
Therefore, O Springtime beauties,
During the flower of your youthful years,

Ne soiez superbes, ny fieres,
Pour ce qui dure peu de tans.   20
Croiez que le feu qui s'alume
Par vos regards, arréte peu,
Si une favorable plume
N'atise doucement ce feu.
Et vous, Monsieur, que le Pimandre   25
Atire, embraze, émeut, époint,
Sagement vous faites entendre
De quelles fléches il vous point.

    3

Puisqu'il vous plait de me louer,
Je n'ay besoin d'autre Poete,
Et plus grand heur je ne souhaite
Sinon de vostre m'avouer.
Je ne desire point de voir
Qu'un Petrarque chante ma gloire,
Puisque dedans vostre memoire
Il vous plait de me recevoir.
L'on voit plusieurs Hommes chanter,
Epris d'une flame gentille,
Mais de Femme aimant une fille,
Nulle autre s'en peut vanter.

    4

Cete amitié par vous represantée
Et que vos vers redisent si souvent,
N'est pas en moy, vous l'avez mise au vent,
Je ne veux point d'une Amour éventée.

    6

Pour adoucir la solitude
Qui vous retient en vostre étude,
D'un Bouquet je vous fais presant,
Desirant qu'il vous soit plaisant.
Il n'est pas de grande dépanse,   5
Et peut servir de recompanse
A ces Bouquetz bien façonnez,
Que déjà vous m'avez donnez.
Les Fleurs en sont de bonne augure,

Be neither arrogant nor proud,
Of what lasts but a short while.   20
Believe me, the fire that is lit
By your gaze will soon die out
If a talented pen
Does not gently stoke it.[63]
And you, Monsieur, whom the *Pimander*[64]   25
Attracts, sets on fire, moves, and inspires,
You wisely make known
By which arrows it stings you.

3 [On a female friend's love and friendship for the author]
Since it pleases you to praise me,
I need no other Poet,
And I wish no greater happiness
Than to call myself yours.
I do not wish to see
A Petrarch sing my glory,
Since within your memory
It pleases you to hold me dear.
One finds many Men
In love with a sweet flame,
But a Woman loving a girl,
No other can pride herself on that.

4 [To an unwelcome suitor]
This friendship that you vaunt,
That your verses so often repeat,
I don't share, you divulge it to the winds,
I refuse a wind-puffed Love.

6 [To René Brochart][65]
To lighten the solitude
That keeps you in your study,
I offer you a Bouquet,
Hoping it will please you.
Although not a costly one,   5
It will serve as reward
For all those well-fashioned Bouquets
That you've often given me.
Its Flowers are of good omen,

L'odeur en est fort douce et pure.   10
Je ne veux point que le Muguet
Aparoisse dans ce Bouquet,
Ny que l'amoureuse Clytie
Y face jaunir la Sousie,
Ny qu'Hyacinth' y trouve lieu;   15
Car bien qu'il fust aymé d'un Dieu,
C'estoit un joueur ordinaire,
Dont la façon ne me doit plaire.
Je n'y veux point la Fleur d'Adon,
Ny de celuy que son brandon   20
Brula dans l'onde crystaline,
Aimant trop sa beauté divine,
Ny de cet Ajax coleré
Qui se trouvant desesperé
Pour les armes du Peleide   25
Fut de soy-méme l'homicide.
Celles-là sont Fleurs de mal-heur,
Ces autres sont Fleurs de valeur.
Je veux que la Rose incarnate
Y montre sa Fleur delicate,   30
Et que le Damas rougissant
Y soit en Grace paroissant.
Je veux que l'unique Pensée
S'y montre premiere advancée,
Et que le prophete Laurier   35
Soit de ce bouquet le pilier.
Je veux la Marguerite belle
Qui tient le nom d'une Pucelle,
Et d'une perle; aussi je veus
Le Mastic, le Thim odorens,   40
Et que la fraiche Marjolaine
Y répande sa douce halaine.
J'y veux le Romarin fleuri,
L'Espy de l'Hyver favori,
Qui dessoubz la glace nuysante   45
Retient une odeur si plaisante.
J'y veux la Giroflée aussi:
Et vous y veux, mon cher souci,
Ma fleur sur toutes estimée,

Their aroma sweet and pure. 10
In this Bouquet I do not want
The Lily of the valley[66] to appear,
Nor that love-stricken Clytia[67]
Who turned into a yellow Marigold,
Nor the Hyacinth to find a place in it; 15
For although he was loved by a God,[68]
He was an ordinary player,
Whose behavior does not please me.
Neither do I want the Flower of Adonis,[69]
Nor the one whose firebrand 20
Burned in the crystalline source
Because he loved his divine beauty too much,[70]
Nor that choleric Ajax
Who, in despair
Over the armor of Achilles, 25
Killed himself.[71]
These are Flowers of unhappiness,
While the others are Flowers of great worth.
Instead I'll select the ruby-red Rose
To display its delicate Flower, 30
And the reddening Damson
To appear there in all its Grace.
I'd like the unique Pansy
To be the first to be noticed,
And the prophetic Laurel[72] 35
To be the bouquet's center.
I'll select the beautiful Marguerite,
Who bears the name of both a Maiden
And a pearl; and also I want
The Mastic, the aromatic Thyme, 40
And the fresh Marjoram
To spread its gentle scent.
I'll find you the flowery Rosemary,[73]
A favorite among winter's plants,
Which beneath the harmful ice 45
Retains such a pleasing aroma.
I'll also pick the Gillyflower;
And you, my sweet marigold,
Whom I esteem above all others,

Vous seule qui étes nommée   50
D'un Dieu, d'un mois, et d'une fleur,
Et portez du Ciel la couleur.
O Fleurs de ce jour épanies,
Jamais ne soiez-vous fanies,
Soiez presage de bon-heur   55
A celuy qui vous fait honneur.
Qui vous aime, caresse, et baise,
Puisse toujours vivre à son aise.

9

Si Numa défandoit de pourtraire les Dieux,
En exemptant de l'Art les formes eternelles,
Qui represantera vos Graces immortelles,
Et vostre Esprit divin, rare presant des Cieux?
L'on a veu d'autrefois d'un art laborieux
Parrasius, Zeuxis, Protogenes, Apelles,
Raporter aux mortelz des figures si belles
Que leurs espris étoient derobez par les yeux.
Il ne faut seulement represanter les faces
De qui les dous atraitz tirent hors de leurs places,
Par les sens trahissans, les volages espris.
Mais toutes les beautez, demeurant en vostre ame,
Vous alumez aux cueurs une celeste flame,
Et plus sain est celuy qui plus en est epris.

10

Cousine, mon cher souci,
Je te demande une excuse,
En ofrant un grand-merci
A ta gracieuse Muse.
Vraiment, je te sçay bon gré   5
D'avoir incité ma plume
Pour dire l'honneur sacré
De l'amour qui nous alume.
Celant l'agreable neu,
Où nos cueurs se viennent rendre,   10
C'est cacher un luysant feu
Dessoubs une obscure cendre.
La purité de tes meurs,
La douceur de ton langage,

You alone are named   50
For a God,[74] for a month, and for a flower,
And reflect Heaven's glow.
O Flowers, today in full bloom,
May you never wilt,
Shine forth as omens of happiness   55
To him who does you such honor.
May he who loves, caresses, and prizes you
Always live in delight.

    9 [Sonnet to Marie de Lavau][75]
If Numa prohibited the making of effigies of the Gods,
By exempting from Art the eternal forms,[76]
Who then will paint your imperishable Graces,
And your divine Mind, rare gift of the Heavens?
In the past, we've seen with what a laborious art
Parrhasius, Zeuxis, Protogenes, and Apelles[77]
Showed mortals figures of such beauty
That the sight stole their spirits away.
One must not merely represent faces
Whose enticing attractions, by their traitorous senses,
Seduce fickle minds.
But all your beauties, firmly planted in your soul,
Enable you to ignite in hearts a celestial flame.
And it's better for someone to fall in love with them.

    10 [To Madeleine Chémeraut][78]
Cousin, dearest,
I ask you to excuse me,
By offering the thanks I owe
Your gracious Muse.
I'm truly grateful   5
That you have inspired my pen
To reveal the sacred and honorable
Love that unites us both.
For to conceal such an agreeable bond,
So deeply rooted in our hearts,   10
Is like hiding a brightly burning fire
Beneath a darkened ash.
The purity of your morals,
The sweetness of your words,

Montrant des pensers tous meurs   15
Dedans un fleurissant age,

Meritent que le Bon-heur,
D'une Ame sage et sçavante,
Voulant chanter ton honneur,
L'honneur d'elle-mesme chante.   20
Bien qu'en cela mon pouvoir
N'égale point ta pensée,
Je m'éjouis de me voir
Toujours par toy devancée.
D'une si sainte amitié   25
Je reçoy toute la gloire,
Mais toy, plus digne moitié,
Prens l'honneur de la victoire.

     11
Ma Cousine, je voy
Tes belles traces
Qu'heureuse je reçoy,
Des mains des Graces.
Regardant ton écrit   5
Plain d'allegresse,
Je sans que mon Esprit
Le tien caresse.
Combien que de tes yeux
Loin je demeure,   10
Si te voy-je en mains lieux
En moins d'une heure.
Le Cors lourd et massif
N'est pas nous-méme,
Mais c'est l'Esprit naïf   15
Que le Ciel aime.
Ton Esprit pur et beau
Que tant j'honore,
Résemble ce flambeau
Qui le jour dore.   20
L'un éclaire cet air
Que l'on respire,
L'autre éclaire un parler
Que l'on admire.

Displaying such mature thoughts   15
In a youthful frame,

Merit that the Happiness
Of a wise and learned Soul,
Wishing to sing your honor,
Sings its own.   20
Although in this my ability
Does not equal your learning,
I rejoice in seeing myself
Continually outdone by you.
Of such a mutual sacred friendship,   25
I receive all the glory,
But you, my more worthy half,
Take the honor of the victory.

    11 [To Madeleine Chémeraut]
Cousin dearest, I'm reading
Your beautiful letters
That happily I receive
From the hands of the Graces.
Looking at these writings   5
Filled with happy thoughts,
I sense my Mind
In communion with yours.
However far from your gaze
I find myself,   10
I see you in all sorts of places
In under an hour!
The heavy and massive Body
Is not us ourselves,
For it is our inner Mind   15
That Heaven loves.[79]
Your pure and beautiful Spirit
That I honor so much,
Resembles the torch[80]
That gives light to day.   20
The latter illuminates the air
That we breathe,
The former illuminates the speech
That we admire.

12

Ainsi que l'onde pousse l'onde,
Que la nuit va suivant le jour,
Le Soleil, ornement du monde,
Chasse les ombres à son tour.
Et comme nous voyons leur étre   5
Reglé par un cours éternel,
Ainsi le mourir et le naitre
Entre nous est perpetuel,
Puisque la Matiere et la Forme
Par un assidu changement   10
De l'un en l'autre se transforme,
Changeant de face en un moment.
La Pyramide Ægyptienne,
Et le Colosse Rhodien,
En perdant leur forme ancienne   15
Pourtant ne sont reduitz à rien.
L'on voit d'une ville pillée
Une autre prendre acroissement,
Par les ruines d'Aquilée,
Venise print commancement.   20
Voions-nous un plaisant visage
Changer son vermeil en palleur?
Nature, bonne mere et sage,
En va mettre un autre en valeur.
Ce n'est point le tans qui s'envole,   25
C'est la douce Fleur des beaux Ans,
Mais par l'air de vostre parole
La Vertu triomphe du Tans.
Bien que d'une louange feinte,
Dont vous étes le vray Sonneur,   30
Vous donniez une gloire peinte
Prenant le veritable honneur:
Si est-ce que la Renommée
Ne peut chanter vos vers tant dous,
Que moy par leur Grace animée   35
Ne vole au ciel avecques vous.
Et plus vous me voiez indigne
De tant de belles fictions,
Et plus vostre Muse divine

12 [To an admirer]
Just as one wave sends off another,[81]
As night follows day,
So the Sun, our world's embellishment,
Drives away in turn all shadows.
And as we see the world's existence   5
Regulated by an eternal course,
So death and birth
Are perpetually with us,
Since Matter and Form
Through constant change   10
Transform themselves one into another,
Changing their appearance in an instant.
The Egyptian Pyramid
And the Colossus of Rhodes,[82]
In losing their ancient form   15
Are not, however, reduced to rubble.
We see from one plundered city
Another built up in its place,
From the ruins of Aquileia,
Venice had its beginnings.   20
Do we now see a pleasing face
Change its vermilion to paleness?
Nature, good and wise mother,
Puts another beautiful one in its place.
It is not time that flies away,   25
But rather the sweet Flower of our beautiful Years;[83]
Yet by the grace of your very words,
Virtue triumphs over Time.
Although with feigned praises,
Of which you are the real author,   30
You give me a fictitious glory,
You, in fact, reap all the honor for yourself:
Fame can no more
Sing your sweet verses,
Than I can fly to the heavens by your side   35
On account of their Grace.
And the more you see me unworthy
Of such fancy fictions,
The more your divine muse

Est riche en ses inventions.   40
Si bien que vostre Poësie
Vers vous m'aquite prontement,
Payant à vostre courtoysie
Le pris de vostre jugement.
Mais, pourtant, je ne me dispanse   45
De payer mon humble devoir,
Car le Ciel fait la recompanse
Pour ceux qui manquent de pouvoir.

18

Pour voir toutes beautez du Cors et de l'Esprit,
Tournez vos yeux sur vous: voiez vostre excellence
Et vous lirez encor cete belle sentence
Qu'Apollon Delphien a mise par écrit.
Pour voir de la Vertu les plus dignes pourtraitz   5
Il ne faut qu'observer vos coutumes louables,
Vos Ecris dous-coulans, vos Discours admirables,
Ce sont de la Vertu les bien-heureux éfaitz.
Vous, Nymphe des Beautez et Graces le sejour,
Produisez devant tous ces tesmoins sans reproches,   10
Que vous et la Vertu étes toujours si proches
Et que sa Deïté brule de vostre Amour.
Puisque l'Aimant se voit aux yeux de son Aimé,
La Vertu voit en vous ses divines lumieres,
Et retenant pour vous les Ames prisonnieres   15
Fait mouvoir mon Esprit par le vostre animé.

23

Comme la lumiere brillante
Du Soleil, ornement des cieux,
Nous rend toute couleur plaisante
Eclairant prontement nos yeux;
Si bien que cete splendeur vive   5
Penetrant doucement un oeil,
Fait que l'objet qui luy arrive
Luy résemble un autre Soleil;
Ainsi vostre Ame sage et belle,
Ayant tourné longtans vers soy   10
Pour voir sa beauté immortelle
La pense voir encor en moy.

Is fertile in her inventions, 40
So much so that your Poetry
Promptly acquits me of my debt to you,
By paying for your courtesy
At the expense of your judgment.
But, nevertheless, I will not forgo 45
Paying off my humble duty,
For Heaven rewards
Those with less ability.

18 [To a learned and virtuous lady]
To contemplate all the beauties of Body and Mind,
Simply turn your eyes on yourself: see your own excellence
And you shall read that beautiful maxim
That Apollo the Delphian put into writing.[84]
To see the most worthy examples of Virtue 5
One need only observe your customary ways,
Your sweet-sounding Writings, your admirable Discourses,
These are the blessed effects of your Virtue.
Nymph, the dwelling of the Beauties and of the Graces,
You produce, before all, these impeccable proofs that 10
You and Virtue are always intimate
And that she burns with your Love.
Just as the loved one is mirrored in the eyes of the Lover,
So Virtue sees in you its divine rays,
And in catching for you Souls as prisoners 15
It inspires my Mind to be quickened by yours.

23 [To Odet de Turnèbe][85]
As the Sun's bright rays,
Ornament of the heavens,
Make every color pleasant to see
And readily fill our eyes with light,
Such that their lively splendor, 5
Gently penetrating one's eyes,
Make the object one perceives
Resemble another Sun,
So your perceptive and wise Soul,
Having for a time contemplated itself 10
To see its immortal beauty,
Thinks it also sees it in me.

Mais des Graces et Vertus rares
Qui vous font admirer de tous,
Les Dieux m'en ont été avares   15
Pour les prodiguer dedans vous.

24

Vostre encre est de ce just qui change l'Homme en Dieu,
Dont Glauque avoit mangé, quand il quita son lieu
Pour les Ondes laissant nostre terre fleurie.
Comme le clair flambeau de ce grand univers
Ternit les moindres feux, la Grace de vos vers
Fait mourir mes écris, et me donne la vie.

29

La Beauté, la doctrine, et la grave douceur,
Qui orne vostre front, vostre esprit, vostre Grace,
Atire doucement, et retient et enlasse
A celuy qui vous voit les yeux, l'Ame et le cueur.
Puis vous avez encor la faveur, le bien, l'heur,
De Vertu, de Fortune, et d'une antique race,
Si que les nourrissons de Smyrne, Thebes, Thrace,
Chantant vostre honneur saint, se feroient grand honneur.
Que doy-je faire donc, sinon par le Silence
Honorer vos valeurs d'une humble reverence,
Baisant vos blanches mains en toute humilité?
Voiant tant de Beautez, de Vertus, de merites,
De sçavoir, de sagesse, et de chastes Charites
Ne demontrer en vous que la Divinité.

30

Les Daemons qui gardoient la poudreuse rüine
Du superbe Palais que bâtit Melusine,
Aiant pitié de voir cet ouvrage tant beau
Prontement demoli, vous inspirent dans l'Ame
Un louable desir d'imiter cete Dame,   5
Et faire un chasteau neuf dessus le vieux chasteau.
Mais voiant que le bois, que le fer, que la pierre
Ne peuvent défier le feu, l'eau, ny la guerre,
Et qu'ilz servent toujours au triomphe du Tans,
Il vous plait bien que l'ancre, et la plume, et le livre,   10
Grave plus dur qu'un Roc, que le Marbre, ou le Cuivre

But the Graces and unique Virtues
That make you admired by all,
Have been sparingly given to me by the Gods   15
Who preferred to shower them upon you.

24 [To Estienne Pasquier][86]
Your ink is of just the kind that changes Man into a God,
The kind that Glaucus[87] ate when he sprang into
The Waves, leaving behind our flowered meadows.
As the bright torch of this great universe
Makes all fires pale, so the Grace of your verses
Brings death to my writings, and to me life.

29 [Sonnet to Jeanne de Bourbon, Abbess of Sainte-Croix][88]
The Beauty, learning, and grave sweetness
That adorns your forehead, your spirit, and your Grace,
Gently attracts, and retains, and embraces
Whoever sees your eyes, your Soul, and your heart.
For in you reside such favor, goodness, and happiness
Of Virtue, Fortune, and an ancient lineage,
That the offspring of Smyrna, Thebes, and Thrace,[89]
In praising your holy honor, would do themselves a great honor.
What must I do then except honor
In Silence your worth with a humble curtsy,
And kiss your white hands in all humility?
Seeing so much Beauty, Virtue, and merit,
Knowledge, wisdom, and chaste Charity
Shows forth in you only what is divine.

30 [To Odet de Turnèbe][90]
The Daemons who guarded the dusty ruins
Of the splendid Palace that Melusina built,[91]
Full of pity at seeing such a beautiful masterpiece
So quickly demolished, inspired in your Soul
A laudable desire to imitate that Lady,   5
And to build a new castle where the old one stood.
But when you saw that neither wood, iron, nor stone
Can withstand fire, water, or war,
And that they always serve the triumph of Time,
It pleased you to choose ink, the pen, and the book,   10
To engrave harder than a rock, than marble or copper,

Ce Fort qui tiendra fort contre l'effort des Ans.
Ce logis étant né de vostre Ame gentille,
Vous y faites venir la sage Logistile,
Les Muses, les Vertus, les Graces, et l'Amour,   15
Je dy l'Amour venu de la Venus celeste;
Et pour rendre à tous yeux sa Gloire manifeste,
Phoebus y fait toujours éclairer un beau jour.
Vous donques, ô ESPRIT ORNÉ DE BEAUTÉ DINE,
Qui atirez du Ciel une troupe divine   20
Pour luy faire illustrer ce brave bâtiment,
Je croy que le plaisir qui vous plait davantage,
C'est l'honneur d'avoir fait cet excelant ouvrage,
Et que vostre Vertu luy serve d'ornement.

       31

Le Feu est le premier de tous les Elemens,
Illustre, pur, et beau, qui par sa vive flame
Eclaire, agite, émeut, les yeux, le cueur, et l'Ame,
C'est l'Esprit des Espris, cause des sentimens.
Vulcan, maitre du feu, ardoit le Dieu des Dieux
Quand sa teste enfanta la grand' Tritoniene,
Sa méme Deité honorant vostre peine
Vous fait chanter des vers qui volent jusqu'aux Cieux.
Comme cet element vous tenez un haut lieu,
Divin, vous élongnez cete masse de Terre,
Ny la Terre, ny l'Eau, ny l'Air ne vous font guerre,
Et ne pouvez bruler, vous qui n'étes que Feu.

       32

Quand vous montrez de me connoitre
Avec un parler gracieux,
Humble vous me voiez paroitre
Salüant doucement vos yeux.
Mais quand vous avez une grace
Dédaigneuse et pleine d'orgueil,
Brave je détourne ma face
Afin de ne voir point vostre œil.
Demandez-vous preuve plus grande
De l'Amitié que je vous doy,
Si vostre bouche me commande,
Et que vostre œil me donne loy?

This fort that will stand strong against the erosion of the years.
To this dwelling, engendered by your noble Soul,
You invite wise Logistilla,[92]
The Muses, the Graces, the Virtues, and Love,   15
I mean the Love that comes from the celestial Venus;[93]
And to display to all eyes her manifest Glory,
Phoebus[94] always makes it a bright day.
To you, therefore, O SPIRIT ADORNED WITH WORTHY BEAUTY,[95]
Who attract from Heaven a divine multitude   20
To bring honor upon this proud edifice,
I believe that the pleasure that more pleases you
Is the honor of having written this excellent work,
And that your Virtue serves as its adornment.

    31 [To Étienne Pasquier][96]
Fire is the first of all the Elements.
Illustrious, pure, and beautiful, with its lively flame
It brightens, moves, and stirs one's eyes, heart, and Soul;
It's the Spirit of Spirits, cause of all feelings.[97]
Vulcan, master of fire, burned within the God of Gods
When from the latter's head came forth great Athena,[98]
That same deity honoring your work
Makes you sing verses that fly up to the Heavens.
Like this element, you hold a high place,
Divine, you leave behind this mass of Earth,
Neither Earth, nor Water, nor Air make war on you,
And you cannot burn, you who are but Fire.

    32 [To an arrogant and disrespectful suitor]
When you will show me that you can address me
With gracious words,
Humble I'll appear to you,
Gently meeting your gaze.
But when you show that you're
Disdainful and filled with pride,
I boldly turn my face away
So as not to meet your eye.
How can you demand a greater proof
Of the Friendship I owe you,
If your mouth commands me,
And your eyes order me around?

33

Dy-moy, ROCHETTE, que fais-tu?
Ha! tu rougis, c'est de la honte
De voir un pourtrait qui surmonte
Ta foible et debile Vertu.
BINET a voulu dextrement　　　　　　　　　5
Represanter une peinture,
Qui est de celeste Nature,
Et la nommer humainement.
Aiant pillé dedans les Cieux
Le pourtrait d'une belle Idée,　　　　　　10
Ne voulant comme Promethée
Irriter le courroux des Dieux:
D'un artifice nompareil
Il a voilé son beau visage
D'un nom obscur, comme un nuage　　　　15
Qui cache les rais du Soleil.
C'est afin de n' étre repris,
Rendant aux Hommes manifeste
Une beauté toute celeste,
Digne des immortelz Espris.　　　　　　20
ROCHE, tu ne sçaurois user
D'un autre plus evident signe
D'étre de tant d'honneurs indigne,
Que ne pouvoir t'en excuser.

34

Si la Beauté, la richesse,
Le sçavoir, la gentillesse,
Decorent vostre Printans,
Faites que la Vertu sage,
Soit dedans vostre courage,　　　　　　5
Fleur de la Fleur de vos ans.
Prenant si seure conduite,
Tout Bien soit à vostre suite,
Voiez longtans le Soleil,
Que par-tout le Ciel vous rie,　　　　　10
Que la terre y soit fleurie,
Et que tout plaise à vostre œil.
Pithon, Diane, Minerve

33 [To Claude Binet][99]
Tell me, ROCHETTE,[100] what do you say?
Ah! You're blushing from shame
At seeing a portrait of yourself that exceeds
Your weak and negligible Virtue.
BINET sought with clever skill,   5
To represent to us a painting
That is of heavenly origin
And to give it a human name.
He stole from the Heavens
The portrait of a beautiful Idea,   10
Not wanting, like Prometheus,
To incite the wrath of the Gods:
With a witty artifice
He veiled its beautiful face
Beneath an obscure name, like a cloud   15
That hides the rays of the Sun.
It was so as not to be criticized
In making manifest to all
This celestial beauty,
Worthy of immortal beings.   20
ROCHE, you could not provide
A more self-evident sign
Of being unworthy of so much honor,
Than your inability to demur.

34 [To a learned lady]
If Beauty, wealth,
Knowledge, and nobility,
Adorn your youthful Spring,
Make it so that wise Virtue
Be found in your heart,   5
Flower of the Flower of your years.
In taking such a sure guide,
May good be your lot,
May you live a long life,
May Heaven smile favorably on you,   10
May the earth flower for you,
And may all be pleasing to your eyes.
May Pithon, Diana, and Minerva[101]

Vous donne, inspire, conserve
La Voix, les Meurs, les Espris: 15
L'Honneur, la Bonté, la Gloire,
Vous rende Heur, Grace, Victoire
En propos, efetz, écris.

35

Tu es indigent, si le tien
Ne peut fournir à tes plaisirs;
Deviens plus pauvre de desirs,
Lors tu seras riche de bien.

36

Comme la docte Guerriere
Alla voir dans sa maison
L'inutile filandiere,
Dépourveue de raison.
Et regardant son ouvrage   5
Feit semblant de l'admirer,
Combien qu'ell' eut au courage
Desir de le dechirer.
Voiant que cete hautaine
Pour quelque subtilité,   10
S'osoit comparer Humaine,
A sa haute Deité.
Elle déguisa sa face
Soubz un petit animal,
Que tout le monde dechasse   15
Comme augure de tout mal.
Ainsi les Muses divines
Se pourroient vanger de nous,
Si nous pensions estre dines
De l'honneur reçeu par vous.   20

37

J'ay une affection à soy toujours semblable,
Qui deux éfetz divers acorde en méme point,
Car il me plait assez de vous étre agreable,
Et ne me déplait pas de ne vous plaire point.

41

Apollon ne veut pas que son Chantre sacré
Chante un humble sujet en si haute harmonie,

Give, inspire, and keep
Your Voice, your Conduct, and your Spirit: 15
May Honor, Goodness, and Glory,
Bring you Happiness, Grace, and Victory
In your words, deeds, and writings.

35 [To a prodigal son]
You are indigent, if your income
Cannot satisfy your pleasures;
Become poorer in desires,
Then you'll be rich in goods.

36 [To admirers of the Dames des Roches]
When the learned Warrior[102]
Went to pay a visit to
The useless weaver,[103]
Deprived of reason,
She looked upon her work   5
And pretended to admire it,
Even though she felt in her heart
The desire to rip it apart.
Seeing that this arrogant girl,
For some subtle reason,   10
Dared to compare her mere Humanity
To her high Divinity,
She covered her [Arachne's] face
Beneath the features of a small animal,
That everyone chases away   15
For fear of it as a harbinger of evil.
Thus the divine Muses
Might avenge themselves,
If we thought ourselves worthy
Of the honor you bestow upon us.   20

37 [To an unwelcome suitor]
My mood and my humor are always the same,
For they react to two different things in the same way:
It pleases me to be agreeable to you,
And it doesn't displease me not to please you.

41[Sonnet to an admirer]
Apollo doesn't want his sacred Songster to sing
Of such a lowly subject as me, with such an harmonious melody,

Prenant pour argument une face fanie
Qui s'en va chacun jour declinant d'un degré.
Un jardin plein de fleurs n'est point si diapré
Que vostre Ame paroit de Graces embellie,
Mais animant pour moy vostre douce Thalie,
Le maitre des chansons ne vous en sçait bon gré.
Hé c'est aussi pourquoy un repentir vous touche,
Si tost que vous ouvrez vostre excellente bouche
Pour louanger ce peu qui peut valoir en moy;
Le Ciel en est jalous: le Ciel en vous s'admire,
Tres digne est le miroir de l'objet qui s'y mire,
Tenant celuy enclos qui l'enclôt dedans soy.

42

Pensant à vostre juste plainte,
Je sans pour vous mon ame attainte,
Ma chère Seur, mais je ne puis
Vous montrer combien me maitrise
La douleur qui vous tirannise   5
Vous faisant soufrir tant d'ennuys.
Vostre passion vehemente
Incessament se represente
Devant les yeux de mon Esprit,
Toutesfois j'aimois mieux me taire   10
Que de chasser cet adversaire
Avec un si mauvais écrit.
Si je pouvois vous donner aide
Avecques quelque bon remede
Comme Zethes et Calaïs,   15
Je forcerois la fause Harpie
Qui du fond d'Enfer est sortie,
De retourner en son païs.
Apres je vous ferois connoitre
Que ce qu'Amour vous fait paroitre   20
De beau, de gentil, et gaillard,
N'est sinon qu'une vaine image
Pour servir bientost de pillage
A la faux de ce grand Vieillard.
Je dirois que la Jalousie,   25
Bourrelle de la fantaisie,

Taking as topic a faded face
That each day gets a little worse.
A garden full of flowers is not as many colored
As your Soul appears embellished by Grace.
But making your gentle Thalia sing on my behalf,[104]
The master of songs[105] doesn't bear you good will.
That's why you should repent,
As soon as you open your excellent mouth
To praise the little that may be of worth in me;
Heaven is jealous because Heaven admires itself in you;
The mirror is worthy of the object that contemplates itself in it,
Holding within it the Heavens that encompass all.

    42 [To a friend, on her unfaithful husband]
Thinking of your justifiable complaint,
My soul goes out to you,
My dear Sister, and words cannot convey
To you how much the pain
That tyrannizes you and makes you suffer   5
So many sorrows also overwhelms me.
Your vehement passion
Is incessantly present
Before the eyes of my Mind.
However, I preferred to keep quiet   10
Rather than to drive this adversary away
With a poorly written piece.
If I could lend you assistance
With some good remedy,
Like Zethus and Calais[106]   15
I'd force that false Harpy
Who has come up from the depths of Hell
To return to her own country.
After which I'd let you know
That what Love seems to make   20
So beautiful, noble, and lively to you,
Is nothing but a vain image
That will soon serve as plunder
For the scythe of Old Man Time.
I'd tell you that Jealousy,   25
That torturer of one's fantasy,

Vient de se défier de soy,
Et qu'une telle defiance
N'est pas digne de l'excellance
Qui acompagne vostre Foy.   30
Connoissez donc vous et les autres,
Ne déprisez les Vertus vostres
Pour admirer celles d'autruy,
Je ne voi Homme qui soit digne
De vous enflamer la poitrine,   35
Tant y ait de Graces en luy.
Vostre Beauté vous rend aimable,
Vostre Chasteté honorable,
Vostre Esprit vous fait admirer,
Vostre bonté vous reconforte,   40
Vostre richesse vous suporte,
L'Epoux seul vous fait soupirer.
Ne l'aymez plus que par mesure,
N'empruntez l'Amour à usure,
N'en rendez point beaucoup pour peu,   45
Aimez-le autant comme il est sage:
Mais ne l'aymez pas davantage,
Selon le Saint ofrez le veu.

43

Les Muses, la Pithon, et les Graces encore,
Ont pillé d'Apollon, de Mercure, des Cieux,
Le sçavoir, le discours, la splandeur qui decore
Vostre divin Esprit, vos propos, et vos yeux.

44

Je croy que l'Amour est Charite de vostre ame,
Qui vous fait rechercher ce dous miel nectarin,
Dont vous puisez la goutte au fleuve Pegasin,
Pour écrire vos vers au Temple de la Fame.
Tel Amour ne vient pas des attrais d'une Dame:
Vostre cueur est si fort, vostre Daemon si fin,
Vostre Esprit si ravi par un Amour divin
Que vous ne craignez point qu'un autre vous enflame.
Or ainsi que l'on voit l'Ægyptien subtil
Par un Oeil, une Lampe, un Peloton de fil,
Demontrer la Prudence, et Splendeur de la vie:

Comes from lack of faith in oneself,
And that such suspicion of self
Isn't worthy of the excellence
That accompanies your Faith.   30
Know then yourself and others,
Don't despise your own Virtues
To go admire those of another;
I see no Man who is worthy
Of inspiring love in you,   35
No matter how gracious and talented he may be.
Your Beauty makes you lovable,
Your Chastity honorable,
Your Spirit makes you admired,
Your goodness comforts you,   40
Your wealth sustains you,
It's only your husband who makes you sigh.
Love him no more than you have to,
Don't borrow Love on interest,
Don't return a lot of love for only a little,   45
Love him only insofar as he deserves it,
But no more than you have to,
According to the Saint tailor the vow.

    43
The Muses, Pithon, and the Graces besides,
Have stolen from Apollo, from Mercury, from the Heavens,
The learning, the speech, and the splendor that adorns
Your divine Spirit, your words, and your gaze.

    44 [Sonnet to a learned lady]
I think that Love is the Charite[107] of your soul
That makes you search for that sweet nectarine honey
Which you draw from the river Pegasine,[108]
To write your verses for the Temple of Fame.[109]
This kind of Love doesn't come merely from a Lady's good looks:
Your heart is so strong, your Daemon so fine,
Your Mind so ravished by a divine Love
That you don't worry that another will set you on fire.
Now just as one sees the subtle Egyptian[110]
With an Eye, a Lamp, a Ball of yarn,
Demonstrate Prudence, and the Splendor of life:

Ainsi vous demontrez par ces images saints,
Dont vos écris tant beaus de toutes pars sont ceints,
La divine Beauté dont vostre Ame est ravie.

A MESSIEURS TENANT LES GRANDS JOURS A POITIERS
Messieurs, offrant des vers à voz sages bontez,
C'est vous faire un presant de legere fumée,
Mais l'Encens fume ainsi brulant sur les Autelz,
Et des souverains Dieux sa vapeur est aimée.
Je vous voy resembler à la Divinité,   5
Comme luisants Soleilz éclairant nostre Terre,
Vous faites les Grands-Jours, et avez merité
Qu'on vous nomme sans fin Dieux de paix et de guerre.
Car vous faites la guerre aux Hommes dépravez,
Bornant par voz Grands-Jours leurs dernieres journées,   10
Et conservez les bons, pour ce que vous sçavez
Que pour garder les bons les Loix sont ordonnées.
Je vous salüe donc, Soleilz de nos Grands Jours,
Et vous rends les mercis de vos recentes Graces,
Excusez de mes vers le trop foible Discours,   15
Ilz sont humbles-hautains en regardant vos faces.
O combien je desire une faveur du Ciel,
C'est que lisant les vers que je vous viens d'écrire,
Vous les puissiez trouver aussi coulants que miel,
Car ainsi je rendrois du Miel pour de la Cire.   20

LA PUCE
Petite Puce fretillarde,
Qui d'une bouchete mignarde
Succotez le sang incarnat
Qui colore un sein delicat,
Vous pourroit-on dire friande   5
Pour desirer telle viande?
Vraiment, nenny. Car ce n'est point
La friandise qui vous point,
Et si n'allez à l'adventure
Pour chercher vostre nourriture.   10
Mais pleine de discretion,
D'une plus sage affection,

So you demonstrate through these sacred images,
That weave themselves into your beautiful writings
The divine Beauty that delights your Soul.

TO THE GENTLEMEN JUDGES AT THE GRANDS JOURS OF POITIERS[111]

Gentlemen, to offer this poem to your infinite wisdom
Is to make you a gift that dissipates into thin air,
But Incense burns thus on church Altars,
And its smoke is appreciated by the sovereign Gods.
I see that you resemble the Divinity,   5
For you are like bright Suns lighting up our Earth,
You put on the Grands Jours, and deserve
That we endlessly name you the Gods of peace and of war.
For you make war on depraved Men,
Putting an end with your Grands Jours to their life,   10
And you protect the good, because you know
That Laws are ordained to guard the good.
So I greet you, Suns of our Grands Jours,
And give you thanks for your most recent Favors,
Excuse the overly negligible worth of my verses,   15
They are humbly haughty when they gaze upon your faces.
O how I desire a favor from Heaven,
Which is that when you read the lines I have just written,
You may find them as flowing as honey,
For then I could return Honey for Wax.[112]   20

THE FLEA[113]

Little wriggling Flea,
Who with your cute little mouth
Sucks the deep red blood
That colors such a delicate breast,
Can one really say   5
You're fond of such a meal?
Truly, no. For it isn't
Gluttony that stirs you,
Nor do you wander aimlessly
To search for food.   10
But full of discretion
And a wiser affection

Vous choisissez place honorable
Pour prendre un repas agreable.
Ce repas seulement est pris   15
Du sang le siege des Espris.
Car desirant estre subtile,
Vive, gaye, promte, et agile,
Vous prenez d'un seul aliment
Nourriture et enseignement.   20
On le voit par vostre alegresse,
Et vos petis tours de finesse,
Quand vous sautelez en un sein
Fuiant la rigueur d'une main:
Quelquefois vous faites la morte,   25
Puis d'une ruse plus accorte,
Vous fraudez le doigt poursuivant
Qui pour vous ne prend que du vent.
O mon Dieu, de quelle maniere
Vous fuiez cete main meurtriere,   30
Et vous cachez aux cheveux longz,
Comme Syringue entre les joncs!
Ah! que je crains pour vous, Mignonne,
Céte main superbe et felonne.
Hé! pourquoy ne veut-elle pas   35
Que vous preniez vostre repas?
Vostre blessure n'est cruelle,
Vostre pointure n'est mortelle,
Car en blessant, pour vous guerir,
Vous ne tuez pour vous nourrir.   40
Vous étes de petite vie:
Mais aymant la Geometrie
En ceux que vous avez époint,
Vous tracez seulement un point,
Où les lignes se viennent rendre.   45
Encor avez-vous sçeu aprendre
Comment en Sparte les plus fins
Ne se laissoyent prendre aux larcins.
Vous ne voulez étre surprise
Quand vous avez fait quelque prise,   50
Vous vous cachez subtilement
Aux replys de l'acoutrement.

You choose an honorable place
To take a pleasant meal.
This meal you draw only   15
From blood the seat of Spirits.[114]
For in wanting to be lithe,
Vivacious, happy, prompt and agile,
You take from only one food
Both nourishment and learning.   20
One can see this because of your delight,
And your little fine feats,
When you leap onto a breast
As you flee the hand's harsh swat.
Sometimes you act as though dead,   25
Then with an even cleverer ruse,
You escape the pursuing finger
Which rather than seizing you grabs a fist full of air.
O my God, what a way you have
Of fleeing that murderous hand,   30
As you hide in the long flowing hair
Like Syrinx among the reeds![115]
Ah! How I fear for you, my dearest,
This arrogant and treacherous hand.
Oh! Why does it not want   35
You to eat your meal?
Your bite is not cruel,
Your wound is not serious,
For in wounding, to heal you
And feed yourself, you don't kill.   40
Your life is short:
But since you like Geometry,
In those whom you have bitten,
You land on one spot alone,
Where lines come together.   45
Also you've learned
How in Sparta the cleverest
Didn't let themselves be captured at their larceny.[116]
Since you don't want to be caught
When you've made some catch,   50
You subtly hide
In the folds of clothes.

Puce, si ma plume étoit digne
Je décrirois vostre origine,
Et comment le plus grand des Dieux,   55
Pour la Terre quitant les Cieux
Vous fit naitre, comme il me semble,
Orion et vous tout-ensemble.
Mais il faudra que tel écrit
Vienne d'un plus gentil Esprit.   60
De moy je veus seulement dire
Vos Beautez, et le grand martire
Que Pan soufrit en vous aimant,
Avant qu'on veit ce changement,
Et que vostre face divine   65
Prit céte couleur ebenine,
Et que vos blancs pieds de Thetis
Fussent si gréles et petis.
Puce, quand vous étiez Pucelle,
Gentille, sage, douce, et belle,   70
Vous mouvant d'un pied si leger
Pour sauter et pour voltiger,
Que vous eussiez peu d'Atalante
Devancer la course trop lente;
Pan, voiant vos perfections,   75
Sentit un feu d'affections
Desirant vostre mariage.
Mais quoy? vostre vierge courage
Aima mieux vous faire changer
En Puce, afin de l'étranger,   80
Et que perdant toute esperance
Il rompit sa perseverance.
. Diane sçeut vostre souhait,
Vous le voulûtes, il fut fait:
Elle voila vostre figure   85
Sous une noire couverture.
Depuis fuiant toujours ce Dieu,
Petite, vous cherchez un lieu
Qui vous serve de sauvegarde,
Et craignez que Pan vous regarde.   90
Bien souvent la timidité
Fait voir vostre dexterité,

Flea, if my pen were worthy,
I'd describe your origins,
And how the greatest of the Gods,   55
Leaving the Heavens for the Earth
Caused the birth, or so it seems to me,
Of Orion and you all at once.[117]
But such a writing would have
To come from a nobler Mind.   60
I only want to tell of
Your Beauty, and of the great martyrdom
That Pan endured because of his love for you,
Before you were changed
And before your divine face   65
Took on an ebony color,
And your white feet like those of Thetis
Became so frail and small.
Flea, when you were a chaste young Maiden,
Noble, wise, sweet, and beautiful,   70
And you moved about on such a light foot,
That leaping and flying about
You would have been able to
Beat Atalanta in her faltering race,[118]
Pan, seeing your perfections,   75
Felt the fire of affection
And wished to marry you.
But then your virgin's bold resolve
Preferred to change you
Into a flea, so as to escape from him,   80
And so that losing all hope,
He would have to break off his pursuit.
Diana[119] knew your wish,
You wanted it, and it was done:
She veiled your face   85
Beneath a black covering.
Since then, fleeing from this God,
Little one, you seek a place
Offering you a safe haven,
And still you worry that Pan can see you.   90
Quite often your timidity
Demonstrates your dexterity,

Vous sautelez à l'impourveüe
Quand vous soubsonnez d'estre veüe,
Et de vous ne reste sinon   95
La Crainte, l'Adresse, et le Nom.

EPITAPHE 2
Passant, premier qu'on veit ma belle et chaste vie
Soubz la fatale main de la Parque ravie,
Je resemblois du tout ce pourtrait que tu voy,
Je revy dans celuy qui vivoit dedans moy.
Il est de Marbre dur, j'avois un cueur de Marbre,   5
Plus fier, plus endurci, que n'est le cueur d'un arbre.
Il est blanc comme nege: et le Lait, et les Lys
Cedoient à la blancheur de mes traitz embellis
De mil' et mil' atraitz: il est froid, et ma face
Enflammant tant d'Espris sembloit étre de Glace.   10
Il est dous et poly, je l'étois tout ainsi;
Il est sourd, j'étois sourde, et sans avoir souci
Des Cueurs passionnez en l'Amoureux martire,
J'appaisois, comme il fait, d'un regard, d'un soûrire:
Je ne santis jamais la Flame, ny le Trait   15
Du jeune Archer ailé, non plus que ce pourtrait.

For you leap about suddenly
When you suspect you've been seen,
And all that remains of you is   95
Your Fear, your Skill, and your Name.

EPITAPH 2[120]
Passerby, before my beautiful and chaste life was
Ravished by the fatal hand of Fate,
I looked like this tombstone you see,
I live again in that which used to live in me.
It is made of hard Marble, and I had a heart of Marble,   5
Prouder, harder, than even the heart of a tree.
It is white as snow, but even Milk and the Lily
Could not compare to the whiteness of my traits embellished
And attractive to many; it is cold, and though my face
Inflamed many a suitor, it looked like Ice.   10
It is soft and polished, as I also was;
It is deaf, and I also was deaf, and indifferent
To the impassioned Hearts martyred by Love,
I appeased them, here with a gaze, there with a smile;
I never felt either the Flame or the Arrow   15
Of the young winged Archer,[121] and neither does this tombstone.

IV

THE DIALOGUES OF CATHERINE DES ROCHES FROM *LES ŒUVRES* (1579) AND *LES SECONDES ŒUVRES* (1583)

You must study, spend time with books, take pleasure in reading. Then, as books start occupying more and more of your thinking, they will drive away all these vain and frivolous thoughts from your mind.

— Catherine des Roches, *Dialogue between Iris and Pasithée*

INTRODUCTION

In his study of Renaissance writing manuals, Jonathan Goldberg emphasizes
that women's training in the use of the pen did not disturb social relations
and hierarchies: much like the ornamental skills of the needle and gold
threads, drawing and playing the lute, the pen was meant to keep woman's
fingers busy so that by copying texts written or dictated by others, "thoughts
swift and unsettled," in Vives's words, would not take over her mind.[1] Literacy and writing thus provided an education in docility. In *De ratione studii
puerilis* (On a Plan of Study for Children, 1523), Vives specifies that a young
girl—in this case Princess Mary Tudor, daughter of Catherine of Aragon and
of Henry VIII—should "write down with her fingers anything the tutor may
dictate";[2] furthermore, she is to copy out *dialogues* about items found in households "which she requires daily to concern herself about, so that she may be
accustomed to name them in Latin, *e.g.*, clothes, parts of the house, food, di-
visions of time, musical instruments, house-furniture."[3] Her learning is to re-

---

1. Jonathan Goldberg, *Writing Matter: From the Hands of the English Renaissance* (Stanford: Stanford
University Press, 1990), 141; Vives, *Education of a Christian Woman*, 59.

2. Vives, *Plan of Studies for Girls*, in *Vives and the Renascence Education of Women*, ed. and trans. Forster
Watson (New York: Longmans, Green, 1912), 141; cited by Goldberg, *Writing Matter*, 145.

3. Vives, *Plan of Studies for Girls*, 143.

inforce her socially constructed femininity and ensure the nonnegotiability of differences between men and women. Such iteration, however, has its flip side: it betrays the anxiety that attended placing the pen in female hands. Literacy for women could mean empowerment, as it did for men. As Goldberg states, "even the differences that mean to guarantee the exclusion of women cannot finally be stabilized in the duplicative regimes of copy."[4]

Catherine des Roches exemplifies this ideological contradiction in female literacy in two dialogues on women's education written in 1581 and 1582 and published in *Les Secondes Œuvres*. In the first of these, *Dialogue between Placide and Severe*, Placide, a humanistically enlightened bourgeois, holds an argumentative conversation on the merits of educating girls with his neighbor Severe, a misogynist merchant. Placide is the father of a learned daughter named Pasithée, and Severe is the father of a flighty and ignorant daughter named Iris. Placide presents the educational views of Erasmus and Vives, who defended female education as a means of transforming a young girl into a sweet-tempered wife and companion. When asked how Pasithée has benefited from her learning, Placide responds that she is obedient to him and that, unlike Iris who refuses "d'arrester au logis, d'avoir soing du ménage" (to stay at home and take care of her housework), she remains in her room playing her lute and pondering "les belles Sentences de Plutarque et de Seneque" (the beautiful Maxims of Plutarch and Seneca).[5] He has followed the guidelines of Plutarch's *Precepts of Marriage* and Xenophon's *Oeconomicus*, two of the most influential texts on women's domestic and economic roles, which he now heartily recommends to Severe. Through ventriloquism (Placide becomes the author's representative) and an adept use of Ciceronian *refutatio*, as well as a good dose of Lucianic and Erasmian humor, Des Roches wins critics over to her side: she dissolves irreconcilable opposites by suggesting that a woman can sew and read, be attentive to her *ménage* (household) and write. The social roles advocated for women in this dialogue reflect the conservative (writing) manuals of the period.

The sequel *Dialogue between Iris and Pasithée* on the other hand subtly undermines Placide's explicitly cautious premises.[6] While Pasithée seems to be everything Placide describes her to be, she is in fact much more than an obe-

---

4. Goldberg, *Writing Matter*, 145.

5. *Dialogue de Placide et Severe, Secondes œuvres*, 190, 192 (and see below).

6. On closer reading, Placide expresses views that are far less conservative than at first sight: to Severe's outburst that a "femme sçavante" (learned woman) is a "monstre," Placide paradoxically lauds such "monstrous" women for their vow of perpetual virginity and their desire to "get along without men"; he asserts that women should be allowed to use the spindle and the pen for "l'un de ces exercices aide l'autre. Pallas les avoit tous deux" (each of these activities assists the other.

dient upper-gentry daughter. Her very (aristocratic) name, carrying enormous prestige in Italian lyric and Pléiade poetry,[7] hints at a transformed relation to bourgeois ideological constructions of femininity. Unlike her namesake in Pontus de Tyard's Neoplatonic dialogues *Solitaires* (1552 and 1555), she is the teacher in a master-pupil dialectic where she assumes an authority reserved only to a male pedagogue. She is therefore strikingly different from the few women speakers who appear in French philosophical dialogues of the 1550s—in Pasquier's *Monophile* (1554), Pontus de Tyard's *Solitaire premier* (1552) and *Solitaire second* (1555), Louis Le Caron's *Dialogues* (1556), for instance—and in some forty cinquecento Italian dialogues.[8] These female interlocutors are learners who direct the discussion (as in Castiglione's *Book of the Courtier*) rather than leaders and teachers. They conform to acceptable conversational feminine behavior and to the overarching concern of *sermo* (conversation) to maintain decorum and behavior suitable for women.[9] Exceptions to these are contemporary women widely famed for their knowledge who take a spirited lead in the dialogues in which they are featured,[10] and three sixteenth-century women writers who produced dialogues containing exclusively women speakers, the Italians Olympia Morata (whom Des Roches includes in Placide's list of contemporary intellectual women)

Pallas practiced them both.); and he argues that truly learned women do not chase after men: "sans avoir [de mari], elles se déportent honnestement, ou en aiant, les gouvernent paisiblement" (if they remain single, they behave honorably, or if they do marry, they live in peace with their husbands). To Severe's disparaging comment that the exemplary virtuous women Placide mentions to his daughter are from another age, the latter evokes five contemporary female intellectuals whose works Des Roches had likely read and admired.

7. As Francis Yates states, "within Pasithée, the fourth Grace, are packed all the nine Muses and the three Graces" (*French Academies of the Sixteenth Century* [London: Wartburg Institute, 1947], 133). Pasithée as a pseudonym had currency in court circles where Claude-Catherine de Clermont (1543–1603), maréchale de Retz, was addressed as Dictynne or as Pasithée, and the learned Marguerite de France (1523–76), sister of Henri II, was referred to either as Charite or as Pasithée. Des Roches's Pasithée is closer in spirit and in educational training to her aristocratic court sisters than to the daughters of her own class. Like her creator, she has the ambitions of the socially mobile *noblesse de ville* (urban nobility).

8. For a listing of these, see Virginia Cox, "Seen but Not Heard: The Role of Women Speakers in Cinquecento Literary Dialogue," in *Women in Italian Renaissance Culture and Society*, ed. Letizia Panizza (Oxford: Legenda, 2000), 385–400.

9. Women's speech in the private sphere is connected with the Ciceronian concept of *sermo* (private conversation), which should be light and witty and concern household matters or learning. See Robert W. Cape Jr., "Roman Women in the History of Rhetoric and Oratory," in *Listening to Their Voices. The Rhetorical Activities of Historical Women*, ed. Molly Meijer Wertheimer (Columbia: University of South Carolina Press, 1997), 117–18.

10. The poet Vittoria Colonna appears in Francesco De Holanda's *Diálogos de Roma* (ca. 1549) and Tarquinia Molza in Francesco Patrizi's *L'amorosa filosofia* (1577); see Cox, "Seen but Not Heard," 388.

and Moderata Fonte, as well as the Portuguese humanist Luisa Sigea, also cited by Des Roches.[11]

Pasithée stands in for the male teacher/lover in Renaissance dialogues where the female pupil seeks to possess her teacher's learning while he courts his student.[12] Pasithée's courting of Iris, however, subtly undercuts the heterosexual plot: on the one hand, she advises her pupil to "[embellir] vostre ame" (beautify your soul) so as to be "uniquement aimée par un Amy sage, accort, et sçavant" (uniquely loved by a wise, discreet, and learned friend); in this manner she will come closer to being a "sçavante vertueuse" (virtuous learned woman) like Cassandra Fedele, who was praised by Angelo Poliziano as "le sainct honneur de l'Italie" (the saintly honor of all of Italy). But on the other, she counsels her to live without love and "vous proposez les mal-heurs qui viennent pour aimer" (think about all the misfortunes that come with love). She elevates as model the "femme sçavante" (learned woman) for whom "les lettres" (learning) helps to "drive away" gallant men of the sort that plague Iris's life. She offers friendship with women and the possibility of a safe haven, a sort of "school," where women can teach and learn from each other. Her courting of Iris—she plays the lute for her, sings love songs to her, watches and applauds her dancing the "volte," a popular court dance imported from Italy—is intended to show that being a "femme savante" in no way leads to an ascetic "book-lined cell."[13] Pasithée's modern version of the learned woman mirrors the ethos of social recreation prevalent in coterie cul-

---

11. Olympia Morata, "Dialogue between Lavinia della Rovere and Olympia Morata" (1550) and "Dialogue between Theophila and Philotima" (1551–52), in *Complete Writings of an Italian Heretic*, 100–103, 118–26; Moderata Fonte, *The Worth of Women* (1600), ed and trans. Virginia Cox, Other Voice in Early Modern Europe (Chicago: University of Chicago Press, 1997); Luisa Sigea, *Duarum virginium colloquium de vita aulica et privata* (Conversation between Two Virgins on Courtly and Private Life, 1552), ed. Manuel Serrano y Sanz (Madrid: Biblioteca de Autores Españoles, 1903), 41–71, published only in 1903 despite encomiums for it during Sigea's lifetime. See also Louise Sigée [Luisa Sigea], *Dialogue de deux jeunes filles sur la vie de court et la vie de retraite*, ed. and trans. Odette Sauvage (Paris: Presses Universitaires de France, 1970). Des Roches had probably read or knew of her bucolic poem *Sintra* published in Paris in 1566.

12. Leone Ebreo's *Dialoghi d'amore* (Dialogues on Love, 1535) epitomizes the teacher's quest for union of both soul and body that confirms the spiritual union already established through reason.

13. The expression symbolizes fifteenth-century Italian learned women's socially enforced confinement in "self-constructed prisons, lined with books." Margaret King, "Book-Lined Cells: Women and Humanism in the Early Italian Renaissance," in *Beyond Their Sex: Learned Women of the European Past*, ed. Patricia Labalme (New York: New York University Press, 1980), 74. On Pasithée's sensory and pleasure-oriented modern view of the learned woman, see Cathy Yandell, " 'Des ames sans cors, et des cors sans ames': la pédagogie dialectique de Catherine des Roches," in *Lectrices d'Ancien Régime*, ed. Isabelle Brouard-Arends (Rennes: Presses Universitaires de Rennes, 2002), 557–66.

ture; it adapts an aristocratic courtly and urban *savoir mondain* (worldly knowledge) to a sociability that will attain its fullest expression in seventeenth- and eighteenth-century salons. Like the storytellers in Marguerite de Navarre's *Heptameron* who debate and converse like interlocutors in a literary circle, so Des Roches's dialogues imitate the literary and performative dynamics of coterie conversation. They anticipate in this way Madeleine de Scudéry's *conversations*.[14]

The historical grounding, practicality, Lucianic parody and wit, comic characterization, and theme of female independence in the pedagogic dialogues are all in evidence in Catherine des Roches's first five dialogues published in *Les Œuvres*. These pieces, akin to medieval debates where allegorical figures contest various problems, are very much in the tradition of humanist dialogues that rationally examine conflicting arguments in the search for truth. They seek to persuade through concrete examples drawn from everyday experience.[15] As in the humanist dialogue, they are connected by the overarching quest for the reconciliation of antagonistic entities. Old Age and Youth (dialogue 1) mimic a mother-daughter relationship gone sour as Youth, a flighty Iris figure, seeks lovers and Old Age counsels her on the brevity of life. The iconoclastic violence of the religious wars is evoked in *Dialogue between Virtue and Fortune;* Fortune changes her character in order to assist Virtue in saving Poitiers from further destruction. In *Dialogue between the Hand, the Foot, and the Mouth,* the stay-at-home feminine Hand argues with the restless masculine Foot about who is to be most valued; a third party, the reasonable Mouth, imposes harmony through persuasive discourse about the importance of peace among citizens, for "les querelles des citoyens causent la ruine d'une ville" (quarrels among citizens cause the downfall of a city). Des Roches's speaker thus appeals to orthodox morality on gender relations and applies the traditional political analogy of parts of the body not to the body politic but rather to the governance of a city.[16]

A similar concern with gender relations and urban social disorder sur-

14. On this new dialogic model, see Nicole Cazauran, "Un nouveau 'genre d'écrire:' les débuts du dialogue mondain," in *Marguerite de Navarre, 1492–1992*, ed. Nicole Cazauran and James Dauphiné (Mont-de-Marsan: Éditions InterUniversitaires, 1995), 537–91, cited by Delphine Denis, ed., *"De l'air galant" et autres conversations. Pour une étude de l'archive galante* (Paris: Champion, 1998), 20 n. 43.

15. On the humanist dialogue, see David Marsh, *Classical Tradition and Humanist Innovation* (Cambridge: Harvard University Press, 1980).

16. Ann R. Jones, "The Muse of Indirection: Feminist Ventriloquism in the Dialogues of Catherine Des Roches," in *The Dialogue in Early Modern France, 1547–1630: Art and Argument,* ed. Colette H. Winn. (Washington, D.C.: Catholic University of America Press, 1995), 199–200.

faces in *Dialogue between Poverty and Hunger,* the most frequently anthologized of Des Roches's dialogues. As in Louise Labé's *Debate of Folly and Love* (1555), where Love treats Folly with blatant disrespect ("Your youth, your sex, your behavior give you away, but above all your ignorance"),[17] male Hunger attacks female Poverty for her garrulity and lack of reason. Poverty snaps back: "Who says such things but big, loud men? They dare not spend their time with courteous and learned women for fear that these women will judge them for who they are."[18] Poverty goes on to critique Hunger for stirring rapaciousness and greed among professionals (treasury officials, lawyers, judges, and merchants) and ends with a stark reminder of the hunger suffered by the peasants of Poitou on account of the civil wars. The *Dialogue between Love, Beauty, and Physis* presents Catherine des Roches's striking suggestion of a possible "third way" or "third status" (more fully developed in her heroine Pasithée) that would allow intellectual women to choose freely a single life dedicated to study.[19] Mother Physis enables her daughter Beauty to escape from Love's sexual aggression, the "violence of the times," and the snares of the "poets' love sonnets" by taking refuge with Pallas Athena: "ainsi," states Beauty, "je me sauveray de la tyrannie d'Amour par les livres, par les ouvrages, et par les yeux de la Meduse" (that way I'll escape from Love's tyranny through books, needlework, and the eyes of Medusa).

Lastly, Beauty's independence of mind is enacted in the *Dialogue between Sincero and Charite,* where Charite (a salon pseudonym for Catherine des Roches) assumes the active role of the virtuous chaste woman who teaches and refines her lover. Rather than adhering to the conventional (Petrarchan) portrayal of a passive beloved serving her lover's poetic interests, Des Roches constructs a female intellectually dominant partner who gently satirizes her lover's unself-conscious use of Neoplatonic platitudes. She foreshadows Pasithée's role as mentor teaching her student to be more like her: chaste, eloquent, self-aware in love *and* in life.

Literacy and writing for Catherine des Roches became tools to question

17. Louise Labé, *Debate of Folly and Love,* trans. Anne-Marie Bourbon (New York: Peter Lang, 2000), 27.

18. "Qui dit ce propos sinon des hommes lourds et grossiers? Lesquels n'[osent] frequenter les femmes gentilles et bien apprises, de crainte qu'elles les estiment tels qu'ils sont."

19. Unlike the Dimesse, Italian single women who wished to serve God outside convents, Pasithée embodies a secular ideal of female independence that is strikingly similar to Corinna's concept of the single self in Moderata Fonte's *Worth of Women.* On the Dimesse, see Gabriella Zarri, "The Third Status," in *Time, Space, and Women's Lives in Early Modern Europe,* ed. Anne Jacobson Schutte et al. (Kirksville, Mo.: Truman State University Press, 2001), 181–99; Virginia Cox, "The Single Self: Feminist Thought and the Marriage Market in Early Modern Venice," *Renaissance Quarterly* 48, no. 3 (1995): 513–81.

the status quo and envisage new social demands for women. As Eva Kushner points out, a radical note is sounded in Des Roches's dialogues: Des Roches made "social change [her] prime or direct aim."[20] Des Roches is a moralist more in line with the thinkers of the seventeenth century than with the humanist dialogue writers of her own century. Her writing is rooted in the social and moral problems faced by women of her class. The dialogical nature of her writing enabled her to reflect upon a given historical situation, endow each of her characters with a true-to-life existence, and allow the reader to follow the entire course of the argument.

༃

DIALOGUES FROM LES ŒUVRES (1579)

1

Dialogue between Old Age and Youth

OLD AGE Why, who is this young wanton, crowned with flowers, who runs around and jumps so happily? She's carrying a lute in her hands, and sings along to her playing, and quite often leaves it all to admire herself in some mirror. Alas! If she felt but a portion of the troubles that accompany me, she'd forget all about her happiness.

YOUTH So many thoughts crowd my mind that I don't know where to begin. Wouldn't it be better . . . ? Ah no, no, I'll go and sing myself a song, then I'll think about the rest.

> The lovely springtime of my carefree youth
> Cures the dangerous wound of Love;
> That child's power, more than human,
> Is sustained by my powerful hand.
>   What good would it be if its ardent flame
> Burned blood, heart, body, and soul,
> While I, the world's sustainer,
> From this great evil did not reap a great benefit?
>   If a lover who lacks wisdom
> Is disdained by a wise mistress,
> I teach him ten thousand inventions,

---

20. Evan Kushner, "The Dialogue of Dialogues," in *The Dialogue in Early Modern France, 1547–1630: Art and Argument,* ed. Colette H. Winn (Washington, DC: Catholic University of America Press, 1995), 279.

So he may succeed in his intentions.
   If a lover who lacks riches
Is scorned by a rich mistress,
I give him a running river of gold,
And Pluto's precious treasure.
   But those who to old age are held captive,
No one can rejuvenate their frailty;
Even Love would be intimidated,
His torch put out, his arrows broken.

OLD AGE All right, so far I've forced myself to endure all her little vanities, but since it's against me she's carrying on, I'll ask her why.

YOUTH O Lord! Who sends me this decrepit old woman, with her glassy eyes and her forehead wrinkled like a prune? She has no teeth in her mouth because of the cold that has swept them all out. And what is she doing with that staff? Is it to support herself or to hit someone? Should I flee? No, what could she possibly do to me? I'll wait for her. Since I know that she'll get very angry with me, I'll deliberately feed her anger. So, how shall I begin? I'm going to talk to her. God protect you, my good mother, would you like to dance with me while I sing you a song?

OLD AGE Go away, you little pretender, I'll have nothing to do with you or your songs. You were just now speaking so unkindly of me that I'll make you beg for my forgiveness for having said those words.

YOUTH Now then, now then, don't be such a boor, come on over and dance if you think it's a good idea, and give your wooden horse a rest.

OLD AGE Don't make fun of my horse, he's stronger than you think.

YOUTH Ha! I think he's quite strapping, but where did you get him? Is he a jennet from Spain, or a Clydesdale from Germany, or a hackney from Brittany?

OLD AGE I'll not tell you where he's from; it's enough for you to know that he can hurt you.

YOUTH Well then, good woman, could he be from the race of Diomedes' mares, which fed on human flesh?[21] If that were so, I'd quickly take my leave. All the same, I have no doubt that he's related to

---

21. Diomedes, king of Thrace, had strangers in his land eaten by his mares. Hercules put an end to his practice.

Seius's horse, for he brought death to his master, and this one here is swiftly taking you to yours.[22]

OLD AGE Who told you I was about to die? I assure you that you'll die before me, since you were born before me.

YOUTH You want to make me believe, then, that I came into the world before *you*, who are the mother of old Demogorgon?[23]

OLD AGE Which would make you his grandmother.

YOUTH O you hideous old hag!

OLD AGE O you young fool!

YOUTH You were just saying that I was older than you, and then you called me young. I think you're raving mad.

OLD AGE Oh please! I said you were born before me, not that you were older. If the oldest necessarily had to age, eternity would fall into decay.

YOUTH If aging is the beginning of perishing, you are near the end, just as I said.

OLD AGE I don't grow older, for I've always been old, and was so even the day I was born. If I had, in fact, lost some of my strength and vigor, you would be right to hold such a theory.

YOUTH So, you've never been otherwise?

OLD AGE No.

YOUTH Ah, unhappy the one who resembles *you*!

OLD AGE Listen, if you get me angry, I'll exact my revenge on you.

YOUTH What could you possibly do to me?

OLD AGE I'll hit you with this staff so hard that your blond hair will lose its tincture and turn from gold into silver, your teeth of ivory will turn to ebony, your rosy complexion will become pale, and the flicker in your eyes will die away.

YOUTH I'm not afraid of you, since I'm well aware that middle age keeps you apart from me by always standing between the two of us, as springtime and autumn stand between winter and summer.

---

22. Seius's horse passed into legend to denote a gain that brings with it misfortune. See the adage "Equum habet Sejanum" (He must keep Sejus's horse), in Erasmus, *Adages, Collected Works of Erasmus*, trans. Margaret Mann Phillips and R. A. B. Mynors (Toronto: University of Toronto Press, 1989), vol. 32, 1.10.97.

23. This ominous-sounding name, used by fifteenth-century writers to denote the primeval god of ancient mythology, originated with a medieval scribe's misspelling of the name Demiurge. Boccaccio copied the word in *Genealogia deorum* (1531) (New York: Garland Reprints, 1976), book 14, Proem, 15. The Demiurge in Plato's *Timaeus* is the creator of the visible world.

OLD AGE Ah, but this middle age gives me the means by which to entrap you, for it resembles a Quartermaster who marks for me the dwellings where you live, and very often when I am annoyed at your pride, I send him to drive you away from handsome people who worship you, so that you're forced to find room with someone ugly.

YOUTH Whether we dwell with the beautiful or the ugly, they always find me pleasing, whereas they're always angry with you.

OLD AGE true that some find me horrific; but that's because they've abused you, allowing themselves unbridled pleasure. That's what causes their extreme pains for which I receive the blame, even though I'm not even responsible for them. There lies the reason for their woes and for mine: if they had been temperate in their youth, they would have found old age peaceful.

YOUTH You rebuke others for the evils you shower upon them. We both know full well that you are detested, because you rob people of their zest for life in a way far worse than normal thievery; for thieves can use the money they take, but you wouldn't know what to do with the gracious traits you lay hold of.

OLD AGE All I want to do is to take these graces away from one person so that another can have them; but those who live in excess are asking for it.

YOUTH Indeed! So that's how you treat this innocent earth, and all her inhabitants! After my favor has given her a new gown, and I've made her produce all sorts of flowers, herbs, and fruits for the nourishment of her children, you strip her of her bounty, and cruelly take her gown from her, even as winter is approaching.

OLD AGE My influence is no less necessary than yours. And just as the good Lord enclosed a pair of every kind of animal in Noah's ark, so they would continue on after the flood,[24] I enclose in the heart of the land, during the rigorous cold, the seeds of what she must produce in the next season; and if for a time I didn't make her sparse, she could not produce so generously afterward.

YOUTH So that's how you are the source of its niggardliness, just as I'm the source of its bountifulness: that's what makes *you* so odious and *me* so pleasant. Now see how much people must prefer me to you.

OLD AGE My Lord, how vainglorious you are! Don't you know that we are both creatures of the same Creator, who brought us both forth into the world for the same purpose?

---

24. Genesis 6:13–22.

YOUTH I do know this; but among all the parts in a whole, there are always some that are more excellent than others. Indeed, in the human body, people say that the heart and the lungs are the noblest parts, compared with the spleen and the liver. As to what's on the outside, one can't compare the hand and the foot to the eye and the mouth, father and mother of Philosophy. Nor would I compare you and me, although we belong to the same master who has commanded us to sustain (with his help) the world in its first state, you to dismember, with all your power, what I've done, and me to give it a force by which it is continually reborn: in this way we are never idle.

OLD AGE Really, you're quite a talker; now if you were as reasonable as you are wordy, you'd win.

YOUTH Have I said something that seems unreasonable since I've begun talking with you?

OLD AGE I don't know. I'll judge you according to how you explain what you've just now said. Now, why do you call the eye and the mouth the mother and father of Philosophy?

YOUTH And why are you trying to learn something about the very thing that you can't use? For since you have neither light in your eyes nor teeth in your mouth, you can neither look around nor speak a single word with conviction.

OLD AGE It's the meaning of the word that gives it conviction, and not how it's pronounced. So say what you like, I'll not take away from the grace of your words by repeating them.

YOUTH Well then, I'll explain so I can get away from you. Before the appearance of any written science, the eye, gazing upon the starry skies, was reading in the heavenly map the admirable power of the Creator of the universe. That's how Philosophy came about: it awakened the soul's nascent understanding by making it look for the sovereign God, who remains the only true wisdom. Since then this soul, filled with an infinity of beautiful ideas, has happily given birth to them through the mouth.[25] But adieu, good woman, I'm leaving; I've stayed too long in this place.

OLD AGE Listen to me a little bit, please.

YOUTH can't. O what a beautiful group of young girls has just arrived! I'm going to join them.

---

25. The notion of the soul that rises from ignorance to truth is found in Plato's *Republic* 516 ff. On the ascension of the soul by degrees from the beauty of the body to the Idea of the Beautiful, see Plato, *Symposium* 210–11.

OLD AGE It's strange that everyone flees me like this to follow after Youth. Even those who aren't youthful search for her in others although she avoids them. They don't know what the Sage said: even a live dog is better off than a dead lion.[26] Their own youth has died away, and they'll never be able to recover it, whereas I'll always be alive to direct them into the hands of Fate. While all those beautiful ladies are embracing my enemy, I'm going to hide in some solitary place, and wait there until it's my turn to receive their favors. There's a church. I'll go there to say my prayers without worrying that anyone will come to look for me, given my horrible ugliness, which I'll describe a bit while I remember what I look like, for I often forget.

> I'm not surprised if my hideous face,
> Sunken eyes, and spiteful voice
> Cause so much terror to the world; nor am I surprised
> If upon seeing me from afar so ugly and decrepit,
> Rather than approach, all flee
> And run away at a fast step.
> Who wouldn't hate me, when my obvious frailty
> Robs beautiful youths of their good looks,
> The most healthy and robust of their strength,
> Brave captains of their valor and honor,
> Great Kings of their power; I drag them all away,
> To enlist them among the ranks of the elderly.
> If I have brought to ruin the high Pyramids,[27]
> The gardens of Babylon, the Colossus, and the maze from where
> Without the thread one could never leave,
> Jupiter's portrait, Mausolus's tomb,
> Diana's temple, and if with one word
> I can abolish the power of the strongest,
> Must you be astonished if I'm offensive?
> Should it surprise you that I'm odious,
> Since I am always pillaging and yet keep nothing?
> The beauty and the grace I steal from the young

26. Ecclesiastes 9:4: "For all those who live there is hope; and even a live dog is better than a dead lion."

27. The seven wonders of the world included the pyramids of Egypt, the hanging gardens of Semiramis in Babylonia, the colossus of Rhodes, Phidias's statue of Zeus, the tomb of the Mausoleum, and the temple of Diana; in place of the lighthouse of Alexandria, the author mentions the labyrinth of the Minotaur.

I return to nature so that she can refashion
And maintain the world in its original form.
   Through dying a thousand times and a thousand times being
      reborn,
Nothing is lost; all things keep their being,[28]
As they always experience the many changes that come;
But those whom pleasure, that gentle delight of life,
Maintains and cherishes, make me more hateful,
For they refuse to obey my commands.

YOUTH Now that Old Age has left, and she can no longer rebuke me for anything I say, I'd like to tell these Ladies a secret I learned
from her. But then people will accuse me of being a gossip for stealing
the words of some and telling them to others. So I think I'd better tell
it only to myself. I'll not divulge it to anyone else if that's possible, and
will keep it to myself.

   I've only said it to myself; and then I suspect,
That I have become my own enemy,
By sharing a secret I've sworn to keep.
I'll not reveal it; but can I keep quiet?
All right, I'll say it; but is it really possible
That I'd betray both my thoughts and myself?
   Now then! I'll say it; no, I won't. Ha! I think
That by not saying it, I'll lose patience;
And if I say it I'll regret it dearly;
If I don't say it, I'll be greatly troubled;
But then what? If I say it I'm altogether certain
Of never being able to take my secret back.
   I'll not say it for fear of contradicting myself;
Truly I'll say it for could it really hurt anyone?
I'll not say it for fear of getting upset.
I'll say it anyway, what could be the harm?
I'll not say it, for one must learn to keep quiet;
A secret is no longer a secret if it can't be kept.[29]

---

28. The Heraclitean notion of the mutability of the universe is frequently invoked in Ronsard's early verse, one of the main sources of the Dames des Roches' writings.

29. Keeping a secret is a frequent theme in ancient and Renaissance humanist writings. See Plutarch, *Concerning Talkativeness, Moralia* 506e–507b; Alciati, *Silentium* (Silence), emblem 11, *Book of Emblems,* 28; Barbara Bowen, *Words and the Man in French Renaissance Literature* (Lexington, Ky.: French Forum, 1983), 9–26.

2

DIALOGUE BETWEEN VIRTUE AND FORTUNE[30]

VIRTUE Greetings, Fortune, I've been looking for you for a long time to ask you to do me a favor.

FORTUNE I'm not looking for *you*, Virtue, nor do I wish to do anything for you, for you constantly foil all my plans and ruin much of my work.

VIRTUE But understand that if I'm looking for you, it's not because I need you. In all things I rely only on myself, without turning to one side or the other, because I want help from no one else.

FORTUNE Then you shouldn't even have wasted your steps coming to find me, since you want nothing to do with me.

VIRTUE It's true that I want nothing to do with you, but I merely wish to present you with a request that will be both an honor to you and agreeable to me, should it please you to grant it.

FORTUNE And what is it?

VIRTUE I ask you to be gentle with those who favor me; if you do this, you'll be held in much higher esteem.

FORTUNE Really, you've got good reasons to want to reform my injustices. Be gone, you can do things your way and I'll do them my way.

VIRTUE The Egyptians had a law.

FORTUNE I don't care about the Egyptians or their law, and I'm surprised you do, seeing how they took so little account of you. I remember that I locked up the Egyptian Sesostris in a house where he would have burned to death if you hadn't counseled his wife, the Queen, to save him even though it meant the loss of their children.[31] And then she didn't order a temple built for you, as the Romans did for me, feminine Fortune, in memory of Volumnia.[32]

---

30. The probable source of this dialogue is Plutarch's *On the Fortune of the Romans, Moralia.* Plutarch depicts Fortune and Virtue personified, just having argued over the paternity of the Roman Empire. The debate ends as the two rivals agree to work together. Rome is the fruit of their efforts. For Catherine, Poitiers replaces Rome.

31. Sesostris, Egyptian king of the twelfth dynasty, was saved with his wife from a burning palace at the cost of the death of their two children. See Herodotus, *History* 2.107.

32. In *On the Fortune of the Romans, Moralia* 318f, Plutarch contrasts the rarity of temples consecrated to Virtue with the abundance of temples to Fortune. Among these, he cites the temple of "The Fortune of Women," dedicated to Coriolanus's mother, Volumnia, who saved Rome from his invading army. See Plutarch, *Coriolanus, Lives* 4.33–38.

VIRTUE I build instead my sacred temples inside virtuous souls, and demand no sacrifice other than that of their will. But if it had pleased you just now to lend me *your* will, I would have told you about an Egyptian law that condemned with a punishment or a fine those who saw evil being done and who did nothing to stop it. That's why I'm trying to make you take a bit more notice of those who are good, so that you can be more humane toward them.

FORTUNE And I'm trying to tell you to go find better luck with those "holy" people who think so highly of you; you wouldn't find it hard to satisfy so few of them. Personally, I'll stick to my usual pleasure of incessantly turning my wheel. I love to humble the great ones as I did to Dionysius,[33] and exalt the least as I did to Agathocles.[34] I'm the Queen of men and I want to control them absolutely; even those who obey you are all subject to me.

VIRTUE Yea, perhaps their wealth, but not their persons.

FORTUNE I can control their lives as well as their possessions. I made Aegeus jump into the sea because his son's ship had not changed its sails,[35] and I saved Arion, pulling him from the raging waves and allowing him to drift to a safe port.[36]

VIRTUE All right, you may have power over their wealth and their lives, but not over their minds.

FORTUNE Ha! I leave that to you! Make good use of your privilege, I don't think you'll have many devotees. But say, look at your feet; they're supported by a cube whose form corresponds to only one element; if you look at me, I'm elevated on a sphere designed to resemble this great universe.[37] These two images show how much greater my power is than yours, since I'm the master of almost everyone, and you don't even govern a fourth of the world.

33. Dionysius the Younger, tyrant of Syracuse from 367 to 357 BCE. See Plutarch, *Timoleon, Lives* 6.16.

34. A young man from Syracuse with populist tendencies and the son of a potter, Agathocles (born 361 BCE) was credited by Diodorus Siculus (*Library of History*, LCL, 21.16.5) with having restored self-government to the people. See Plutarch, *Sayings of Kings and Commanders, Moralia* 176e; Justin, *History* 21.1–7.

35. When Theseus returned from Crete, he forgot to raise the agreed-upon sign on his ship. Aegeus, his father, believing his son dead, threw himself into the sea.

36. Arion, a musician from Lesbos, was saved from the sea by a dolphin who carried him safely to shore.

37. Fortune stands precariously upon a sphere symbolizing its fickle nature, while Virtue sits upon a cube. See Alciati, *Ars naturam adiuvans* (Art to the Aid of Nature), emblem 98, and *In occasionem* (About chance), emblem 121, *Book of Emblems*, 118, 144–45.

VIRTUE I don't doubt your power. But I'm vexed at the fact that being able to do what you please, you do evil rather than good.

FORTUNE All I do is good; my joy and delight are my only laws.

VIRTUE Duty is mine. Now listen, I'm talking to you.

FORTUNE I've run out of time.

VIRTUE Stay a bit longer, please.

FORTUNE I don't want to. Stop it! You're going to make me fall.

VIRTUE No, I'm not, I'll support you. Look how you've just betrayed your weakness: supported as you are by a sphere and a broken staff, you're always in danger of falling.

FORTUNE No matter, I always gain new strength when I fall, as did Antheus.[38] But your pillar is more secure than is mine; yes, in all honesty, I could not knock it down.

VIRTUE That's because it's built to the same standards as altars are.

FORTUNE But even altars are sometimes destroyed; the Poitou region bears good witness to this, principally her capital city, where there remained not one in its entirety.[39]

VIRTUE Alas, you're right. These altars were destroyed against my will, because quite often they served my purposes. Those who ruined them were enemies of virtue and learning both. They had only some vain guise of supposed religion, and they were less religious in fact than those they claimed they wanted to reform. It became quite clear that they were guided strictly by greed, and not by devotion: they went first for the church treasuries, pretending to wish to reduce the ceremonies,[40] like the tyrant who, to correct the pomp of Apollo and of Aesculapius, took the robe from the one and the beard from the other;[41] but I pray to God that what they stole in this poor city may be like what the gold of Toulouse was to the soldiers of Cepio.[42]

FORTUNE That's fine with me as soon as I've raised men higher so that their fall may be all the more perilous.

VIRTUE No, I beg you, don't harm them more than is necessary;

---

38. The giant Antheus was invulnerable as long as he was touching his mother, the Sun. See Hyginus, *Fabula*, fable 31.

39. An allusion to the destruction of the churches of Poitiers by Huguenot armies in June 1562.

40. An allusion to the Protestant reform of Christianity.

41. Dionysius the Younger, tyrant of Syracuse, who ruled for twelve years from 367 BCE, stripped a statue of Apollo of a golden dress and a statue of Aesculapius of a golden beard.

42. "Aurum habet Tolossanum" (He has gold from Toulouse), a maxim denoting a gain that is of little benefit. See Erasmus, *Adages, Collected Works*, vol. 32, 1.10. 98. The allusion is to the sack of Poitiers in 1562 by the Huguenot armies of the comte de Grammont.

you've done too much for them as it is and they show you no gratitude.
But from now on, help me instead to defend Poitiers. I will not be ungrateful to you for this favor. Now, following the custom of the Spartans, let us sacrifice to the Muses, in hopes that our kindness will not
be forgotten.

FORTUNE Yes, but for all the good we'll do, the honor will be
given to you and I will not be praised.

VIRTUE Not true, I assure you. Just as the ancients built only one
temple in honor of both Pollux and Castor, even though Jupiter was
the father of the one, and Tyndaraeus of the other, so I want us to be
honored together, although I do consider myself God's beloved daughter, and you his servant.

FORTUNE So that's the reason I have to obey my master's daughter; but can Fortune do anything reasonable? In teaming up with you
I worry about losing my identity and about forgetting what I normally do.

VIRTUE Ah, don't worry, I have not come looking for you with
such an intention. It's to help me save Poitiers that I ask your assistance,
and that you do harm to those who would harm her. For in doing them
evil, you *will* in fact be doing good. So make the outcome of all their
undertakings the opposite of what they wish. In the meantime, come
and hear my prayer to God, and you may add another to it if you feel
so inclined.

> O Lord whose providence
> Holds all in its obedience,
> Lend us, O God our sovereign,
> Your favorable and powerful hand,
>   So we may be able to defend
> This people willing to offer you
> Its life, its body, and its heart,
> Sacrificed for your honor.
>   Take care of her [Poitiers's] gracious women,
> Look out for her chaste girls,
> Protect also the men
> Who revere your goodness.
>   If some enemy attempts
> To knock down our walls,
> If someone is looking for ways
> To take our citizens by surprise,

Confound him with a judgment
That punishes the traitorous spirit,
As it has the proud and cruel heart
Of the incredulous Pharaoh.[43]

Fortune, would you care to say a few words?
FORTUNE Why yes! I'd be pleased to second you in this worthy
endeavor.

God who, unmoved, moves this entire great world,
Starting and stopping the vagabond course
Of so many bright-shining stars, ornaments of your Heavens;
As you watch, unperturbed, fearful humans here below,
May it please you to hear my reverent prayer,
That proceeds from a humble and devoted heart.
Lord, although I am fickle and shallow,
I pay homage nonetheless
To your majesty, always recognizing
That from you alone do I hold my scepter and my reign,
That it pleases you to see me constant in inconstancy,
And to name me Fortune, whose course is so variable.
If my favors were longer lasting,
The faith owed to you would be ill proven;
People would no longer think of you as the Great Being;[44]
We would completely forget to do service to you,
And this world would become a school for every vice;
That's why, Lord, I change in an instant.
I sometimes appear arrogant and cunning;
Then I become all of a sudden gracious and benign;
But all I do is for the purpose of obeying you,
Provided that I'm humble to you and obedient;
I don't mind being called both traitor and unkind,
And it does not displease me to be hated.
O God! If what I do is agreeable to you,
Please grant my requests similar
To those of Virtue: please bring peace

---

43. Exodus 7–11.
44. Title of God, "The Being, or the One Who Is," Deuteronomy 32:39; Plato, *Timaeus* 28a,
29a–b; Louis Le Caron, *Dialogues*, ed. Joan Buhlmann and Donald Gilman (Geneva: Droz, 1986),
175.

To our poor Poitiers, and if someone makes ready
And dares to attack her, may he feel on his head
The blow that Pyrrhus felt in Argos.[45]

There, Virtue, are you satisfied?

VIRTUE Yes, in part, and I'll be so completely if you act as well as you talk.

FORTUNE One might say you distrust me.

VIRTUE No, for your lack of assurance assures me; you've grown accustomed to spending very little time at any point [of the wheel]; so that having already done much harm to our Poitiers, I hope that in the future you'll be kinder to her.

FORTUNE But why are you so interested in her?

VIRTUE Because I'm revered by several who live there.

FORTUNE I don't think there are too many of those.

VIRTUE The good are never numerous; so it's said that if anyone wants to be counted among the virtuous, that one must seek solitude. Even though few honor me, these few are very worthy people.

FORTUNE As for me, I don't think anyone in this entire world loves me. The very same people to whom I do the most good think that it's because they deserve it, like that Greek general[46] to whom I handed over entire cities while he slept, and yet he disavowed me, saying I had no part in his victory. But I've had my revenge on him, for since then he's had no successes.

VIRTUE Quite often you disappoint the hopes of those who love you, and this causes some of them to hide the affection they have for you, because they're not sure to what end you're leading them. I eagerly receive all those who seek me even if they might have neglected me, like Polemon. I still welcome them with open arms.

FORTUNE Because you've always been good, it's not hard for you to stay that way. I'd now like to follow you, were it in my power to do so; but I worry that if I give up my former self to become better, I'll be even more slandered than Sulla when he resigned his dictatorship, and contempt will be heaped upon me by those who think I've injured them.[47]

45. Pyrrhus, king of Epirus, perished at Argos when a tile was dropped on his head. Plutarch, *Pyrrhus, Lives* 9.34.

46. This "Greek general" is probably Polemon (king of Pontus), who is mentioned in the next few lines. See Plutarch, *Antony, Lives* 9.38.61.

47. Fortune hesitates to give up her rights, contrary to Sulla (138–78 BCE) who, considering himself fortunate, voluntarily had himself deposed from the dictatorship. See Plutarch, *Sulla, Lives* 34.6.

VIRTUE O Fortune, my friend, if you wish to reform your way of life from now on, I'll guide you to a safe place, where you'll be well received by an excellent person who loves me a lot.[48] You'll be safe from all dangers, as you stay near me, and you'll no longer have the trouble of continually turning a wheel, like poor Ixion.[49]

FORTUNE My trouble is pleasant to me, and it seems that you should rather be telling me that in turning my wheel, I'm like these intelligent heavenly beings who make the Heavens go round.[50]

VIRTUE The moving of the heavens is beneficial, but that of your wheel is dangerous; while the former is good, because it helps and conserves our world, yours is bad, because it brings destruction and ruin.

FORTUNE You can't deny that in doing evil to some, I also do good to others, in the same way that the sun, in giving day to those who are opposite to us, creates night for us by its absence. But I see what your problem is: you're envious of my power, because I do both good and evil, and you can only do one of those two.

VIRTUE If I were envious I would not be Virtue, for envy is a great vice. Please don't hold such an opinion of me, and don't think of yourself more highly for being able to do both good and evil. The enemy of humankind would in that case be half praised along with you. As for your notion that I'm powerless, saying that I can't do evil, I take such blame for praise, and if we remain together for some time, I hope you'll see that my power, my duty, and my will are so united that they'll never be separated.

FORTUNE The sweetness of your words has so won me over that I never want to be separated from you.

VIRTUE You would do well to favor sometimes with your presence those who hate me, so they may not be completely unhappy.

FORTUNE Ha! I protest that I'll never love those who hate you, and if for a time I show myself more amiable toward them, in the end they'll experience my rigors even more. Because from now on, you can take me wherever you wish, and I assure you that I value nothing more in this world than obeying you.

VIRTUE For the time being, let's keep Poitiers safe, just as we have decided. Meanwhile, some good opportunity to introduce you to that excellent person I spoke to you about will come our way; notwith-

---

48. A reference to Madeleine des Roches, whom Catherine praises at the end of this dialogue and in the *Dialogue between Poverty and Hunger*.

49. Ixion, king of Thessaly, was attached by Zeus to a flaming wheel that turned perpetually.

50. Plato, *Timaeus* 34a.

standing your disfavor, she has climbed so high up my ladder of virtue that your greatness could not add much to hers.

FORTUNE Then I mustn't present myself there for fear of being scorned.

VIRTUE But you'll be even more appreciated; because you'll win honor in giving away your gifts, and maybe in enjoying such a beautiful gain you'll always want to behave yourself with discretion, uplifting the most virtuous.

FORTUNE In truth I'm wrong to favor men of little value. But as for not making the same mistake again, I'd like to begin walking in your very footsteps, because I know full well that it's better to be guided by a clear-sighted person than to lead a great number of the blind.[51]

3

DIALOGUE BETWEEN THE HAND, THE FOOT, AND THE MOUTH[52]

HAND Lord, how I could go on complaining about my master! I work daily for him, but all the same he pays so little attention to me that he gives me no garment whatsoever and makes me sweat in the summer and freeze in winter, while this villain, Foot, is so well dressed.

FOOT Well, well, I could have patiently listened to your whining and tried to console you, but now I know that you're very malicious and that you complain more about my good luck than about your misery.

HAND Ha, sweetheart! It's easy for you to talk, while I work every day spinning the wool and silk you're dressed in, or cutting out the slippers you use to caper about in front of the Ladies.

FOOT How can you not reproach me for my faults, as if you could

---

51. A proverb; see Matthew 15:14 and Luke 6:39.

52. The principles of complementarity and hierarchy in the social order, as well as the analogy between the body politic and different parts of the human body, are found in various political treatises of the period. Des Roches applies the anatomical analogy to the city rather than the republic. Probable sources include Plutarch's *On Brotherly Love, Moralia* 6; 1 Corinthians 12; Livy, *The Early History of Rome* 2.32, cited by Janet Smarr, "A Female Tradition? Women's Dialogue Writing in Sixteenth-Century France," in *Strong Voices, Weak History: Early Modern Women Writers and Canons in England, France, and Italy,* ed. Pamela Joseph Benson and Victoria Kirkham (Ann Arbor: University of Michigan Press, 2005), 41 n. 17; and the abundant medical literature on the science of the human body, especially the hand, considered by Aristotle the "instrument of instruments" (*Problemata* 30.5.955b and *De anima* 3.8.432a I). On the hand, see the recent *On Hands: Memory and Knowledge in Early Modern Europe,* ed. Claire R. Sherman (Seattle: University of Washington Press, 2000).

know what they are, when you even reproach me for what I do right? But tell me, please, who would bring you wool, silk, and gold if I didn't go and fetch them for you?

HAND Who could turn gold into clear and pure thread if it weren't for me, who am mistress of all the arts.

FOOT Say instead that you're their servant, that's much closer to the truth; for it's the mind that invents them, and then commands you to execute them as it sees fit. So you don't do anything but by obedience; your actions aren't guided by any discretion or reason that may be found in you.

HAND And what do you know about reason, you who are placed so far away from her? I think that nature, because she saw how contrary you are to her, decided to place reason at one extremity of the body, and you at the other.

FOOT That was so as to deprive you of reason altogether. You've certainly heard it said that the burning rays of the sun heat the earth when it's in the constellations of Cancer or Leo and that at such a time, all the cold air retreats to the middle region of the atmosphere. In the same way reason is the sun for man, remaining as it were in the heaven of his brain; from there it illumines all *my* actions, while all sorts of foolishness ends up in or near you. What foot, besides that of Philoctetes,[53] has ever caused its master to lose his life, while there have been thousands of hands that have caused thousands of deaths to thousands of men, and many others would have perished on account of the actions of their hands, if my diligence in fleeing had not saved them. So then, don't find it strange if people accord *me* more honor than *you*. Remember, Mercury wears golden sandals on his feet and yet does not wear gloves.[54]

HAND Oh how nasty you are! You dare compare yourself to the winged feet of a god? You who were just now playing the Philosopher, don't you know that those who exalt themselves will be humbled?[55]

FOOT Actually, I couldn't be placed lower than I am; but please, stop being envious of my position. Consider that if I'm given shoes and sandals, it's not simply to look good, but also to protect myself from

---

53. Philoctetes, guardian of Hercules' bow and arrows, violated the oath he had taken to keep secret his master's burial ground by striking it with his foot; he was punished with a wound to his heel.

54. Mercury's attributes are the caduceus, the wide-brimmed hat, and winged sandals.

55. Luke 18:14.

mud, stones, and thorns that are found along roads. Also, the master to whom we belong has to worry about losing me, for no other part is more necessary to him than me.

HAND I'd like you to know that he needs *me* more than he needs *you*. He couldn't put a single thing in his mouth without my help.

FOOT And who but me fetches his food for him?

HAND But don't you realize that if it were really necessary, I could get down on the ground and try to walk?

FOOT Try it.

HAND All right then.

FOOT But then you'll stay down like me, supporting the body by the force of your arms as I've supported it.

HAND That's fine.

FOOT It's not good to get mixed up in something that one doesn't know how to do; watch out, I beg you, so that what happened to Phaethon when he tried to drive a borrowed chariot doesn't happen to you.[56]

HAND You compared yourself to Mercury, and now you're comparing yourself to the Sun.

FOOT Of course not, I'm comparing you to his son! Now let's see then how you get along with your new trade. O God, how you're working at it! O God, how I worry that you'll make me tumble!

HAND I will *not*. No, just stay still.

FOOT Listen, who is that who's threatening us?

HAND It's the mouth of our master. My God! What are we going to do?

MOUTH What's this, what's all this about? What kind of household is this, you worthless scoundrels? Are you trying to pervert the order of the Creator who put eyes in the highest part of the body, so that through them we might see his most excellent works? Shush now! Shush! Each of you return to your usual place and tell me who started this chaos.

FOOT It's the hand who complains about her condition because she envies the honor that you give me.

MOUTH But what does she lack, this ungrateful wretch? Our Master is hardly up in the morning when he lifts his hand to his head, the noblest part of his body, and quite often has it hold an ivory comb to straighten out his hair.

---

56. Phaethon, son of the Sun, tried to drive his father's chariot, but the chariot ran amuck and he was struck dead by Zeus.

HAND That's to render him service.

MOUTH When he's in the company of learned men and lords, everything remarkable that he sees, he reveals to his hand that often writes it down.

HAND That's to show him honor.

MOUTH If he sees some beautiful Ladies, he uses his hand to lift his hat to greet them.

HAND That's to please him.

MOUTH If he's at his place of worship, he lifts his hands to Heaven to say his prayers.

HAND That's to appease God on his behalf.

MOUTH If he's at table eating, his hand is always the first to dip into the plate.

HAND That's for his benefit.

MOUTH If he's lying down in bed, his hand is most often on his chest.

HAND That's for his health.

MOUTH If someone brings him money, the Hand is the first to touch it, count it, and lock it away, as its sole guardian, while the rest of us can get some only if it pleases the Hand to give us some.

HAND My master has to use me in this because none of you is right for this duty. But you're not mentioning the fact that I'm often employed in the vilest and most dishonest things anyone could think of.

MOUTH And you're not mentioning that you're constantly washed and perfumed with sweet-smelling water. And besides, I beg you, since you're complaining so much about your misfortunes, think also a little about the good things that happen to you every day. Don't get discouraged at your present state, but instead try to improve it without envying the garments that you yourself gave to the Foot. Look into acquiring some for yourself, too; we'll be much better off for it, for we want to live in peace, since we know that quarrels among citizens cause the downfall of a city.[57] In the same way, disagreements between us could destroy our master. Let's look out then for his well-being more than for our own, and realize that the good that's his alone is also ours.

FOOT Truly, we must believe what the Mouth tells us.

HAND There you are again, speaking without being asked.

MOUTH Foot, there's no reason for you to encroach upon the Hand's domain; you must think yourself inferior to her. And you, Hand, although you're placed higher, don't become arrogant, for you

---

57. Another allusion to the destruction caused by the religious wars.

too are a servant just like the Foot. Therefore, recognizing that you're in the same position, help one another and get along amiably together.

HAND I'm happy to follow from now on your good advice, and I thank you for the trouble you've taken to settle our arguments. And, Foot, I no longer want to quarrel with you; if you have something for me to do, I'm at your service, to wash you, or to put your shoes on.

FOOT Ah! I thank you humbly; I'm delighted to hear you say such good words. As for me, you'll always find me ready to serve you, if you'd like to stock up on gloves or rings.

HAND Very well, very well, I'd like that, but the Mouth must state how much it wants to pay, because I won't do anything without its advice.

4

DIALOGUE BETWEEN POVERTY AND HUNGER[58]

POVERTY I heard the other day that Jupiter was preparing a banquet for the wedding of a Nymph he once loved, and even though I wasn't invited, I began to head in that direction, thinking that I might find at the tables in the back some place for you, Hunger, my friend.

HUNGER Then why didn't you call on me to accompany you there?

POVERTY I wanted to find out what was going on for fear of bringing you there in vain.

HUNGER How were you received?

POVERTY Alas! Worse than I could have imagined. As soon as those Gods and Goddesses saw me, they began to run away, clinging tightly to their jewels: Jupiter hid his scepter, Venus her belt, Mercury his winged shoes, Apollo his harp, and Love his arrows, saying that Poverty would surely bring misfortune.

HUNGER And then what? Is Love afraid of you? Doesn't he know that you're his mother?[59]

POVERTY Ah! dear friend, he pretended not to. He was the first to say while chasing me out that I was interrupting the entire party, and

---

58. This dialogue bears the influence of Louise Labé's *Debate between Folly and Love*, associated with Plato's *Symposium* and Erasmus's *Praise of Folly*. It poses the question of social inequality, exacerbated in times of war and famine, and is enriched by the claim that women can exercise reason and discretion.

59. In Plato's *Symposium* 203a–c, Love is born from the union of Porus (Plenty) and Penia (Poverty).

that his daughter Voluptuousness would be forced to flee if I stayed there for any length of time, because she and I can't get along together.

HUNGER Love didn't want you to be recognized as his mother?

POVERTY Indeed, that's why I never mentioned it.

HUNGER Do you think it was in your power to keep it quiet? If you had openly admitted Love was your son, his subjects would have become contemptuous of him. For you have no vessels of gold to give him out of which to make a statue like the one that King Amasis made for himself.[60]

POVERTY True enough, I don't have gold at my fingertips, but I sometimes have reason to prevent me from saying what I mustn't say.

HUNGER It's often said that women abound in words, but lack reason.[61]

POVERTY Who says such things but big, loud men? They dare not spend their time with courteous and learned women for fear that these women will judge them for who they are;[62] so instead they look for women who are like them. And then by asking them foolish questions, they compel these women to answer less well than they normally do, only to conclude that all women speak alike and that the little they say is too much! But I've hardly ever known a woman who perished because of what she said, whereas an infinite number of men, on account of their boasting, have caused their own ruin. If the "Lioness of Athens" had not learned to remain silent, preferring to bite her tongue off rather than reveal the names of those who wanted to topple the dictatorship, she wouldn't have been awarded a bronze statue with which she was honored after her death.[63]

60. Pharaoh Amasis had a golden statue of himself forged so that he would be venerated. See Herodotus, *History* 2.172. Christine de Pizan voices the same criticism in *The Book of the City of Ladies* 1.8.8.

61. For many early modern theoreticians, women either lack reason altogether or possess a faculty of reason inferior to that of men. For a broad discussion of women and reason, see Michèle Crampe-Casnabet, "A Sampling of Eighteenth-Century Philosophy," in *A History of Women in the West: Renaissance and Enlightenment Paradoxes*, ed. Natalie Zemon Davis and Arlette Farge (Cambridge: Harvard University Press, 1993), 3:315–47.

62. Christine de Pizan voiced the same criticism: "Those men who have attacked women out of jealousy are those wicked ones who have seen and realized that many women have greater understanding and are more noble in conduct than they themselves, and thus they are pained and disdainful." *Book of the City of Ladies* 1.8.8.

63. Leaena (Greek for lioness), surnamed the Lioness of Athens, was the mistress of Aristogiton, the tyrannicide. The plot failed, but Leaena refused to reveal the names of the conspirators; the Athenians erected a monument of a tongueless lioness in her honor. See Plutarch, *Concerning*

HUNGER That was so long ago! You probably couldn't find today a woman of the sort you just described.[64]

POVERTY May God grant that no other render such a wretched proof of her virtuous silence. Believe me, those who speak well also know how to keep quiet, and one can find as many excellent women in the world now as at any point in history.

HUNGER Well then, tell me who they are, and how many there are.

POVERTY There are so many that I can't count them. All the same I know one who on her own possesses more grace than all others combined. To speak of her is to speak of all those women who deserve praise.

HUNGER What's her name?

POVERTY I wish to veil it with the honor of silence,[65] for fear that to utter that name would be to profane it. Suffice it to know that she is made admirable by the virtue of her conduct, the nobility of her mind, the greatness of her learning, and the sweetness of her words.

HUNGER Do you speak with her often?

POVERTY Sometimes at her gate.

HUNGER Don't you enter her house?

POVERTY Not to stay there, for I'd be a nuisance to her, and I don't wish to bother her if it is within my power not to do so. But just as happened with my son [Cupid] when he sought to wound the Muses, that upon seeing them so intent on their varied occupations, he lost all will to harm them, so I, when I see from afar the worthy activities of this virtuous Lady, lose all will to bother her, because I see in her a good number of the traits of my former host Aristides. It's true that I'm almost as hated by her as I was loved by him, but nonetheless I don't cease to honor her.

HUNGER Since you're so unwelcome at her house, I too would have very little chance at being received.

POVERTY Ah! Truly I advise you not to go there; she knows how to resist you and all other passions.

Talkativeness, Moralia 6.505d–e; Castiglione, *Book of the Courtier,* book 3, section 23; Vives, *Education of a Christian Woman* 11.108; Alciati, *Nec quaestioni quidem cedendum* (One must never yield to questioning), emblem 13, *Book of Emblems,* 30.

64. Des Roches repeats the same rhetorical ploy in her *Dialogue between Severe and Placide:* when Severe tries to discredit Placide's allusion to exemplary intellectual women from antiquity on grounds that none of the same caliber can be found in his own time, Placide answers with a catalogue of even more remarkable contemporary women writers and poets.

65. Des Roches refrains from stating her mother's name out of deference and admiration.

HUNGER Oh, I hate meeting such people, I'd worry about finding Epimenides' meal there.[66]

POVERTY She constantly says that virtue without fortune is too weak, and that fortune without virtue is too shallow, so she calls on them both together to be protected from you and from me.

HUNGER Well, let's leave her alone then and find out which home you could enter to find a meal.

POVERTY Oh God! Where on earth can I go? I'm so weak that I can barely stand up.

HUNGER I'm in fine shape and I walk quite easily; let's go to the home of Porus. Perhaps he'll do us some good, for the sake of the son you have in common.

POVERTY My friend, he acts as if he doesn't know me and has never seen me before.

HUNGER Perhaps he doesn't remember meeting you. But remind him of it now; his memory could come back to him, at least if he wasn't drunk at the time.

POVERTY He wasn't drunk. No, that's just gossip. Nectar, which is of divine origin, doesn't make people drunk like foul-smelling wine that clouds up one's senses and one's reason. But just as those who were caught speaking ill of King Pyrrhus used the excuse that they were drunk, and that they would have maligned him even more had they not run out of wine,[67] so Porus, who was ashamed that his lasciviousness had led him toward me, poor wretch that I am, said that he had drunk too much, wishing by this fault to excuse an even greater one.[68]

HUNGER Well, since he wasn't drunk, he'll recognize you.

POVERTY Yes, but he'll drive me away by hitting me with his staff. Don't you know that the rich are almost always proud and disdainful?

HUNGER Well, where do you want to go?

POVERTY I'll just sit down beside some door, as I'm accustomed to doing.

HUNGER Cursed be whoever follows *you!*

---

66. Epimenides, one of the Seven Wise Men, often abstained from eating. See Plutarch, *Dinner of the Seven Wise Men, Moralia* 2.157d–e.

67. Plutarch, *Pyrrhus, Lives* 9.8.12.

68. In Plato's *Symposium* 203a–c, Penia, or Poverty, voluntarily mates with Porus when he is dulled with drunkenness. The striking reversal of roles here attributes to Poverty, the female character, the qualities of temperance and virtue, and makes her a victim of male aggression.

POVERTY You'll come too in spite of yourself, even though I wish you'd stay away, for I'm sure you're the one who makes me so hated.

HUNGER But it's because of you that I'm so miserable. If you weren't around, people would satisfy me with the best meals.

POVERTY Oh, you wretch! Don't you know that the rich and the greedy treat you much worse than others?

HUNGER And where shall I go, then, poor as I am?

POVERTY You could go to the royal Court, and sit at the table with the lords.

HUNGER Oh, oh, really! They're too focused on eating; they would have already eaten everything by the time I'd arrived.

POVERTY Then go find the Treasury officials.

HUNGER No, I shall not; even though they quite often have fine meals, they sometimes pay so much attention to games of chance that in deference to them they cheat their appetite out of what it's owed.

POVERTY Go then, if you wish, to the Judges, and begin whispering in their ears.

HUNGER Your advice isn't wise. A Judge must be able to hear well, and it's said that a hungry man has no ears.[69]

POVERTY Wouldn't it be better if you went to see the Counselors at law?

HUNGER They would advise me to leave and would make use of their positions to thwart me.

POVERTY Go then to the Attorneys to learn their fancy ways of speaking.

HUNGER They would say nothing good with me around; bagpipes make no sound when they're empty, and Attorneys can't plead their cases well when they're hungry.

POVERTY All right, go see the merchants.

HUNGER I'd better not stay with them, for in little time I'd make them so weak that they could neither go to market nor make use of their usual wiles.

POVERTY What's that to you?

HUNGER In all honesty, it's because you would immediately come along and prevent them from being kind to me at the very moment when they might feel like it.

POVERTY Do you think that I'm so opposed to you?

69. Lawyers and judges are often represented in Renaissance literature as devoured by an insatiable greed.

HUNGER It's not that you consciously wish to harm me, but you would cause them to lose their means of helping me.

POVERTY Ah ha! What a fuss you make for a wretched beggar! Go, go hide in Pandora's box![70]

HUNGER Why you old lice-infested hag, go hide in the depths of Tartarus! All you do is harmful to the world; more so even than me, who am sometimes sought after by the sick, and by those who no longer want to live. Ah! I get angry at being accompanied by you sometimes, who are the hate and the horror of all men!

POVERTY Poverty must always be humble, so I'll respond modestly and without anger by saying that if you never followed me, I'd not be as hated as I am. All the same, since Fate has bound me to you, I must patiently endure the inconveniences that come upon me because of *you*. But I beg of you, flee from me as much as you're able, and I'll also flee from you with all of my power, even so we'll have too much time together. Now tell me, where are you going from here?

HUNGER I'm going to visit the peasants of Poitou; it seems that they feed on hunger the way others die from it. Ever since the war brought me there, I haven't moved.

POVERTY That is where I normally abide; I must return there before long.

HUNGER Don't come there so soon, then; wait until I've eaten their provisions, so that, having nothing left to eat, they'll lose their desire to drink, for they had very little wine this year.

POVERTY Go, and may God be with you! I won't be far behind.

HUNGER Please don't be in a hurry, we'll do just fine without you.

5

DIALOGUE BETWEEN LOVE, BEAUTY, AND PHYSIS[71]

LOVE Well, well, what do I see? What glistening splendor is making its way through my blindfold? Ah! yes, it's Beauty. If I can just hold onto her once, I'll not let her easily escape from my rule.

---

70. In Hesiodic mythology, Pandora, the first woman, was the "gift" of the gods to men, designed to bring them misfortune.

71. For likely sources, see the debate of Love and Beauty in Plato's *Phaedrus* 250–57, and Louise Labé's *Debate of Folly and Love*. Des Roches shares Boccaccio's view that Cupid's attributes (his gaze, bow, arrows, and torch) should be judged negatively: "De cupidine I martis filio, qui genuit Voluptatem" (On the ambition of the son of Mars who engendered Sensuality, *Genealogia deorum* 2.4). This dialogue inspired Marie Le Gendre's *Dialogue des chastes amours d'Eros, et de Kalisti*, in *L'Exercice de l'âme vertueuse*.

BEAUTY O! how unfortunate I am to encounter here the worst enemy I have in this world! If his blindfold doesn't make me invisible to him, I'm in danger of being captured. O Lord! I think he sees me. Here he comes flying after me. Where can I flee?

LOVE Where are you going so quickly, Beauty? I want to speak with you, please. Won't you wait a minute?

BEAUTY If that's all you want, I'm ready to hear you. But I'm afraid of your hands much more than your words.

LOVE Well, if you're not afraid of what I say, then accept at least my assurance that I won't harm you.

BEAUTY In whose name do you swear not to injure me? Tell me so that I may know who is protecting me.

LOVE I swear by my bow.

BEAUTY And what is your bow made of if not the ebony of my eyebrows? If you're not worried about injuring my whole person, you'll hardly worry about taking a false oath by just one part of me.

LOVE In that case I swear by my arrows.

BEAUTY Indeed, but from where do you get your arrows[72] if it isn't from my facial features?

LOVE All right, then. I swear by my torch.

BEAUTY Your torch's heat and light come from the fire of my eyes.

LOVE Well then, if all my power comes from you, why are you so afraid of me?

BEAUTY Love, don't you know full well that it's from me that people take their weapons to wound me? The snares in which I often find myself trapped are the very hairs of my head that are disguised by poets' love sonnets. Seeing these hairs so well ordered, I want to take them, and find myself captured by my own hairs which betray their innocent mistress, rendering her a prisoner in your hands.

LOVE Then complain only about yourself, for you give to others the means by which to harm you; don't blame me.

BEAUTY I'd have no opportunity to complain of either me or others, if you didn't take from me that with which you strike lovers. Once wounded by you, these men look for where the blow came from, and when they see me nearby, so resembling that which just struck them, they think that I alone inflicted their wound, and then they want to exact their revenge on me alone; to do this, they take the arrows you shot at them and throw them back at me, some with love poetry wrapped

---

72. The term "traict" means both an arrow and a facial feature. This play on words is lost in translation.

around them, others with courteous words, still others with golden tips more piercing than either iron or steal; and *you* are the one who teaches them all these malicious tricks.[73]

LOVE I beg you, Beauty, don't blame me for all of your problems. All I want to do is make sure your perfections are seen and admired. But why don't you go live in those great palaces, where you'll find better protection.

BEAUTY Ha! really it's not there that I can be safe, Love. Not long ago I went there to see those rich men, but you filled the entire place with courtiers who wanted to kidnap[74] my hostess and me!

LOVE What harm could your would-be assailants have done to you? You're an immortal Goddess.

BEAUTY Don't you think that being imprisoned is harm enough? Quite often I find myself hurt by the rudeness of those who courted me ever so humbly, and although I'm immortal in myself, I seem to perish in those people whom I've favored, and am forced to vanish, either through the violence of the times, or because of their maltreatment by those who imprison me.

LOVE Would you like me to take you to the home of my mother, Poverty?[75] Not many people would look for you there.

BEAUTY No, no, thank you, I wouldn't want to stay with her too long.

LOVE Well, come with me then, and I'll take you to some other place.

BEAUTY I want nothing to do with you. Be on your way. Do you think I'd want to be led by someone who's blind?

LOVE I clearly showed that I wasn't blind when I saw you. Rest assured that Love always sees clearly in the presence of beauty; but those who love ugly people and in their foolishness think them beautiful are truly blind,[76] and they think I am as well, even though that's wrong, as you've been able to see.

---

73. For a similar disapprobation of the notion that feminine beauty bewitches and deceives men, see Hélisenne de Crenne, *Renaissance Woman*, 94, third invective epistle: "Surely it is pointless for you to say that feminine beauty with its sumptuous dress is both vain and dangerous. To lend substance to your argument you remind us yet once more of the perils into which men have fallen in the past for having been fascinated by women's beauty."

74. *Desrober* means both to steal and to disrobe. The term thus indicates sexual aggression akin to rape.

75. Love is the offspring of Penia (Poverty) and Porus (Plenty). See Plato, *Symposium* 203a–c.

76. Plato, *Symposium* 206d, 209b.

BEAUTY Well, why do you wear that blindfold if not to hide your bad eyesight?

LOVE It's one of my tricks, so that when men see me wearing it, they never suspect that I can make war on them.

BEAUTY What? You're a traitor? I'm getting away from you!

LOVE Oh, please don't. What good would it do you to flee? You can't outrun my wings.

BEAUTY Go away! Go away! don't follow me, away with you, I say! But I think I see someone who can chase you away from me just in time: the eldest daughter of the Almighty Creator. Yes, it's Physis herself.[77] May God protect you, my mother. I beg you, if you please, get rid of this troublesome fellow; wherever I am, he pesters me and never leaves me alone.

LOVE Physis, my good mother, if ever I did anything to please you, I ask you to show me your gratitude now and command this lady to stay with me always, so that her graces will make me more pleasing to mortals.

BEAUTY Don't allow this, my mother.

PHYSIS Listen to me, my children, neither one of you has any power without the other. Beauty, you'd never be accepted or desired without Love. And you, Love, you'd never be prized or revered without beauty. So, my children, since you complement each other so well, be united as well in your wills, and live peacefully together.

LOVE That will be fine, my mother.

BEAUTY And I think it's fine to accompany Love, but I don't want him always with me.

PHYSIS How is that possible, my daughter?

BEAUTY I mean that Love will never be found in any place except where there is beauty, but beauty will sometimes be in the places where Love is not.

PHYSIS And must Love be found only with beautiful people?

BEAUTY Well, yes, if he wishes, my mother, I don't really care. I simply beg you to show me a place where I can be alone without him.

PHYSIS Go where Diana[78] is worshiped, and hide beneath the veils of the holy sisters. Love won't look for you there.

---

77. *Physis* is Greek for nature. As eldest daughter of the Creator, she is reminiscent of Physis in the *Romance of the Rose*, where she presides over the human reproduction of the species. She is a conservative figure who mediates God's will on earth.

78. Virgin goddess of the hunt, protector of women, identified with the Greek Artemis.

BEAUTY O, my mother, he almost never moves from there! I don't think I could be *less* safe anywhere else in the world, for the less beauty is seen, the more strongly she is desired.[79] I'll go take refuge with Pallas,[80] if that's agreeable to you; that way I'll escape from Love's tyranny through books, needlework, and the eyes of Medusa.[81]

PHYSIS Well go then, that's fine with me.

LOVE And what about me, mother, can't I go there, too?

PHYSIS If you do, you'll remain a prisoner, even though you imprison others.

LOVE All right, then, I'll wait until she leaves that place.

BEAUTY And I, mother, with your permission, I'll go live in my temple of freedom.

6

DIALOGUE BETWEEN SINCERO AND CHARITE[82]

SINCERO Forgive me, please, Madame, for my boldness in asking that you show your good graces toward me. It's not that I think I deserve them, but because of their name and yours,[83] they must be freely given. I'm of the opinion that you should be more generous to me than to another who is less lavish toward you with his affections.[84]

CHARITE What, Sincero, are you lavish with yours? Truly, since you're such a poor manager, I no longer wish to give you my good *graces*, because after having wasted your own goods, you could lose mine by your negligence.

SINCERO Don't worry about that, my lady, you'll never see me careless with anything belonging to you. When it pleases you to give me part of the graces I ask for, you'll at the same time have them all at

---

79. The satire of convents as places where according to Erasmus "virginity is often in considerable danger" recurs frequently in humanist writings. See Erasmus's colloquies *The Girl with No Interest in Marriage* and *The Repentant Girl*, in Rummel, *Erasmus on Women*, , 25–38.

80. Pallas Athena or Minerva, goddess of war, wisdom, and learning, identified with Minerva, goddess of female handcrafts.

81. In Greek myth, one of the three Gorgons. Anyone who looked at her was turned to stone.

82. In this dialogue, the author criticizes several concepts from courtly and Petrarchan lyric, namely, the exchange of hearts which is obligatory for the beloved, the psychology of the "innamoramento" (falling in love), and the Neoplatonic notion of poetry as truly representing the love that inspires it.

83. Play on Charite's name meaning one of the three Graces.

84. An unabashed appeal to the Ficinian maxim "Whoever is loved ought to love in return." Ficino, *Commentary on the Symposium*, speech 2.8.

your disposal, for you possess me, and all I possess. Now because I've nothing that's not yours, and my singular wealth is to lose myself in order to find myself again in you, since I have bequeathed my liberty to your beautiful eyes, suns of my soul, and have lavished on you my heart and my affections, I act like those who for a time lose the earth to gain the Heavens. Likewise, your excellent virtues and divine beauty, having guided me to the paradise of your perfections, guide me still to the Heaven from where they originate.

CHARITE You astonish me, heaping on me like this more courtesies than reasons. Since the moment you began praising me, I haven't known what face to make, nor what was safer for me, to keep silent or to speak. If I speak, and refuse the praises you give me, it looks as if I want to give you the occasion to come back with even better compliments. If I keep quiet, you'll think that my silence admits all that you say in my favor.[85]

SINCERO It will be very easy for you, Madame, to rid yourself of this trouble, and me of a much greater one. You only have to reply and agree with everything I say to you and ask for.

CHARITE I am content provided that all your words are reasonable, and your request an honest one.

SINCERO My lady, I still persevere with what I said and with my first request. I ask that your graces, since it sometimes pleases them to guide me to Heaven, should not disdain to guide me on earth as well.

CHARITE Since you can't yet guide yourself on earth without the help of others, why do you seek out Heaven as well?

SINCERO You are the cause, Madame, for I am guided there by you, and you by me.

CHARITE don't remember ever having been there. But you might refresh my memory by telling me what was the most marvelous thing I saw on this voyage.

SINCERO You saw nothing as perfect as yourself. But since you were embarrassed in contemplating your own beauty and graces, these kept you from seeing what was presented to your eyes. As for the day you went, I won't tell you which one it was, because not a day passes by that you and I are not brought there together.

---

85. Des Roches refers to the necessity for decorum in women's speech, a matter frequently addressed by contemporary sociolinguists such as Castiglione (*Book of the Courtier* 3.5): the *donna di palazzo* "must observe a certain mean (difficult to achieve and, as it were, composed of contraries) and must strictly observe certain limits and not exceed them."

CHARITE It seems to me that you're making up a long fable.

SINCERO On the contrary, I'm telling you the truth.

CHARITE Recount to me, please, this miraculous event.

SINCERO Any miracle that concerns you can be believed, my lady. Therefore I'm going to begin to tell you marvels about yourself. It's said that of all the things that exist here on earth, their forms are in Heaven:[86] there is an Idea of goodness, an Idea of beauty, and there is a destiny, which is second in power to divine providence. Destiny then, having ordained the hour of your birth, when the more benign planets watched one another with an amiable aspect, called on the Fates,[87] and commanded them to weave the most beautiful life they could choose. The three sisters were obedient to this command, and Nature, by the will of her father, put the finishing touches on it, and modeling you after the most beautiful Idea, she made you so accomplished that she herself was amazed at her work. But some time later she became ever more astonished, because the Idea of your beauty, looking all around, and seeing nothing as agreeable to her as you, desiring to be always in your company, bound herself to you in such a way that it was impossible to get her back. Immediately the Gods assembled their council to deliberate what to do. Some were of the opinion that you should be retained in heaven, but Destiny disagreed, and Clotho had already begun to spin her thread. The others said that they could let you come to earth, then suddenly pull you back up. But Nature didn't wish to permit the sudden ruin of such a beautiful work of art, for she herself brought you into the world so that she could be admired through your excellent qualities. Since then the Gods, when they saw that the richest adornment had been taken from their abode, complained without end of their loss. To make up for this in some other way, they heard that Venus's son was the best painter to be found, and that in lieu of paintbrushes he made use of his arrow alone. They sent for this little God, and telling him of their trouble, beseeched him to find a remedy by coming down to earth to search for a portrait of what had so pleased them in Heaven. Then Love prepared himself to obey his elders, but not finding a tableau that was worthy of holding your beautiful features, he stopped for a long time to look at the sincerity of

86. On the Forms, see Plato, *Timaeus* 5b–e; *Phaedrus* 249c.

87. In Greek mythology, the three Parcae or Fates wove human life: Clotho ("spinner") held the distaff, Lachesis ("apportioner") drew the thread, and Atropos ("inflexible") cut it short.

my thoughts, and since it seemed to him that I was suitable enough to execute his project, he engraved your beauty so vividly on my heart that neither your rigor, nor time, nor death could erase you from me. Thus Love, having placed your portrait within my soul, lifts it up to Heaven, so that the Gods, contemplating you in my soul, may no longer be envious of the condition of us mortals. And that is how, my lady, by the power of your beauty I approach the Heavens.

CHARITE I think, rather, that through the favor of your words you take my name up to Heaven, Sincero, and bring it back down when it suits you. Now because you desire to be thought a lover and a poet, you can pretend without being rebuked, and I who have nothing to do with either poetry or love can surely listen to you without putting much faith in your words.[88]

SINCERO My lady, since you have neither love for me nor much faith in my words, I have no reason to expect a great deal from you. However, the less hope I have, the more I desire that what happened to your Idea would happen to you, and that having fallen madly in love with your portrait, it would please you, for the love of it, to love *me* as well.

CHARITE If my portrait brought you as much good as I've heard you say, you would never ask me for anything, but you would remain quite happy receiving so great an honor on my account.

SINCERO lady, the more I owe you, the more I want to owe you, so that my obligation, surpassing all means of ever being able to satisfy itself, will make me your prisoner.

CHARITE All right then, as my prisoner, I order you to be silent and to save speaking for some other occasion.[89]

SINCERO Since it pleases you, my lady, I shall honor silence with silence.

---

88. A reference to the Platonic linking of love to poetry (see Plato, *Symposium* 196a). Des Roches distances herself from this notion, as she does in her rebuttal to critics who accuse her of daring to write about a real-love experience (see *Epistle to Her Mother* [see chap. 2]).

89. An ironic retort which Sincero misinterprets: he thinks that the silence about which Charite speaks is that of the courtly lover in the presence of his lady.

DIALOGUES FROM *LES SECONDES ŒUVRES* (1583)[90]
DIALOGUE BETWEEN PLACIDE AND SEVERE

PLACIDE Here comes our neighbor Severe, with an amazingly scowling face; he must have seen someone at home who made him angry, and he's complaining to anyone who will listen.

SEVERE O! What trouble it is to have Wives or Daughters to rule over! Truly, I'm not surprised that a renowned Philosopher thinks it wise to keep them at the level of reasonless Animals.[91] And if ever a poor man has found himself afflicted by their annoyances, I'm the one. I have a disorderly, disobedient, disdainful Wife and a long-winded, dissembling, and insolent Daughter. I have to put up with the chagrin of the former and the vanity of the latter. But I see old man Placide coming this way, who has the same useless charge as I do in his own home—a nuisance of a Daughter, that is—so he should be able to tell me how he treats her, so I can follow his example, if I think it's a good one. I think I'll go say hello to him, although it normally isn't my custom to greet anyone. Good evening, Placide.

PLACIDE God be with you, Lord Severe, you and all those whom you love.

SEVERE Believe me when I say that such a greeting is by no means universal; for the only one I love in this world is myself; and I have little occasion to love anyone.

PLACIDE Goodness! Haven't you reason to hold your Wife dear?

SEVERE Ah! It's easy for you to say so because you no longer have yours. How I wish with all my heart that I were as happy as you! Yours is dead, but mine, who is only absent, by her unpleasant life makes me die at all hours.

PLACIDE We have very different opinions of our Wives, who were perhaps even more different from each other.

SEVERE I wouldn't think there would be much of a difference: *For all are adversaries to Men.*

PLACIDE *But all are necessary to Men.* And if I didn't see the desirable

---

90. Internal evidence indicates that the *Dialogue between Placide and Severe* was composed in 1581 soon after the death in childbirth of Diane de Morel, one of the three learned daughters of the Parisian humanist Jean de Morel. Placide mentions her death at the end of the dialogue. The sequel *Dialogue between Iris and Pasithée* was written the following year: Pasithée refers to the defeat of the French during a naval battle with the Spaniards on 26 July 1582.

91. See Aristotle, *On the Generation of Animals* 2.3.737b I; *Politics* 1.5.1254b I.

portrait of my Wife in the physique and habits of my Daughter, I would languish in this harsh life.

SEVERE You were *such* a good husband! But speaking of your Daughter, how is she behaving herself?

PLACIDE As I wish, and as it seems to me she ought.

SEVERE Mine goes against her duty and my will. I've never seen such an incredible gadabout; she wishes to see in a day both hemispheres, as cranes do! No matter how much I order her to stay at home and take care of her housework, it's impossible to restrain her. No sooner have I left home than she is at the window, out the door, in the street, and off visiting someone. She never rests, and neither do I. So tell me, what is your daughter doing now, where is she?

PLACIDE In her room.

SEVERE Alone?

PLACIDE No, she is accompanied by souls without bodies, and by bodies without souls, making the first move about in a winged chariot, and giving spirit and movement to the latter.

SEVERE It seems as if you're making her out to be some sort of Medea.[92]

PLACIDE Not at all, actually I am speaking of a Daughter who is as sweet and debonair to her Father as Medea was cruel and evil to hers.[93]

SEVERE What riddles are you talking about, then? I can't understand them.

PLACIDE But you soon will, they're easy. These Bodies enlivened by her are Lutes and Violas that her hand causes to resonate, and the Souls she takes up into the winged chariot are the beautiful Maxims of Plutarch and Seneca, flying on the wings of her thoughts and words.

SEVERE What's this, Placide? You permit her to read such Authors? Aren't you worried about profaning them, by allowing a Girl's mouth to utter their names?

PLACIDE These Philosophers were of the opinion that the least impure people were the most capable of these disciplines. If this is so, Wives and Daughters are much more worthy of education than Men, since they're more sober, chaste, and peaceable.

SEVERE Your words disappoint me. You speak as though the im-

92. Medea, a legendary magician, went from place to place in a winged chariot.

93. Medea, daughter of Aeetes, king of Colchis, betrayed and abandoned her father when she fled with Jason, leader of the Argonauts.

becility of these little Beasts could be compared to the intellectual prowess seen in us men daily. And besides, by giving them permission to read anything they like, you are giving them license to do whatever they want.

PLACIDE I agree, but since they are guided by good books, they won't want to do anything unreasonable.

SEVERE As if reason could be found in them!

PLACIDE

Those who have even a little reason
Make it flourish through Learning,
But reason soon abdicates
To the evils brought about by Ignorance.

Whether Women seem foolish or wise to you, I think that we should allow them to read, so that the foolish ones can become a bit less foolish, and the wise ones even wiser, thanks to books which are very necessary for them if only to keep them at home alone where they would remain otherwise idle.[94]

SEVERE O what misfortune it is to see a learned Woman![95]

PLACIDE Oh? What's that? Please explain.

SEVERE Why, she's a monster!

PLACIDE Quite the contrary, learned women are often the most excellent things in the world. You see, monsters are not always proof that Nature has made a mistake, but rather they show how great her power is. Iocasie's "monstrous" Beauty, Grace, Virtue, and Learning gained her admiration among men, and gave her the means necessary to live without them her entire life, forever remaining a virgin.[96]

SEVERE Indeed! I'd be delighted if all learned women remained unattached, and I will never advise Men to go looking for them.

PLACIDE Now tell me, Lord Severe, are you happily married?

SEVERE About as unhappily as could be.

PLACIDE And is your wife learned?

SEVERE Oh no, she is but a fat beast, who does not know how to honor her husband, or how to manage her household, which is the only thing I want her to learn—not how to spend time with books. She needs no other Instructor but my voice.

94. A common argument in pedagogical and feminist treatises on women's education.

95. "Femme savante" in the original.

96. Iocasie is unknown to me.

PLACIDE Indeed, but as you say, you have been taking the trouble to persuade her to do these things for quite some time, and you have not made much progress; so either your labors are fruitless or your complaints are false.

SEVERE My complaints are not false, but Women are very much so, as I find daily.

PLACIDE You are deserving of this evil that befalls you, since the cure is within your grasp, but you do not want to take hold of it. Ischomachus's Wife would teach yours to do her duty if you had her read Xenophon's *Oeconomicus*.[97]

SEVERE Hee, hee, if I found her in similar circumstances, I would let her know that her hand must reach only for the distaff and never for a book.

PLACIDE Each of these activities assists the other. Pallas practiced them both.[98]

SEVERE These are silly myths. Women must never study.

PLACIDE Why do you so hate the innocent Muses? And who set you about trying to drive them from your chamber, from your table, from your fireside, seeing as how they cost nothing and offer instead numerous benefits?

SEVERE I know that books are absolutely useless to Women.

PLACIDE As they are to Men.

SEVERE You're making fun of me. Will women study Theology, stand at the pulpit, preach a sermon to the people, and earn benefices?[99]

PLACIDE No, but they will learn God's Word, because it orders Wives to obey their husbands, just as in Genesis.[100] And when they have children, it will be much easier for them to bring them up in the fear of God, of their Fathers, and of themselves.[101] In fact, they will be happily guided by the precepts of virtue, which are the richest benefices one can acquire.

SEVERE I would prefer to have a simple Wife, rather than one

---

97. Isomachus succeeded in making his very young wife his greatest ally by educating her himself. See Xenophon, *Oeconomicus*, ed. and trans. Sarah Pomeroy (Oxford: Clarendon Press, 1994).

98. Pallas Athena is the goddess of wisdom and the domestic arts.

99. Common feature of the Catholic polemic against Reformed women who dared to reason on Scripture.

100. Genesis 3:16.

101. 1 Timothy 2:15.

with wily opinions. After learning what you would have them learn, they would judge themselves too strong.

PLACIDE Simpleminded women of feeble understanding resemble these thin clouds which, for fear of disappearing, flee the Star of day; or if it shines through them, no trace of its rays is left. But as a thick cloud absorbs the light of the Sun and then reflects outward and intensifies the beautiful face that illumines it, so the prudent Woman, who strengthens her mind with the discourses of moral Philosophy, humbly receives the image her Husband wishes to give her, so that his beloved portrait always appears in her thoughts, words, and all her actions.[102]

SEVERE You speak such marvels that I permit my Wife and daughters to read the Holy Scriptures, provided they read nothing else.

PLACIDE I tell you that *all* subjects are necessary for them, just as they are for us.

SEVERE Oh don't tell me they should study law![103]

PLACIDE They must not be ignorant of it.

SEVERE Ah ha! You've ruined everything, Placide. Your lack of judgment will cause me to take back what I just said and forbid on account of their foolishness that which I would have permitted because of my affection for you.

PLACIDE And will you reprimand the people of God for being judged by Deborah?[104]

SEVERE I speak not of Hebrew Law, but rather of Roman Law.[105]

PLACIDE All right then, must a woman to please her husband renounce the Velleien Law without understanding it?[106] You are aware,

102. On the wife as a mirror to her husband, see for example, Plutarch, *Advice to Bride and Groom, Moralia 2;* Francesco Barbaro, *On Wifely Duties,* trans. Benjamin Kohl, in *The Earthly Republic,* ed. Benjamin Kohl and R. G. Witt (Philadelphia: University of Pennsylvania Press, 1976), 179–228; Erasmus, *The Institution of Marriage,* in Rummel, *Erasmus on Women,* 98.

103. A widespread opinion. Montaigne rejects the idea that women can be "intent on rhetoric, astrology, logic, and similar drugs, so vain and useless for their needs." *The Complete Essays of Montaigne,* trans. and ed. Donald W. Frame (Stanford: Stanford University Press, 1958), 3.3, 624.

104. Deborah, prophetess and judge in Israel, thirteenth century BCE, emblem of the valiant woman. See Judges 4–5.

105. Beginning in the sixteenth century, the return of Roman law reinforced the inequality of the sexes to the benefit of men since it imposed the *potestas patris,* which demanded the absolute obedience of the wife and the children.

106. Women engaged to be married and ignorant of the law often renounced in their marriage contract the Roman law of the Senatus Consul Velleien which protected them from all solicitations from the husband or an indebted child to sell their property. The author critiques husbands who take advantage of the ignorance of their wives.

aren't you, that those in this country who have wealthy Wives let them know that they can give their furnishings and acquired goods, with a third of their inheritance, to their surviving husband, since customary law permits it? Men profess three types of learning, which they then practice: Theology, Jurisprudence, and Medicine. I am of the opinion that you should also teach women the means by which to cure sickness, so that they hold all areas in common with us. The one who was the disciple of the scholar Herophilus demonstrated that she learned medicine for the benefit of others.[107] There are still today women who help their young children, comfort their neighbors, and cure their servants through the use of certain domestic remedies that experience makes known to them.

SEVERE Women who know so many beautiful things are often vainglorious; they disdain their husbands and make fools of them. As I learned the other day from a tapestry, which was hung on the fireplace of Achariste, my neighbor. There was in the middle of the piece a pompous Woman, sitting on a throne, holding a pen in her hand and a book under her feet; around the tapestry was written:

When a Woman knows how to speak well
And makes a profession of writing,
She disdains all Authors
Who of the arts were inventors.

Nothing pleases her, everyone makes her angry,
Always pensive she is brooding over
Some word of great weight,
Which she marks with her fingers.

She says her Mother is crazy,
Her Father has nothing good to say,
Her Brother knows nothing useful,
Her Sister will never learn a thing.

If her neighbor is somewhat beautiful,
She is nothing compared to her,
Whose grace and knowledge
Surpass all that can be seen.

When she is married,
She claims to be wise

---

107. An allusion to Agnodice, legendary Greek heroine who was the first to disobey the law that prohibited women from practicing medicine. See Catherine des Roches's narrative poem *Agnodice* (see chap. 2).

In governing her household much better
Than the most ancient of Men.
  So flee the learned Woman,[108]
Rather seek one with nothing in her mind,
The former will only scorn you,
While the latter will let herself be ruled.

There you have it, Placide, that is what I've learned, and it seems to me worthy of note.

PLACIDE So now you carefully welcome the smoky authorities found on chimney curtains?

SEVERE Must one not learn wherever possible?

PLACIDE One must look for truth whenever possible; but what you recount is an error that reason and experience show to be such.

SEVERE Experience shows that Women who exceed the Common lot do not love their husbands very much.

PLACIDE I will take as an example two excellent Roman women, Emponina and Arria,[109] who, being unwilling to outlive their husbands, courageously followed them to death.

SEVERE It would be difficult to find such women these days.

PLACIDE Yes, because by forbidding them to read books, you keep from their sight examples that could inspire them to feel this equally deep affection for you.

SEVERE But those women who are able to do so often want to speak, and I get angry when there's so much cackle.

PLACIDE I remember hearing my Daughter Pasithée sing a song she had written for a young Man who had the same words for Women as you do, stating that Silence must seal their mouths. The song goes like this:

  I believe that Silence
Is a mere shadow of true distinction,
  While discreet Eloquence
Is the light of true understanding.
  When a graceful word
Which knows how to devise skillfully,

---

108. "Femme savante" in the original.

109. Emponina, a Roman matron devoted to her husband (Plutarch, *Love Stories, Moralia* 10.613a–b); Arria, wife of Caecina Paetus, killed herself when she was unable to save her husband, a prisoner in the revolt of Camillus Scribonianus (Pliny, *Epistles* 3.16; Martial, 1.13).

Can in a virtuous life
Legitimize all things,
　Ladies who wish to live well,
Desiring to learn and understand,
Seek out virtue and books,
And marry their actions to learning.
　If these examples seem natural
And have any persuasive power,
If they take hold of the one who contemplates them,
Leading them by means of a gentle law:
　See the sons of Cornelia,[110]
Who render their name immortal,
By following the Philosophy
Of such a rare maternal example.
　And look at Cleobulina,[111]
Who wisely persuades
Her Father to show himself worthy
Of such a rich government.
　See faithful Portia,[112]
Collection of all the virtues,
Who in death as in life,
Wished to follow her dear Brutus.
　Now you know that Ladies
Are worthy of philosophizing,
Seeing such a number of Women
Triumph in the midst of men.
　If still, kind sir, you persist
In this common misjudgment,
May some thoroughly foolish Mistress

---

110. According to Cicero (*Brutus* 211), Cornelia also became a model letter writer. On Cornelia as rhetorician, see Glenn, *Rhetoric Retold*, 66–67. Daughter of Scipio Africanus and mother of the Gracchi, Cornelia, after the death of her husband, dedicated herself to the education of her sons, thereby becoming a model of Roman motherhood. Plutarch, *Tiberius and Gaius Gracchus, Lives* 10.1; Agrippa, *Declamation on the Nobility and Preeminence of the Female Sex*, 73; Gournay, *Equality of Men and Women*, in *Apology for the Woman Writing and Other Works*, 78.

111. Daughter of Cleobulus, one of the Seven Wise Men of ancient Greece, who thought that girls should be educated. Cleobulina (her other name is Eumetis) was renowned for her intelligence. See Diogenes Laertius, *Cleobulus, Lives* 1; Plutarch, *Dinner of the Seven Wise Men, Moralia* 2.148c–e; Vives, *Education of a Christian Woman*, 66.

112. Portia, daughter of Cato of Utica (95–46 BCE), killed herself upon learning of the death of her husband Brutus at the Battle of Philippi. Plutarch, *Brutus, Lives* 53; Boccaccio, *Famous Women*, 82.

Soon run away with your heart.
　　May all that you do for her
Be it serving her, pleading, or shouting,
Never succeed in pleasing her,
Nor in freeing you from her grasp.

You see, Lord Severe, the kind of punishment that noble Women demand of those who have injured them.

SEVERE Truly, they've had their revenge on me; for I'm bound head and foot to a foolish woman, who incessantly rebukes me.

PLACIDE Cure the both of you: drive the anger from your spirit, and the ignorance from hers.

SEVERE I'm afraid that after studying, she would want to order me around.

PLACIDE *Precepts of Marriage* and *Virtuous Deeds of Women* will teach her to obey you.[113]

SEVERE Being cleverer, I am afraid she would deceive me.

PLACIDE What deception could she use on you that would not also be harmful to her? Knowing the worth of honor, she'll fear the shame that such conduct would bring. Moreover, you know that idle thoughts cause lascivious wills. And Women who give themselves over to study will be neither lascivious nor idle. After finding out what books teach with neither anger nor flattery (for they are masters who teach very candidly), they endeavor to fulfill their duties to their husbands, their households, their families, and their parents, remaining humble, modest, and dutiful to all that belongs to them. They have no time for immodest behavior.

SEVERE That I know, for all women who are shamed by their faults are mindless, and only know how to satisfy dishonest feelings. But under the guise of a well-kept chastity, learned women harshly contradict their husbands, if the latter do something these women don't like.

PLACIDE Less than other women, I assure you. If you are around young people, you'll hear it said all the time, "My Father wants it like this, but my Mother doesn't, and she always gets her way." Now these Mothers are really ignorant. You should hear the most lighthearted of them praise themselves, saying, "This house would have been ruined without me, my Husband would have become a knave, my Mother-in-law a strumpet for not knowing how to keep house. O how I was made just for this! Since I've been here, I've raised the value of the land, I've retired debts, acquired mills." And meanwhile the ones who say such things know how to do nothing except spend their time uselessly feasting or partying.

SEVERE You impress me with a kind of Truth that I didn't know before, even though it was daily before my eyes, so that I'm considering changing my Daughter Iris's diet to make her learn something good. Her ever-changing manner has earned her the name she has. But perhaps, hearing you, she'll change for the better, provided that her Mother isn't opposed to the idea, for she has told me in the past, speaking of learned Girls: "What use is it for a Woman to understand literature and Music? I didn't learn any of this and I'm just as wise as any other woman. I don't want my Daughter to know more than I do. And besides, what good will it do her? Will she get married any sooner?"

PLACIDE Ho, ho, that's quite a statement. So she thinks educating a Girl serves the ends only of greed or love. Truly, if one judges all that is good to be useful, Girls will be able to benefit from taking part in such praiseworthy activities. After all, we mustn't believe that virtuous Girls will want to use their grace and beauty to develop any amorous liaisons with which to enslave Men. For they well know that "A Woman who seeks out Love deserves to have men flee from her." Therefore the modest ones wouldn't want to undertake anything indecent. All of their attractive qualities are intended not to win them a Husband, but rather to enable them, if they remain single, to behave honorably, or if they do marry, to live in peace with their husbands. Even the most aggressive women are tempered by gentleness, and gentleness increases through Reason, Reason through Knowledge, Knowledge through Books. Therefore I maintain that books must be made available to Women, as the most faithful company they can ever find.

SEVERE I'm surprised that your Daughter likes them so much, since you approve of them, because I thought she would have followed the way of other girls, which is always to rebel against the wishes of their Fathers.

PLACIDE Mine was happily born for me. That's why I want to give her an instruction that is worthy of her natural goodness.

SEVERE You want to work a miracle.

PLACIDE I don't want to undertake anything miraculous. Miracles are the work of God, and not of Man. I only want to nurture my Daughter in a chaste and fulfilling solitude, giving her as an example the illustrious virtues of the excellent Ladies I wish her to emulate.

SEVERE Like those Sibyls who gained renown in past times!

PLACIDE Actually no, like the wise learned women who are famous in our own time. I don't try to set before her eyes those whom the ancients honored. I leave out wise Eumetis,[114] Arete the great,[115] beautiful and graceful Eudoxia,[116] learned Theodora,[117] even though the sincerity of their minds and the subtlety of their writings make them admirable. It suffices me to portray those of which our century is rich, such as learned Sigea, whose beautiful poem "Sintra" girds the pleasant sojourn of the Muses,[118] and Laura Terracina,[119] whose name is upheld throughout the universe and can never be brought back down to earth. But what will I say of Morata, who truly earned from Heaven the name of Olympia?[120] And how will I convey the reverence I feel for the memory of the beautiful, graceful, and virtuous Ippolita Torella, whose

114. Eumetis, or Cleobulina, daughter of Cleobulus, one of the Seven Wise Men of Greece. Cleobulina is rarely mentioned in catalogues of illustrious women. Lucrezia Marinella does refer to her in *The Nobility and Excellence of Women and the Defects and Vices of Men*, 84.

115. Arete, daughter and disciple of the philosopher Aristippus of Cyrene.

116. Or Eudocia (d. 460), wife of the Emperor Theodosius II.

117. Theodora (ca. 497–548), empress of the East, wife of Justinian I, possessing superior intelligence and great energy, was the driving force behind her husband's government.

118. Luisa Sigea (1522–60), lady in waiting and governess of the Infanta Maria of Portugal, dedicated to the latter in 1548 her Latin poem *Sintra* which she sent to Pope Paul III, accompanied by an epistle in five languages. This earned her a response, dated January 1547, also written in five languages. The poem was published in 1566 in Paris by Denys du Pré. On Sigea, see Odette Sauvage, "Recherches sur Luisa Sigea," *Bulletin des études portugaises* 31 (1970): 33–176; Inès Rada, "Profil et trajectoire d'une femme humaniste: Luisa Sigea," in *Images de la femme en Espagne aux XVI*e et XVIIe siècles, ed. Augustin Redondo (Paris: Presses de la Sorbonne Nouvelle, 1994), 339–49.

119. Laura Terracina (1519–ca.1577), Neapolitan poetess, author of nine volumes of poetry published between 1548 and 1561. In her *Discorso sopra tutti i primi canti di "Orlando Furioso"* (Commentary on all the first cantos of "Orlando Furioso," 1549), she defends women from their enemies, but regrets that there are so few devoted to literature. On Terracina, see Jaffe, *Shining Eyes, Cruel Fortune*; Nancy Dersofi, "Laura Terracina," in *Italian Women Writers: A Bio-Bibliographical Source Book*, ed. Rinaldina Russell (Westport, Conn.: Greenwood Press, 1994), 423–30.

120. Born in Ferrara, Olympia Fulvia Morata (1526/27–1555) joined the court of the Duchess Renée de France where she became a study companion of Anna d'Este. After joining the Reformation, she married a German Lutheran doctor. She died of the plague in Heidelberg. Catherine des Roches could have become familiar with her Latin works thanks to Agrippa d'Aubigné who visited her salon during the Grands Jours of 1579. Agrippa d'Aubigné praises Morata in a letter to his daughters (*Œuvres complètes*, 853). On Morata, see Albert Rabil, "Olympia Morata," in Russell, *Italian Women Writers*, 269–78; Morata, *Complete Writings of an Italian Heretic*.

doleful Elegies gave so much pleasure and pain to her absent husband?[121] In what way can I worthily esteem Sincere Proba,[122] who in stealing the verse of excellent Virgil accommodates the most beautiful of them to the divine mysteries? She thus makes the one who robs seem more just, and the one who is robbed seem richer. Nor must I forget Clemence Isaure, whose generous endowment gives to Toulouse each year the beautiful flower of the Eglantine to whoever composes the best Christian hymn.[123]

SEVERE Have you finished?

PLACIDE Not at all, for I haven't yet spoken of those who adorn France, but I fear that my lowly voice would offend their high value. I do, however, remember having noticed many whose infinite graces are worthy of infinite honor. Those still alive will become known to posterity and prevent their names from dying out by the perfection of their virtue and learning. Others, whom time and death have cut down prematurely, will resemble the Amaranth, which never loses its beauty.[124] But who is this who shows herself to me with such gentle melancholy? Ah ha! It's brilliant Diana,[125] whose graceful face had hardly appeared in its fullness when cruel Fate made her disappear into

121. Ippolita Torella (1499–1520), daughter of Guido Torelli, married Baldassare Castiglione in 1516, in Mantua, and died in childbirth.

122. The Roman aristocrat Faltonia Betitia Proba (ca. 322–ca. 370 CE), a convert to Christianity, composed her *Cento Vergilianus de laudibus Christi* in ca. 360 CE by rearranging lines from Virgil into a composition or a commentary with a new meaning. Proba appears frequently in catalogues of learned women. See Pizan, *Book of the City of Ladies* 1.29.1; Boccaccio, *Famous Women*, 97; Anna Maria van Schurman, *Whether a Christian Woman should be Educated*, ed. Joyce Irwin, Other Voice in Early Modern Europe (Chicago: University of Chicago Press, 1998), 52.

123. Clémence Isaure, legendary founder of the Floral Games of Toulouse. See Broomhall, *Women and the Book Trade*, 147–48.

124. The amaranth, a purplish red and velvet-smooth autumn flower that does not wilt, becomes for the Dames des Roches the emblem of the poetic immortality acquired by the learned woman. "Amaranthe," the name of the principal female protagonist in Des Roches's pastoral *Bergerie*, is a learned woman who combines the reason of Pallas Athena and the poetic creativity of Apollo. She takes her name, suggestive of immortality, from the nymph Amaranta in Sannazaro's *Arcadia*, the prototype of the pastoral mode in the Renaissance.

125. One of the three daughters of Jean de Morel, seigneur de Grigny, a good friend of Erasmus, whose learned wife, Antoinette de Loynes, held around 1550 a salon frequented by jurists from the Paris Parlement, humanists, and poets. The three daughters were educated by the humanist Charles Utenhove. Diane de Morel was married, then died in 1581. See Samuel Will, "Camille de Morel: A Prodigy of the Renaissance," *Publications of the Modern Language Association* 51 (1936): 83–119. On Loynes, see Catherine M. Müller, "Éloges au féminin: la voix nouvelle d'Antoinette de Loynes (poétesse et traductrice) dans le *Tombeau* de Marguerite de Navarre (1551)," *Versants* ("La littérature au féminin") 46 (2004): 49–63.

a perpetual eclipse. O beautiful, chaste, and learned Diana, may your bright light long illumine my dark words, which I shall end here with a sad sigh, caused by my justifiable regret for your death. Lord Severe, excuse me, please, the night and weariness make me bid you farewell.

SEVERE Well, well, another time I'll ask you who was this one you miss so much. But in the meantime I commend myself to you; tomorrow I'll send my Daughter to see yours, at least if that meets with your approval.

PLACIDE She'll be quite welcome.

DIALOGUE BETWEEN IRIS AND PASITHÉE

IRIS My desire to hear and see you would have brought me to you earlier, Pasithée, had it not been for my Father who had forbidden it, and who now orders me to come. I hope you clearly see what kind of man he is.

PASITHÉE Don't be surprised by his changeableness, Iris. Perhaps he forbade it and then ordered you to come for one and the same reason: what's good at one time may not be at another.

IRIS What? Are you trying to excuse his inconstancy?

PASITHÉE Not only do I excuse Inconstancy, but I applaud it, knowing that we are in this world born, fed, and sustained by it. See the day-giving Sun, which by its inconstant course gives light to the entire universe without ever stopping in one place. See the Moon its Sister, which changes its face at every moment. Take a look at the beautiful Goddess whose name you bear, her dress is always changing.[126] Remember that fire is constantly transformed into air, air into water, water into earth which in the long run shrinks and changes into its higher kin.[127] And we who call ourselves citizens of the Elements, who are indeed composed of them, why shouldn't we like inconstancy, since we follow the inconstant nature of our first parents?[128]

IRIS One can surely be inconstant with others, but not with oneself.

126. A reference to Iris, messenger of the gods, who wore a dress which in sunlight had the colors of the rainbow.

127. On the Heraclitean doctrine of the metamorphosis of fire into air and water into earth, see Diogenes Laertius, *Heraclitus, Lives* 9.9; Plato, *Phaedo* 78b–79a, *Timaeus* 28a–c, *Symposium*, 207a–208b.

128. "Our first parents" are Eve and Adam, whose "inconstant nature" led them into temptation. Genesis 3.

PASITHÉE Iris my dear, try to imagine a person, all of whose parts looked alike without any variation: hair, eyes, complexion, and mouth all of the same color. You'd recognize how unpleasant it would be to see such a creature, compared with one adorned with an inconstant variety of colors, with golden hair, a white forehead, brown eyebrows, hazel eyes like the French, or black like a Greek, or maybe celestial blue, such as noble Petrarch gave to his excellent Laura. The other day I saw some poetic verses in the hands of Philide, depicting all the beautiful parts of a face by means of various flowers that, thanks to their inconstant colors, decorate a Garden.[129]

IRIS Do you remember them, Pasithée?

PASITHÉE Why yes, and I'll gladly recite them, if you'd like to hear them.

IRIS Please.

PASITHÉE Listen, then.

> You resemble a gentle springtime,[130]
> Adorned with flowers and foliage,
> The flowering of your young years
> Shines in your lovely face.
>   When I see the golden blossom
> Of beautiful loving Clytia,[131]
> I compare it to the golden curls
> Of your luminescent hair.
>   When I see the growing fleur de Lis,
> Which in whiteness surpasses all others,
> I see the whitening ivory
> Of your forehead, temple of grace.

---

129. The Heraclitean philosophy on the inconstancy and mutability of all created things provides Des Roches with a strategy for disrupting rigid views on women since it promotes a greater openness of spirit. A case in point is Des Roches's onomastic play on Iris's name. At once denoting a flower and Iris, the messenger of the gods, her name symbolizes the fact that feminine beauty is founded not on similitude but on difference; in the same manner, all women should not be relegated, as in misogynist logic, to the same mold. Des Roches is criticizing detractors for accusing women of inconstancy. She may also have had in mind Pontus de Tyard's Pasithée who expresses concern to her interlocutor that women are often accused of inconstancy and flightiness. Pontus de Tyard, *Solitaire premier*, ed. Silvio Baridon (Geneva: Droz, 1950), ll. 46–47.

130. This love song in the form of a blazon reminds the anonymous annotator of Ronsard's *Chanson en faveur de Mademoiselle de Limeuil* (1564) in the *Nouvelle Continuation des Amours, Œuvres complètes*, ed. Laumonier, 12:163–70. Des Roches's rendition diverges from Ronsard's sensual treatment.

131. Loved by Phoebus, Clytia was changed into a heliotrope.

When I see the narrowly bent leaf of
The Hair of Venus,
I see the small engraved curve
Of your thin eyebrow.
    When I see the beautiful flower of Iris
Shatter its celestial flame,
I see the gentle laughter of Love,
In your eyes, messengers of the soul.
    When I look at the vermilion hue
Of a fresh, blooming Rose,
I think I see this same hue
By which your face is beautified.
    When I see a beautiful Damask chosen
And touched by a ray of Sunlight,
I think I see the crimson
Of your coral lips.
    When I look at a small bud
That half-opens in the morning,
I see this lovely little chin
Which rounds off your face.
    When I see the branches extending from
The roots of a young Bay tree,
I see your singularly beautiful body,
Dwelling of your divine soul.

It seems to me, Iris, that these lines capture your beauty.

IRIS That's not Nirée's opinion. He compares me to that other Iris one can see in the sky. He says she heralds rain and I tears, that she is delicately curved while I'm misshapen, that she's the opposite of the Sun while I'm that of Reason, that she's changing and I unsettled, that her beauties are false and mine are feigned.

PASITHÉE This comparison is appropriate, but very poorly expressed. You truly do resemble the celestial Iris. For she is sent by God to men as an omen of peace and happiness, and you are the happy sign of chaste love.[132] She curves to fit the Heavens, but you turn your soul into a circle of self-contemplation. She looks into the Sun but you look toward Reason. She changes like the seasons of the year, just like us who change constantly from one day to the next. Her beauty can't be

132. "Honnête amour" in the original.

false, because true light reflects those upon whom it shines, and yours is not feigned, because an honest gaze, judging it, takes such great pleasure in seeing it. Truly then, I think that this presumptuous man has not seen you enough to really know you, or that spite has caused him to say these things.

IRIS It could be.

PASITHÉE What happened between the two of you?

IRIS O, Pasithée, it would take a long time to tell it all. You see, I loved him once in the past.

PASITHÉE And why don't you love him anymore?

IRIS My Mother put a stop to it, because she wanted to marry me to the rich son of Chrysobole. She drove Nirée away from me, and at about that same time I was beginning to fall in love with Charidore, but he would never entertain the idea of an alliance with me.

PASITHÉE My God, what are you saying? And your Mother was talking about marrying you to another?

IRIS Yes, but the marriage never took place because my Father didn't want to give a big enough dowry. I loved Achryse, and he didn't ask for much, but people said he was too poor. Since then, I've loved countless others, none of whom were up to my Father's standards. He's the most terrible man imaginable. If he merely sees me in the street, he screams at me and carries on about it all day long. Now I love kind Eole, but I can't let him know that because of my father.

PASITHÉE So you love Eole; I'm worried that he'll disappoint you. He's so full of hot air; the wind pursues the cloud, and you're a pleasing cloud, Iris. Be careful about what you do.

IRIS It's true he hasn't rejected me; on the contrary he escorted me right up to your door, and gave me a love Song that I can't entirely understand; here, read it, Pasithée.

PASITHÉE

    My beautiful Iris, my Love,
  Your singular beauty
  And its pleasing glow,
  Make it a beautiful day within me.
    When you turn your eye away,
  Hiding its lively flame from me,
  I sense nothing in my soul
  But weariness, sorrow, and pain.
    So toward me be
  Humane and compassionate,

Because your marvelous gaze alone
Triumphs over my faith.
  I beg you, may the rigor
Of your unbending Father
Neither render you more austere,
Nor more cruel to my heart.

PASITHÉE Eole is quite right to praise your qualities, but I don't know why he decided to complain about your Father. For it certainly seems that is what he's doing.

IRIS Everyone complains about him, Pasithée, because he gives everyone a reason to.

PASITHÉE What! Even your Mother?

IRIS I don't know who has the more reason to complain: him about my Mother or my Mother about him; they're both wrong. They're always getting angry at each other, or at my Brother, my Sister, or me, even though I'm the only one to bring a semblance of order to the household.

PASITHÉE Oh? Why do they scold you, then?

IRIS Because I'm never home.

PASITHÉE If they want you at home, why are you never there?

IRIS When I'm there for too long, I get bored.

PASITHÉE Well then, try doing a little needlework to keep you there in spite of yourself.

IRIS But you don't realize that I want to see Eole, and he can't stand being cooped up.

PASITHÉE Iris, do you want to do the right thing? Then free yourself from the rigors of love, and from your parents' tyranny.

IRIS How do I do that, Pasithée?

PASITHÉE There once lived in Argos a lady named Telesilla, who cured herself of a bodily indisposition by dedicating herself to the Muses.[133] Make a similar vow, and they will cure you of your passion of Spirit.

IRIS I don't know what you mean by that.

---

133. Telesilla, an Argive poet (fifth century BCE), was cured of a sickness by vowing to dedicate herself to the Muses (Plutarch, *Bravery of Women, Moralia* 3.245d–f). Tradition credited her with arming the women of Argos after the defeat of the city by Cleomenes. See Pausanias, *Description of Greece* 2.20.8–10. Nine fragments of her work, all dedicated to the women, have survived. Telesilla is praised in the epistle of Angelo Poliziano to Cassandra Fedele, and in the dedicatory epistle of the works of Olympia Morata. See Cassandra Fedele, *Letters and Orations*, 90; Morata, *Complete Writings of an Italian Heretic*, 71.

PASITHÉE: That you must study, spend time with books, take pleasure in reading. Then, as books start occupying more and more of your thinking, they will drive away all these vain and frivolous thoughts from your mind.

IRIS One time I read a book that told fortunes that my father had brought back home.

PASITHÉE Do you know its title?

IRIS It had none.

PASITHÉE Who wrote it?

IRIS I think his name was Almanac. I thought it was wonderful, but my head started to hurt, so I stopped reading it.

PASITHÉE Ah, I should think so. Now the books I'm referring to do not cause headaches, rather they have the opposite effect.

IRIS You're not talking about that beautifully bound book that Eole was reading the other day, are you?

PASITHÉE Well, I don't know. What was it called?

IRIS I don't remember.

PASITHÉE What was it about?

IRIS I can't remember that, either.

PASITHÉE Was it in verse or in prose?

IRIS I didn't look.

PASITHÉE When was it published?

IRIS I don't know. But it was certainly beautiful.

PASITHÉE So you only saw it, Iris, without learning anything from it?

IRIS That is true.

PASITHÉE You would have pleased your Eole by reading it a little. And surely he must have shown it to you thinking that you would want to read it.

IRIS I'd take great pleasure in reading, but my Father doesn't allow it.

PASITHÉE But if you truly wanted to, it would be so easy for you to have books and to study without his knowing it! When he forbids you to go on visits so often, you pay no attention to him. It's a shame, however, that your beauty is not accompanied by the cultivation of your mind, which lasts far longer.

IRIS That's what Nirée says, that my beauty will pass, like a flower. The other day he put this on a piece of paper that I have in my purse. He told one of our servants to come and give it to me. Take a look. Would you like to read it?

PASITHÉE Yes, quite.

> If I formerly have,
> Cruel Love, paid homage to your power,
> I now leave your laws behind,
> Freeing myself from your deplorable service.
>> Honor and virtue
> Have saved me from this doleful life,
> Where you, obstinate monster,
> Enslaved my thoughts for so long.
>> Goodbye, flower of Springtime,
> Who commanded my youthful thoughts,
> I see as the years go by,
> Your beauty lost, and my past loves.

But why does he say that, Iris? You were never more beautiful than you are now.

IRIS I think so too, but he says otherwise.

PASITHÉE Well then, his eyes have deteriorated, but not your face, or maybe he's denying the truth he knows about you.

IRIS I wouldn't know what to do about this.

PASITHÉE Don't you worry that Eole will speak to you in the same way someday?

IRIS Ah, if I knew it, he wouldn't be the first to break the bond of love; I could love plenty of other men besides him. Do you know this foreigner, who calls himself Lord Felix?[134] People say he's happy and rich in everything, and I think he loves me, for we spoke for quite some time the other day at a party.

PASITHÉE And what did he say to you?

IRIS All sorts of lovely things.

PASITHÉE Like what?

IRIS I couldn't understand him very well, because he was speaking in the manner of his own country.

PASITHÉE And what did you say in reply?

IRIS Nothing.

PASITHÉE So you pronounced no reprehensible words. But your friendship is by no means finalized, since the one who could be understood said nothing, and the one who did speak wasn't understood.

IRIS Do you think I should love Eucrit instead? He greets me so

---

134. A Spanish or Italian nobleman, according to the annotator.

courteously. It's true Eole is in better shape than him, and makes me dance the *volte*.[135]

PASITHÉE Has Eucrit offered himself to you?

IRIS No, not really.

PASITHÉE Then I would advise you not to love anyone yet. Wait for some discerning Man to present himself at your service, led to love you because he is in some way similar to you.[136]

IRIS When will this happen, Pasithée? Would you please read my palm? Do you know how?

PASITHÉE A discreet Girl, able to bring happiness to the one she loves, can't be judged as such simply by looking at her palm, Iris; it's her Mind that reveals her to be wise in all her actions. Such Minds are sought out only by those who resemble them; and those they attract they retain, as I've heard it said in these lines:

> Fair Lady, do not fear scorn,
> Even though several winters tarnish your beauty;
> Adorn your mind with Virtues and Grace,
> For Virtue retains what the eye has captured.

IRIS I don't see, however, that people esteem virtuous learned women[137] so much; to the contrary, men thoroughly mock them.

PASITHÉE Well yes, ignorant men do. But the most learned and best educated men have for them a friendship filled with honorable reverence. Think of what Angelo Poliziano said as he admired

> That Cassandra Fedele
> Saintly honor of all of Italy.[138]

And following the example of this noble Virgin, you should live modestly and speak advisedly, so that if your beauty attracts men, your

---

135. A new dance that came from Italy to the French court in 1572, the *volte* was highly esteemed by the youth and the ladies. Moralists such as Vives categorized dancing as "trivial and foolish" (*Education of a Christian Woman*, 71).

136. Ficinian doctrine of similarity from which love is born. See Ficino, *Commentary on Plato's Symposium*, speech 2.8.

137. "Femmes savantes" in the original.

138. On the letter of praise that Angelo Poliziano addressed to Cassandra Fedele, a learned Italian woman (1465–1558), see Fedele, *Letters and Orations*, 90; Margaret King and Albert Rabil Jr., eds. *Her Immaculate Hand: Selected Works by and about the Women Humanists of Quattrocento Italy* (Binghamton, N.Y.: Medieval and Renaissance Texts and Studies, 1983), 126–27.

Graces will retain them in a relation of good will, such that they can rightly say: amorous servitude frees me from all vice.

IRIS So what should I do, Pasithée?

PASITHÉE Iris, you must read.

IRIS But my Father forbids it. He says it's useless.

PASITHÉE Learn to write well.

IRIS My Mother doesn't want me to. She claims she's wise enough without it.[139]

PASITHÉE Play the lyre.

IRIS My Brother makes fun of me for it; he says it's a waste of money.

PASITHÉE Learn to speak properly.

IRIS What? Don't you think I speak well enough? Haven't I spoken good words to you?

PASITHÉE Ah, I'm truly pleased with them, Iris. What I'm telling you is only to keep you from complaining anymore about the inconstancy of your Lovers. For if you take my friendly advice, you'll be able to live well without having a Suitor.[140] If, on the other hand, you are loved, it will be by an honest Man[141] who will be faithful to you. People want to love those who are like them.[142] Men of wit and learning are better at loving because they have a stronger imagination. Love is created by images carried from the beloved to the lover. The eye and the ear are the windows through which love slips into the heart. The love of corporal beauty takes hold through the gaze, and that of beautiful souls enters by the ear. So beautify your soul if you desire to be

---

139. Mothers traditionally did not encourage their daughters' literary instruction even in the most well-to-do homes. Christine de Pizan's mother opposed her penchant for studying because she "wished to keep her busy with spinning and silly girlishness, following the common custom of women" (Pizan, *Book of the City of Ladies* 2.36.4). Marie de Gournay's mother had such an "aversion . . . en telles choses" (an aversion for such things) that Gournay had to educate herself for the most part in her spare time. See *Copie de la vie de la Damoiselle de Gournay* (1616), in Marie de Gournay, *Fragments d'un Discours féminin*, ed. Elyanne Dezon-Jones (Paris: José Corti, 1988), 137; Marie de Gournay, *Apology for the Woman Writing and Other Works*, 6. One can thus measure the exceptional attitude of Madeleine des Roches toward her daughter.

140. A declaration that the author applies to herself in her *Epistle to Her Mother* (see chap. 2), in sonnet 12 of *Sonnets from Charite to Sincero* (see chap. 2), and in letter 42 of her *Missives* (see chap. 5).

141. "Honnête homme" in the original.

142. On the Aristotelian principle of reciprocity and resemblance in friendship and love, see *Nicomachean Ethics* (LCL vol. 19), 1159b2, 1166a1. The following explanation develops Ficinian notions on Neoplatonic love. See Ficino, *Commentary on the Symposium*, speech 2.8.9.

uniquely loved by a wise, discreet, and learned Friend. Otherwise, live without love and think about all the misfortunes that come with love; how many poor Mistresses are aggrieved, having lost their Suitors to this unfortunate trip to Portugal.[143] Ah! Our Chariclée shed so many tears over the departure of her lover that it was such a pity to see her, for she worried that the Daughter of Necessity would wound his heart that she had so gently won. I remember hearing that she retired to the country to flee social life, and that there, while walking alone, she sang a Song, which I've been able to learn.

IRIS Sing it then, I beg you, Pasithée, because now I feel like dancing.

PASITHÉE Iris, your request is so persuasive that I can't refuse what you ask, so I'll say this: do your best to accommodate it to your dance.

> Nymphs, hostesses of these woods,
> Who hold your court in secret,
> You have heard the sweet voice
> Of my virtuous Philarete:
> No longer will you hear anything so sweet,
> As was his graceful voice,
> Even though Pan, who is forever by your side,
> Defies bright-shining Apollo.
> And you, small silvery Clain,[144]
> Who with your curling waves
> Gently murmur without end,
> As you flow into the next valley,
> You see nothing as pure
> Within your crystalline sources,
> And touch nothing as hard
> As you strike your adamantine Rocks.
> How firm is the heart
> Of my beloved Philarete
> How pure, and constantly
> In the bonds of a Love so discreet!
> And you, O beautiful greening meadow,
> Who, peppered with so many flowers,

---

143. When Portugal was invaded by the Spanish army on orders of Philip II, Catherine de Médicis, who claimed dynastic rights to the throne of Portugal, sent in French naval forces commanded by Philippe Strozzi. The battle, on 26 July 1582, ended in disaster for the French.

144. River that flows through Poitiers.

Carpet the riverbank,
Neighbor of troops of fish,
   You never produced flowers,
As beautiful and pleasing,
As those born from the tears
Of my love, when away he goes.
   Your Hyacinth, your Adonis,[145]
Loved by a God and by a Goddess,
Pale in comparison to him
Whose nobility dwarfs theirs.
   And you, gentle amorous Zephyr,
Who kiss the newly flowered Rose,
Do not think yourself more happy
As you caress Flora the Beautiful
   Than I am to see
The sweet rain of tears,
Which Philarete makes to fall,
Showing that his departure saddens him.
   A gently floating sigh,
Witness of his sad thoughts,
Comforts my soul,
After having injured it so.
   I am happy to see him wounded
In a chaste and amorous war,
I complain at seeing him forced
To abandon his dearly beloved land.
   O Heaven which hold him prisoner
In a climate so far from ours,
Give him back to me healthy and refreshed,
He belongs to me, even though he's yours.
   And you, Song, leave
Solitary Chariclée:
When you entertain her,
Her solitary musings are troubled.

Well, Iris, what do you think? Is it easy to dance to?
   IRIS No, not really, Pasithée; I think it's too—well, I don't know,
it's not—not enough . . .

---

145. Youths changed into flowers (Ovid, *Metamorphoses* 10.162 ff. and 345 ff).

PASITHÉE You mean it's not lively enough?

IRIS Yes, yes, that's it.

PASITHÉE I can sing a livelier one.

IRIS O, please do, but play the Viol as well.

PASITHÉE I'm happy to do it for love of you. I'll sing the Song of beautiful Alcyon:[146] it's a lively one.

IRIS All right, please begin, because I have to leave soon.

PASITHÉE

> May all be peaceful and gentle
> On this riverbank,
> May the waves be calm,
> The sky without storm.
>   May pink-tinted Dawn
> Spread her flowers,
> And may happy destiny
> Descend from the sky.
>   The radiant Sun
> Drives away the clouds,
> So by our eyes
> Its beauty may be seen.
>   The beautiful azure chariot
> Of the Nereids
> Pierces through the waves
> With a moderate speed.
>   The amorous Dolphins
> Are at the water's edge
> And sweet-smelling Zephyr
> Reaches us,
>   Flattering with his gaze
> His beautiful Flora,
> Who everywhere makes
> Flowers to bud.
>   To hear my song
> Each one prepares,
> Even the Fish
> Will celebrate.
>   One taken by the snare

146. Alcyon, daughter of Eolus and wife of Ceyx, king of Trachis; the latter died in a shipwreck. In her despair, Alcyon was changed into a bird with a melancholy song. Ovid, *Metamorphoses* 11.410 ff.

Frolics and jumps,
To the tune of my voice,
Sometimes high, sometimes low.
     Who would not be moved
In thought,
By the dream that I had
Last night.
     I saw the Child Love,
His bow and his arrows,
He was scouting around
With his sparks.
     His branding iron was beautiful,
His flame gentle,
Happy were his torch,
His bow, and his quiver.
     He shoots instantly
His lively flames,
And scorches
Beautiful souls.
     His fire, luminous and bright,
Comes down to earth
Like a flash of lightning
But without thunder.
     So let us revere this God,
You noble companions,
Praying that everywhere
He may command us.

Alcyon's gentle voice gave much Grace to this Song. Please excuse me, Iris, if I've not done it justice.

IRIS It's very beautiful, Pasithée, but I'm glad it wasn't longer, because I wanted to hear it all, and I've got to leave.

PASITHÉE Why are you in such a hurry?

IRIS As I looked out your window, I saw Eole pacing in the street down below.

PASITHÉE Wait for him to come here to pick you up and bring you back home.

IRIS Oh, he won't come inside. He doesn't want to talk with you because you're a learned woman.[147]

147. "Savante" in the original.

PASITHÉE Ha, ha, really now, I can do without him, and all others like him. I don't think that girls study letters in vain, because literature helps them to drive away gallants of his sort.

IRIS He did tell me, though, to ask your opinion of the Song he gave me.

PASITHÉE The Song is pleasant enough because it's about you. But Eole didn't make it up, for he simply copied what he saw in your face.

IRIS My Lord, how well you speak, Pasithée! I'd come to your school every day if I had the time! I take all the pleasure in the world when I discuss things with you. I must, however, take my leave, because Eole is calling me, and it's also late. I kiss your hands, Pasithée.

PASITHÉE I commend myself to your Grace, Iris.

V

SELECTED LETTERS OF
MADELEINE DES ROCHES
AND CATHERINE DES ROCHES
FROM *LES MISSIVES* (1586)

I insist that from now on, neither my headaches, nor my stomach pains, nor my recurrent fever will prevent me from going where my desire leads me: because it is your will that I follow you, here I am, my Daughter.

— Madeleine des Roches, *Epistle to My Daughter*

My deepest desire is that they [letters] may be agreeable to you, Mother, and I humbly beseech you to love them more than their beauty deserves, so they don't go lacking for support.

— Catherine des Roches, *To My Mother*

INTRODUCTION

The publication of the Dames des Roches' missives, the first printed letters actually sent by women in French literary history, represents an inaugural moment.[1] As Janet Altman indicates, "moments when women did publish their own letters, or when their letters were appropriated as cultural models by publishers, are significant."[2] The Des Roches' dialogic intrafamil-

---

1. Helisenne de Crenne's *Epistres familieres et invectives* (1539), while constituting the first printed letters in prose written in French, are not considered missives. The prevailing critical view is that Crenne composed "a story, through letters." See *A Renaissance Woman: Helisenne's Personal and Invective Letters*. For Jean-Philippe Beaulieu, the *Epistres* are a "une reprise partielle des enjeux et des conflits des *Angoysses*" (partial return to the themes and conflicts of [Crenne's novel] the *Angoysses*." *Les Epistres familieres et invectives de ma dame Hélisenne*, ed. J.-P. Beaulieu (Montréal: Presses Universitaires de Montréal, 1995), 14. Several of Marguerite de Navarre's letters to her brother François Ier were published in 1547 by Marguerite herself, but they were of a more personal nature and not originally written for publication. My thanks to Régine Reynolds-Cornell for pointing this out to me.

2. Janet Gurkin Altman, "Women's Letters in the Public Sphere," in *Going Public: Women and Publishing in Early Modern France*, ed. Elizabeth Goldsmith and Dena Goodman (Ithaca: Cornell University Press, 1995), 101.

ial correspondence in the prefaces to their first two works finds its most inclusive outlet in their last collaborative venture: there they answer in tandem, Madeleine first, followed by Catherine, the many individuals who formed part of their entourage. Madeleine's dedicatory epistle attests to Catherine's growing literary authority; Catherine's subtle shift in pronouns, from "her" to "my mother" in the title of her dedicatory letter (see the epigraph at the start of this chapter), underscores her leadership role as she reveals in her letter the editorial circumstances and decision-making process that led to their (final) joint enterprise. Madeleine's premonitory fears of a less than successful reception and Catherine's cavalier pose in regard to the publication of her letters participate in a similar use of the modesty topos that lies at the heart of their conception of the *lettre mondaine* (civility letter). Missives in high-gentry and noble urban networks functioned primarily as rhetorical markers of class. They were central to a codified system of social relations in which one wrote letters to exchange civilities. Interactions, whether in person or in letters, were governed by the conventions of *honnêteté* and *mondanité* (worldly civility), polite, well-bred behavior. The Des Roches' missives exemplify above all the letter of compliment.[3]

Missives in the early modern period were generally not considered private property. As Jane Couchman observes, the letters, journals, and memoirs of important female political figures were preserved because they were "public texts." To address children, relatives, or friends about home, illnesses, or their religious faith was not viewed as "more personal" than to write about political alliances or state matters.[4] Whether to public figures, family members, or friends, letters were subject to circulation, confiscation, and publication with or without the author's consent. They were read aloud in gatherings, circles, and salons to be admired and critiqued since they were considered a "written conversation" reflecting above all the conventions of civility.

In her prefatory epistle as well as her two letters to her editor Abel L'An-

---

3. On the letter of compliment, Luc Vaillancourt remarks: "Fruit du croisement de diverses traditions épistolaires, curieux mélange d'affectation et de naturel, de conventionnalisme et d'invention, ce type de lettre jouera un rôle déterminant dans le développement de la prose conversationnelle en France" (As fruit of the mixing of diverse epistolary traditions, as a curious mixture of affectation and naturalness, of conventionality and invention, this type of letter will play a determining role in the development of conversational prose in France). *La lettre familière au XVIe siècle. Rhétorique humaniste de l'épistolaire* (Paris: Champion, 2003), 318.

4. Jane Couchman, "What Is 'Personal' about Sixteenth-Century French Women's Personal Writings?" *Atlantis* 19, no.1 (1993): 16–22. Margaret Ezell notes that letters in the early modern period were "highly conventional public forms of address" meant to display the writer's rhetorical graces. *Writing Women's Literary History* (Baltimore: Johns Hopkins University Press, 1993), 34.

gelier,[5] Catherine appears more interested in the publication of her newly finished translation *Le Ravissement de Proserpine* (The Rape of Proserpina) than in that of her letters. Using the rhetorical humility trope, she thinks of these as a "chose si legere" (such a light thing) whose "obscurité" is unworthy of the "feu luysant" (sun's gleaming light). Besides she sent them a long time ago and they are so "peu desirables" (undesirable) that she herself is annoyed at having kept them. It seems that Abel L'Angelier wanted them published. He had reedited Étienne du Tronchet's epistolary best-seller *Lettres missives et familieres* (Familiar Letters and Missives) in 1577 (and again in 1578, 1580, 1582, 1584, 1585; Du Tronchet's missives were originally printed in 1568–69), and he was about to publish the first edition of Étienne Pasquier's *Lettres* (1586).[6] L'Angelier placed the Des Roches' missives first, then followed them with the translation and named the volume with a strategic marketing title which Catherine herself suggested in her cover letter: "My Mother didn't want to name this little book, because she hoped you would become its godfather. So give it whatever title you think best, be it Missives, or Letters, or Epistles, for the readers' curiosity will perhaps make it sell faster. So please treat it as if it were your own."[7]

A striking feature of the Des Roches' letters, one that seems in direct conflict with the proud rhetorical assertion of their worth in their other works, is their constant depreciation of themselves the better to praise their interlocutors' virtues. They elevate their correspondent by downgrading themselves. This was a common strategy in male and female epistolary writing. Madeleine for instance excuses herself for adapting a word from Ariosto's epic, claiming that this should be permitted to her "as one who lacks wit, invention, and facility with words."[8] Catherine states to a learned woman that "as I have no grace that could make me worthy, I'll try, if at all possible, to gain

5. Letter 70 (see below) is the cover letter accompanying the manuscript of *Les Missives*. Along with letter 69 (see below), also to L'Angelier, it provides a rare example of a sixteenth-century woman writer's correspondence with her editor.

6. Although Pasquier claimed to be the first in France to publish his private letters in the vernacular, thereby relegating the Dames des Roches to second place and conveniently omitting Du Tronchet, the *privilège du roi* indicates otherwise. The privilege of the Des Roches' missives is dated 1 March 1586, that of Pasquier's letters 7 June 1586. For Pasquier's boast, see his *Lettres familières*, ed. Dorothy Thickett (Geneva: Droz, 1974), 187.

7. "Ma mere n'a point voulu nommer ce petit livre, desirant que vous en soiez parain. Nommez-le donc ainsi que bon vous semblera, du tiltre du Missives, ou de Lettres, ou d'Epistres, pource que la curiosité des hommes en rendra peut-estre la despesche plus prompte. Vous en ferez (s'il vous plaist) comme du vostre." Letter 70, *Missives*, 211 (and see below).

8. "À moy qui defaut d'esprits, d'inventions et de paroles." Madeleine, letter 6, *Missives*, 96 (and see below).

some esteem from your favor,"[9] and to an erudite male friend she explains: "You say that you cannot worthily praise me. Truly I believe it, but it's because I'm unworthy of praise; and because your excellence praises only that which is as excellent as itself."[10] Both mother and daughter speak poorly at times of their letters. Madeleine thanks a correspondent for the pleasure she received from reading his "lettres douces et gracieuses" (gentle and gracious letters) but adds that she cannot reciprocate in her replies because these are "defaillant de sujet et de stile" (lacking in subject and style).[11] Catherine states in her preliminary epistle to her mother that her letters will be seen by some "qui les despriseront encore plus que je ne fais" (who will scorn them even more than I do); she asks a correspondent to excuse her reply for "les fillets en sont mal tissus" (its threads are poorly woven);[12] and to her suitor Claude Pellejay who had sent her his *Hymn of Beauty* in her honor, she indicates: "Monsieur, my only purpose in taking up the pen is to let you know that I have some knowledge of myself, and that I am not the one who has inspired you to bring to light this hymn of beauty; rather you've wished to represent in it the beauty of your mind, which alone has been the worthy progenitor of such excellent offspring."[13]

The Dames des Roches, however, are supremely conscious of playing a *de rigueur* game with their correspondents. As Luc Vaillancourt aptly notes, the dialectic of self-abasement with its concomitant exaltation of the other plays into the strategic quest for social distinction: "It is evident that there is a great deal of pride in such humility."[14] Such self-conscious gamesmanship is perceptible when Madeleine, after excusing herself for having asked a scholar to "correct" her epitaph on the death of the comte de Brissac, asserts that she cannot accept one of his suggested word changes. To attenuate her refusal, she invokes the Aristotelian distinction between form and matter: "Je

---

9. "Ainsi, n'ayant aucune grace pour me faire valoir, j'essaieray, s'il m'est possible, de gaigner quelque estime par la faveur des vostres." Letter 14, *Missives*, 156 (and see below).

10. "Vous dites que vous ne me pouvez dignement loüer. Vra. ement je le croy, mais c'est pource que je suis indigne de loüange: et puis vostre excellence ne loüe que ce qui est excellent comme elle." Letter 26, *Missives*, 166 (and see below).

11. Madeleine, letter 2 (see below).

12. Catherine, letter 13 (see below).

13. "Monsieur, je n'ay pris la plume, sinon pour vous faire cognoistre qu'en partie je me cognois, et sçay bien que ce n'est point moy qui vous aye esté occasion de mettre en lumiere l'hymne de la beauté, mais vous avez voulu representer par elle celle de vostre esprit, qui seul a esté digne cause de tant d'excellens enfans que ceux qui en sont issus." Letter 23, *Missives*, 163 (and see below).

14. "On le voit, il y a beaucoup d'orgueil dans cette humilité." Vaillancourt, *La lettre familière au XVIᵉ siècle*, 326.

sçay que mes vers mal polis reçoivent nature qui est femelle, et refusent l'art qui est masle" (I know that my ill-fashioned verses are female by nature, and refuse art which is male). Then, in a clever witticism, she declares that she should not be holding company with such (male) art while her husband is absent, and she concludes by recommending the latter's "personne et affaires" (person and affairs) to her correspondent.[15] In a missive to an admirer, Catherine shows that she is no dupe of his pose of humble deference toward her. Since "l'humilité est la grace des graces" (humility is the grace of graces), he has humbled himself by displaying how little he esteems his own "pensées et paroles" (thoughts and words). But in effect, "vous monstrez par vos louables coustumes que les effaits suivent en vous le desir de la vertu" (you show with your praiseworthy manners, that you are indeed virtuous).[16] Such deferential posing is endemic to correspondences in elite circles. Kristen Neuschel, Sharon Kettering, and Arlette Jouanna among others have shown that in the early modern period the continual exchange of recognition with others was a means to securing a noble's identity.[17] Substance equated style, and formulaic expression conveyed meaning.

The Dames des Roches' missives reflect the purposes for which most noble letters were written. They seek to maintain contact with distant friends or relatives, as in Catherine's note to her cousin Françoise Chémeraut, who left Poitiers with her mother and sister because of an outbreak of the plague.[18] They value friendship. Catherine especially praises female friendship, closely linked in her mind with female learning and writing. To a friend noted for her "eloquence," she begs God to bless her with "la sainte amitié que vous m'avez jurée" (the holy friendship that you've sworn to me); she considers another friend "un miracle entre les autres filles" (a miracle among young girls) for her learned letters, and wishes for the continuation of "l'amitié que vos lettres me promettent" (the friendship your letters promise me).[19] They recommend family members to professionals and political figures who could be useful to them: Catherine recommends her cousin, "ce gentil-

15. Madeleine, letter 4 (see below).

16. Catherine, letter 27 (see below).

17. Kristen B. Neuschel, *Word of Honor: Interpreting Noble Culture in Sixteenth-Century France* (Ithaca: Cornell University Press, 1986); Kettering, "Gift-Giving and Patronage in Early Modern France"; Arlette Jouanna, *Le devoir de révolte. La noblesse française et la gestation de l'État moderne* (Paris: Fayard, 1989).

18. Catherine, letter 43 (see below).

19. Catherine, letters 14, 49 (see below). On the linking between female friendship and "écriture féminine," see Colette H. Winn, "Aux origines du discours féminin sur l'amitié: Marguerite de Navarre, *La Coche* (1541)," *Women in French Studies* 7 (1999): 9–24.

homme qui m'est affectionné parent" (a nobleman who is a very dear relation of mine), to a well-placed Parisian professional whose help she enlists in securing the attention of the famous attorney general Jacques Faye d'Espeisses.[20] Madeleine addresses several letters to lawyers for a favorable outcome to her lawsuits.[21] They wrote to offer their services, as in Madeleine's opening letter to a noblewoman whom she thanks for her invitation "to write on your behalf," offering "to serve you in such a manner" again.[22]

As in humanist correspondences, the Des Roches write often about sending and receiving books which were the most common gifts circulated among learned friends.[23] These were also a means to patronage. In exchange for the rich gifts that the ambassador to Constantinople Jacques de Germigny has sent them, they reciprocate by offering him "un petit livre de nostre façon" (this little book of ours).[24] As both this example and the choice of titles for their volume noted above reveal, mother and daughter were keenly interested in marketing strategies for their books. They hoped to gain publicity and further sales. Catherine's address to a noblewoman who has sent her a payment for copies of *Les Œuvres* and/or *Les Secondes œuvres* also includes a reminder to publicize them "par les lettres ou propos de vous" (in your letters or conversations).[25] Both accepted commissions to write poems on behalf of others, men and women, for which they received occasional payments. Madeleine sends a sonnet requested by a noble widow to whom she offers her "affectionné service" (affectionate service), and she thanks another widow for her payment to Catherine for an epitaph for her husband.[26]

Several letters address seemingly more personal matters such as bouts of ill health and migraines suffered by various family members,[27] a friend's complaint about the infidelities of her husband,[28] epidemics of the plague in the Poitiers region and in Paris,[29] and an unwanted suitor to whom Catherine makes clear her desire to remain free. To the latter, she declares in no uncer-

---

20. Catherine, letter 29 (see below).
21. Madeleine, letters 9, 12, 13, 14, 26 (see below).
22. Madeleine, letter 1 (see below).
23. Natalie Zemon Davis, *The Gift in Sixteenth-Century France* (Madison: University of Wisconsin Press, 2000), 36.
24. Madeleine, letter 25 (see below).
25. Catherine, letter 19 (see below).
26. Madeleine, letters 7 and 22 (see below).
27. Madeleine, letter 24 (see below; Catherine, letters 20, 21, 22, 25, 39, 53 (see below).
28. Catherine, letter 45, *Missives*, 187–88.
29. Catherine, letter 43 (see below); Madeleine, letter 26 (see below).

tain terms: "So you should know, Monsieur, that I would not consider myself free if I were to cause servitude in another.... So I don't want a suitor, nor do I need a companion or a master."[30] These references to familial situations, however, should not be construed as autobiographical. In letters founded on a rhetoric of civility, the writer seeks not to establish an intimate rapport with the addressee but to manifest an exemplary sociability and *savoir dire*. This is indeed the case with the majority of letter manuals and epistolary collections of the period. Étienne Pasquier eliminated from his letters references to private or domestic issues in order to create a literary work in which moral, political, and historical reflections are paramount. So too the Des Roches are concerned with creating an exemplary anthology to achieve a universalizing effect. To that end, they eliminated names, dates, and temporal or spatial references to present an epistolary model. They drew on the literary tradition of the familiar letter as defined in Erasmus's influential *De conscribendis epistolis* (1522). Erasmus urges letter writers to practice the virtues of pleasing the addressee through an *apte dicere*, or style adapted to both the sender and the receptor, through decorum and language characterized by artful simplicity and charm, *brevitas*, and learned allusions. The Des Roches explore as well the gamut of possible subjects suggested by Erasmus: letters of thanks, recommendation, information, supplication, invitation, consolation, blame and commendation, requests, and excuses.

In their correspondence, the Dames des Roches invoke themes consistently found throughout their oeuvre such as the need to write to overcome the effects of time, loss, and death, the acquisition of virtue through letters, the pairing of friendship with learning, and especially the refusal to acquiesce to silence, the so-called "ornament of women." They exercise their right to speech. "Silence," affirms Catherine, "bears witness only to itself: its veil is sometimes as sorrowful as that of the clouds when they prevent us from seeing the glistening splendor of the sun."[31]

◦⟫

30. "Sçachez doncques (Monsieur) que je n'aurois pas opinion d'estre assez libre, causant la servitude en un autre.... Or ne desirant point de serviteur, je ne demande non plus ny compagnon ny maistre." Letter 44, *Missives*, 186–87 (and see below).

31. "Le silence ne tesmoigne gueres que de luy-mesme; et son voile est quelquefois autant ennuieux que celuy des nues, quand elles nous empeschent de voir la luisante splendeur du Soleil" Letter 26, *Missives*, 167 (and see below).

SELECTED LETTERS OF MADELEINE DES ROCHES
EPISTLE TO MY DAUGHTER

If a remarkable poet's legend has immortalized Aeneas for having rescued his father and the images of his gods from the flames that were burning Ilion,[32] with how much more reason should the history books of a not ungrateful century make honorable mention of you, my Daughter.[33] For your deep faith shows that you bear in your heart the image of our great God. And by the flight of your pen,[34] without begging for help from anyone else,[35] you have taken the trouble to rescue me from the Cimmerian nights[36] in which ignorance and old age kept me buried. You resemble the green twig which in its youthful grace is cherished by the gentle breeze, lively streams, and the tempered rays of the Sun: and paying for the good it receives by the fertility of its ever-multiplying flowers, it never forgets the old stump that gave it a little formless matter. Even better, the little twig is always scrupulous to hide the stump's defects, and to defend it from the violence of the winds, of thunder, and passing time. Thus, my Daughter, I see you filled with endless love and piety, as you inspire my soul and my heart to some praiseworthy undertaking. It is now the third time that your strength encourages me to speak in public, and I can't help but feel a little frightened as I remember the Mantuan's tale.[37] He relates that the Almighty, after he had punished our first father for

32. Aeneas, surprised in Troy by the Greeks, fled through the burning city carrying old Anchises on his back, his son in his arms, and the city's most sacred gods. See Virgil, *Aeneid* 2.

33. An extraordinarily bold statement for the time. Women, especially from the gentry, were not to be known for themselves; they were given access to a (limited) education "on grounds that it fostered understanding in marriage and in society," and as Rousseau put it some two centuries latter, "to make themselves more agreeable to the men in their lives." Martine Sonnet, "A Daughter to Educate," in *A History of Women in the West*, vol. 3: *Renaissance and Enlightenment Paradoxes*, ed. Natalie Zemon Davis and Arlette Farge (Cambridge: Harvard University Press, 1993), 103, 110.

34. The "winged pen" in Pléiade theory symbolizes the unfettered imagination and intellect.

35. Madeleine's pride in her daughter's intellectual achievement is crystallized in her use of the saying "sans mendier l'aide d'autruy" (without begging for help from anyone else). This invocation to self-help occurs in several instances in which the Des Roches challenge their female contemporaries to use their pens to overcome the destruction of time and death. See Madeleine's ode 3, ll. 52–54 (see chap. 1), and Catherine's *Epistle to Her Mother* (see chap. 2).

36. The Cimmerians were a mythic people who lived in a land where the sun never shone. Ulysses went there to conjure up the dead and to question the blind Tiresias. See Homer, *Odyssey* 11.16.

37. The parable that follows is adapted from the *Eclogues* of Baptista Spagnuoli, known as the Mantuan. See Baptista (Spagnuoli) Manteanus, *Adulescentia. The Eclogues of the Mantuan*, ed. and trans. Lee Piepho (New York: Garland, 1989), eclogue 6: *Cornix. A Dispute between Townsmen and Country Folk*, ll. 56–193. Madeleine's apprehension concerns the publication of the *Missives*, their third collaborative venture.

his disobedience and had chased him from the Paradise of delights,[38] made him a tiller of the land, charging him to take care of it, and to grow and multiply. God then went back to heaven, man remained on earth which, newly created by the divine hand, became so fertile that our ancestors, with little trouble, enjoyed its plentiful bounty; in a short time they gave birth to a great number of beautiful children. The Lord, who cared for them, wanted to pay them a more courteous visit than the first time; Adam found out, and advised his wife of the coming of the master. She, knowing how much chastity is the adornment of women, began to think that this fault of not having kept it well enough was somehow connected with the taking of the forbidden fruit. Therefore, seeking to cover up her error, she quickly hid some of her children in the haystack, in the barn, or in the manger. Her other children she took time to wash, get ready, and dress. The Lord promptly shed his glory to take on the form of lowly humanity, which received him in all humility. He looked on these new children with a benign and favorable eye. He bestows on the one the monarchy, on another a fiefdom, and on the third a principality. The mother, now full of joy, calls to her those of her children whom she had not so well prepared. God, whose powerful hand never rests, gave each gifts of understanding, prophecy, oracles, knowledge of how things change and evolve, and universal laws. When she saw this second set of children so well rewarded, Eve quickly pulled the others from their hiding place, hoping that there would still be enough riches for them. But the Lord had already left and did not see the third set of brothers, even though they were no less agreeable than the first. You know, my Daughter, exactly what this tale pertains to; nevertheless if you are resolved to keep going, I'll say like this Roman: "I am healthy, Brutus!";[39] and I insist that from now on, neither my headaches, nor my stomach pains, nor my recurrent fever will prevent me from going where my desire leads me: because it is your will that I follow you, here I am, my Daughter.

    1 [To a noble woman to whom she offers her services][40]
I thank you that in asking me to write on your behalf,[41] you've taken possession of my soul, which has been devoted to you for a long time now. Should it please

---

38. Adam, Genesis 3.

39. This "Roman" is Caius Ligarius who, when sick one day, was visited by Brutus who said to him: "Ah! Ligarius, this is no time to be sick." Ligarius responded, "But Brutus, if you have in your head some scheme worthy of you, I'll soon be better." Plutarch, *Brutus, Lives* 11.

40. The numbering of the letters follows that in my edition of *Les Missives*.

41. The Dames des Roches were frequently asked to write poems on behalf of patrons from whom they received monetary or other rewards.

you, Madame,[42] that I continue to serve you in such a manner, I'll think of myself even more highly, and will find myself all the more ready for your service. This is what I desire above all else and I very humbly kiss your hands.

2 [To a male addressee, thanking him for his letters]
O how I treasure the memory you have of me, which produces so many beautiful and honorable words that prove your excellence in virtue, learning, and courtesy. Truly, Monsieur, I approve more than ever the authority of those who say that nothing in and of itself is fortunate or unfortunate, since although your absence is a bitter and unhappy matter, your (gentle and gracious) letters, on the other hand, which are caused by it [the absence], bring me so much pleasure. However, I can't convey such pleasure in my replies because these are lacking in subject and style. The one whose name resembles the names for the north and west winds[43] delivered your message to me through another. And believe me those drugs were good, for they were put outside to air out;[44] but for fear of over-airing the graces of the messenger, I'll not speak further. It will suffice me to humbly greet yours, which are the complete opposites of his.[45]

4 [To a scholar, on the correction of her verse][46]
I am quite grieved, Monsieur, over the trouble I've caused you without wishing it; for I swear to you that I've never asked any living person to make you do something that could annoy you, or distract your noble mind from its normal exercises which are so beautiful and worthy. And I dare say that I'm a little concerned that my verses (having received your skillful and exacting correction) could disdain me as their author. But then, everyone can see by reading them that I will not be rebuked by Apelles for the mistake of Protogonus.[47] It has happened that this drudgery has befallen you, and you corrected them,

42. In Madeleine des Roches's day, women bore titles of honor analogous to those of men, designating a woman's social class rather than her marital status. The title "Madame" was reserved for women of the highest rank, and that of "Mademoiselle" for the lesser gentry.

43. Madeleine des Roches uses a pun to hint at the identity of the letter bearer whose name likely contained the word *vent* (wind).

44. Meaning that the contents of the letter were so good that the addressee read it aloud to others.

45. A backhanded compliment to say that the addressee surpasses the present messenger's qualities.

46. This scholar is in all probability a member of her coterie and perhaps the famous philologist Joseph-Juste Scaliger who was often asked by friends to edit their writings and correct their Latin verses so as to make these conform to the classical models so familiar to him. See Jean Plattard, "Le séjour de J.-J. Scaliger en Poitou," *Bulletin historique et philologique* 44 (1926–27): 118.

47. Apelles, the greatest of Greek painters, was the first to recognize Protogonus's talent. But in the end, he preferred his own paintings to those of Protogonus, which "lacked the charms that lifted his own toward heaven." Plutarch, *Demetrios, Lives* 22.6.

for which I thank you with all my heart, and I gladly receive your critique. But I beseech you not to force my conscience over the word *caterve* because I am persistent and proud.[48] I know that my ill-fashioned verses are female by nature, and refuse art which is male.[49] Also it would be even more unfitting for me than ever to practice such an art in the absence of Monsieur de la Villée my husband,[50] whose person and affairs I commend to you, humbly beseeching you, Monsieur, if it is in your power to help him, that he may be in your good graces.

6 [To the same addressee, on the correction of her verse]
Truly, I would be upset if, due to such a noble letter as yours, I stood condemned for three faults: ingratitude, ignorance, and stubbornness. Ingratitude toward you, corrector of my mistake, ignorance for not having caught it, and stubbornness for not wanting to change it. Not that I want the goddess Truth to be inclined in my unfavorable favor. I am not so presumptuous as to think that I never err, nor do I hold myself in such low esteem as to think that I always make mistakes; and if I have erred with *proterve*, the divine Ariosto, who doesn't like too much Latin in his vernacular, uses this term to embellish one of the lines of his first canto.[51] Since such thievery is praised in so great a poet, will it not also be permitted to me as one who lacks wit, invention, and facility with words, especially in this time of war when pillage is practiced by all? So please don't allow the sweetness of your so well-spoken words to turn to sourness; and believe me when I say that I wish, desire, and seek to be advised, taught, and instructed when it is needed. I hope no less to have a part in your good graces, if it pleases you to do me such an honor, as I pray that God on high, Monsieur, will be liberal to you in dispensing His.

---

48. Reference to Madeleine des Roches's choice of the word *caderve* (cadaver), a deformation of *caterve* (troop), which rhymes with *proterve* (arrogant), in her *Epitaphe de Monsieur le Comte de Brissac* (*Œuvres*). This letter was composed soon after the death of Timoléon de Cossé, count of Brissac, killed during the siege of Mussidan in Périgord on 28 April 1569.

49. According to Aristotle, form animates and organizes matter, an inert mass. While form is masculine, matter is feminine. See Aristotle, *On the Generation of Animals* 1.20.728aI, 729aI; *Physics* 1.9.192a22; and Thomas Aquinas, *Summa theologica* Ia192.I. The misogynist Gasparo in Castiglione's *Book of the Courtier* (3.15.217) propounds the same view: "man is as the form and woman as the matter; and therefore, just as the form is more perfect than the matter—nay, gives it its being—so man is far more perfect than woman." Madeleine des Roches critiques such a standard view.

50. François d'Éboissard, seigneur de La Villée, a lawyer by profession, enjoyed great respect in Poitiers. Between 1565 and 1570 he was elected one of the seventy-five *bourgeois* of the city. He died during the summer of 1578.

51. Madeleine des Roches defends her choice of the word *proterve* (meaning "ungrateful"), which she used in her *Epitaphe de Monsieur le Comte de Brissac* (*Œuvres*). For Ariosto, see *Orlando Furioso* 1.51.8.

7 [To a widow for whom the author has composed a sonnet]

Just as ignorance should seal one's lips, as you say, Madame, so knowledge should give one leave to open them: therefore that is what now opens yours. I say this because the word is the image of one's thoughts, and writing is the image of the word.[52] So then your missive, which represents (as it is so beautifully written) the rare perfections of your divine mind, touches my soul by way of my eyes in such a way that I, who in the past had the honor of hearing you speak and found myself enthralled by your wise discourses, remain entirely at your excellent service. That's why I can't make any judgment in the controversy you speak of independent of the one you pronounce; for as a daughter, as a married woman, and now as a widow, you've always shown a most perfect virtue, and virtue is the source of happiness. So I'll beseech the graces who accompany you, that it may please them to welcome the affectionate service of my Daughter and me , shown by the Sonnet I've composed according to your command and that I'm sending you; I hope that my obedience and my diligence toward you will provide ample excuse for my insufficiency.

9 [To a lawyer]

I'll not apologize for sending you only one letter for the two that you've written to me, for that would be to lay blame, and I don't want to be thought ungrateful for the honor and pleasure that I receive from you. For I worry that sending you two letters written twice as poorly may cause you double annoyance. I certainly hope that the Age of Saturn[53] and *Messire* Philippe de Commines[54] are helping you in navigating this sea of lawsuits. I say this because without them there can be neither good wind nor tides. If in this, as in anything else, I can be of service to someone as honorable as you, I'll employ myself with all my heart as I humbly desire to be commended to you; and I swear to you, Monsieur, that this is my deepest desire.

12 [To a lawyer][55]

My desire to take counsel from your honorable qualities makes me hope for your favors, for I think that you are obligated to someone as good-willed as

---

52. An allusion to poetic writing as a "speaking picture," a notion current in the poetic arts of the time. See Aristotle, *Poetics* 25.1460b; Horace, *The Art of Poetry*, ll. 361–65.

53. Saturn came to symbolize the Golden Age. His temple, at the foot of the Capitoline hill, served as the treasure of the Roman people; it contained the tables of the law and the records of decrees of the Senate.

54. By citing the historian Philippe de Commines (ca. 1447–ca. 1511), Madeleine des Roches seeks to impress upon her correspondent that the search for truth, and not deceitful rhetoric, ought to guide him in conducting his affairs and lawsuits.

55. The following three letters are directed to the same lawyer, who had charge of one of Madeleine des Roches's lawsuits. This one may have been the lawsuit that burdened her for thirteen years.

me, to your promise, and to your sincere goodness, which makes you in turn lend help and succor to those who humbly ask these of you. Help me then, if you please, to find a satisfying and agreeable end to this lawsuit, whose continuation has seemed to me so bitter and regrettable. I pray to God that He may keep you happy, Monsieur, you and Madame your companion, to whom my Daughter and I send our warmest greetings.

13 [To the same lawyer]

I couldn't hope for any less from your courtesy, nor could you promise me more in my time of need than what your letters assure me of; I now have no more pressing affair than the case you're attending to. I hope to see it soon brought to a happy end thanks to your prudence, and to the justice of my cause, which humbly I commend, along with myself, to your graces.

14 [To the same lawyer]

You've displayed such infinite generosity toward me that there remains no way for me to repay you; hence, it would now be more fitting for me to apologize to you for my first annoying solicitations[56] than to repeat them a second time. However, since my debt to you is made honorable by your worthiness, being a sign that it has not been unpleasant for you to please me, I dare ask you to take care of my lawsuit, which is presently in the hands of Monsieur de La Vau.[57] I'd like you to remind him of it so that, as an honest Counsel for my defense, he may give a favorable report, especially for the sake of my Daughter, who greets your good graces, humbly beseeching you, Monsieur, to accept from her the same greeting and the same request. I pray that God may keep you in His holy care, and me in your memory.

17 [To a lawyer]

The singular virtues that adorn you and the divine grace so evident in your writings are such that, after reading what it pleased you to send me, I want to read what you've written to others. But upon reading the letters you sent to your cousin, I see that you're suspicious of me, almost to the point of complaining about me. You were hoping that for a Spartan missive I would respond with an Iliad.[58] I know that your words are so full of reason and good sense that the lines I write cannot equal them in value. But it's up to God alone to practice geometry; I'm content to follow the ancient law that commanded that people give an eye for an eye and a tooth for a tooth.[59] I thus give you

56. "Importunitez" in the original.

57. Probably Jean de La Vau, a lawyer in the Paris Parlement, whose name appears at the beginning of the civil register of the judges of the Grands Jours of Poitiers of 1579.

58. That is, that in exchange for a short letter, the author would respond with a long one.

59. Exodus 21:24.

back one for one. I really can't believe that you, who practice Jurisprudence, would want to commit such a grave crime against your profession by making people pay double and asking two for one! Rather, as you continue with your customary generosity, please receive, Monsieur, my apology for my incapacity, with the humble commendation of my Daughter and me.

18 [To a female addressee, on her gift]
I honor you infinitely, Madame, for the perfect qualities you possess, and because you represent such a fine portrait of the Graces, for you return two gifts for one. But this praise which I give to your worth could in turn cause blame to fall upon me, as it may seem that it is out of stinginess that I give so little to your excellence, even though I receive so much in return. However, I apologize in regard to the gift I've received from your generous hand, which does no less honor to you than it benefits me who, with my daughter, greet you and thank you most humbly.

19 [To Abel L'Angelier][60]
You pretend to have failed me, Monsieur, in order to show how well you know how to graciously make an excuse for a mistake. But I won't accuse you of that laudable laziness that the Spartans said belonged to the nobility, even though we have other laws that are lethal to idleness, like the Athenians, whom you know how to imitate so well with subtlety of words and writings.[61] My Daughter who, like me, follows Hernias's opinion,[62] doesn't want you to be condemned on account of your graciousness. But so as not to hinder what in your soul, even without action, surpasses the actions of all others, she exempts you from the care of her writings, and of mine.[63] Besides, she has arranged for them to see the light of day,[64] or at least the shade since there is only a little bit of light in them;[65] such as they are, I nonetheless hope you like them, and that you give me a part of your good graces.

60. A letter to the Parisian publisher Abel L'Angelier on his refusal to publish *Les Secondes Œuvres* (1583).

61. Athens, mistress of the Greek seas and commercial capital, held for a long time onto her intellectual and artistic supremacy. In spite of her good humor, the author is annoyed that L'Angelier did not agree to publish the second volume of her works.

62. In *Sayings of the Spartans, Moralia* 3.221c, Plutarch reports that "Hernias was at Athens when a man there was found guilty on a charge of not having any occupation, and, when he heard of this, he bade them point out to him the man who had been convicted of the freeman's crime!"

63. That is, even though L'Angelier has not published the volume, the author compliments him for his superiority over all other publishers.

64. That is, to publish them.

65. According to Jean Balsamo, Abel L'Angelier refused to publish *Les Secondes Œuvres* because he found "little light" in them, as Madeleine apparently suggests here (*Abel L'Angelier and Françoise de*

20 [To a young lawyer][66]

So it seems, young Pallas, that you have carefully garnered the teachings of old Evander who stated that one judges a person by the company he keeps:[67] indeed, you have sought out the noblest people in France so that, in admiring them, you might be admired by them. Know that since your departure, I haven't received a single letter that has given me as much pleasure as your last one, because it assures me of your prompt return; and this hope does me so much good that I'll give up writing for thinking [about it]. I pray that God may give you his grace, and I beg you, Monsieur, to keep for me some place among your family, whom I humbly greet.

22 [To a female addressee who has just sent the author a gift]

I know quite well, Madame, how familiar the virtues are to you, and even generosity. My Daughter did not need to have this proven once again with your latest gift; she received the letter, the gift, and the notice of what she must do for the epitaph of Monsieur your husband who, beyond several praiseworthy qualities that made him so estimable, the good fortune of having married you made him honorable among all persons of honor, you whose name and goodness distinguish you above all others, and who will always be first in my thoughts.

23 [To an unwelcome male addressee][68]

As I received, read, and pondered your words, I remembered that the ambiguity of the oracle deceived the King of the Lydians because this simple and unsuspecting man took to heart the literal rather than the figurative message of a shrewd and subtle god.[69] Thus you, Monsieur, you whose keen mind and

---

Louvain [1574–1620] [Geneva: Droz, 2002], 78). However, Madeleine's allusion, belonging to the authorial humility topos, is a play on the preceding "broad daylight," a reference to her having found another publisher. Other more likely explanations for L'Angelier's refusal are that *Les Secondes Œuvres* is focused mostly on Poitiers; or that he may have been too busy at the time. See the volume editor's introduction.

66. A letter to a young scholar who came to the Grands Jours of Poitiers and, thanks to his participation in the flea contest, wrote poems praising various illustrious lawyers. The young poet could have been Raoul Cailler (b. 1561), Nicolas Rapin's nephew, and a young lawyer from Poitiers.

67. Pallas, son of Evander, regarded in Roman legend as the first to construct a settlement on the site of the future city of Rome. Evander's mother, Carmenta, or Nicostrata, was credited with the invention of the Latin alphabet; see Madeleine des Roches's ode 3, ll. 68–72 (see chap. 1).

68. This addressee had sent the Dames des Roches a letter that was not well received.

69. Croesus, king of the Lydians (reigned ca. 560–46 BCE), asked the oracle of Pythia at Delphi if he would hold onto the monarchy for long. The oracle replied that he would be king as long as a "mule" was kept at a distance from his throne. Croesus interpreted the oracle literally,

elegant poetry place you among Apollo's friends,[70] are deceiving me unless you write in a joking mood, as if dedicating your letters to that deity to whom fearful Apuleius sacrificed in Hypate.[71] You say that you must never see me or always see me. People like you, who in the springtime of life have garnered so many agreeable and varied traits, must never frequent simple and straight-forward people like us, my Daughter and me; nor must they sacrifice petty pleasures for the sake of private life. And you have conducted yourself in such a way that were it not for this deforming mirror that makes a large body seem but a dot, you would recognize that you have been in our company for such a short time that your presence could give you no cause for friendship nor your absence give you any cause for regret.

24 [To a male addressee, on her late response]
Monsieur, the rosemary is no more shaken by winds, waves, and storms than am I by the fever, languor, and stomach pains that have violently seized my sad home. These have prevented me from doing as you do, eating, drinking, and writing a letter that is worth two, as you say of yours; which is not the opinion I have of this one. But since, as Mother and Daughter, we are never divided (for we have only one will), we need only one response to commend ourselves to you. We hope that your mother will emulate Penelope,[72] who wanted no other second husband than saintly regret for her first husband. May she devote herself wholly to you, her only Telemachus.[73]

25 [To Jacques de Germigny, baron of Germoles][74]
Monsieur, since you brought to perfection and accomplished such a promi-nent and important charge as the one which has for so long kept you far from France, the glory of this deed follows you everywhere, like a shadow that is always following your solid virtue. But we have been participants, my Daugh-ter and I, in the pleasure you received upon your joyful return, because we so affectionately wished for it. You have, thanks to God, returned to your sweet

---

but it turned out that the "mule" was Cyrus, king of the Persians, born of a noblewoman and of a father of lower station. See Herodotus, *History* 1.55–56, 92.

70. Apollo, god of poetry and music.

71. This deity is the god of laughter to whom the inhabitants of Hypate offered sacrifices. See Apuleius, *Metamorphoses* (*Golden Ass*) 1.3.11.

72. Penelope waited for Ulysses for twenty years; her fidelity made her famous.

73. Son of Ulysses and Penelope, the only offspring of their marriage. Homer, *Odyssey* 1–4.

74. Jacques de Germigny (1532–86), baron de Germoles, senior member of the Council of State, master of the *hôtel du roi*, diplomat, was sent by Henri III as ambassador to Constantinople where he spent five years, from 26 September 1579 to 7 August 1584. This letter was written soon upon his return. Catherine addressed response 16 (*Secondes œuvres*, 295–97) to him, and Madeleine composed on behalf of his wife, Jeanne Boulet, a poem on his absence (*Pour Madame la Baronne de Germole, sur l'absence de son mary, Missives,* 133–35).

fatherland, to your faithful friends, to your wise and virtuous companion who has run your household so prudently that the best-ordered republics in the world would wish a similar government; so the ambassador of Turkey has testified, we've heard it assured. And wasn't it enough for us to hear all this, to read your eloquent and gracious letters in which you show your high opinion of us, without adding to it such precious gifts that their wonderful effects cure the most injured of bodies? Nonetheless they make our souls sick, because we cannot worthily acknowledge such a gift, much less reciprocate it, as Hesiod advises and liberality commands.[75] Thus finding ourselves guilty of the first vice hated by the ancients, which we call being in debt, we don't want to be held accountable for the second one of which they were horrified, which is lying; for it would be enough to constitute a lie, to hide ungratefully the truth of the honorable favors that we've received from you and from Madame your wife. We feel that we are eternally indebted to you for them. And as we desire to settle this with you, if at all possible, we send you this little book of ours,[76] without thinking, however, that this could help to pay off our debt; because if you receive it joyfully, you will make us even more obliged to you, Monsieur, whose graces we humbly acknowledge.

26 [To a male addressee, on her lawsuit]
Since the air around the river Seine has been so unhealthy of late,[77] and we have seen so many illustrious people abandon their beloved land to go elsewhere, I had strongly hoped that our city [of Poitiers] might be for you a rampart against danger,[78] for she seems to promise this good to whoever approaches her. The climate here is so temperate that Galen would have ordered it to the healthiest and the sickest, the former to maintain their health, the latter to recover theirs.[79] But since our Clain[80] was unable to incline you

---

75. Hesiod, *Works and Days*, ll. 349–51.

76. Since Jacques de Germigny returned in the summer of 1584, the book offered to him is likely a copy of *Les Secondes Œuvres*.

77. The water of the Seine river, drunk by the majority of the residents, was reputedly unhealthy on account of the waste dumped into it and its putrid smell. The author is alluding here to one of the many epidemics of the plague that ravaged Paris.

78. The length and sheer dimensions of Poitiers's ramparts made them famous. Travelers such as the seventeenth-century magistrate Robert du Dorat observed: "Cette ville est si vaste en l'enceinte de ses murailles qu'il n'en est point de si grande en toute la France après Paris" (This city's ramparts are so vast that there are none to rival them in all of France except those of Paris). Favreau, *Histoire de Poitiers*, 182.

79. Galen of Pergamum (129–99 CE), a Greek physician, whose outstanding influence on medicine in ancient and modern times was considerable. He wrote works on hygiene and dietetics in which he examined the various influences of air, food, movement, rest, and so on. The first edition of his works appeared in Latin in Venice in 1490.

80. The river Clain that passes through Poitiers.

in its favor, seeing that I am as far from hope as I am close to my desire to see you, I humbly beseech you, Monsieur, do not banish from your memory the promise that it pleased you to make to me to take care of my lawsuit.[81] If you don't care to remember it on my account, for I don't merit such remembrance, at least do it for your own sake, since you promised. That way you will show to all that you are of one mind, and you will be even more worthy of the excellent traits you've received from God, to whom unity is sacred, and in whose favor my Daughter and I humbly greet your graces with unity of thought.

SELECTED LETTERS OF CATHERINE DES ROCHES
DEDICATORY EPISTLE TO MY MOTHER[82]

1

My Mother, as a citizen of this world, I thought I needed to give something in return to my hosts: and so finding myself with these letters in hand, I asked myself to which one of the four elements[83] I should offer them, since it seemed to me that such a light thing as these lines mustn't enter into the heart of the earth, which is so heavy. Furthermore, their obscurity is not worthy of the sun's gleaming light. The translucent air would make their shortcomings obvious, and the transparent water would make these seem much bigger. So to whom will I offer these letters, seeing that they are so undesirable that I myself am annoyed at having kept them? But then again, why do I want to repay my debt at the expense of those letters that have already earned the name Missives, and that were sent a long time ago to many persons of honor? And what do I have to fear from their destruction, except what I desire in their favor, that is, that the wet ink and paper, which takes on its color and aspect from wetness, will lend them a chariot to take them into the air. There they will be seen by some who will scorn them even more than I do, and they will then be thrown into the fire which, having purged them and reduced them to ashes, will faithfully return them to the earth. So before they undergo these many changes, my deepest desire is that they may be agreeable to you, Mother, and I humbly beseech you to love them more than their beauty de-

---

81. A reference to one of Madeleine's many lawsuits.

82. This is the first time that Catherine uses the possessive "ma Mère" instead of "sa Mère" when addressing her mother in a dedicatory epistle, an indication of her own growing authority and literary independence.

83. That is, air, fire, water, and earth. In what follows, Catherine des Roches offers an extended metaphor on these elements, as she discusses what she ought to do with her letters.

serves, so they don't go lacking for support. You'll find among them few addressed to you; in this fact my happiness is manifest, which does not permit you to be far from my presence and even less from my thoughts, which will always be close, ready, humble, and devoted to serving you. Mother, I'll beseech God Almighty to make you live longer than me, so that you may resemble heaven which, having been created first, must end last.

2 [To an admirer]

The ancients who wrote about the gods that are said to inhabit Mount Olympus were people of great authority, and seeing that human passions were immortal among mortals, they covered such affections with a graceful veil and gave them the title of divinities. In the same way you, Monsieur, by thinking more highly of me than I deserve, with the favor of your graces honor the little worth found in me and hide my imperfections under the pleasant cloud of your beautiful writings. But just as Homer and Virgil made a name for themselves and are more renowned than Achilles and Aeneas,[84] so your infinite virtues, although very generous, reserve more honor for you than praises for me. Nevertheless, having received them, I humbly thank you.

6 [To a thankless addressee]

If my counsel, persuasion, and words have been of no use whatever to you, you owe me nothing for them; but if they have benefited you in some way, how do you figure that you are now discharged of the obligation, which is of such a nature that the better one pays it off, the more one owes for it?

13 [To a male addressee, on her tardy reply]

Monsieur, I have more desire than leisure to respond to you, because at the same time that your messenger gives me your letters, he waits for mine. Therefore I humbly beseech you to excuse me if the threads of my letter are poorly woven; keep in mind that I worry less about being thought ignorant than about being considered too proud on account of my silence which I neither want nor ought to use with you, whose graces and virtues I'll always revere.

14 [To a learned female addressee][85]

Mademoiselle, because you've attained the highest level of that admirable eloquence which in the past has made the invincible son of Alcmena famous,[86] I'm not surprised that you deign to imitate him when he voluntarily

84. Achilles, a hero in Homer's *Iliad*; Aeneas, protagonist of the *Aeneid*.
85. A letter of thanks to a woman who has sworn a *sainte amitié* (sacred friendship) to the author.
86. Alcmena is the mother of Hercules. This is a reference to the legend of the Gallic Hercules used to extol the virtues of eloquence.

made himself a prisoner of his prisoner.[87] In the same way you, whose virtues have long held me in thrall, graciously assure me that you are my slave, wishing, by doing me honor, to honor your prison. And even though I don't think I have those perfections that you say have triumphed over your liberty, I don't mourn their loss since I rejoice that they are in you. Thus, as I have no grace that could make me worthy, I'll try, if at all possible, to gain some esteem from your favor, which will endlessly shine in my soul; and because I desire the torch to become worthy of such a flame, I beg God to keep you healthy and happy, and to bless me with the holy friendship that you've sworn to me.

15 [To a male addressee][88]

Being irresolute, it would be improper for me to want to make others decide, especially you who are so affable. Truly, since our last conversation, I have probed my thoughts several times; but I find they haven't changed and that they're just as irresolute as they were at that time. So there's no change in me, besides the fact that over the last year I've become poorer and richer by a year, having lost a year as far as the future is concerned, but gained one for the past. However, just as I haven't changed in what does not matter, I've remained constant in what is praiseworthy, for I esteem the honest opinion that I hold of your qualities to which I am strongly obliged; because in passing through the Alps to see Italy, you kept in your memory the *Roches*[89] of Poitiers. For this grace that I have received from you, I pray to God that He may keep you healthy and happy; I humbly beseech you, Monsieur, to kiss the hands of Mademoiselle your Mother in my name, and I infinitely commend myself to your infinite grace. And greet for me your beautiful and virtuous sister, whom I revere without ever having seen her, and to whom I desire as much good as if I were as closely related to her as she is to you.

17 [To a female addressee, on her friendship]

Mademoiselle, it seems to me that the end of something so well begun and even better continued couldn't possibly be good, because it shouldn't have an end. That's the reason I never want to end the obliging friendship I have for you with such excellent cause. But since you assure me that you're well assured of my friendship, I don't want to affirm anymore, except that as long as I live, I'll be yours, and I beseech you to have as much faith in me as I have in you.

---

87. A reference to Omphale, queen of Lydia, to whom Hercules became enslaved.

88. A letter possibly addressed to a suitor whose attentions the author firmly discourages.

89. A play on words. The French *rocher* means boulder.

19 [To a female addressee, on the books the author sent her][90]
Madame, if good luck had given me the means to please you, the pleasure that I would have in pleasing you would be reward enough for me. But since I recognize my inability no less readily than your qualities, I know that I could never do anything for you that would merit the least thanks. I've received the money you sent me as payment for my books, and I thank you for your offer [to sell copies to others?] on their behalf. I'll be content to see or hear the most excellent comments that you can make [about them] in your letters or conversations, you who are an example for others of one who conducts herself and speaks well.[91]

20 [To a female addressee, on Madeleine des Roches's illness]
I'll not say that my misfortune[92] has prevented me from writing you, but rather that it's the reason for telling you in my letter what I can't tell you in person because I'm so far from you, bereft of your gentle and amiable company, and of your gentle words. I'm left only with the memory of them, which I will keep alive until your return and which is my greatest pleasure. I don't know what news to send you; we see no soldiers.[93] Mars is not in this city, and you have taken Minerva from her, whom you'll soon return to us, Mademoiselle, if you please: or I'll say that Diotima has not sufficiently taught you how to love.[94]

21 [To a female addressee, on her mother's illness]
I have great cause to [blame and] pardon writing, not being able to convey to you by its means anything that will much please you. I can only write to you what I know, and I know nothing other than that my Mother, overcome with sickness, is now in bed, more displeased at not seeing you than at her sickness, which she hopes will soon end. When I'm with her, I'm like someone who is passing an awful sleepless night, awaiting the next day. Please, if you can't help us, you can at least have pity on us. And I pray to God that He may fulfill your desires, for you're the most accomplished *Damoiselle* I know.

---

90. A letter of thanks for the payment of books the author sent. These are likely copies of *Les Œuvres* or the *Les Secondes Œuvres*.

91. Catherine des Roches is interested in the publicity the addressee can give to her books.

92. A reference to her mother's sickness. See also letters 21 and 22, above.

93. Poitiers seems peaceful, thanks to a lull in the civil wars.

94. Diotima, priestess of Mantinea, taught Socrates the doctrine of love. See Plato, *Symposium* 201f–212a.

22 [To a female addressee, on her mother's illness]

Mademoiselle, I can't describe to you the least part of our ills, they're so numerous. So I'll tell you, the only respite we have from them (if I can call respite what so aggrieves us) is that they follow one another so closely that the last ones don't even allow us to think about the first ones. They're all caused by my Mother's sickness, which troubles her moods and my rest. We have, however, found a way to have some respite to read your letters and to write back; I'll finish this letter, praying that He who begins, maintains, and ends all things, may add to your graces as much happiness and pleasure as I at this hour suffer sorrow.

23 [To Claude Pellejay][95]

Monsieur, my only purpose in taking up the pen is to let you know that I have some knowledge of myself, and that I am not the one who has inspired you to bring to light this hymn of beauty; rather you've wished to represent in it the beauty of your mind, which alone has been the worthy progenitor of such excellent offspring, even of these last verses with which you've been pleased to enrich and honor me. Now because I want to enjoy this agreeable gift of yours, I'll finish this letter so as to be able to concentrate better on your writings. I only want to assure you that I accept your hymn as a present of great value, and receive the praises you bestow upon me, just as you've received from heaven the perfections that make you praiseworthy.

24 [To a learned male addressee, on his praise of Cassandra Fedele]

The good fortune of Cassandra Fedele[96] can well be equaled by her excellent perfections, because she was so highly esteemed by Angelo Poliziano that long after her death he made her renown live on.[97] Angelo was no less fortunate than she, because he was familiar with the divine traits that made her admirable, and in praising them (he, as you say) surpassed himself. Therefore,

---

95. A letter of thanks to Claude Pellejay (1542–1613), a suitor of Catherine des Roches, who dedicated to her an unpublished *Hymn of Beauty* of a thousand alexandrine lines. A native of Poitiers, Claude Pellejay was the son of the prosecutor André Pellejay and a close neighbor of the Dames des Roches. He studied mathematics in Paris under Pierre Forcadel, became secretary to the duc d'Anjou, the future Henri III, and was later *maître des comptes*. This letter is exemplary of Catherine des Roches's ability to sidestep a compliment while at the same time seeking to thank her addressee for the high esteem he accords her.

96. Cassandra Fedele (1465–1558), one of the most renowned women scholars of Italy. See Fedele, *Letters and Orations*.

97. On the letter of praise which Angelo Poliziano wrote to Cassandra Fedele, see Fedele, *Letters and Orations*, 90–91. Catherine des Roches holds up Fedele as a model for young women in her *Dialogue between Iris and Pasithée* (see chap. 4).

he was immortalized by her, and she by him.[98] But Monsieur, you yield neither to the former nor to the latter, since having known both of them by the writings of one only, you've so well drawn the portrait of the portrait[99] of this excellent virgin, that the Graces themselves are obliged to you for the honor you do to one who was so dear to them. And the payment you'll receive from them is that they'll make you all the more honored, the more they see you esteem the one who was so worthy of esteem.

25 [On the illness of François Éboissard][100]

Just as your last letter assured me that my displeasure displeased you, so can I affirm in this letter that I will always be joyful concerning your joy, and happy for your happiness. And because you wish to hear my and my Mother's thoughts, words, and actions: know that our thoughts are sad, our words pitiful, and our labor endless. We're taking care of my father, sick with a fever that seized him two weeks ago. And as we wait for our tears to turn to laughter, I'll take pleasure in remembering you, whom I will always keep in my thoughts.

26 [To an erudite male friend]

Monsieur, I thank you for remembering my mother, because thanks to her you've thought of me who don't deserve it except for being a little twig from such a tree. You say that you cannot worthily praise me. Truly I believe it, but it's because I'm unworthy of praise, and because your excellence praises only that which is as excellent as itself. It's your duty to praise the stars and the heavens, as much for the knowledge you have of their courses and movements as for having received from them such an accomplished soul. It's your duty cleverly to praise the cleverness that has brought your perfections to perfection. It's your duty to praise God who gives you a spirit embellished with so many virtues. And it's my duty to revere these virtues in you and in all who hold them dear. It's also my duty to thank you for wanting the successful outcome of our affairs. It's furthermore my duty to wish that your merit be esteemed by all, not only because you're worthy of that esteem, but because you're from the same region I am, and because silence bears witness

---

98. The theme of *exegi monumentum* (I have built a monument), important in the poetry of the Pléiade, is a major influence on the writings of the Dames des Roches.

99. That is, Poliziano's depiction of Fedele.

100. A letter about the fatal illness of François Éboissard, seigneur de La Villée, second husband of Madeleine des Roches, who died in 1578 at the age of fifty-eight of a lung infection. This letter must have been written during the summer of 1578.

only to itself:[101] its veil is sometimes as sorrowful as that of the clouds when they prevent us from seeing the glistening splendor of the Sun. But for fear of dazzling myself in such a great light, I'll close my eyes and my letter, after having prayed that divine providence grant you a happiness equal to your worth.

27 [To a male admirer, on his praises of her]

A worthy man can't praise something that's not worthy of praise without offending Truth, princess of all virtues. You also, who hold her dear, worry about having displeased her by praising me more than I deserve, and you're searching for a way to appease her. And because you recognize that humility is the grace of graces, you've thought to make your peace with truth by donning humility, such that in humbling yourself as much as possible, you show how little you esteem your thoughts and words. Blaming now your mind, now your inventiveness, one might say that you tacitly confess the error which you have voluntarily committed (at least that's what I think), solely to prevent the jealousy the Gods would have felt toward you, because it's said that they are the only ones who can't err. In regard to what you say about having nothing in you that's virtuous except the desire to be virtuous, it seems that in this you imitate Philoctetus who with his foot indicated the place where Hercules' arrows were, while at the same time claiming that he didn't know.[102] In the same way you show with your praiseworthy manners that you are indeed virtuous, even though your modesty makes you say the contrary. Now I beseech you, you who are Logistilla's most favored friend,[103] that it please you to beg her to make me worthy of a part of the praises that you bestow upon me, and then the truth that you've offended will be better able to forgive you.

29 [To a male addressee whose help she seeks]

Monsieur, you've been so accustomed to lend your helpful hand not only to me, but to all those of my lineage, that I thought this custom had become a law such that you would in no way want to break it. That's what makes me willing to ask for your help for this nobleman who is a very dear relation of

---

101. Silence, so unfavorable to honor and literary immortality, is a frequent theme in the Des Roches' writings; see Catherine's letter 61 (see below) and Madeleine des Roches's *Epistle to the Ladies* (see chap. 1).

102. Philoctetus, guardian of Hercules' bow and arrows, violated his oath to keep secret his master's burial place by hitting the spot with his foot.

103. Pure and chaste Logistilla, heroine of Ariosto's *Orlando Furioso*, represents noble thinking and reason. See *Orlando Furioso* 7.1–69.

mine. He has an upcoming lawsuit against a great Lord, whose name he will tell you. And because many sacks are full of this quibbling, I don't want to fill my letter with it. I only want to beseech you to help my cousin, and to ask Monsieur Depaisse to be in his favor also.[104] For just as I remain assured of your loyalty toward me, I am assured of his loyalty toward you, whom my mother and I humbly greet.

38 [To a male addressee whose missive she has not received]

The Missive that you mention at the start of your last letter has not reached me. And if you did send it off, I think the courier lost it. I've only received two of your letters, and you have a response to the first, with which, it seems, you're not satisfied. I want this one to please you more, and to match the graciousness of your letter. But I also worry that I'll run out of compliments if I put too many in my letters.[105] So I prefer to write according to my customary habit, and wonder why you ask for grace, you, Monsieur, who have so much of it. Because if you don't recognize yours, you are unworthy of possessing it; and if you do recognize it, it's not right for you not to be content with it. As far as I'm concerned, I'm not at all envious of it; but I desire that your grace always continue to perfect itself, and that you remember that you've acquired more honor with books than with arms.[106] Nevertheless if you've decided to march under Mars's ensign, I don't want to dissuade you; but I beseech you not to take along this guest who stays in your household. It would be improper for her to follow an army, at least if her portrait resembles her at all.[107]

104. Jacques Faye, seigneur d'Espeisses (1543–90), studied law at Poitiers, became *conseiller* in 1567, *commissaire aux enquêtes* in 1570, and accompanied the duc d'Anjou (future Henri III) to Poland in 1574. Upon his return to France in 1575, he bought the post of attorney general from Barnabé Brisson (1531–91), president of the Grande Chambre in the Paris Parlement and one of the jurists of the Grands Jours in Poitiers. He later became *maître des requêtes* for the Council of State and worked to strengthen the liberties of the Gallican Church. Jeanne Faye, one of the members of his extended family, wrote verse; Marot dedicated one of the poems of his *Estrennes poétiques* to her.

105. The author prefers to exchange her courtesies in person.

106. A reference to the topos of *Arms and Letters*. Political commentators of the period argued that education was necessary to save the nobility of the sword and keep it virtuous. The humanists and the Pléiade poets, for their part, enlarged the notion of noble honor to include all those able to profit from letters and handle the pen. Thus, bookish culture became more and more "the distinctive sign of the new model of the nobleman." Jouanna, *Le devoir de révolte*, 44.

107. Convinced of the superiority of letters, the author hopes perhaps that the female guest (or spouse?) of her noble correspondent also shares her opinion and that she will not accompany him to war. The meaning of these last lines, however, is unclear.

39 [To Madeleine Chémeraut][108]

My cousin and dear friend, when I think of the pleasure I was accustomed to receiving from your sweet and amiable company, and of the event that has prevented me from seeing you now, I cry for past pain. But I ache even more on account of your present pain, which upsets me as much as it hurts you. If you continue to be sick for a long time, without fear of being reminded of what was, I'll come see what is, because I want to be your companion in your suffering, as well as in your happiness. May God be with you, and may you remember me.

42 [To an admirer of her works who also knows Ronsard]

Since my return to Poitiers, I've had so little leisure that I have not had the time to be pained by your neglect, or by you for having given me the occasion for it, even though it's more difficult to serve well than to love well. You're obliged to do neither the former nor the latter any more than you wish. Actually, I've hardly thought of my book[109] which, now that it belongs to the readers, I no longer consider as my own. Nonetheless, since Monsieur de Ronsard called Sincero the honor of the citizens of Poitiers, I've come to regard the latter with more compassion than friendship, on account of the judgment that such a great person has made.[110] Truly, Monsieur, when I think of how Poitiers is simply a mere city in Poitou, Poitou merely one province of France, France such a small part of Europe, Europe the lesser third of the earth, the earth a mere geometric point in the heavens, I consider Sincero quite insignificant, not that I despise him, for he is my creature,[111] but I am not envious of Charite's happiness in owning such a friend. I've answered Monsieur de Ronsard's sonnet, and I'm sending you a copy. I return line for line, but not grace for grace. You'll apologize to him for me, please, and my excuses for disturbing you.

---

108. This letter was probably written to Madeleine Chémeraut, Catherine des Roches's cousin, whom she ordinarily addresses with the less formal *tu* and to whom she wrote several letters and *responses*. Madeleine Chémeraut, a poet, came from one of the most prominent families in Poitou.

109. That is, *Les Œuvres* (*Works*).

110. It was probably in September 1575 that Ronsard, during his stay in Conflans at the summer residence of Nicolas de Neufville, seigneur de Villeroy (ca.1543–1617), and his wife Madeleine de L'Aubespine, composed a sonnet in honor of Catherine des Roches's "Sincero." Ronsard's sonnet and Catherine's response have been lost. See Ronsard's "A Conflans," *Œuvres complètes*, ed. Céard et al.; Michel Simonin, *Pierre de Ronsard* (Paris: Fayard, 1990), 320. Ronsard's sonnet praising Sincero indicates that Des Roches's sonnet sequence circulated in manuscript form for a few years among court coteries before its eventual publication. Ronsard likely penned his poem for a coterie gathering at the Conflans residence.

111. In her *Epistle to Her Mother* (see chap. 2), Catherine des Roches argues her right to compose love poetry based on imagination rather than experience. She thereby asserts her right to be an

43 [To Françoise Chémeraut][112]

Madame and dear cousin, if the fear of that dangerous evil[113] has so much power over you that it can speed up your desired return, I think I'd find some sweetness in such bitterness, that is if you return healthy and content, even though you've been guided by fear, so often a sure guide that warns us of what we must flee and where we must go. Now as one who thinks herself familiar with fear, and having some credit with her,[114] I beg her to incite you to return. I beseech you also that it please you to believe what she tells you on my behalf. On her behalf, in response to my prayer, and for the sake of your rest, return as early as possible. Bring back your gracious Trio to the little house my Mother and I keep; which belongs to you as much as to us. Humbly greet for us my aunt, yourself, and my cousin your sister.

44 [To an unwelcome suitor][115]

I thought that my silence, together with my Mother's letter, would have served as a sufficient answer to yours. But since you wish my Letter to mirror my thoughts,[116] I will convey that thought as clearly as I can. So you should know, Monsieur, that I would not consider myself free if I were to cause servitude in another. And just as I like being free, so do I appreciate freedom in the people I hold dear. So I don't want a suitor, nor do I need a companion or a master. It will be quite sufficient for me if virtue deigns to rule my life, good fortune attends me, and learning and writing serve me to express what is in my soul, where I've found affectionate regards to send you, if it pleases you to receive them.

49 [To a learned noble lady][117]

Madame, I received your learned and gracious letters with much honor and pleasure, seeing myself esteemed by someone as respected as you who seem

---

author and, as Evelyne Berriot-Salvadore notes, to affirm "the intellectual aptitude of women for literary creation." *Les femmes dans la société française de la Renaissance,* 459.

112. This letter was probably addressed to Françoise Chémeraut, sister of Madeleine Chémeraut, whom the author addresses with the more formal *vous,* as she is not as close to her as to her sister Madeleine. Françoise Chémeraut received from the Dames des Roches a less considerable legacy than her sister (see Diller, *Dames des Roches,* 26).

113. The plague. From 1580 to 1587, epidemics of plague returned annually to French cities, reaching a climax in 1585.

114. That is, fear.

115. A missive to a suitor who, in spite of both Catherine des Roches's silence and a harsh letter from her mother, persists in failing to understand Catherine's desire to remain free from amorous attachments.

116. In classical epistolary rhetoric, a letter was defined as a *sermo absentium* or a substitute for a conversation between two people absent from each other.

117. A letter to a noblewoman renowned for her talents as a writer, a painter, and a musician.

a miracle among young girls. And even though I don't think I deserve the praises you bestow upon me, I don't want to stop receiving them as a gift from you. For since these praises are yours, you can give them to me who am also yours. Thus when they reach me, your praises will never be very far from you, since my thoughts follow you everywhere to contemplate your agreeable beauty, and the nobility of your divine spirit adorned with the perfections of your poetry, the sweetness of your music making, and the beauty of your paintings. I know, Madame, that you can with the pen and the brush grant immortality to mere mortals, thus making yourself immortal as well.[118] But the more virtues I recognize in you, the bolder I become in asking you, in the name of all of your virtues, that it please you to continue the friendship your letters promise me, and receive in exchange my humble service, with my mother's and my affectionate regards.

53 [To a male addressee, on the illness of her mother]
Monsieur, the more occasions I've had to write to you, the less it's been convenient for me to write until today, when my Mother, somewhat relieved of her illness, gives me this leisure. During the worst of her harsh pain, I sometimes said to myself as I thought of you: "What shall I do to let him know?" And then again, "What should I do to hide it from him? He might be grieved at my grief, and I worry about upsetting him." During this inner debate, along with so many others raging within me, I saw these terrible days go by with their increasing toll of continual fevers; but then my mother gave me hope that, in freeing herself from them, she might be cured. So, God willing, I await the happy day when she will at last be healthy. She and I humbly greet you, praying the divine goodness to grant you his graces.

61 [To a male addressee on his eloquence]
Since desire accords so well in you with hope, why have you given me the former without the latter? I desire and yet can't hope to write to you as well as I ought; but in this you deserve all the praise and the blame, for you've demonstrated your ability and my lack. Believe me, Monsieur, your letters have made me feel the praiseworthy anger that Molon[119] felt for that great Roman orator when he saw him leave no means of speaking well after him because he had opened and then closed his treasure of eloquence.[120] So to ad-

118. The topos of *exegi monumentum*, dear to the Dames des Roches.

119. Apollonius Molon, famous orator, whom Cicero heard first in Rome, then in Rhodes, and whom he praises in his *Brutus* 91.316.

120. Plutarch recounts that Molon one day asked Cicero to give a speech in Greek. When he had done it, everyone praised him. But Molon remained pensive and said to Cicero: "I praise and admire you, but I grieve at Greece's fate, as I see that the only advantages which remained ours—

mire your eloquence, I must remain silent. But I won't: for without words one can't honor the honor found in speech.[121] But what shall I do? Must I speak? Yes, and *speak little about Carthage*.[122] Thus my words will be brief and my will eternal to revere your graces and virtues which my Mother, my cousin, and I humbly greet.

64 [To an addressee to whose praises she feels indebted][123]
Monsieur, I'm no longer in debt because I constantly banish it, offering up as much as I am able the praise that is due to your unique worth. But yet I'm truly mistaken, for the more I pay my debt, the more I owe, since your excellence is such that in honoring you I do myself honor. God forbid, however, that I should believe that you remember me because you're unable to do otherwise; for I would not then be so grateful for your kind memory. I don't want to think either that you judge me like someone who is colorblind; I would do wrong to your good judgment and to the little good that I recognize in me, who greet you in all humility.

69 [To Abel L'Angelier][124]
Monsieur, that amiable Proserpina who, thanks to you, will soon see our French sky,[125] wishes to send you greetings, and perhaps to complain about me because, having made even narrower, I don't know just how, the beautiful black and white dress[126] she's received from your generous courtesy, I am still so late in dressing her in it. My mother's illness has made me imagine with such dread the dark underworld that I haven't been able adequately to describe it. Now my mother is beginning to find a bit of rest for herself, and

---

that is, culture and eloquence—have also, thanks to you, passed on to the Romans." Plutarch, *Cicero, Lives* 4. See the same allusion in Du Bellay, *Deffence et Illustration de la langue françoyse*, ed. Henri Chamard (Paris: Didier, 1970), 1.7.43–44.

121. For this important motif in the work of the Dames des Roches, see Catherine's letter 26 (see above) and Madeleine des Roches's *Epistle to the Ladies* (see chap. 1).

122. The formula is by Sallust: *De Carthagine silere melius puto quam parum dicere* (Of Carthage, I would rather say nothing than too little), *Jugartha* 19.2; see Quintilian, *De Institutio oratore* 2.13.14. Des Roches likely read this allusion in Du Bellay's dedicatory letter on "the incomparable learning, virtue and conduct" of Cardinal Jean du Bellay, whose greatness the author prefers to cover "under the veil of silence. For on such a weighty matter it is better to say nothing (as on Carthage according to T. Livy) than to say little." *Deffence et Illustration de la langue françoyse*, 1.7.43–44.

123. This sample courtesy letter, a predecessor of *précieux* salon civility, is replete with formulas of sociability and indirect "artificial" language. Skilled writers of these *lettres de compliment* had to master such turns of phrases.

124. The author addresses her final two letters to her editor Abel L'Angelier to apologize for her tardiness in sending him her translation of the *Rape of Proserpina*.

125. That is, will soon be published.

126. The ink of print.

leisure for me, and I've now been able to transcribe Claudian's first two books, and I hope to finish the third very soon if Fate does not cut the thread of my life, or hers who is the life of my life.[127] And I pray God will not permit it, nor yours, which I esteem and honor above all.

70 [To Abel L'Angelier][128]

Monsieur, I've so much to tell you that I don't know where to begin. And when I have started, I'll have a hard time stopping this talk with you. The daughter of Ceres has gone forth in the hope of finding you. I beg you humbly to welcome her, but dare not recommend that you take good care of her, as I worry about showing a lack of trust in you in whom everyone should trust. But I am also unable not to recommend her, since I feel great affection for her. You will readily find that the company I give her is more sizable than beautiful.[129] But when putting her household in order, drive from it all those useless servants that bring neither pleasure to her nor honor to me. My mother didn't want to name this little book, because she hoped you would become its godfather. So give it whatever title you think best, be it Missives or Letters or Epistles, for the readers' curiosity will perhaps make it sell faster. So please treat it as if it were your own. And whichever of my writings you find least worth reading, simply throw them into the fire.[130] But I beseech you, never throw into the water of forgetfulness the honorable remembrance you have of my Mother and me, who greet you with all humility.

127. The author uses the same formula in her *Epistle to Her Mother* (see chap. 3): "Now knowing that I have received from you not only this mortal life but the life of my life, I follow you everywhere as the shadow follows the body."

128. This letter accompanied the completed manuscript of the volume of *Les Missives.*

129. A reference to the letters and other poems in the volume.

130. The allusion pertains to the extended metaphor on the four elements in the author's dedicatory missive to her mother (see above).

NOTES

CHAPTER ONE

1.   These elite women would have consisted of the wives of the magistrates and jurists from the Paris Parlement who were Abel L'Angelier's regular clients (his bookstall
was located in the great hall of the Palace of Justice in Paris); members of humanist
circles such as the one that met during the 1560s and 1570s in Jean de Morel and his
wife Antoinette de Loynes's household (Catherine may have corresponded with Diane de Morel, the youngest of the three erudite Morel daughters); and possibly aristocratic members of the court and of Parisian coteries such as the literary circles of
Madeleine de l'Aubespine, dame de Villeroy, and of Claude-Catherine de Clermont,
the maréchale de Retz, although the latter were more likely to have read the Dames
des Roches' poems in court manuscript collections than in print. On court women's
access to literary texts, see Broomhall, *Women and the Book Trade*, 28–29, 131–38.

2.   On Henri III's visit to Poitiers in 1577, see the volume editor's introduction.

3.   "J'ay voulu en ce petit tableau où je me suis depeinte, arrester ma parolle, pour
vous asseurer de l'amitié entière que j'ay tousjours portée à vous (Mesdames) si aucunes de vous daignez lire mes humbres vers," *Epistle to the Ladies, Œuvres* (see below).

4.   "Le silence, ornement de la femme, peut couvrir les fautes de la langue et de l'entendement." Ibid.

5.   "Quelque langue de Satyre, / Qui tient banque de mesdire, / Dira tousjours, il suffit: / Une femme est assez sage / Qui file et faict son mesnage; / L'on y fait mieux son
profit." Ode 3 (see below).

6.   "Mais quelque chose plus digne / À la dame Poïtevine / Que le brave acoutrement: / Jà desjà ell' faict coustume / De choisir l'ancre et la plume / Pour l'employer
doctement." Ibid.

7.   This third view, originating in the early modern period with Christine de Pizan,
is defended in the sixteenth century by male and female French writers in a wide va-
riety of genres, from for instance Martin Le Franc's *Champion des dames* (ca. 1485) and
Agrippa's *Declamation on the Nobility and Preeminence of the Female Sex* (1529), to Montaigne's
Essays (1580–88), Marie de Gournay's *Equality of Men and Women* (1622), Artus
Thomas's, *Qu'il est bien séant que les filles soient sçavantes* (1600), and Charlotte de Brachart's
Harengue... qui s'adresse aux hommes qui veuillent deffendre la science aux femmes (1604). In the   273

seventeenth century, Cartesian emphasis on universal reason led several thinkers (Gournay, Anna Maria van Schurman, François Poullain de la Barre, and Gabrielle Suchon) to argue the cause of logical feminism. See Elsa Dorlin, *L'évidence de l'égalité des sexes. Une philosophie oubliée du XVIIe siècle* (Paris: L'Harmattan, 2000). The works by Agrippa, Gournay, Poullain de la Barre, and Schurman have appeared in the Other Voice in Early Modern Europe series.

8. Catherine's "sagesse" refers primarily to her chaste decorum. Étienne Pasquier, on his visit to the Des Roches' coterie during the Grands Jours, remarks in a letter to a colleague that Catherine "est une Dame qui ne manque point de response: et neantmoins il ne sort d'elle aucun propos qui ne soit digne d'une *sage* fille" (is a woman who never lacks an answer. And yet no word ever comes from her that is unsuitable for a well-behaved girl). *Lettre à Pierre Pithou, Lettres*, vol. 6, letter 8, in Des Roches, *Missives*, 348.

9. "Il ne suffit pourtant d'estre bien nées; / Le sens acquis nous rend morigenées, / . . . La lettre peut changer le vitieux, / La lettre accroist le cueur du vertueux." *Epistle to My Daughter* (see below).

10. "Dès enfance / Amour, conseil, support, obeissance." Ibid.

11. Marie de Romieu (ca. 1545–90), a contemporary of similar bourgeois origins as the Dames des Roches, expresses in her dedicatory letter to her brother her disgruntlement in having to write in a hurry "n'ayant pas le loisir, à cause de nostre mesnage, de vacquer (comme vous, dedié pour servir aux Muses) à chose si belle et divine que les vers" (not having the leisure, on account of our household, to devote myself [like you who are dedicated to serving the Muses] to such a beautiful and divine thing as writing verse." *Premières œuvres poétiques* (1581), ed. André Winandy (Geneva: Droz, 1972), 4. Catherine never voiced a similar complaint.

12. In Greek, the Daemon or "divine spirit" is commonly interpreted as "he who allots" and is used in poetry to mean "god" or "the gods."

13. "Et le Dœmon, qui l'œuvre a commencée, / Guide si bien l'effect de ta pensée, / Que tesmoignant à la postérité / Combien d'honneur tu auras merité, / Tu sois un jour par vertu immortelle, / Je t'ay tousjours souhaitée estre telle." *Epistle to My Daughter* (see below). On Madeleine's equating virtue with learning, see the volume editor's introduction.

14. "Toujours vostre esprit s'amuse / Aux saints labeurs de la Muse, / Qui en despit du tombeau / Rendra vostre nom plus beau." Ronsard, *La Charité* (1563), *Œuvres complètes*, ed. J. Céard, D. Ménager, M. Simonin, 2 vols. (Paris: Gallimard, Bibliothèque de la Pléiade, 1993), ll. 584, 17–20. Cited by Claudie Martin-Ulrich, *La 'persona' de la princesse au XVIe siècle: personnage littéraire et personnage politique* (Paris: Champion, 2004), 175 n. 1.

15. Smith, *Culture of Merit*, 17–21.

16. On Madeleine des Roches's lawsuits, see the volume editor's introduction.

17. "Pour mon pays, je n'ay point de puissance, / Les hommes ont toute l'autorité, / Contre raison et contre l'equité." *Epistle to My Daughter* (see below).

18. Kendall Tarte argues that Des Roches could have known Pizan's *City of Ladies* since Pizan seems to have been the only one to refer to Carmenta as a lawgiver. "Early

Modern Literary Communities: Madeleine des Roches's City of Women," *Sixteenth-Century Journal* 35, no. 3 (2004): 760 n. 36.

19. On the Des Roches' political affinities with the Politiques party, see the volume editor's introduction.

20. "Ce n'est le Bisantin, l'Espaignol, ou Romain, / Ce n'est pas l'Escossois, l'Anglois, ou le Germain / Qui nous ont mis au sac, cause de tant de plaintes. / C'est le mutin François qui a faict le deroy, / Ne craignant d'offencer un jeune et juste Roy, / Apres avoir polu toutes les choses sainctes." Sonnet 15 (see below).

21. "D'autant que nostre prince a surmonté en armes / L'Espaignol, les Anglois, et les Romains gens-d'armes, / La Togue de la France aura le premier prix." Sonnet 9 (see below).

22. "Par l'amour maternelle, / Par le doux suc tiré de la mamelle, / Et par les flancs qui neuf mois t'ont porté." (see unnumbered sonnet below).

23. Kirk Read, "Mother's Milk from Father's Breast: Maternity without Women in Male French Renaissance Lyric," in *High Anxiety: Masculinity in Crisis in Early Modern France*, ed. Kathleen P. Long. Sixteenth Century Essays and Studies (Kirksville, Mo.: Truman University Press, 2002), 71–92.

24. "Sucer le laict savoureux / De ta feconde mammelle!" cited in ibid., 72.

25. "Naisve" in the original. Cotgrave's synonyms are "naturall, right, proper, true, no way counterfeit." *A Dictionarie of the French and English Tongues* (London, 1611), introduction by William Woods (Columbia: University of South Carolina Press, 1968).

26. Silence as an emblem of feminine virtue is common in moralist conduct books of the period.

27. Reason and speech were considered the distinguishing marks of man, raising him above animals in the cosmic scale of being.

28. The original "puis" instead of the more correct "depuis" is used to maintain the decasyllabic line

29. The term "équité," from jurisprudence, indicates natural justice which tempered legal justice when the latter was considered too severe. For the Roman statute that prohibited women from holding civil and public office, see Ian Maclean, *The Renaissance Notion of Woman: A Study in the Fortunes of Scholasticism and Medical Science in European Intellectual Life* (Cambridge: Cambridge University Press, 1980), 77–81.

30. Madeleine des Roches dealt with a lawsuit that lasted some thirteen years.

31. These four lines, apparently a quotation, express the humanist commonplace that art (study) perfects nature, and that virtue is a primordial condition for right living and fruitful learning. The last line is a play on the proverb "L'habit ne fait pas le moine" ("'Tis not the habit [but the heart] that makes a man religious," Cotgrave, *Dictionarie of the French and English Tongues*).

32. See note 12 above.

33. To maintain the decasyllabic line schema, the author shortened "acquis" to "quis" (acquired).

34. Des Roches's nine odes, from which odes 1, 3, and 4 have been selected, recall the apogee of the genre in the 1550s and 1560s when Ronsard and the Pléiade school

published poetic collections consisting uniquely of odes. The genre fell out of favor soon thereafter. While Madeleine's odes consist of four-line, five-line, six-line, and even eight-line stanzas, the preferred stanza had six lines. See François Rouget, *L'apothéose d'Orphée. L'esthétique de l'ode en France au XVIᵉ siècle de Sébillet à Scaliger* (1548–1561) (Geneva: Droz, 1994), 36.

35.   Pandora, the first woman according to Greek myth, opened a jar containing evils and diseases from which men had hitherto been free; these evils escaped to afflict humankind. See Hesiod, *Works and Days*, ll. 69–106.

36.   The term "equité" indicates natural justice or fairness.

37.   Eros, god of love, was born from the union of Expediency (Porus) and Poverty (Penia) in the garden of the gods. See Plato, *Symposium* 203b–c.

38.   The Muses.

39.   According to Plato, the human soul is formed from the same fire as the stars with which it can enter into communion through contemplation.

40.   In Pléiade theory, poetic inspiration dies out if it is not sustained through creative practice. See Graham Castor, *Pléiade Poetics* (Cambridge: Cambridge University Press, 1964), chap. 4.

41.   The next six stanzas are reminiscent of Cornelius Agrippa's *Declamation on the Nobility and Preeminence of the Female Sex*, ed. and trans. Albert Rabil Jr., Other Voice in Early Modern Europe (Chicago: University of Chicago Press, 1996), 94–95.

42.   Madeleine denounces the "loix d'Hymenée" (marriage laws) as *the* major obstacle to women seeking to become poets.

43.   Pyrrha, daughter of Pandora and wife of Deucalion, was mother of the human race. After the flood, Pyrrha and Deucalion created human beings by throwing stones over their shoulders. Pyrrha's stones became women, while those of Deucalion became men. See Ovid, *Metamorphoses* 1.315–415 and Hyginus, *Fabulae: The Myths of Hyginus*, trans. Mary Grant (Lawrence: University of Kansas Publications, 1960), fable 153.

44.   In Pléiade theory, the "winged pen" is a symbol of the freedom of the imagination and of the intellect.

45.   Phalaris of Acragas in Sicily (sixth century BCE) was proverbially known for his cruelty. In the spurious epistles attributed to him, however, he appears as an enlightened patron of the arts. See "Aux filles de Stesichore," in *Les epistres de Phalaris, et d'Isocrates. Avec le manuel d'Epictete* (Anvers: Christophe Plantin, 1558), 107v–110v. M. des Roches ironically implies that it would be a miracle if men imitated Phalaris, who was partially redeemed for his admiration of learned women. The daughters of Stesichorus are mentioned in the preface to the second and third editions of Olympia Morata's collected works (1562, 1570); see *The Complete Writings of an Italian Heretic*, ed. and trans. Holt N. Parker, Other Voice in Early Modern Europe (Chicago: University of Chicago Press, 2003), 71. Catherine des Roches includes Olympia Morata in her catalogue of contemporary learned women writers in *Dialogue between Placide and Severe* (see chap. 4).

46.   Emblem of the poetic immortality acquired by the learned woman.

47.   The theme of (male) envy against learned women is a leitmotif in the writings

of the Dames des Roches. See Catherine's narrative poem *Agnodice* where the allegorical figure Envy attempts to destroy women's health and minds by blocking their path to books and learning.

48.   The annotator added "est" to maintain the seven-syllabic line.

49.   A reminder of biblical ancient Israel's repeated rejection of her prophets.

50.   The original "banque de mesdire" refers to news that usually reached commercial sites first, such as banks.

51.   Martin of Tours (ca. 315–ca. 399), patron saint of France.

52.   A formulaic injunction in the writings of the Dames des Roches. See for example Catherine's plea in her dedicatory *Epistle to Her Mother* (see chap. 2) to her female contemporaries to take the trouble to write, and Madeleine's praise of Catherine's "winged pen" that rescued her mother from "ignorance and old age" "without begging for help from anyone else," *To My Daughter* (see chap. 5).

53.   From 1546 to 1554, Poitiers played host to a group of talented young poets who originally came to study law and who were dubbed the "Clain Poets," from the river Clain that flows through the city. Several of these poets later joined Ronsard in Paris to form the group of the Pléiade. Madeleine fashions in ode 3 a "learned school" that like a "rich Temple" includes only women.

54.   Carmenta (or Nicostrata), a prophetic goddess, mother of Evander, king of Arcadia and Rome's first settler, was credited with the invention of the Latin alphabet and of "certain laws, enjoining men to live in accord with right and reason, following justice." Christine de Pizan, *The Book of the City of Ladies*, trans. Earl Jeffrey Richards (New York: Persea, 1982), 1:33, 37, 38.

55.   Ancient Italo-Roman grain goddess whose daughter Proserpina was abducted by Pluto, god of the underworld. Ovid states that "prima dedit leges" (Ceres first gave laws) (*Metamorphoses* 5.343); Virgil mentions her instituting laws (*Aeneid* 4.58). See also Herodotus, *History* 6.134. Christine de Pizan credits her with teaching men the use of laws (*City of Ladies*, 1:38). Boccaccio mentions her primarily as the inventor of agriculture (*Famous Women*, ed. and trans. Virginia Brown [Cambridge: Harvard University Press, 2001], 5).

56.   Pallas, surname of the Greek goddess Athena, later identified with the Roman goddess Minerva.

57.   The nine Muses, Greek goddesses who originally presided over music and poetry in general.

58.   Corinna, a Greek lyric poet from Tanagra, in Boeotia, beat her fellow countryman the poet Pindar (518–438 BCE) in a poetic contest. See Pausanias, *Description of Greece* 9.22.3 (LCL 4.265–67); Plutarch, *De gloria atheniensium*, *Moralia* 4.348a; Agrippa, *Declamation on the Nobility and Preeminence of the Female Sex*, 82; François de Billon, *Le fort inexpugnable de l'honneur du sexe feminin*, introd. M. A. Screech (New York: Johnson Reprint, 1970), 2.2.30v.

59.   A Virgilian warrior, dedicated to the goddess Artemis (Diana), who fought on the side of the Latins against Aeneas. See Virgil, *Aeneid* 11.535–600; Boccaccio, *Famous Women*, 39; Pizan, *City of Ladies*, 1:24; Agrippa, *Declamation on the Nobility and Preeminence of the Female Sex*, 74.

60.   Queen of the Scythians, who conquered Cyrus, king of Persia. See Valerius Maximus, *Memorable Doings and Sayings* 9.10.1; Herodotus, *History* 1.206–16; Boccaccio, *Famous Women*, 49; Agrippa, *Declamation on the Nobility and Preeminence of the Female Sex*, 86.

61.   An anonymous virtuous and chaste woman (perhaps one of several female members of his extended family) whom the Latin poet Ausonius (ca. 310–ca. 394 CE) praises; see his *Parentalia* 1.2.5.

62.   The panegyric on the victory of the learned ladies of France over the monster of ignorance is frequent in Pléiade poetry.

63.   Wordplay on "Femme" (woman) and "Fame" (renown). The author delights in emphasizing the virtues as female figures (female because of the Latin gender). Renaissance feminist works frequently used this metaphorical association to heighten the dignity of women.

64.   A poisonous snake, the Hydra had numerous heads; when one was cut off, another grew in its place. See Ovid, *Metamorphoses* 9.69–75. Madeleine des Roches suffered from ill health and repeated bouts of migraine headaches to which she refers in a number of her letters.

65.   In Greek mythology, Scylla and Charybdis were monsters who trapped sailors on opposite ends of the straits of Messina, between Italy and Sicily.

66.   One of the four humors or elements of the human body. See Plato, *Timaeus* 82a.

67.   A striking adaptation of the Petrarchan motif of the "ship." See Petrarch, *Petrarch's Lyric Poems: The Rime Sparse and Other Lyrics*, ed. and trans. Robert Durling (Cambridge: Harvard University Press, 1976), sonnet 189 and canzone 80.

68.   The numbering follows that of my edition of *Les Œuvres*. This sonnet is likely addressed to Catherine for whom the author reserves the more informal second person *tu*. Madeleine ends her collected works of 1579 with two sonnets (see below) addressed as well to her daughter.

69.   Astrea, the constellation Virgo, identified with Justice.

70.   The Roman emperors Nero (37–68 CE) and Domitian (51–96 CE) persecuted the early Christians; Briareus, a giant, son of Uranus (Heaven) and Gaia (Earth), was buried beneath Mount Etna by Zeus.

71.   In sonnets 2 and 3 Madeleine des Roches reflects on the necessity to conduct one's life according to God-given reason. In sonnets 4 through 8, she bemoans her ill health and legal difficulties. She calls on death to release her from pain, then dwells on the insufficiency of her faith, the incapacity of doctors to heal her, and her friends' disapproval and lack of empathy. The allusion in the first line of this sonnet may be to her thirteen-year lawsuit.

72.   This "late-coming happiness" is, according to an anonymous contemporary annotator of *Les Œuvres*, Madeleine's second marriage.

73.   A reference to the transcendence of the body in its reach for the supreme Good. See Plato, *Phaedo* 66b–67b.

74.   In sonnets 9 through 14, the author evokes her strongly nationalist and monarchical convictions. Sonnet 9 expresses the theme of the *translatio studii et imperii*, the transferal of learning and dominion from the ancients to the moderns.

75.   The Romans.

76.   The Roman toga, symbol of virility and honor.

77.   François d'Alençon, duc d'Anjou, Henri III's younger brother, who, in August of 1579, went to England with the intention of marrying Queen Elizabeth I. The marriage negotiations were several years in the making; Albert de Gondi, maréchal de Retz, husband of Catherine de Clermont, was sent to the English court as early as 1573 to discuss the marriage. Plans were terminated in 1581. See Jullien de Pommerol, *Albert de Gondi, Maréchal de Retz* (Geneva: Droz, 1953), 106; Debra Barrett-Graves, "'Highly touched in honour': Elizabeth I and the Alençon Controversy," in *Elizabeth I: Always Her Own Free Woman*, ed. Carole Levin, Jo Eldridge Carney, and Debra Barrett-Graves (Aldershot: Ashgate, 2003), 43–60.

78.   Philip II (1527–98), king of Spain, had married Mary Tudor (Queen Mary I) (1516–58).

79.   A sonnet praising Charles IX (1550–74) or Henri III (1551–89) whose sole legitimacy, insists the author, is founded on their maintaining the rule of law.

80.   In sonnets 15 through 20, the author attacks the "rebel" Huguenots, denouncing their violence, their doctrines, and their "wily preachers."

81.   Aquitaine is located in southwestern France, in the region of Guyenne, where the Protestant Queen Jeanne d'Albret (1528–72) held her court at Nérac.

82.   This sonnet was written in 1562, after the sack of Poitiers, pillaged on 28 May by the five thousand Protestant Gascon troups of the comte de Grammont. Churches and monasteries were burned, including a portion of the relics of Saint Radegonde (ca. 520–87), who founded the convent of Sainte Croix in Poitiers. Orleans, Tours, and Blois were also attacked.

83.   Cambyses, king of Persia (529–21 BCE), son of Cyrus, committed sacrilegious and criminal acts while in Egypt. See Herodotus, *History* 3.27–29; Justin, *Epitome of the Philippic History of Pompeius Trogus*, trans. J. C. Yardley (Atlanta: Scholars Press, 1994), 1.1.9.

84.   Brennus, leader of a Celtic people from Gaul who in 280–79 BCE conquered Greece. He was defeated at Delphi and committed suicide in 278. See Justin, *History* 24.6–7.

85.   Belshazzar, king of Babylon, profaned the objects in the Temple of Jerusalem and died the same day. See Daniel 5.

86.   Persian general under Xerxes, captured and crucified by the Greeks for his violation of Protesilaus's temple. See Herodotus, *History* 7.33, 9.116–20.

87.   In sonnets 21–23, Madeleine underscores the necessity of acquiring through learning the virtues of prudence, good judgment, and humility. The monster Typhon, or Typheus, was the youngest son of Gaia (the earth) and of Tartarus. See Ovid, *Metamorphoses* 5.321.

88.   Plato, *Phaedo* 79a–c.

89.   In Ariosto's *Orlando Furioso*, Ruggiero falls in love with the magician Alcina, the incarnation of sensual love. Finally liberated, he journeys to the country of the pure and chaste Logistilla, who represents noble thoughts and reason. See *Orlando Furioso* 7.1–69.

90.   The sun.

91.   Allusion to the Platonic opposition between the black horse of sensuality and the white horse of reason. See *Phaedrus* 253d.

92.   In the ten intervening sonnets 24–34, Madeleine des Roches writes about her lawsuit (24), the flourishing of the arts and sciences in France (25, 26), the crucial choice of good preceptor for one's children (28), and the need to transcend the prison of the soul (29, 33, 34).

93.   A sonnet on the death of a dear friend.

94.   Cotgrave defines *privauté* as "privacie, private familiaritie or friendship, inward conversation or acquaintance." *Dictionarie of the French and English Tongues.*

95.   Married to Madeleine Neveu in 1550, François Éboissard died in 1578.

96.   Title given to a lawyer.

97.   The Greek Fates (Latin Parcae), represented as three old women spinning the thread of life.

98.   The Day of Judgment.

99.   This poem, added to the 1579 edition, was composed following the destruction of two of the Dames des Roches' townhouses during the siege of Poitiers in 1569.

100.   On the generosity of Henri III, see Jacqueline Boucher, *La cour de Henri III* (Rennes: Éditions Ouest-France, 1986), 85–87. The king's relationships with his subjects were based on a mentality of gift giving. On magnanimity as one of the principal attributes of kingship, see Smith, *Culture of Merit*, chap. 1; Sharon Kettering, "Gift-Giving and Patronage in Early Modern France," *French History* 2, no. 2 (1988): 131–51.

101.   Third king of Israel (ca. 971–31 BCE), son of David, first dynastic ruler and master sage.

102.   An allusion to the royal couple's infertility, which, after 1580, became a national obsession. See Boucher, *La cour de Henri III*, 16–18.

103.   These last two sonnets, added to the 1579 edition, close Madeleine des Roches's collected works.

104.   The god Apollo was associated with light, music, and poetry, Saturn with blight and desolation.

105.   In Greek myth, Cadmus, the legendary founder of Thebes, killed a dragon. His daughters all met with disaster. He was the ancestor of Acteon and Pentheus, who also encountered hard times.

106.   The original "escorce" refers to the bark of a tree.

CHAPTER TWO

1.   "[Beaucoup diront volontiers que] je ne devoy point escrire de quelque suject que ce soit, mesme en ce temps que nous voyons tant de Poëtes en la France." *Epistle to Her Mother, Œuvres* (see below).

2.   Grahame Castor, *Pléiade Poetics: A Study of Sixteenth-Century Thought and Terminology* (Cambridge: Cambridge University Press, 1964), chap. 8.

3. *Sonnets of Sincero to Charite*, sonnet 11.

4. Jones, *Currency of Eros*, 75.

5. Jacqueline Bouchet, *Société et mentalité autour de Henri III*, 4 vols. (Paris: Champion, 1981), 3:111, and *La cour de Henri III*, 119.

6. On this conflation, see Yandell, *Carpe Corpus*, 183. Louise Labé's speaker represents herself also as a woman warrior "loving only Mars and books," *Elegy III*, in *Louise Labé's Complete Works*, trans. and ed. Edith R. Farrell (Troy, N.Y.: Whitston, 1986), 95.

7. "Requise en mariage par une infinité de personnages d'honneur, toutefois elle met toutes ces requestes sous pieds: resoluë de vivre et de mourir avec sa mere." Étienne Pasquier, *Lettre à Pierre Pithou*, in Des Roches, *Missives*, 349.

8. As Suzanne Broomhall points out, Claude Bectone (or de Bectoz, 1480–1547), Anne de Marquets (ca. 1533–88), and Charlotte de Minut (published in 1587), also unmarried women writers in France during the sixteenth century, were nuns. *Women and the Book Trade*, 89.

9. The expression "tomber en quenouille" (to fall beneath a woman's rule) was invoked in the controversy over the Salic Law which forbade women from inheriting the crown. Marie de Gournay critiques the law in *Equality of Men and Women*, in *Apology for the Woman Writing and Other Works*, ed. and trans. Richard Hellman and Colette Quesnel, Other Voice in Early Modern Europe (Chicago: University of Chicago Press, 2002), 84.

10. Robert Clemens, *Picta Poesis: Literary and Humanistic Theory and Renaissance Emblems* (Rome: Storia e Letteratura, 1960), chap. 7, "Pen and Sword"; Gisèle Matthieu-Castellani, *La quenouille et la lyre* (Paris: José Corti, 1998), chap. 2, "Le fuseau et la plume."

11. On needlework as a sign of virtue for noblewomen, see Ann R. Jones and Peter Stallybrass, eds., *Renaissance Clothing and the Materials of Memory* (Cambridge: Cambridge University Press, 2000), chap. 6.

12. "Aussi n'ay-je point quitté pour elle [la plume] mes pelotons, ny laissé de mettre en œuvre la laine, la soye, et l'or quand il en a esté besoing, ou que vous me l'avez commandé," *Epistre à sa Mère*, *Œuvres*, 184–85 (see below).

13. Louise Labé, *Élégie III*, in *Œuvres complètes*, 1:33, cited by Jones and Stallybrass, *Renaissance Clothing*, 148.

14. Brantôme, *Recueil des Dames, poésies et tombeaux*, ed. Étienne Vaucheret (Paris: Gallimard, Bibliothèque de la Pléiade, 1991), "Catherine de Médicis," 37, cited by Jones and Stallybrass, *Renaissance Clothing*, 153.

15. "D'assembler d'égal compas / Les aiguilles, et le livre, / Et de doublement ensuivre / Les deux mestiers de Pallas." *Pour elle mesme*, in *Œuvres complètes*, ed. Céard, Ménager, and Simonin, 2:284, cited by Martin-Ulrich, *La 'persona' de la princesse au XVIe siècle*, 176.

16. Rebhorn, *Emperor of Men's Minds*, 14.

17. Yandell, *Carpe Corpus*, 182.

18. A similar introspection occurs in Gabrielle de Coignard's sonnet 14 where she orders her verse to "stay quiet in my room" and "enclosed in my coffer." She did not

publish her verse, preferring to devote her writing solely to God, "Not wanting to give my labors to any other." *Spiritual Sonnets: A Bilingual Edition*, ed. and trans. Melanie E. Gregg, Other Voice in Early Modern Europe (Chicago: University of Chicago Press, 2004), 53.

19.   On the Des Roches' skillful use of the humility topos, see chap. 5.

20.   Danielle Clarke, *The Politics of Early Modern Women's Writing* (London: Longman, 2001), 192.

21.   Male envy of learned women is frequently denounced by pro-woman writers in the *Querelle des femmes* such as Christine de Pizan in *The Book of the City of Ladies*, 1:18; Helisenne de Crenne in her third invective letter, in *A Renaissance Woman: Helisenne's Personal and Invective Letters*, ed. and trans. Marianna M. Mustacchi and Paul J. Archambault (Syracuse: Syracuse University Press, 1986); Lodovico Ariosto in *Orlando Furioso* (37.8.6); Lucrezia Marinella, *The Nobility and Excellence of Women and the Defects and Vices of Men*, ed. and trans. Anne Dunhill, introduction by Letizia Panizza, Other Voice in Early Modern Europe (Chicago: University of Chicago Press, 1999), chap. 6.

22.   Helisenne de Crenne invokes the same argument in her first invective letter: "I shall, therefore, speak of love (not because I have learned this through experience, but because literature has taught me to understand)." *Renaissance Woman*, 84.

23.   Xenophon (ca. 428–ca. 354 BCE), Greek historian and disciple of Socrates, describes the perfect king in his *Cyropaedia*; Cicero, the perfect orator in *The Orator*; and Castiglione, the perfect courtier in *The Book of the Courtier*. See the source of this passage in Castiglione's *Book of the Courtier*, trans. Charles Singleton (New York: Anchor Books, 1959), dedicatory epistle, section 3.

24.   Genesis 2:18–24.

25.   A possible allusion to the Greek historian Zosimus (late fifth century CE), author of a history of the Roman emperors.

26.   "Serfs," meaning both servants and slaves. This parallels the previous line on the Turkish slaves.

27.   Plutarch, *Sayings of Spartan Women*, Moralia 3.240e.

28.   One of the three Parcae who regulated the length of each individual's life from birth to death by means of a thread. Clotho held the distaff, Lachesis drew the thread, and Atropos cut it.

29.   Catherine des Roches refers here not to spinning, associated with lower-class women, but to needle and tapestry work, activities reserved for women of the upper gentry and aristocracy.

30.   Avoiding idleness, a staple of conduct books of the period, is frequently invoked as a justification for writing in women's prefaces.

31.   The word "nepveux," from the Latin *nepotes*, meaning "descendants," is a play on Madeleine Neveu's patronym. This amusing reference is inevitably lost in translation.

32.   Genesis 49:14. Catherine des Roches's six dialogues precede at this point the sonnets of Sincero to Charite. I have placed these in chapter 4.

33.   Reminiscent of Petrarch, *canzone* 126, l. 55, "She was surely born in Paradise!"

34. On the gaze in Neoplatonic love poetry, see Marsilio Ficino, *Commentary on Plato's Symposium on Love,* trans. Sears Jayne (Dallas: Spring Publications, 1985), speech 2.9.

35. Ibid., speech 2. 8.

36. The motif of the poem as unworthy of the beloved is frequent in Petrarchan lyric. See *Petrarch's Lyric Poems,* sonnet 21, ll. 3–4: "but it does not please you to gaze so low with your lofty mind."

37. "Honneste," when applied to a woman, indicates her chastity and virtue.

38. Iris, virgin daughter of Thaumas and Electra, was represented with wings, dressed in thin silk which in sunlight shone like the rainbow.

39. The legend of the phoenix reborn from its own ashes is a common motif in Petrarchan verse.

40. Reminiscent of Petrarch's *canzone* 80, "He who has decided to lead his life," and sonnet 189, "My ship laden with forgetfulness."

41. The "meaningless error" recalls Petrarch's "giovenile errore." See *Petrarch's Lyric Poems,* sonnet 1, l. 3 and Pontus de Tyard's "erreurs de ma jeunesse" in *Les erreurs amoureuses,* ed. John McClelland (Geneva: Droz, 1967), sonnet 1, l. 14. See also Louise Labé, *Élégie III,* in *Complete Works,* ed. Farrell, l. 6.

42. The invocation of impossible natural occurrences is standard in Petrarchan poetry; see for example, *Petrarch's Lyric Poems,* sonnet 57, ll. 5–8: "Alas! Snow will be warm and black," and sonnet 195; Maurice Scève, *Délie,* ed. I. D. McFarlane (Cambridge: Cambridge University Press, 1966), no. 17, "Plus tost seront Rhosne, et Saone desjoinctz," 128; Jean-Antoine de Baïf, *Les amours de Francine,* ed. Ernesta Caldarini (Geneva: Droz, 1966), book 1, sonnet 103, book 2, sonnets 47, 79, 82.

43. In Petrarch's *canzoniere,* it is the lover-poet who bestows renown upon his lady; see sonnet 61, ll. 12–13: "and blessed all the pages where I gain fame for her." In Louise Labé's *Elégie II,* ll. 61–74, on the other hand, Labé's speaker, thanks to *her* writings, wins honor and renown for her lover. Peletier du Mans highlights Labé's startling reversal of Petrarchan orthodoxy in his prefatory sonnet *Aus poëtes de Louize Labé:* "Tant qu'en louant sa dine poësie, / Mieus que par vous par elle vous vivez" (So much so that by praising her worthy verse, / Better than by you, by her you live on). Louise Labé, *Œuvres complètes,* 141.

44. Alcestis, having sacrificed herself in her husband's place, represents one of three great examples of love cited by Phaedrus in Plato's *Symposium* 179b–e; see also Ficino, *Commentary on the Symposium,* speech 1.4. The author rejects such a feminine model of connubial love.

45. Two "chansons" (songs), omitted here, end Sincero's sonnet sequence.

46. The combination of wealth and virtue is frequent in conduct manuals for the nobility of the time. Wealth, inherited or rewarded, indicated the generosity of the possessor. See Castiglione, *Book of the Courtier* 1.42–47, for the learning, elegance, and refined conversation that characterize the virtuous courtier.

47. A formulaic saying in Ficino's work; see *Commentary on the Symposium,* speech 6.10

in particular. The author repeats "sincérité" to reinforce her demand for absolute fidelity on the part of her lover.

48. An allusion to Pausanias's Celestial Venus in Plato's *Symposium* 180c–182a; see Ficino, *Commentary on the Symposium*, speech 2.7.

49. Charite's insistence on "amitié saincte" is essential to her self-representation as an irreproachable chaste woman. This notion of the lady as a moral guide of "honneste civilité" is also developed in courtly and Petrarchan lyric. See Plato, *Symposium* 210–12.

50. The fifth letter of the Greek alphabet. An expression denoting a little-traveled path.

51. The nine Muses.

52. The benevolent magician who saves Ruggiero from the snares of the enchantress Alcina by revealing to him this fairy's disguised beauties. See Lodovico Ariosto, *Orlando Furioso*, 7.38.

53. Claude Pellejay, who is thought to be the real-life model for Sincero, was known for his skills as musician and poet.

54. Ficino, *Commentary on the Symposium*, speech 2.8.

55. Henri d'Anjou had been elected in 1573 to the Polish throne, which he abdicated upon the death of his brother, Charles IX. He left Cracow for France on 16 June 1574 to become the new king of France. He had with him a large retinue of servants, secretaries, and noblemen. Claude Pellejay, a possible real-life model for Sincero, was among these as a secretary. See Diller, *Dames des Roches*, 44; Brunel, *Un poitevin poète*, 1:289.

56. An implied criticism, common in anti-Petrarchan literature, of women who subject their suitors to a hopeless love.

57. An allusion to the "jeu de paume" (handball or tennis) courts and to the fencing galleries of the Palais Royal in Paris. The "jeu de paume," in great vogue at the Valois court, was an indicator of social status.

58. The three Pauline virtues, 1 Corinthians 15.

59. A "chanson" (song) from Charite to Sincero follows at this point, not given here.

60. The sonnet sequence ends with *La rose à Charite* (Charite's Rose), an adaptation of two poems by Anacreon; see Anacreon, in *Greek Lyric* (LCL), 2:44, 55.

61. These stanzas, which celebrate the virile practices and legendary chastity of the Amazons, were likely composed for Henri III's court visit during three months in Poitiers in 1577. Des Roches may have been inspired by Ronsard's *Pour le trophée d'Amour* and *Pour le trophée de la Chasteté* in *Élégies, Mascarades et Bergerie* (1565), *Œuvres complètes*, ed. P. Laumonier, R. Lebègue, and I. Silver (Paris: Hachette-Didier, 1914–74), 13:218–21.

62. The myrtle is Venus's emblem, the laurel Apollo's.

63. Martesia (or Marpesia), a queen of the Amazons, is referred to in catalogues of famous women. See Boccaccio, *Famous Women* 11; Christine de Pizan, *City of Ladies*, 1.16.1; Antoine du Four, *Les Vies des femmes celebres*, ed. G. Jeanneau (Geneva: Droz, 1970), 30, 40.

64.   An implicit reference to Omphale, a Lydian queen who purchased Hercules as a slave. While she took to wearing his lion skin and to brandishing his club, he, in contrast, wore a long robe and spun linen thread at her feet.

65.   See Ronsard, *La quenoille*, in *Œuvres complètes*, ed. Laumonier et al., 10:122–23; Theocritus, *The Distaff*, idyll 28 in *The Idylls of Theocritus*, trans. Thelma Sargent (New York: W. W. Norton, 1982), 115–16; Coignard, *Spiritual Sonnets*, sonnet 122.

66.   "Souci," an expression of anguish, but also of love, frequently addressed to the beloved.

67.   A justificatory commonplace in women's writings.

68.   The concept of the book as child, referring to writing as self-perpetuation, is a frequent trope in the Renaissance and Baroque periods. See for instance Ronsard, *À son livre* (To His Book), *Œuvres complètes*, ed. Laumonier et al., 7:315–25; Aubigné, *L'auteur à son livre* (The Author to His Book), *Les Tragiques*, in *Œuvres complètes*.

69.   Cleobis and Biton, prize-winning athletes, harnessed themselves to a wagon with their mother riding in it so that she could arrive in time at the temple for a feast of Hera. Their mother then prayed that the goddess reward them with the greatest happiness possible. When the young men lay down to rest in the temple, they died in their sleep, thus preserving their youth, beauty, and strength in the moment of triumph. Statues were dedicated in their honor. See Herodotus, *History* 1.31. A *Chanson de la musique* (Song on music) follows this poem, not given here.

70.   A poem written soon upon the return in June 1574 of the new monarch Henri III who had been in Poland for nearly six months.

71.   Catherine des Roches protects herself from potential criticism that she is courting the king for monetary gain. In her quatrain *To G. P.* (see below), she denounces those who accuse her of selling her verses to royalty.

72.   A reference to Charles VII (1403–61), who took advice from the warrior maiden Joan of Arc (ca.1412–31).

73.   Catherine de Médicis.

74.   François d'Alençon (1554–84), Henri III's younger brother.

75.   See Cicero, *Republic* 1.40.64–65.

76.   Joseph-Juste Scaliger's Greek translation of this poem and Scévole de Sainte-Marthe's Latin translation follow (Des Roches, *Œuvres*, 302–9). Catherine also includes three poems to Queen Louise de Vaudémont, *À la Royne* (To the Queen), *À elle mesme luy presentant l'hymne de l'eau* (To the Same Presenting Her the Water Hymn), *Hymne de l'eau à la Roine* (Water Hymn to the Queen) (*Œuvres*, 310–23); and one to Catherine de Médicis, *Imitation de la mere de Salomon, À la Roine Mere du Roy* (Imitation of the Mother of Solomon, To the Queen Mother of the King) (*Œuvres*, 324–26).

77.   A suspicion of venality also fell upon Louise Labé, who protested: "A faire gain jamais ne me soumis" (I never resorted to gain), *Elegy III*, 1. 24.

78.   The immediate source of this poem is Proverbs 31:10–31.

79.   Housewifely work and the writing of poetry have much in common according to Catherine des Roches, who suggests a homological relation between writing and

sewing by referring to the Horatian motto *dulce et utile*. See Horace, *The Art of Poetry*, ll. 333–46.

80.   In Greek myth, Echo pined away for Narcissus; when she died, her voice remained, repeating the last syllables of spoken words. See Ovid, *Metamorphoses* 3.343 ff. The allusion is to court ladies often disparagingly contrasted, in praises of rural life, to the domestic woman.

81.   On the four cardinal virtues, see Plato, *Symposium* 196c–d; Ficino, *Commentary on the Symposium*, speech 4.5.

82.   Hyginus tells the story of the Athenian virgin Agnodice who disguises herself as a man to study medicine and invents the field of obstetrics. She reveals her true identity to her women patients and later to their husbands, who have accused her of corrupting their wives. The latter's intervention saves her, and "the Athenians amended the law, so that free-born women could learn the art of medicine." See Hyginus, *Fabulae*, fable 274.

83.   Genesis 4:9–16.

84.   That is, Greece.

85.   Theseus had to fight against his cousins who tried to obtain power by force; see Plutarch, *Theseus, Lives* 1.6–13.

86.   Athenian statesman (died ca. 468 BCE) known as "The Just," who came into conflict with Themistocles when the latter rose to power and as a consequence was ostracized in 482. See Herodotus, *History* 8.79, and Plutarch, *Aristides, Lives* 2.5–6.

87.   Themistocles (ca. 524–ca. 459 BCE), celebrated statesman of the Athenian democracy, was condemned to death and fled to the court of Artaxerxes, king of Persia. See Plutarch, *Themistocles, Lives* 2.27–31.

88.   Miltiades (ca. 550–489 BCE) died in prison; see Plutarch, *Aristides, Lives* 2.26.5, and Herodotus, *History* 6.136.

89.   On the death of Socrates (469–399 BCE), see Xenophon, *Apology of Socrates* 24–34; Plato, *Phaedo* 116b–118a.

90.   Phocion (fourth century BCE), Athenian general and statesman during the reign of Philip II of Macedon and his son Alexander, was elected to office forty-five times. When democratic rule was (briefly) restored in Athens in 318, he was put to death on a charge of treason. See Plutarch, *Phocion, Lives* 8.37. In Plutarch's version, it is Phocion's wife who buries her husband's ashes (37.5).

91.   Among the torments is that of childbirth.

92.   "Gentille" has the old meaning of noble.

93.   Glaucus, a fisherman, was changed into an immortal sea god when he ate a certain stalk. See Ovid, *Metamorphoses* 13.940–50. Agnodice uses an herb owned by Apollo, god of poetry. As muse and healer, she brings health to her female patients by giving them access to books and learning.

94.   An allusion to Castor and Pollux; see Theocritus, *The Dioscuri*, idyll 22.1–27.

95.   The Muses.

96.   The volume ends with *Antithese du somme et de la mort* (Antithesis between Sleep and

Death) (*Œuvres*, 340–42), and four epitaphs (*Medée, Clitemnestre, Lucrece, Niobe*) (*Œuvres*, 342–46) translated from Bernardo Accolti, *Verginia. Comedia* (Vinegia, 1530). *Un acte de la tragicomedie de Tobie, où sont representées les amours et les noces du jeune Tobie et de Sarra, fille de Raguel* (One Act of the Tragicomedy of Tobias, where are represented the love and the wedding of the young Tobias and Sarra, daughter of Raguel) (*Œuvres*, 347–82), six sonnets, and a song from Sincero to Charite were added to the 1579 edition of *Les Œuvres* (383–88).

CHAPTER THREE

1. Anthony Grafton and Lisa Jardine, *From Humanism to the Humanities: Education and the Liberal Arts in Fifteenth- and Sixteenth-Century Europe* (London: Duckworth, 1986), 57, cited by Clarke, *Politics of Early Modern Women's Writing*, 44 n. 23.

2. Clarke, *Politics of Early Modern Women's Writing*, 23; Ann R. Jones, "Nets and Bridles: Early Modern Conduct Books and Sixteenth-Century Women's Lyrics," in *The Ideology of Conduct: Essays in Literature and the History of Sexuality*, ed. Nancy Armstrong and Leonard Tennenhouse (New York: Methuen, 1987), 39–72.

3. Yandell, *Carpe Corpus*, 192.

4. Ann R. Jones, "Surprising Fame: Renaissance Gender Ideologies and Women's Lyric," in *The Poetics of Gender*, ed. Nancy K. Miller (New York: Columbia University Press, 1986), 80.

5. Whereas a French translation of Seneca's major work *De clementia* appeared only in 1595, translations of Epictetus's *Discourses* were published in 1544 and again in 1567 (the latter by the Huguenot playwright from Poitou André Rivaudeau), and a translation of Marcus Aurelius appeared in 1570.

6. Sonnet, *Secondes Œuvres*, 106–7.

7. *Secondes Œuvres*, 108–18.

8. They also appeared under a different title: *QUATRAINS DE CATHERINE DES ROCHES AUX Poëtes chante-Puce* (*La Puce de Madame Des-Roches. Qui est un recueil des divers poemes Grecs, Latins et François, composez par plusieurs doctes personnages aux Grans Jours tenus à Poitiers l'an M.D.LXXIX* [Paris: Abel L'Angelier, 1582,1583], fols. 44v–45v) and *CATHERINE DES ROCHES À E. PASQUIER* (*La Puce*, fol. 79v). On the episode of the flea, see the volume editor's introduction.

9. Étienne Pasquier, *La Puce, Jeux Poétiques, François et Latins. Composez sur la Puce aux Grands Jours de Poictiers l'an MDLXXIX, dont Pasquier fut le Premier Motif, in La Jeunesse d'Estienne Pasquier et sa suite* (The Flea, Poetic Games, in French and Latin. Composed on the Flea at the Grands Jours of Poitiers in 1579, for which Pasquier provided the main impetus), in *La Jeunesse d'Estienne Pasquier et sa suite* (Paris, 1610), 565–82.

10. For reasons of space, I have translated only a majority of the poems composed during the Grands Jours. Left out are Catherine's verse translations of Pythagoras's *Golden Verses* and *Symbols* in *Les Secondes Œuvres*, two short prayers for before and after a meal, two canticles to the Virgin, two epitaphs, and her pastoral verse drama *Bergerie*.

11. On the mock encomium, see Annette Tomarken, *The Smile of Truth: The French Satirical Eulogy and Its Antecedents* (Princeton: Princeton University Press, 1990).

12.   A standard rhetorical and humanist education in the Renaissance included poetry as a de rigueur means of entry into the elite. Writing poetry, especially impromptu verse which most of the Grands Jours lyrics are, thus had the function of showcasing the writer's ingenuity, talent, and *savoir dire.*

13.   Tilde Sankovitch, "Inventing Authority of Origin: The Difficult Enterprise," in *Women in the Middle Ages and the Renaissance: Literary and Historical Perspectives,* ed. Mary Beth Rose (Syracuse: Syracuse University Press, 1986), 227–43.

14.   Jones, *Currency of Eros,* 54.

15.   Helen Solterer, *The Master and Minerva: Disputing Women in French Medieval Culture* (Berkeley: University of California Press, 1995), 6–7.

16.   The *groupe marotique* is named after the poet Clément Marot (1496–1544).

17.   Marie-Françoise Piéjus, "La création du féminin dans le discours de quelques poétesses du XVIe siècle," in *Dire la création. La culture italienne entre poétique et poïétique,* ed. D. Budor (Lille: Presses universitaires de Lille, 1994), 79–90.

18.   Howard Kalwies, "The *Responce* Genre in Early French Renaissance Poetry," *Bibliothèque d'Humanisme et Renaissance* 65 (1983): 77–86.

19.   Odet de Turnèbe, *Sonets sur les ruines de Luzignan,* in *La Puce,* fols. 71–74. The castle had been destroyed in 1574 on orders from Catherine de Médicis.

20.   Ibid., fol. 74v.

21.   Logistilla, a chaste heroine in Ariosto's *Orlando Furioso* (7.1–69), represents noble thoughts and embodies reason. This epic poem was enormously popular in the Parisian coteries of Catherine de Clermont and Madeleine de L'Aubespine, where it was selectively imitated and reproduced in anthologies and poetic albums.

22.   On the rarity of depictions of female-female desire, see Maddalena Campiglia, *Flori, A Pastoral Drama,* ed. Virginia Cox and Lisa Sampson, trans. Virginia Cox, Other Voice in Early Modern Europe (Chicago: University of Chicago Press, 2004), 23.

23.   "Je n'ay besoin d'autre Poete, / Et plus grand heur je ne souhaite / Sinon de vostre m'avouer. / . . . L'on voit plusieurs Hommes chanter, / Epris d'une flame gentille, / Mais de Femme aimant une fille, / Nulle autre s'en peut vanter." Response 3 (see below).

24.   See Cathy Yandell, " 'L'Amour au féminin?' Ronsard and Pontus de Tyard Speaking as Women," in *Ronsard. Figure de la variété. En mémoire d'Isidore Silver,* ed. Colette H. Winn (Geneva: Droz, 2002), 65–83; Pierre de Bourdeille, sieur de Brantôme, *Les dames galantes,* ed. Maurice Rat (Paris: Garnier, 1960), 122, 126; Madeleine Lazard, *Pierre de Bourdeille, seigneur de Brantôme* (Paris: Fayard, 1995), 243–44. In the gendered discourse of the day, lesbianism was considered less subversive than sodomy, which was judged by the church and the state. See Floyd Gray, *Gender, Rhetoric, and Print Culture in French Renaissance Writing* (New York: Cambridge University Press, 2000), chap. 5; and Judith Brown, *Immodest Acts: The Life of a Lesbian Nun in Renaissance Italy* (New York: Oxford University Press, 1986), 9–10.

25.   *The Flea* (see below).

26.   Orest Ranum, "The Refuges of Intimacy," in *A History of Private Life,* vol. 3: *Passions of the Renaissance,* ed. Roger Chartier, trans. Arthur Goldhammer (Cambridge: Harvard

University Press, 1989), 258; Jonathan Dewald, *Aristocratic Experience and the Origins of Modern Culture: France, 1570–1715* (Berkeley: University of California Press, 1993), 110–11.

27. Éliane Viennot comments that Marguerite de Valois's letters to her close friend Henriette de Clèves, duchesse de Nemours, "[prennent] la forme de véritables déclarations d'amour" (take the form of veritable declarations of love). Marguerite de Valois, *Correspondance 1569–1614*, ed. Éliane Viennot (Paris: Champion, 1998), 42.

28. Todd Olsen, "'La Femme à la Puce et la puce à l'oreille:' Catherine des Roches and the Poetics of Sexual Resistance in Sixteenth-Century French Poetry," *Journal of Medieval and Early Modern Studies* 32, no. 2 (2002): 327–342.

29. In *The Same City to the King* (see below), Madeleine's feminine speaker ventriloquizes Poitiers as she pleads for a parlement, a sovereign court that would guarantee the city a relative autonomy from royal interference. On this poem, see the volume editor's introduction.

30. A reference to the etiquette of chaperonage.

31. In ode 1, which precedes this poem, Madeleine des Roches expresses her faith in God in the face of an uncertain and ever-changing world.

32. This ode was written in the springtime of 1578, shortly before the death of François Éboissard, the author's second husband.

33. Arete was the name of the daughter of the Greek philosopher Aristippus (ca. 435–350 BCE), who replaced her father as head of the Cyrenaic school; it also means "excellence" in Greek. See Marie de Gournay, for whom Arete "had the pen of her father, the soul of Socrates, the tongue of Homer." *Equality of Men and Women*, 79, and *A History of Women Philosophers*, ed. Mary Ellen Waithe (Bloomington: Indiana University Press, 1996), 1:197–201.

34. Muse of astronomy and geometry, represented with a compass and a globe.

35. Fabled singer, musician, and poet.

36. Amphion received the gift of a lyre from Hercules and devoted himself to music. When theorizing about eloquence, Renaissance writers often recount the myths of Orpheus and Amphion as the first orators and civilizers.

37. Gallic Hercules, symbol of inspired eloquence and political power. See Andrea Alciati's influential emblem (1531) of the Gallic Hercules that includes the caption "Eloquentia fortitudine praestantior" (Eloquence excels force), *A Book of Emblems: The Emblematum Liber in Latin and English*, ed. and trans. John F. Moffitt (Jefferson, N.C.: McFarland, 2004), 208.

38. Madeleine's two townhouses destroyed during the siege of Poitiers in 1569 by the troops of Admiral Gaspard de Coligny.

39. An allusion to Catherine des Roches.

40. The following three sonnets were written during the 1579 Grands Jours of Poitiers.

41. The Dorian, principal mode of ancient music; in plainchant, it is the most somber mode (D minor). In the next line, "the Hellenic phrase" is a metonym for the

Greek or learned style. The author means that her somber and sad "song" is neither as brilliant nor as erudite as the addressee, who extols her, makes it out to be. She is doubtless addressing a scholar specialized in philology and Greek literature.

42.   The passage from chaos to order is found in platonic cosmography (see Plato, *Timaeus* 27b–33a). The "discordant accord" plays a central role in the concept of the harmony and music of the spheres.

43.   "Rochers" in the original. This is a pun on Madeleine and Catherine des Roches's matronym.

44.   A reference to Prometheus who stole seeds of fire from "the sun's wheel" and brought them to humans. Zeus chained Prometheus on the Caucasus and sent an eagle to devour his liver, which was regenerated each day.

45.   Eumetis, or Cleobulina, daughter of Cleobulus, one of the Seven Wise Men of Ancient Greece; see Plutarch, *Precepts of Marriage, Moralia* 2.145e.

46.   Aspasia of Miletus (fourth century BCE) taught Pericles the art of oratory. See Plato, *Menexenus* 236; Plutarch, *Pericles, Lives* 3.24.1–7. On Aspasia's rhetorical gifts, see Cheryl Glenn, *Rhetoric Retold: Regendering the Tradition from Antiquity through the Renaissance* (Carbondale: Southern Illinois University Press, 1997), and "Locating Aspasia on the Rhetorical Map," in *Listening to Their Voices. The Rhetorical Activities of Historical Women*, ed. Molly Meijer Wertheimer (Columbia: University of South Carolina Press, 1997), 19–41; and Madeleine Henry, *Prisoner of History: Aspasia and her Biographical Tradition* (New York: Oxford University Press, 1995).

47.   Diotima, priestess at Mantinea, taught Socrates the doctrine of love. See Plato, *Symposium* 201f–212a. On Diotima and Aspasia, see Waithe, *History of Women Philosophers*, 1:75–116.

48.   Daemon (or Daimon) refers to an irresistible fate.

49.   Renowned Greek legislators.

50.   The author draws on Neostoicism, an intellectual movement that formulated an ethic of constancy for help in times of trouble.

51.   A pass with a grotto in a high rocky embankment, frequented in the days of Rabelais by rowdy crowds of university students.

52.   A reference to Catherine, whose thoughts, so united with those of her mother, echo hers.

53.   Greek goddess, personification of justice.

54.   The magistrates and poets attending the Grands Jours.

55.   Madeleine's ode "La mesme ville au Roy" (The Same City [of Poitiers] to the King) in which she requests the king to establish a parlement in Poitiers, and an epitaph in memory of an anonymous gentleman who died defending the city during the 1569 siege, appear at this point in *Les Secondes Œuvres*, 101–5.

56.   Poem against the Huguenot armies.

57.   A pun on La Charité-sur-Loire, a city in the Nièvre region. The Edict of Boulogne (11 July 1573) took La Charité from the Huguenots to whom it had been given under the Peace of Saint-Germain (8 August 1570).

58.   Prometheus, who stole fire from the sun, gave it to mankind. Madeleine des Roches, unlike Prometheus, had no need to steal her poetic inspiration for she received it as a gift from God. Catherine thereby defends women's creative power as a legitimate gift.

59.   The olive tree, an emblem of peace and harmony, was the favorite tree of Pallas Athena, goddess of wisdom and patron of the arts and the sciences.

60.   The golden bough was divulged to Aeneas not by Deiphobus but by the Cumean Sybil (Virgil, *Aeneid* 6.494 ff.). However, Aeneas did meet the shade of Deiphobus in his descent to Hades. The golden bough was a symbol of the strength and knowledge needed to explore Hades.

61.   Pythagoras, Greek polymath, philosopher, and mystic of the sixth century BCE. Catherine des Roches's translations of Pythagoras' *Golden Verses* and *Symbols* immediately follow this dedicatory epistle.

62.   The numbering follows that in my edition of *Les Secondes Œuvres.*

63.   At the very start of her response sequence, under the guise of warning young gullible female readers of the rhetorical wiles of suitors, the author lets it be known that she is no dupe of the rhetoric of compliment in the numerous *carpe diem* poems addressed to her by her admirers. She praises her current addressee for his wisdom in the manner he approaches her.

64.   A work by that name attributed to Hermes Trismegistus, an Egyptian sage who foretold Christianity and whose wisdom inspired Plato and the Platonists. The Hermetic core in Renaissance Neoplatonism was an important factor in the revival of magic. Hermes Trismegistus believed speech to be as precious as immortality. See Agrippa, *Declamation on the Nobility and Preeminence of the Female Sex*, 60, and Brian Copenhaver, *Symphorien Champier and the Reception of the Occultist Tradition in Renaissance France* (The Hague: Mouton, 1978).

65.   René Brochart, sieur des Fontaines, earned a law degree in 1580, was made a counselor in the law courts of Poitiers in 1586, the city's mayor in 1589, and alderman of the *conseil particulier de la Ligue* in 1590. His sister Jeanne became the mother of the philosopher René Descartes. Brochart was the Dames des Roches' legal representative and the executor of their estate.

66.   *Muguet* also has the sense of "fop" or "gallant."

67.   A young girl loved by the Sun, who then spurned her for love of Leucothoe. Clytia revealed her rival's affair to Leucothoe's father and for this was buried in a deep ditch where she died.

68.   Hyacinth, a young man of great beauty, was loved by Apollo who transformed him into a jacinth flower; see Ovid, *Metamorphoses* 10.170 ff.; Hyginus, *Fabulae*, fable 271.

69.   Adonis, mortally wounded by a wild boar, was changed into this flower by Aphrodite; see Ovid, *Metamorphoses* 10.516 ff.

70.   Narcissus; see ibid. 3.342 ff.

71.   In the second legend of the hyacinth, the flower is born of the blood of Ajax, son of Telamon, when he kills himself; see ibid. 13.383 ff.

72. Emblem of Apollo, evoking glory.

73. The rosemary symbolizes constancy.

74. The "violette de Mars" is often evoked in Ronsard's poetry.

75. Marie de Lavau, daughter of Jean de Lavau, a judge of the Grands Jours. She and her father likely attended the Des Roches' coterie. This poem is not included in the volume of *The Flea*.

76. Numa Pompilius, in legendary Roman history, was the successor of Romulus as second king of Rome (715–673 BCE). According to tradition, he carried out numerous reforms. On Numa's interdiction, see Plutarch, *Numa, Lives* 8.13–15.

77. Famous Greek painters who worked in the late fifth and fourth centuries BCE.

78. Responses 10 and 11 are addressed to Madeleine Chémeraut, Catherine des Roches's beloved cousin. Daughter of the lawyer Barthélemy Chémeraut and of Perrine Chasteigner, Madeleine was baptized at Poitiers on 30 July 1544. Madeleine Neveu was one of her godmothers. Madeleine Chémeraut, a poet in her own right, is praised by Marie de Romieu in her *Brief Discourse: That Woman's Excellence Surpasses that of Man* (1581), trans. Marian Rothstein, in *Writings by Pre-Revolutionary French Women: From Marie de France to Elizabeth Vigée-Le Brun*, ed. Anne Larsen and Colette Winn (New York: Garland, 2000), 144.

79. Reference to the transcendence of the body: see Plato, *Phaedrus* 66b–67b; Ronsard, *Hymne de la Mort, Œuvres complètes*, ed. Laumonier et al., 8:164, l. 50.

80. The Sun.

81. According to Heraclitus (ca. 540–480 BCE), the unity of the world depends on the balance between opposites: change in one direction leads to change in the other. Hence "all things are in a state of flux." See *Fragments*, trans. T. M. Robinson (Toronto: University of Toronto Press, 1987), 12, 49, 91a.

82. Two of the seven wonders of the ancient world.

83. A critique of the *carpe diem* topos, a staple of contemporary love poetry. The author asserts that since physical beauty is ephemeral, a lover should be attracted to the beauty of the beloved's soul rather than to her fleeting physical attractiveness. On this poem, see Yandell, *Carpe Corpus*, 206.

84. At Delphi, the most important of Apollo's oracular shrines, an inscription read: "Know Thyself."

85. Odet de Turnèbe (1552–81), son of the famous humanist Adrien de Turnèbe, cousin of Estienne Pasquier (1529–1615), was a lawyer in the Paris Parlement, then president of the Cour des comptes. Catherine includes in the *Secondes Œuvres* at least eleven responses (19, 20, 23 to 28, 30, 31, and 33) which she wrote during the Grands Jours of 1579. Response 23 is included in the collection of *La Puce* under the title, "RESPONSE AU SONET PRECEDENT FAITE sur le champ" (Response to the preceding sonnet, invented on the spot) (fol. 37v). Odet de Turnèbe's sonnet, to which this poem is a response, praises Catherine des Roches's "excellent speech" and "sweet voice."

86. Estienne Pasquier, a reputed lawyer and a deputy at the Estates General in 1588. This poem, a response to a sextet Pasquier had written, is included in the volume of *La Puce* (fol. 5).

87. A fisherman changed into an immortal sea god when he ate an herb owned by Apollo, god of poetry. See Ovid, *Metamorphoses* 13.940–50.

88. A sonnet possibly in praise of Jeanne de Bourbon (1542–1624), daughter of Louis II de Bourbon, duc de Montpensier, who is characterized as offspring of an ancient lineage. She became abbess of the convent of Sainte-Croix in Poitiers. The author had also dedicated to her a *CANTIQUE DE L'HEUREUSE VIERGE MERE DE DIEU* (Canticle of the Virgin Mary; *Secondes Œuvres*, 144–46).

89. That is, Homer, Amphion, and Orpheus.

90. A response to sonnet 11 in Turnèbe's sequence "SONETS SUR LES RUINES DE LUZIGNAN PAR ODET DE TOURNEBU" (Sonnets on the Ruins of Lusignan) written during the Grand Jours and published in *La Puce*, fols. 71v–74v.

91. The castle of Lusignan, built according to legend by the half-woman, half-siren Melusina, had become a Protestant stronghold and was destroyed in 1575 by the Catholic troops of the duc de Montpensier. Turnèbe, a habitué of the Des Roches' salon during the Grands Jours, addressed to Catherine ten sonnets in which the ruined castle becomes a melancholic image for war-torn France and a metonym for the poet-lover's broken heart.

92. Chaste heroine of Ariosto's *Orlando Furioso* (7.1–69), Logistilla represents noble thoughts and reason.

93. Reference to Plato's Heavenly Venus in the *Symposium* 180c–182c.

94. An epithet of Apollo, god of light, identified with the sun.

95. Anagram of Odet de Turnèbe.

96. Included in the volume of *La Puce*, this response is to a sonnet by Étienne Pasquier on the occasion of Catherine des Roches's recitation of her *Hymne de l'eau à la Roine* (Water Hymn to the Queen), published in *Les Œuvres*, 313–23.

97. A reference to the Heraclitean doctrine of fire as the principal origin of all things.

98. Athena sprang forth in full armor at birth from the head of Zeus.

99. Claude Binet (1533–1600), a lawyer in the Paris Parlement and later lieutenant general of Auvergne.

100. Little rock.

101. Pithon was a goddess of rhetorical persuasion and eloquence; Diana, a virgin and eternally young, was the goddess of the hunt and the protecting deity of the Amazons who resembled her in her chastity and independence; Minerva was the virgin goddess of war and of the intellect.

102. Pallas Athena, goddess of wisdom and learning.

103. Arachne, a woman of Lydia who challenged the goddess Athena to a contest in weaving. She had depicted in her web the loves of the gods, and Athena, angered at her presumption, tore the web in pieces and beat the weaver. Arachne in despair hanged herself, but Athena turned her into a spider. See Ovid, *Metamorphoses* 7.1–143.

104. As one of the Charites (Graces), Thalia presided over vegetation; as one of the Muses, she presided over light verse.

105. Apollo.

106.   In Greek mythology, the sons of Boreas, the north wind, took part in the expedition of the Argonauts to recover the Golden Fleece, in the course of which they delivered King Phineus from the Harpies, birds with women's features.

107.   Or Grace.

108.   The fountain Hippocrene.

109.   A pun on fame and *femme*, meaning woman.

110.   An allusion to the hieroglyphs of the legendary Horapollo. The first Latin edition dates from 1505. See *The Hieroglyphics of Horapollo*, trans. George Boas (New York: Bollingen, 1950).

111.   In *La Puce* this poem appears under the added title *ELLE MESME AYANT OBTENU ARREST* (The author having obtained judgment), fol. 77v. Catherine thanks the judges for granting her a favorable outcome to a lawsuit.

112.   An allusion to the wax of the seal that appears on the copy of the *arrest* (judgment).

113.   Catherine's poem opens the volume of *La Puce*.

114.   In the medical sense, etherlike luminous substances that are born of blood and give life to the body.

115.   An Arcadian dryad pursued by the god Pan. Just as he was about to catch her, she changed herself into a reed on the banks of the Ladon River. As the winds made the reeds sigh, Pan joined these together to make a musical instrument which he called the Syrinx, in memory of the nymph. See Ovid, *Metamorphoses* 1. 687–723.

116.   Spartan boys were practiced thieves. See Plutarch, *Lycurgus, Lives* 17–18.

117.   The constellation of Orion is seen in the month of October, during which the flea poems were composed. The Grands Jours took place between 10 September and 18 December 1579.

118.   The huntress Atalanta refused to marry any man who could not defeat her in a race. Hippomenes, taking up the challenge, won by dropping three golden apples at intervals; Atalanta could not resist the temptation to stop and pick them up. Ovid, *Metamorphoses* 10.666–80.

119.   Virgin goddess of woodlands and protector of women.

120.   The anonymous annotator identifies this epitaph as that of Catherine des Roches. The volume of the *Secondes Œuvres* ends with seven songs, three sonnets, and two more epitaphs.

121.   Cupid.

SERIES EDITORS'
BIBLIOGRAPHY

PRIMARY SOURCES

Alberti, Leon Battista. *The Family in Renaissance Florence*. Translated by Renée Neu Watkins. Columbia, S.C.: University of South Carolina Press, 1969.

Arenal, Electa, and Stacey Schlau, eds. *Untold Sisters: Hispanic Nuns in Their Own Works*. Translated by Amanda Powell. Albuquerque, N.M.: University of New Mexico Press, 1989.

Astell, Mary. *The First English Feminist: Reflections on Marriage and Other Writings*. Edited and with an introduction by Bridget Hill. New York: St. Martin's Press, 1986.

Atherton, Margaret, ed. *Women Philosophers of the Early Modern Period*. Indianapolis, Ind.: Hackett Publishing, 1994.

Aughterson, Kate, ed. *Renaissance Woman: Constructions of Femininity in England: A Source Book*. London and New York: Routledge, 1995.

Barbaro, Francesco. *On Wifely Duties*. Translated by Benjamin Kohl. In *The Earthly Republic*, edited by Benjamin Kohl and R. G. Witt, 179–228. Philadelphia: University of Pennsylvania Press, 1978

Behn, Aphra. *The Works of Aphra Behn*. 7 vols. Edited by Janet Todd. Columbus, Ohio: Ohio State University Press, 1992–96.

Boccaccio, Giovanni. *Famous Women*. Edited and translated by Virginia Brown. The I Tatti Renaissance Library. Cambridge, Mass.: Harvard University Press, 2001.

———. *Corbaccio or the Labyrinth of Love*. Transated by Anthony K. Cassell. 2d rev. ed. Binghamton, N.Y.: Medieval and Renaissance Texts and Studies, 1993.

Booy, David, ed. *Autobiographical Writings by Early Quaker Women*. Aldershot and Brookfield, UK: Ashgate Publishing, 2004.

Brown, Sylvia. *Women's Writing in Stuart England: The Mother's Legacies of Dorothy Leigh, Elizabeth Joscelin and Elizabeth Richardson*. Thrupp, Stroud, Gloceter: Sutton, 1999.

Bruni, Leonardo. "On the Study of Literature (1405) to Lady Battista Malatesta of Moltefeltro." In *The Humanism of Leonardo Bruni: Selected Texts*, translated and with an introduction by Gordon Griffiths, James Hankins, and David Thompson, 240–51. Binghamton, N.Y.: Medieval and Renaissance Studies and Texts, 1987.

Castiglione, Baldassare. *The Book of the Courtier*. Translated by George Bull. New York: Penguin, 1967.

———. *The Book of the Courtier*. Edited by Daniel Javitch. New York: W. W. Norton, 2002.

Clarke, Danielle, ed. *Isabella Whitney, Mary Sidney and Aemilia Lanyer: Renaissance Women Poets*. New York: Penguin Books, 2000.

Crawford, Patricia, and Laura Gowing, eds. *Women's Worlds in Seventeenth-Century England: A Source Book*. London and New York: Routledge, 2000.

"Custome Is an Idiot": Jacobean Pamphlet Literature on Women. Edited by Susan Gushee O'Malley. Afterword by Ann Rosalind Jones. Chicago and Urbana: University of Illinois Press, 2004.

Daybell, James, ed. *Early Modern Women's Letter Writing, 1450–1700*. Houndmills, England, New York: Palgrave, 2001.

Elizabeth I: Collected Works. Edited by Leah S. Marcus, Janel Mueller, and Mary Beth Rose. Chicago: University of Chicago Press, 2000.

Elyot, Thomas. *Defence of Good Women: The Feminist Controversy of the Renaissance*. Edited by Diane Bornstein. Facsimile Reproductions. New York: Delmar, 1980.

Erasmus, Desiderius. *Erasmus on Women*. Edited by Erika Rummel. Toronto: University of Toronto Press, 1996.

Female and Male Voices in Early Modern England: An Anthology of Renaissance Writing. Edited by Betty S. Travitsky and Anne Lake Prescott. New York: Columbia University Press, 2000.

Ferguson, Moira, ed. *First Feminists: British Women Writers 1578–1799*. Bloomington, Ind.: Indiana University Press, 1985.

Galilei, Maria Celeste. *Sister Maria Celeste's Letters to her father, Galileo*. Edited and translated by Rinaldina Russell. Lincoln, Neb., and New York: Writers Club Press of Universe.com, 2000.

———. *To Father: The Letters of Sister Maria Celeste to Galileo, 1623–1633*. Translated by Dava Sobel. London: Fourth Estate, 2001.

Gethner, Perry, ed. *The Lunatic Lover and Other Plays by French Women of the 17ᵗʰ and 18ᵗʰ Centuries*. Portsmouth, N.H.: Heinemann, 1994.

Glückel of Hameln. *The Memoirs of Glückel of Hameln*. Translated by Marvin Lowenthal. New Introduction by Robert Rosen. New York: Schocken Books, 1977.

Harline, Craig, ed. *The Burdens of Sister Margaret: Inside a Seventeenth-Century Convent*. New Haven: Yale University Press, abr. ed., 2000.

Henderson, Katherine Usher, and Barbara F. McManus, eds. *Half Humankind: Contexts and Texts of the Controversy about Women in England, 1540–1640*. Urbana, Ill.: University of Illinois Press, 1985.

Hoby, Margaret. *The Private Life of an Elizabethan Lady: The Diary of Lady Margaret Hoby 1599–1605*. Phoenix Mill, England: Sutton Publishing, 1998.

Humanist Educational Treatises. Edited and translated by Craig W. Kallendorf. The I Tatti Renaissance Library. Cambridge, Mass.: Harvard University Press, 2002.

Hunter, Lynette, ed. *The Letters of Dorothy Moore, 1612–64*. Aldershot and Brookfield, UK: Ashgate Publishing, 2004.

Joscelin, Elizabeth. *The Mothers Legacy to Her Unborn Childe*. Edited by Jean leDrew Metcalfe. Toronto: University of Toronto Press, 2000.

Kaminsky, Amy Katz, ed. *Water Lilies, Flores del agua: An Anthology of Spanish Women Writers from the Fifteenth through the Nineteenth Century*. Minneapolis: University of Minnesota Press, 1996.

Kempe, Margery. *The Book of Margery Kempe*. Translated and edited by Lynn Staley. A Norton Critical Edition. New York: W.W. Norton, 2001.

King, Margaret L., and Albert Rabil, Jr., eds. *Her Immaculate Hand: Selected Works by and about the Women Humanists of Quattrocento Italy*. Binghamton, N.Y.: Medieval and Renaissance Texts and Studies, 1983; second revised paperback edition, 1991.

Klein, Joan Larsen, ed. *Daughters, Wives, and Widows: Writings by Men about Women and Marriage in England, 1500–1640*. Urbana, Ill.: University of Illinois Press, 1992.

Knox, John. *The Political Writings of John Knox: The First Blast of the Trumpet against the Monstrous Regiment of Women and Other Selected Works*. Edited by Marvin A. Breslow. Washington: Folger Shakespeare Library, 1985.

Kors, Alan C., and Edward Peters, eds. *Witchcraft in Europe, 400–1700: A Documentary History*. Philadelphia: University of Pennsylvania Press, 2000.

Krämer, Heinrich, and Jacob Sprenger. *Malleus Maleficarum* (ca. 1487). Translated by Montague Summers. London: Pushkin Press, 1928; reprint New York: Dover, 1971.

Larsen, Anne R., and Colette H. Winn, eds. *Writings by Pre-Revolutionary French Women: From Marie de France to Elizabeth Vigée-Le Brun*. New York and London: Garland Publishing, 2000.

de Lorris, William, and Jean de Meun. *The Romance of the Rose*. Translated by Charles Dahlbert. Princeton: Princeton University Press, 1971; reprint University Press of New England, 1983.

Marguerite d'Angoulême, Queen of Navarre. *The Heptameron*. Translated by P. A. Chilton. New York: Viking Penguin, 1984.

Mary of Agreda. *The Divine Life of the Most Holy Virgin*. Abridgment of *The Mystical City of God*. Abridged by by Fr. Bonaventure Amedeo de Caesarea, M.C. Translated from the French by Abbé Joseph A. Boullan. Rockford, Ill.: Tan Books, 1997.

Mullan, David George. *Women's Life Writing in Early Modern Scotland: Writing the Evangelical Self, c. 1670–c. 1730*. Aldershot and Brookfield, UK: Ashgate Publishing, 2003.

Myers, Kathleen A., and Amanda Powell, eds. *A Wild Country out in the Garden: The Spiritual Journals of a Colonial Mexican Nun*. Bloomington, Ind.: Indiana University Press, 1999.

de Pizan, Christine. *The Book of the City of Ladies*. Translated by Earl Jeffrey Richards. Foreward by Marina Warner. New York: Persea Books, 1982.

———. *The Treasure of the City of Ladies*. Translated by Sarah Lawson. New York: Viking Penguin, 1985.

———. *The Treasure of the City of Ladies*. Translated and with an introduction by Charity Cannon Willard. Edited and with an introduction by Madeleine P. Cosman. New York: Persea Books, 1989.

Russell, Rinaldina, ed. *Sister Maria Celeste's Letters to Her Father, Galileo*. San Jose and New York: Writers Club Press, 2000.

Teresa of Avila, Saint. *The Life of Saint Teresa of Avila by Herself*. Translated by J. M. Cohen. New York: Viking Penguin, 1957.

Travitsky, Betty, ed. *The Paradise of Women: Writings by Englishwomen of the Renaissance*. Westport, Conn.: Greenwood Press, 1981.

Weyer, Johann. *Witches, Devils, and Doctors in the Renaissance: Johann Weyer, De praestigiis daemonum*. Edited by George Mora with Benjamin G. Kohl, Erik Midelfort, and Helen Bacon. Translated by John Shea. Binghamton, N.Y.: Medieval and Renaissance Texts and Studies, 1991.

Wilson, Katharina M., ed. *Medieval Women Writers*. Athens, Ga.: University of Georgia Press, 1984.

————, ed. *Women Writers of the Renaissance and Reformation.* Athens, Ga.: University of Georgia Press, 1987.

Wilson, Katharina M., and Frank J. Warnke, eds. *Women Writers of the Seventeenth Century.* Athens, Ga.: University of Georgia Press, 1989.

Wollstonecraft, Mary. *A Vindication of the Rights of Men and a Vindication of the Rights of Women.* Edited by Sylvana Tomaselli. Cambridge: Cambridge University Press, 1995.

————. *The Vindications of the Rights of Men, The Rights of Women.* Edited by D. L. Macdonald and Kathleen Scherf. Peterborough, Ontario, Canada: Broadview Press, 1997.

Women Critics 1660–1820: An Anthology. Edited by the Folger Collective on Early Women Critics. Bloomington, Ind.: Indiana University Press, 1995.

Women Writers in English 1350–1850. 15 volumes published through 1999 (projected 30-volume series suspended). Oxford: Oxford University Press, 1993–1999.

Wroth, Lady Mary. *The Countess of Montgomery's Urania.* 2 parts. Edited by Josephine A. Roberts. Tempe, Ariz.: MRTS, 1995, 1999.

————. *Lady Mary Wroth's "Love's Victory": The Penshurst Manuscript.* Edited by Michael G. Brennan. London: The Roxburghe Club, 1988.

————. *The Poems of Lady Mary Wroth.* Edited by Josephine A. Roberts. Baton Rouge, La: Louisiana State University Press, 1983.

de Zayas Maria. *The Disenchantments of Love.* Translated by H. Patsy Boyer. Albany, N.Y.: State University of New York Press, 1997.

————. *The Enchantments of Love: Amorous and Exemplary Novels.* Translated by H. Patsy Boyer. Berkeley: University of California Press, 1990.

SECONDARY SOURCES

Abate, Corinne S., ed. *Privacy, Domesticity, and Women in Early Modern England.* Aldershot and Brookfield, IK: Ashgate Publishing, 2003.

Ahlgren, Gillian. *Teresa of Avila and the Politics of Sanctity.* Ithaca, N.Y.: Cornell University Press, 1996.

Akkerman, Tjitske, and Siep Sturman, eds. *Feminist Thought in European History, 1400–2000.* London and New York: Routledge, 1997.

Allen, Sister Prudence, R.S.M. *The Concept of Woman: The Aristotelian Revolution, 750 B.C.–A.D. 1250.* Grand Rapids, Mich.: William B. Eerdmans Publishing Company, 1997.

————. *The Concept of Woman: Volume II: The Early Humanist Reformation, 1250–1500.* Grand Rapids, Mich.: William B. Eerdmans Publishing Company, 2002.

Amussen, Susan D., and Adele Seeff, eds. *Attending to Early Modern Women.* Newark: University of Delaware Press, 1998.

Andreadis, Harriette. *Sappho in Early Modern England: Female Same-Sex Literary Erotics 1550–1714.* Chicago: University of Chicago Press, 2001.

Armon, Shifra. *Picking Wedlock: Women and the Courtship Novel in Spain.* New York: Rowman and Littlefield Publishers, 2002.

Backer, Anne Liot Backer. *Precious Women.* New York: Basic Books, 1974.

Ballaster, Ros. *Seductive Forms.* New York: Oxford University Press, 1992.

Barash, Carol. *English Women's Poetry, 1649–1714: Politics, Community, and Linguistic Authority.* New York and Oxford: Oxford University Press, 1996.

Battigelli, Anna. *Margaret Cavendish and the Exiles of the Mind.* Lexington, Ky.: University of Kentucky Press, 1998.

Beasley, Faith. *Revising Memory: Women's Fiction and Memoirs in Seventeenth-Century France.* New Brunswick, N.J.: Rutgers University Press, 1990.

Becker, Lucinda M. *Death and the Early Modern Englishwoman.* Aldershot and Brookfield, UK: Ashgate Publishing, 2003.

Beilin, Elaine V. *Redeeming Eve: Women Writers of the English Renaissance.* Princeton: Princeton University Press, 1987.

Benson, Pamela Joseph. *The Invention of Renaissance Woman: The Challenge of Female Independence in the Literature and Thought of Italy and England.* University Park, Penn.: Pennsylvania State University Press, 1992.

Benson, Pamela Joseph, and Victoria Kirkham, eds. *Strong Voices, Weak History? Medieval and Renaissance Women in Their Literary Canons: England, France, Italy.* Ann Arbor: University of Michigan Press, 2003.

Berry, Helen. *Gender, Society and Print Culture in Late-Stuart England.* Aldershot and Brookfield, UK: Ashgate Publishing, 2003.

Bicks, Caroline. *Midwiving Subjects in Shakespeare's England.* Aldershot and Brookfield, UK: Ashgate Publishing, 2003.

Bilinkoff, Jodi. *The Avila of Saint Teresa: Religious Reform in a Sixteenth-Century City.* Ithaca, N.Y.: Cornell University Press, 1989.

Bissell, R. Ward. *Artemisia Gentileschi and the Authority of Art.* University Park, Penn.: Pennsylvania State University Press, 2000.

Blain, Virginia, Isobel Grundy, and Patricia Clements, eds. *The Feminist Companion to Literature in English: Women Writers from the Middle Ages to the Present.* New Haven: Yale University Press, 1990.

Bloch, R. Howard. *Medieval Misogyny and the Invention of Western Romantic Love.* Chicago: University of Chicago Press, 1991.

Bogucka, Maria. *Women in Early Modern Polish Society, against the European Background.* Aldershot and Brookfield, UK: Ashgate Publishing, 2004.

Bornstein, Daniel, and Roberto Rusconi, eds. *Women and Religion in Medieval and Renaissance Italy.* Translated by Margery J. Schneider. Chicago: University of Chicago Press, 1996.

Brant, Clare, and Diane Purkiss, eds. *Women, Texts and Histories, 1575–1760.* London and New York: Routledge, 1992.

Briggs, Robin. *Witches and Neighbours: The Social and Cultural Context of European Witchcraft.* New York: HarperCollins, 1995; Viking Penguin, 1996.

Brink, Jean R., ed. *Female Scholars: A Tradition of Learned Women before 1800.* Montréal: Eden Press Women's Publications, 1980.

Brink, Jean R., Allison Coudert, and Maryanne Cline Horowitz. *The Politics of Gender in Early Modern Europe.* Sixteenth Century Essays and Studies. Volume 12. Kirksville, Mo.: Sixteenth Century Journal Publishers, 1989.

Broude, Norma, and Mary D. Garrard, eds. *The Expanding Discourse: Feminism and Art History.* New York: HarperCollins, 1992.

Brown, Judith C. *Immodest Acts: The Life of a Lesbian Nun in Renaissance Italy.* New York: Oxford University Press, 1986.

Brown, Judith C., and Robert C. Davis, eds. *Gender and Society in Renaisance Italy.* London: Addison Wesley Longman, 1998.

Burke, Victoria E. Burke, ed. *Early Modern Women's Manuscript Writing.* Aldershot and Brookfield, UK: Ashgate Publishing, 2004.

Bynum, Carolyn Walker. *Fragmentation and Redemption: Essays on Gender and the Human Body in Medieval Religion.* New York: Zone Books, 1992.

―――. *Holy Feast and Holy Fast: The Religious Significance of Food to Medieval Women.* Berkeley: University of California Press, 1987.

Cambridge Guide to Women's Writing in English. Edited by Lorna Sage. Cambridge: Cambridge University Press, 1999.

Cavallo, Sandra, and Lyndan Warner. *Widowhood in Medieval and Early Modern Europe.* New York: Longman, 1999.

Cavanagh, Sheila T. *Cherished Torment: The Emotional Geography of Lady Mary Wroth's "Urania".* Pittsburgh: Duquesne University Press, 2001.

Cerasano, S. P., and Marion Wynne-Davies, eds. *Readings in Renaissance Women's Drama: Criticism, History, and Performance 1594–1998.* London and New York: Routledge, 1998.

Cervigni, Dino S., ed. *Women Mystic Writers. Annali d'Italianistica* 13 (1995) (entire issue).

Cervigni, Dino S., and Rebecca West, eds. *Women's Voices in Italian Literature. Annali d'Italianistica* 7 (1989) (entire issue).

Charlton, Kenneth. *Women, Religion and Education in Early Modern England.* London and New York: Routledge, 1999.

Chojnacka, Monica. *Working Women in Early Modern Venice.* Baltimore: Johns Hopkins University Press, 2001.

Chojnacki, Stanley. *Women and Men in Renaissance Venice: Twelve Essays on Patrician Society.* Baltimore: Johns Hopkins University Press, 2000.

Cholakian, Patricia Francis. *Rape and Writing in the* Heptameron *of Marguerite de Navarre.* Carbondale and Edwardsville, Ill.: Southern Illinois University Press, 1991.

―――. *Women and the Politics of Self-Representation in Seventeenth-Century France.* Newark: University of Delaware Press, 2000.

Christine de Pizan: A Casebook. Edited by Barbara K. Altmann and Deborah L. McGrady. New York: Routledge, 2003.

Clogan, Paul Maruice, ed. *Medievali et Humanistica: Literacy and the Lay Reader.* Lanham, Md.: Rowman and Littlefield, 2000.

Clubb, Louise George. *Italian Drama in Shakespeare's Time.* New Haven: Yale University Press, 1989.

Clucas, Stephen, ed. *A Princely Brave Woman: Essays on Margaret Cavendish, Duchess of Newcastle.* Aldershot and Brookfield, UK: Ashgate Publishing, 2003.

Conley, John J., S.J. *The Suspicion of Virtue: Women Philosophers in Neoclassical France.* Ithaca, N.Y.: Cornell University Press, 2002.

Crabb, Ann. *The Strozzi of Florence: Widowhood and Family Solidarity in the Renaissance.* Ann Arbor: University of Michigan Press, 2000.

Crowston, Clare Haru. *Fabricating Women: The Seamstresses of Old Regime France, 1675–1791.* Durham, N.C.: Duke University Press, 2001.

Cruz, Anne J., and Mary Elizabeth Perry, eds. *Culture and Control in Counter-Reformation Spain.* Minneapolis: University of Minnesota Press, 1992.

Datta, Satya. *Women and Men in Early Modern Venice.* Aldershot and Brookfield, UK: Ashgate Publishing, 2003.

Davis, Natalie Zemon. *Society and Culture in Early Modern France.* Stanford: Stanford University Press, 1975. Especially chapters 3 and 5.

————. *Women on the Margins: Three Seventeenth-Century Lives.* Cambridge, Mass.: Harvard University Press, 1995.

DeJean, Joan. *Ancients against Moderns: Culture Wars and the Making of a Fin de Siècle.* Chicago: University of Chicago Press, 1997.

————. *Fictions of Sappho, 1546–1937.* Chicago: University of Chicago Press, 1989.

————. *The Reinvention of Obscenity: Sex, Lies, and Tabloids in Early Modern France.* Chicago: University of Chicago Press, 2002.

————. *Tender Geographies: Women and the Origins of the Novel in France.* New York: Columbia University Press, 1991.

————. *The Reinvention of Obscenity: Sex, Lies, and Tabloids in Early Modern France.* Chicago: University of Chicago Press, 2002.

Dictionary of Russian Women Writers. Edited by Marina Ledkovsky, Charlotte Rosenthal, and Mary Zirin. Westport, Conn.: Greenwood Press, 1994.

Dixon, Laurinda S. *Perilous Chastity: Women and Illness in Pre-Enlightenment Art and Medicine.* Ithaca, N.Y.: Cornell University Press, 1995.

Dolan, Frances, E. *Whores of Babylon: Catholicism, Gender and Seventeenth-Century Print Culture.* Ithaca, N.Y.: Cornell University Press, 1999.

Donovan, Josephine. *Women and the Rise of the Novel, 1405–1726.* New York: St. Martin's Press, 1999.

Encyclopedia of Continental Women Writers. 2 vols. Edited by Katharina Wilson. New York: Garland, 1991.

De Erauso, Catalina. *Lieutenant Nun: Memoir of a Basque Transvestite in the New World.* Translated by Michele Ttepto & Gabriel Stepto. Foreward by Marjorie Garber. Boston: Beacon Press, 1995.

Erdmann, Axel. *My Gracious Silence: Women in the Mirror of Sixteenth-Century Printing in Western Europe.* Luzern: Gilhofer and Rauschberg, 1999.

Erickson, Amy Louise. *Women and Property in Early Modern England.* London and New York: Routledge, 1993.

Ezell, Margaret J. M. *The Patriarch's Wife: Literary Evidence and the History of the Family.* Chapel Hill, N.C.: University of North Carolina Press, 1987.

————. *Social Authorship and the Advent of Print.* Baltimore: Johns Hopkins University Press, 1999.

————. *Writing Women's Literary History.* Baltimore: Johns Hopkins University Press, 1993.

Farrell, Michèle Longino. *Performing Motherhood: The Sévigné Correspondence.* Hanover, N.H., and London: University Press of New England, 1991.

The Feminist Companion to Literature in English: Women Writers from the Middle Ages to the Present. Edited by Virginia Blain, Isobel Grundy, and Patricia Clements. New Haven, Conn.: Yale University Press, 1990.

The Feminist Encyclopedia of German Literature. Edited by Friederike Eigler and Susanne Kord. Westport, Conn.: Greenwood Press, 1997.

Feminist Encyclopedia of Italian Literature. Edited by Rinaldina Russell. Westport, Conn.: Greenwood Press, 1997.

Ferguson, Margaret W. *Dido's Daughters: Literacy, Gender, and Empire in Early Modern England and France.* Chicago: University of Chicago Press, 2003.

Ferguson, Margaret W., Maureen Quilligan, and Nancy J. Vickers, eds. *Rewriting the Renaissance: The Discourses of Sexual Difference in Early Modern Europe.* Chicago: University of Chicago Press, 1987.

Ferraro, Joanne M. *Marriage Wars in Late Renaissance Venice.* Oxford: Oxford University Press, 2001.

Fletcher, Anthony. *Gender, Sex and Subordination in England 1500–1800.* New Haven: Yale University Press, 1995.

French Women Writers: A Bio-Bibliographical Source Book. Edited by Eva Martin Sartori and Dorothy Wynne Zimmerman. Westport, Conn.: Greenwood Press, 1991.

Frye, Susan, and Karen Robertson, eds. *Maids and Mistresses, Cousins and Queens: Women's Alliances in Early Modern England.* Oxford: Oxford University Press, 1999.

Gallagher, Catherine. *Nobody's Story: The Vanishing Acts of Women Writers in the Marketplace, 1670–1820.* Berkeley: University of California Press, 1994.

Garrard, Mary D. *Artemisia Gentileschi: The Image of the Female Hero in Italian Baroque Art.* Princeton: Princeton University Press, 1989.

Gelbart, Nina Rattner. *The King's Midwife: A History and Mystery of Madame du Coudray.* Berkeley: University of California Press, 1998.

Glenn, Cheryl. *Rhetoric Retold: Regendering the Tradition from Antiquity through the Renaissance.* Carbondale and Edwardsville, Ill.: Southern Illinois University Press, 1997.

Goffen, Rona. *Titian's Women.* New Haven: Yale University Press, 1997.

Goldberg, Jonathan. *Desiring Women Writing: English Renaissance Examples.* Stanford: Stanford University Press, 1997.

Goldsmith, Elizabeth C. *Exclusive Conversations: The Art of Interaction in Seventeenth-Century France.* Philadelphia: University of Pennsylvania Press, 1988.

———, ed. *Writing the Female Voice.* Boston: Northeastern University Press, 1989.

Goldsmith, Elizabeth C., and Dena Goodman, eds. *Going Public: Women and Publishing in Early Modern France.* Ithaca, N.Y.: Cornell University Press, 1995.

Grafton, Anthony, and Lisa Jardine. *From Humanism to the Humanities: Education and the Liberal Arts in Fifteenth-and Sixteenth-Century Europe.* London: Duckworth, 1986.

Grassby, Richard. *Kinship and Capitalism: Marriage, Family, and Business in the English-Speaking World, 1580–1740.* Cambridge: Cambridge University Press, 2001.

Greer, Margaret Rich. *Maria de Zayas Tells Baroque Tales of Love and the Cruelty of Men.* University Park, Penn.: Pennsylvania State University Press, 2000.

Gutierrez, Nancy A. *"Shall She Famish Then?" Female Food Refusal in Early Modern England.* Aldershot and Brookfield, UK: Ashgate Publishing, 2003.

Habermann, Ina. *Staging Slander and Gender in Early Modern England.* Aldershot and Brookfield, UK: Ashgate Publishing, 2003.

Hackett, Helen. *Women and Romance Fiction in the English Renaissance.* Cambridge: Cambridge University Press, 2000.

Hall, Kim F. *Things of Darkness: Economies of Race and Gender in Early Modern England.* Ithaca, N.Y.: Cornell University Press, 1995.

Hampton, Timothy. *Literature and the Nation in the Sixteenth Century: Inventing Renaissance France.* Ithaca, N.Y.: Cornell University Press, 2001.

Hannay, Margaret, ed. *Silent but for the Word.* Kent, Ohio: Kent State University Press, 1985.

Hardwick, Julie. *The Practice of Patriarchy: Gender and the Politics of Household Authority in*

Early Modern France. University Park, Penn.: Pennsylvania State University Press, 1998.

Harris, Barbara J. *English Aristocratic Women, 1450–1550: Marriage and Family, Property and Careers.* New York: Oxford University Press, 2002.

Harth, Erica. *Ideology and Culture in Seventeenth-Century France.* Ithaca, N.Y.: Cornell University Press, 1983.

—————. *Cartesian Women: Versions and Subversions of Rational Discourse in the Old Regime.* Ithaca, N.Y.: Cornell University Press, 1992.

Harvey, Elizabeth D. *Ventriloquized Voices: Feminist Theory and English Renaissance Texts.* London and New York: Routledge, 1992.

Haselkorn, Anne M., and Betty Travitsky, eds. *The Renaissance Englishwoman in Print: Counterbalancing the Canon.* Amherst, Mass.: University of Massachusetts Press, 1990.

Hendricks, Margo, and Patricia Parker, eds. *Women, "Race," and Writing in the Early Modern Period.* London and New York: Routledge, 1994.

Herlihy, David. "Did Women Have a Renaissance? A Reconsideration." *Medievalia et Humanistica* NS 13 (1985): 1–22.

Hill, Bridget. *The Republican Virago: The Life and Times of Catharine Macaulay, Historian.* New York: Oxford University Press, 1992.

Hills, Helen, ed. *Architecture and the Politics of Gender in Early Modern Europe.* Aldershot and Brookfield, UK: Ashgate Publishing, 2003.

A History of Central European Women's Writing. Edited by Celia Hawkesworth. New York: Palgrave Press, 2001.

A History of Women in the West.
    Volume 1: *From Ancient Goddesses to Christian Saints.* Edited by Pauline Schmitt Pantel. Cambridge, Mass.: Harvard University Press, 1992.
    Volume 2: *Silences of the Middle Ages.* Edited by Christiane Klapisch-Zuber. Cambridge, Mass.: Harvard University Press, 1992.
    Volume 3: *Renaissance and Enlightenment Paradoxes.* Edited by Natalie Zemon Davis and Arlette Farge. Cambridge, Mass.: Harvard University Press, 1993.

A History of Women Philosophers. Edited by Mary Ellen Waithe. 3 vols. Dordrecht: Martinus Nijhoff, 1987.

A History of Women's Writing in France. Edited by Sonya Stephens. Cambridge: Cambridge University Press, 2000.

A History of Women's Writing in Germany, Austria and Switzerland. Edited by Jo Catling. Cambridge: Cambridge University Press, 2000.

A History of Women's Writing in Italy. Edited by Letizia Panizza and Sharon Wood. Cambridge: University Press, 2000.

A History of Women's Writing in Russia. Edited by Alele Marie Barker and Jehanne M. Gheith. Cambridge: Cambridge University Press, 2002.

Hobby, Elaine. *Virtue of Necessity: English Women's Writing 1646–1688.* London: Virago Press, 1988.

Horowitz, Maryanne Cline. "Aristotle and Women." *Journal of the History of Biology* 9 (1976): 183–213.

Howell, Martha. *The Marriage Exchange: Property, Social Place, and Gender in Cities of the Low Countries, 1300–1550.* Chicago: University of Chicago Press, 1998.

Hufton, Olwen H. *The Prospect before Her: A History of Women in Western Europe, 1:1500–1800.* New York: HarperCollins, 1996.

Hull, Suzanne W. *Chaste, Silent, and Obedient: English Books for Women, 1475–1640.* San Marino, Calif.: The Huntington Library, 1982.

Hunt, Lynn, ed. *The Invention of Pornography: Obscenity and the Origins of Modernity, 1500–1800.* New York: Zone Books, 1996.

Hutner, Heidi, ed. *Rereading Aphra Behn: History, Theory, and Criticism.* Charlottesville, Va.: University Press of Virginia, 1993.

Hutson, Lorna, ed. *Feminism and Renaissance Studies.* New York: Oxford University Press, 1999.

Italian Women Writers: A Bio-Bibliographical Sourcebook. Edited by Rinaldina Russell. Westport, Conn.: Greenwood Press, 1994.

Jaffe, Irma B., with Gernando Colombardo. *Shining Eyes, Cruel Fortune: The Lives and Loves of Italian Renaissance Women Poets.* New York: Fordham University Press, 2002.

James, Susan E. *Kateryn Parr: The Making of a Queen.* Aldershot and Brookfield, UK: Ashgate Publishing, 1999.

Jankowski, Theodora A. *Women in Power in the Early Modern Drama.* Urbana, Ill.: University of Illinois Press, 1992.

Jansen, Katherine Ludwig. *The Making of the Magdalen: Preaching and Popular Devotion in the Later Middle Ages.* Princeton: Princeton University Press, 2000.

Jed, Stephanie H. *Chaste Thinking: The Rape of Lucretia and the Birth of Humanism.* Bloomington, Ind.: Indiana University Press, 1989.

Jones, Ann Rosalind, and Peter Stallybrass. *Renaissance Clothing and the Materials of Memory.* Cambridge, UK: Cambridge University Press, 2000.

Jordan, Constance. *Renaissance Feminism: Literary Texts and Political Models.* Ithaca, N.Y.: Cornell University Press, 1990.

Kagan, Richard L. *Lucrecia's Dreams: Politics and Prophecy in Sixteenth-Century Spain.* Berkeley: University of California Press, 1990.

Kehler, Dorothea, and Laurel Amtower, eds. *The Single Woman in Medieval and Early Modern England: Her Life and Representation.* Tempe, Ariz.: MRTS, 2002.

Kelly, Joan. "Did Women Have a Renaissance?" In Joan Kelly *Women, History, and Theory.* Chicago: University of Chicago Press, 1984. Also in Renate Bridenthal, Claudia Koonz, and Susan M. Stuard, eds., *Becoming Visible: Women in European History.* 3d ed.. Boston: Houghton Mifflin, 1998.

———. "Early Feminist Theory and the *Querelle des Femmes.*" In *Women, History, and Theory.*

Kelso, Ruth. *Doctrine for the Lady of the Renaissance.* Foreword by Katharine M. Rogers. Urbana, Ill.: University of Illinois Press, 1956, 1978.

Kendrick, Robert L. *Celestial Sirens: Nuns and their Music in Early Modern Milan.* New York: Oxford University Press, 1996.

Kermode, Jenny, and Garthine Walker, eds. *Women, Crime and the Courts in Early Modern England.* Chapel Hill, N.C.: University of North Carolina Press, 1994.

King, Catherine E. *Renaissance Women Patrons: Wives and Widows in Italy, c. 1300–1550.* New York and Manchester: Manchester University Press (distributed in the U.S. by St. Martin's Press), 1998.

King, Margaret L. *Women of the Renaissance.* Foreword by Catharine R. Stimpson. Chicago: University of Chicago Press, 1991.

Krontiris, Tina. *Oppositional Voices: Women as Writers and Translators of Literature in the English Renaissance.* London and New York: Routledge, 1992.

Kuehn, Thomas. *Law, Family, and Women: Toward a Legal Anthropology of Renaissance Italy.* Chicago: University of Chicago Press, 1991.

Kunze, Bonnelyn Young. *Margaret Fell and the Rise of Quakerism.* Stanford: Stanford University Press, 1994.

Labalme, Patricia A., ed. *Beyond Their Sex: Learned Women of the European Past.* New York: New York University Press, 1980.

Lalande, Roxanne Decker, ed. *A Labor of Love: Critical Reflections on the Writings of Marie-Catherine Desjardins (Mme de Villedieu).* Madison, N.J.: Fairleigh Dickinson University Press, 2000.

Lamb, Mary Ellen. *Gender and Authorship in the Sidney Circle.* Madison: University of Wisconsin Press, 1990.

Laqueur, Thomas. *Making Sex: Body and Gender from the Greeks to Freud.* Cambridge, Mass.: Harvard University Press, 1990.

Larsen, Anne R., and Colette H. Winn, eds. *Renaissance Women Writers: French Texts/American Contexts.* Detroit: Wayne State University Press, 1994.

Laven, Mary. *Virgins of Venus: Enclosed Lives and Broken Vows in the Renaissance Convent.* London: Viking, 2002.

Lerner, Gerda. *The Creation of Patriarchy and Creation of Feminist Consciousness, 1000–1870.* 2 vols. New York: Oxford University Press, 1986, 1994.

Levin, Carole, and Jeanie Watson, eds. *Ambiguous Realities: Women in the Middle Ages and Renaissance.* Detroit: Wayne State University Press, 1987.

Levin, Carole, Jo Eldridge Carney, and Debra Barrett-Graves. *Elizabeth I: Always Her Own Free Woman.* Aldershot and Brookfield, UK: Ashgate Publishing, 2003.

Levin, Carole, et al. *Extraordinary Women of the Medieval and Renaissance World: A Biographical Dictionary.* Westport, Conn.: Greenwood Press, 2000.

Levy, Allison, ed. *Widowhood and Visual Culture in Early Modern Europe.* Aldershot and Brookfield, UK: Ashgate Publishing, 2003.

Lewalsky, Barbara Kiefer. *Writing Women in Jacobean England.* Cambridge, Mass.: Harvard University Press, 1993.

Lewis, Jayne Elizabeth. *Mary Queen of Scots: Romance and Nation.* London: Routledge, 1998.

Lindenauer, Leslie J. *Piety and Power: Gender and Religious Culture in the American Colonies, 1630–1700.* London and New York: Routledge, 2002.

Lindsey, Karen. *Divorced Beheaded Survived: A Feminist Reinterpretation of the Wives of Henry VIII.* Reading, Mass.: Addison-Wesley Publishing, 1995.

Lochrie, Karma. *Margery Kempe and Translations of the Flesh.* Philadelphia: University of Pennsylvania Press, 1992.

Longino Farrell, Michèle. *Performing Motherhood: The Sévigné Correspondence.* Hanover, N.H.: University Press of New England, 1991.

Lougee, Carolyn C. *Le Paradis des Femmes: Women, Salons, and Social Stratification in Seventeenth-Century France.* Princeton: Princeton University Press, 1976.

Love, Harold. *The Culture and Commerce of Texts: Scribal Publication in Seventeenth-Century England.* Amherst, Mass.: University of Massachusetts Press, 1993.

Lowe, K. J. P. *Nuns' Chronicles and Convent Culture in Renaissance and Counter-Reformation Italy.* Cambridge: Cambridge University Press, 2003.

MacCarthy, Bridget G. *The Female Pen: Women Writers and Novelists 1621–1818.* Preface by Janet Todd. New York: New York University Press, 1994. (Originally published by Cork University Press, 1946–47).

Maclean, Ian. *Woman Triumphant: Feminism in French Literature, 1610–1652.* Oxford: Clarendon Press, 1977.

———. *The Renaissance Notion of Woman: A Study of the Fortunes of Scholasticism and Medical Science in European Intellectual Life.* Cambridge: Cambridge University Press, 1980.

MacNeil, Anne. *Music and Women of the Commedia dell'Arte in the Late Sixteenth Century.* New York: Oxford University Press, 2003.

Maggi, Armando. *Uttering the Word: The Mystical Performances of Maria Maddalena de' Pazzi, a Renaissance Visionary.* Albany: State University of New York Press, 1998.

Marshall, Sherrin. *Women in Reformation and Counter-Reformation Europe: Public and Private Worlds.* Bloomington, Ind.: Indiana University Press, 1989.

Masten, Jeffrey. *Textual Intercourse: Collaboration, Authorship, and Sexualities in Renaissance Drama.* Cambridge: Cambridge University Press, 1997.

Matter, E. Ann, and John Coakley, eds. *Creative Women in Medieval and Early Modern Italy.* Philadelphia: University of Pennsylvania Press, 1994.

McGrath, Lynette. *Subjectivity and Women's Poetry in Early Modern England.* Burlington, Vt.: Ashgate, 2002.

McLeod, Glenda. *Virtue and Venom: Catalogs of Women from Antiquity to the Renaissance.* Ann Arbor: University of Michigan Press, 1991.

Medwick, Cathleen. *Teresa of Avila: The Progress of a Soul.* New York: Alfred A. Knopf, 2000.

Meek, Christine, ed. *Women in Renaissance and Early Modern Europe.* Dublin-Portland: Four Courts Press, 2000.

Mendelson, Sara and Patricia Crawford. *Women in Early Modern England, 1550–1720.* Oxford: Clarendon Press, 1998.

Merchant, Carolyn. *The Death of Nature: Women, Ecology and the Scientific Revolution.* New York: HarperCollins, 1980.

Merrim, Stephanie. *Early Modern Women's Writing and Sor Juana Inés de la Cruz.* Nashville, Tenn.: Vanderbilt University Press, 1999.

Messbarger, Rebecca. *The Century of Women: The Representations of Women in Eighteenth-Century Italian Public Discourse.* Toronto: University of Toronto Press, 2002.

Miller, Nancy K. *The Heroine's Text: Readings in the French and English Novel, 1722–1782.* New York: Columbia University Press, 1980.

Miller, Naomi J. *Changing the Subject: Mary Wroth and Figurations of Gender in Early Modern England.* Lexington, Ky.: University Press of Kentucky, 1996.

Miller, Naomi J., and Gary Waller, eds. *Reading Mary Wroth: Representing Alternatives in Early Modern England.* Knoxville, Tenn.: University of Tennessee Press, 1991.

Monson, Craig A., ed. *The Crannied Wall: Women, Religion, and the Arts in Early Modern Europe.* Ann Arbor: University of Michigan Press, 1992.

Moore, Cornelia Niekus. *The Maiden's Mirror: Reading Material for German Girls in the Sixteenth and Seventeenth Centuries.* Wiesbaden: Otto Harrassowitz, 1987.

Moore, Mary B. *Desiring Voices: Women Sonneteers and Petrarchism.* Carbondale, Ill.: Southern Illinois University Press, 2000.

Mujica, Bárbara. *Women Writers of Early Modern Spain.* New Haven, Conn.: Yale University Press, 2004.

Musacchio, Jacqueline Marie. *The Art and Ritual of Childbirth in Renaissance Italy.* New Haven: Yale University Press, 1999.

Newman, Barbara. *God and the Goddesses: Vision, Poetry, and Belief in the Middle Ages.* Philadelphia: University of Pennsylvania Press, 2003.

Newman, Karen. *Fashioning Femininity and English Renaissance Drama.* Chicago and London: University of Chicago Press, 1991.

O'Donnell, Mary Ann. *Aphra Behn: An Annotated Bibliography of Primary and Secondary Sources.* 2d ed. Aldershot and Brookfield, UK: Ashgate Publishing, 2004.

Okin, Susan Moller. *Women in Western Political Thought.* Princeton: Princeton University Press, 1979.

Ozment, Steven. *The Bürgermeister's Daughter: Scandal in a Sixteenth-Century German Town.* New York: St. Martin's Press, 1995.

———. *Flesh and Spirit: Private Life in Early Modern Germany.* New York: Penguin Putnam, 1999.

———. *When Fathers Ruled: Family Life in Reformation Europe.* Cambridge, Mass.: Harvard University Press, 1983.

Pacheco, Anita, ed. *Early [English] Women Writers: 1600–1720.* New York and London: Longman, 1998.

Pagels, Elaine. *Adam, Eve, and the Serpent.* New York: Harper Collins, 1988.

Panizza, Letizia, ed. *Women in Italian Renaissance Culture and Society.* Oxford: European Humanities Research Centre, 2000.

Parker, Patricia. *Literary Fat Ladies: Rhetoric, Gender and Property.* London and New York: Methuen, 1987.

Pernoud, Regine, and Marie-Veronique Clin. *Joan of Arc: Her Story.* Revised and translated by Jeremy DuQuesnay Adams. New York: St. Martin's Press, 1998 (French original, 1986).

Perry, Mary Elizabeth. *Crime and Society in Early Modern Seville.* Hanover, N.H.: University Press of New England, 1980.

———. *Gender and Disorder in Early Modern Seville.* Princeton: Princeton University Press, 1990.

Petroff, Elizabeth Alvilda, ed. *Medieval Women's Visionary Literature.* New York: Oxford University Press, 1986.

Perry, Ruth. *The Celebrated Mary Astell: An Early English Feminist.* Chicago: University of Chicago Press, 1986.

Rabil, Albert. *Laura Cereta: Quattrocento Humanist.* Binghamton, N.Y.: MRTS, 1981.

Ranft, Patricia. *Women in Western Intellectual Culture, 600–1500.* New York: Palgrave, 2002.

Rapley, Elizabeth. *A Social History of the Cloister: Daily Life in the Teaching Monasteries of the Old Regime.* Montreal: McGill-Queen's University Press, 2001.

Raven, James, Helen Small and Naomi Tadmor, eds. *The Practice and Representation of Reading in England.* Cambridge: University Press, 1996.

Reardon, Colleen. *Holy Concord within Sacred Walls: Nuns and Music in Siena, 1575–1700.* Oxford: Oxford University Press, 2001.

Reiss, Sheryl E., and David G. Wilkins, ed. *Beyond Isabella: Secular Women Patrons of Art in Renaissance Italy.* Kirksville, Mo.: Truman State University Press, 2001.

Rheubottom, David. *Age, Marriage, and Politics in Fifteenth-Century Ragusa.* Oxford: Oxford University Press, 2000.

Richardson, Brian. *Printing, Writers and Readers in Renaissance Italy.* Cambridge: University Press, 1999.

Riddle, John M. *Contraception and Abortion from the Ancient World to the Renaissance.* Cambridge, Mass.: Harvard University Press, 1992.

———. *Eve's Herbs: A History of Contraception and Abortion in the West.* Cambridge, Mass.: Harvard University Press, 1997.

Roper, Lyndal. *The Holy Household: Women and Morals in Reformation Augsburg.* New York: Oxford University Press, 1989.

Rose, Mary Beth. *The Expense of Spirit: Love and Sexuality in English Renaissance Drama.* Ithaca, N.Y.: Cornell University Press, 1988.

———. *Gender and Heroism in Early Modern English Literature.* Chicago: University of Chicago Press, 2002.

———, ed. *Women in the Middle Ages and the Renaissance: Literary and Historical Perspectives.* Syracuse: Syracuse University Press, 1986.

Rosenthal, Margaret F. *The Honest Courtesan: Veronica Franco, Citizen and Writer in Sixteenth-Century Venice.* Foreword by Catharine R. Stimpson. Chicago: University of Chicago Press, 1992.

Rublack, Ulinka, ed. *Gender in Early Modern German History.* Cambridge: Cambridge University Press, 2002.

Sackville-West, Vita. *Daughter of France: The Life of La Grande Mademoiselle.* Garden City, N.Y.: Doubleday, 1959.

Sánchez, Magdalena S. *The Empress, the Queen, and the Nun: Women and Power at the Court of Philip III of Spain.* Baltimore: Johns Hopkins University Press, 1998.

Scaraffia, Lucetta, and Gabriella Zarri. *Women and Faith: Catholic Religious Life in Italy from Late Antiquity to the Present.* Cambridge, Mass.: Harvard University Press, 1999.

Schiebinger, Londa. *The Mind Has No Sex?: Women in the Origins of Modern Science.* Cambridge, Mass.: Harvard University Press, 1991.

———. *Nature's Body: Gender in the Making of Modern Science.* Boston: Beacon Press, 1993.

Schutte, Anne Jacobson, Thomas Kuehn, and Silvana Seidel Menchi, eds. *Time, Space, and Women's Lives in Early Modern Europe.* Kirksville, Mo.: Truman State University Press, 2001.

Schofield, Mary Anne, and Cecilia Macheski, eds. *Fetter'd or Free? British Women Novelists, 1670–1815.* Athens, Ohio: Ohio University Press, 1986.

Schutte, Anne Jacobson. *Aspiring Saints: Pretense of Holiness, Inquisition, and Gender in the Republic of Venice, 1618–1750.* Baltimore: Johns Hopkins University Press, 2001.

Schutte, Anne Jacobson , Thomas Kuehn, and Silvana Seidel Menchi, eds. *Time, Space, and Women's Lives in Early Modern Europe.* Kirksville, Mo.: Truman State University Press, 2001.

Seifert, Lewis C. *Fairy Tales, Sexuality and Gender in France 1690–1715: Nostalgic Utopias.* Cambridge, UK: Cambridge University Press, 1996.

Shannon, Laurie. *Sovereign Amity: Figures of Friendship in Shakespearean Contexts.* Chicago: University of Chicago Press, 2002.

Shemek, Deanna. *Ladies Errant: Wayward Women and Social Order in Early Modern Italy.* Durham, N.C.: Duke University Press, 1998.

Smith, Hilda L. *Reason's Disciples: Seventeenth-Century English Feminists.* Urbana, Ill.: University of Illinois Press, 1982.

————. *Women Writers and the Early Modern British Political Tradition.* Cambridge: Cambridge University Press, 1998.

Sobel, Dava. *Galileo's Daughter: A Historical Memoir of Science, Faith, and Love.* New York: Penguin Books, 2000.

Sommerville, Margaret R. *Sex and Subjection: Attitudes to Women in Early-Modern Society.* London: Arnold, 1995.

Soufas, Teresa Scott. *Dramas of Distinction: A Study of Plays by Golden Age Women.* Lexington, Ky.: The University Press of Kentucky, 1997.

Spencer, Jane. *The Rise of the Woman Novelist: From Aphra Behn to Jane Austen.* Oxford: Basil Blackwell, 1986.

Spender, Dale. *Mothers of the Novel: 100 Good Women Writers Before Jane Austen.* London & New York: Routledge, 1986.

Sperling, Jutta Gisela. *Convents and the Body Politic in Late Renaissance Venice.* Foreword by Catharine R. Stimpson. Chicago: University of Chicago Press, 1999.

Steinbrügge, Lieselotte. *The Moral Sex: Woman's Nature in the French Enlightenment.* Translated by Pamela E. Selwyn. New York: Oxford University Press, 1995.

Stephenson, Barbara. *The Power and Patronage of Marguerite de Navarre.* Aldershot and Brookfield, UK: Ashgate Publishing, 2004.

Stocker, Margarita. *Judith, Sexual Warrior: Women and Power in Western Culture.* New Haven: Yale University Press, 1998.

Stretton, Timothy. *Women Waging Law in Elizabethan England.* Cambridge: Cambridge University Press, 1998.

Stuard, Susan M. "The Dominion of Gender: Women's Fortunes in the High Middle Ages." In *Becoming Visible: Women in European History,* edited by Renate Bridenthal, Claudia Koonz, and Susan M. Stuard. 3d ed. Boston: Houghton Mifflin, 1998.

Summit, Jennifer. *Lost Property: The Woman Writer and English Literary History, 1380–1589.* Chicago: University of Chicago Press, 2000.

Surtz, Ronald E. *The Guitar of God: Gender, Power, and Authority in the Visionary World of Mother Juana de la Cruz (1481–1534).* Philadelphia: University of Pennsylvania Press, 1991.

————. *Writing Women in Late Medieval and Early Modern Spain: The Mothers of Saint Teresa of Avila.* Philadelphia: University of Pennsylvania Press, 1995.

Suzuki, Mihoko. *Subordinate Subjects: Gender, the Political Nation, and Literary Form in England, 1588–1688.* Aldershot and Brookfield, UK: Ashgate Publishing, 2003.

Teague, Frances. *Bathsua Makin, Woman of Learning.* Lewisburg, Penn.: Bucknell University Press, 1999.

Thomas, Anabel. *Art and Piety in the Female Religious Communities of Renaissance Italy: Iconography, Space, and the Religious Woman's Perspective.* New York: Cambridge University Press, 2003.

Tinagli, Paola. *Women in Italian Renaissance Art: Gender, Representation, Identity.* Manchester: Manchester University Press, 1997.

Todd, Janet. *The Secret Life of Aphra Behn.* London, New York, and Sydney: Pandora, 2000.

————. *The Sign of Angelica: Women, Writing and Fiction, 1660–1800.* New York: Columbia University Press, 1989.

Tomas, Natalie R. *The Medici Women: Gender and Power in Renaissance Florence.* Aldershot and Brookfield, UK: Ashgate Publishing, 2004.

Traub, Valerie. *The Renaissance of Lesbianism in Early Modern England.* Cambridge: Cambridge University Press, 2002.

Valenze, Deborah. *The First Industrial Woman.* New York: Oxford University Press, 1995.

Van Dijk, Susan, Lia van Gemert, and Sheila Ottway, eds. *Writing the History of Women's Writing: Toward an International Approach.* Proceedings of the Colloquium, Amsterdam, 9–11 September. Amsterdam: Royal Netherlands Academy of Arts and Sciences, 2001.

Vickery, Amanda. *The Gentleman's Daughter: Women's Lives in Georgian England.* New Haven: Yale University Press, 1998.

Vollendorf, Lisa, ed. *Recovering Spain's Feminist Tradition.* New York: Modern Language Association, 2001.

Walker, Claire. *Gender and Politics in Early Modern Europe: English Convents in France and the Low Countries.* New York: Palgrave, 2003.

Wall, Wendy. *The Imprint of Gender: Authorship and Publication in the English Renaissance.* Ithaca, N.Y.: Cornell University Press, 1993.

Walsh, William T. *St. Teresa of Avila: A Biography.* Rockford, Ill.: TAN Books and Publications, 1987.

Warner, Marina. *Alone of All Her Sex: The Myth and Cult of the Virgin Mary.* New York: Knopf, 1976.

Warnicke, Retha M. *The Marrying of Anne of Cleves: Royal Protocol in Tudor England.* Cambridge: Cambridge University Press, 2000.

Watt, Diane. *Secretaries of God: Women Prophets in Late Medieval and Early Modern England.* Cambridge, UK: D. S. Brewer, 1997.

Weaver, Elissa. *Convent Theatre in Early Modern Italy.* New York: Cambridge University Press, 2002.

Weber, Alison. *Teresa of Avila and the Rhetoric of Femininity.* Princeton: Princeton University Press, 1990.

Welles, Marcia L. *Persephone's Girdle: Narratives of Rape in Seventeenth-Century Spanish Literature.* Nashville, Tenn.: Vanderbilt University Press, 2000.

Whitehead, Barbara J., ed. *Women's Education in Early Modern Europe: A History, 1500–1800.* New York and London: Garland Publishing, 1999.

Wiesner, Merry E. *Working Women in Renaissance Germany.* New Brunswick, N.J.: Rutgers University Press, 1986.

Wiesner-Hanks, Merry E. *Christianity and Sexuality in the Early Modern World: Regulating Desire, Reforming Practice.* New York: Routledge, 2000.

———. *Gender, Church, and State in Early Modern Germany: Essays.* New York: Longman, 1998.

———. *Gender in History.* Malden, Mass.: Blackwell, 2001.

———. *Women and Gender in Early Modern Europe.* Cambridge, UK: Cambridge University Press, 1993.

———. *Working Women in Renaissance Germany.* New Brunswick, N.J.: Rutgers University Press, 1986.

Willard, Charity Cannon. *Christine de Pizan: Her Life and Works.* New York: Persea Books, 1984.

Winn, Colette, and Donna Kuizenga, eds. *Women Writers in Pre-Revolutionary France.* New York: Garland Publishing, 1997.

Woodbridge, Linda. *Women and the English Renaissance: Literature and the Nature of Womankind, 1540–1620.* Urbana, Ill.: University of Illinois Press, 1984.

Woodford, Charlotte. *Nuns as Historians in Early Modern Germany.* Oxford: Clarendon Press, 2002.

Woods, Susanne. *Lanyer: A Renaissance Woman Poet.* New York: Oxford University Press, 1999.

Woods, Susanne, and Margaret P. Hannay, eds. *Teaching Tudor and Stuart Women Writers.* New York: Modern Language Assocation, 2000.

INDEX